DATE DUE

JA 29 '95		
JE 10 '94		
AG 18 '94		
NO 17		
DE 4 '97		
DE 18 '98		
OC 2		
NO 25 '02		
MR 30		

DEMCO 38-296

Iraq

Iraq

David L. Bender, *Publisher*
Bruno Leone, *Executive Editor*
Bonnie Szumski, *Managing Editor*
Carol Wekesser, *Senior Editor*

William Dudley, *Book Editor*
Stacey L. Tipp, *Book Editor*

Current Controversies

R '92

Library of Congress Cataloging-in-Publication Data

Iraq / William Dudley & Stacey L. Tipp, book editors.
    p. cm. — (Current controversies)
    Includes bibliographical references and index.
    Summary: An anthology of articles debating issues surrounding the Persian Gulf War, including its effects on the United States and the Middle East, the justification of military action, the accuracy of the media coverage, and lessons learned from the war.
    ISBN 0-89908-575-X (lib.) — ISBN 0-89908-581-4 (pap.)
    1. Persian Gulf War, 1991.   [1. Persian Gulf War, 1991.]
    I. Dudley, William, 1964- . II. Tipp, Stacey L., 1963- .
III. Series.
DS79.72.I73   1991
956.704'3—dc20   91-30036

Printed on
recycled paper

Contents

No: Military Action Is Not Justified

Chapter 2: Did the Persian Gulf War Strengthen the U.S.?

Yes: The War Strengthened the U.S.

No: The War Weakened the U.S.

The victory of U.S. military forces in the Persian Gulf weakened America's future role in world affairs. U.S. military leaders will not want to jeopardize their refurbished reputation by risking other missions, and economic constraints will continue to hamper America's superpower status.

Chapter 3: What Are the Military Lessons of the Persian Gulf War?

The War Proves the Need for a Strong Military

The War Does Not Prove the Need for a Strong Military

Chapter 5: How Well Did the News Media Cover the Persian Gulf War?

Foreword

By definition, controversies are "discussions of questions in which opposing opinions clash" (*Webster's Twentieth Century Dictionary Unabridged*). Few would deny that controversies are a pervasive part of the human condition and exist on virtually every level of human enterprise. Controversies transpire between individuals and among groups, within nations and between nations. Controversies supply the grist necessary for progress by providing challenges and challengers to the status quo. They also create atmospheres where strife and warfare can flourish. A world without controversies would be a peaceful world; but it also would be, by and large, static and prosaic.

The Series' Purpose

The purpose of the Current Controversies series is to explore many of the social, political, and economic controversies dominating the national and international scenes today. Titles selected for inclusion in the series are highly focused and specific. For example, from the larger category of criminal justice, Current Controversies deals with specific topics such as police brutality, gun control, white collar crime, and others. The debates in Current Controversies also are presented in a useful, timeless fashion. Articles and book excerpts included in each title are selected if they contribute valuable, long-range ideas to the overall debate. And wherever possible, current information is enhanced with historical documents and other relevant materials.

Thus, while individual titles are current in focus, every effort is made to ensure that they will not become quickly outdated. Books in the Current Controversies series will remain important resources for librarians, teachers, and students for many years.

In addition to keeping the titles focused and specific, great care is taken in the editorial format of each book in the series. Book introductions and chapter prefaces are offered to provide background material for readers. Chapters are organized around several key questions that are answered with diverse opinions representing all points on the political spectrum. Materials in each chapter include opinions in which authors clearly disagree as well as alternative opinions in which authors may agree on a broader issue but disagree on the possible solutions. In this way, the content of each volume in Current Controversies mirrors the mosaic of opinions encountered in society. Readers will quickly realize that there are many viable answers to these complex issues. By questioning each author's conclusions, students and casual readers can begin to develop the critical thinking skills so important to evaluating opinionated material.

Current Controversies is also ideal for controlled research. Each anthology in the series is composed of primary sources taken from a wide gamut of informational categories including periodicals, newspapers, books, United States and foreign government documents, and the publications of private and public organizations.

Readers will find factual support for reports, debates, and research papers covering all areas of important issues. In addition, an annotated table of contents, an index, a book and periodical bibliography, and a list of organizations to contact are included in each book to expedite further research.

Perhaps more than ever before in history, people are confronted with diverse and contradictory information. During the Persian Gulf War, for example, the public was not only treated to minute-to-minute coverage of the war, it was also inundated with critiques of the coverage and countless analyses of the factors motivating U.S. involvement. Being able to sort through the plethora of opinions accompanying today's major issues, and to draw one's own conclusions, can be a complicated and frustrating struggle. It is the editors' hope that Current Controversies will help readers with this struggle.

Introduction

The 1991 Persian Gulf War, involving more than a half million U.S. troops, was the largest U.S. military action since the Vietnam War, and the largest ever in that part of the world. But it was not the first time the U.S. had become militarily involved in the Persian Gulf, and it might not be the last. The interests that motivated the U.S. to wage war in 1991 remain, and could possibly spur future U.S. military involvement in the region.

Oil was and is a primary motivation for U.S. involvement in the Persian Gulf. Oil is a vital part of the U.S. economy, accounting for 43 percent of U.S. energy use. In 1990 the U.S. imported half the oil it consumed, with much of this oil coming from nations ringing the Persian Gulf. The eight countries in the region—Iraq, Iran, Saudi Arabia, and the small Gulf states including Kuwait—possess more than two-thirds of the world's proven oil reserves. Millions of barrels of oil are loaded and transported aboard tankers in the Persian Gulf every day.

To protect the flow of oil, the U.S. has worked to ensure that the Persian Gulf countries are both politically stable and willing to cooperate with Western nations in developing and selling their oil. To achieve these goals, the U.S. has had to face different challenges and threats to its interests. As these threats have changed over the years, so have U.S. allies and strategies in the region.

One such threat that dominated U.S. thinking during the 1950s and 1960s was its Cold War rivalry with the Soviet Union. The U.S. feared losing access to the oil-rich Persian Gulf nations to the Soviet Union, and consequently attempted to establish long-standing allies in the region. These attempts had mixed results. During the 1950s Iraq and the U.S. were closely aligned, but in 1958 Iraq's pro-Western monarchy was overthrown by a military dictatorship that opposed the U.S. and established close ties with the Soviet Union. The U.S. responded by forming an alliance with Iraq's historical rival, Iran. This relationship was mutually beneficial to both governments. From the U.S., Iran was able to buy billions of dollars of sophisticated military equipment, modernize its armed forces, and obtain technical assistance to develop its economy. The U.S., in turn, viewed Iran as a bulwark against communism, a check on Iraqi influence, and a dependable supplier of oil.

In 1979, however, the U.S. found itself confronted by a new threat—Islamic fundamentalism. The government of Iran was overthrown by Islamic religious leader Ayatollah Khomeini, and Iran's pro-American monarchy was replaced by an Islamic republic that was highly antagonistic to the U.S. The emergence of Islamic ideology was also a potential threat to the pro-Western governments of Saudi Arabia, Kuwait, and other Persian Gulf countries. Khomeini called on the people of these nations to revolt against their governments, which had cooperated with the U.S. and other Western nations and had violated Islamic principles. The U.S. became fearful that such Islamic revolutions could spread in the Persian Gulf, and so sought ways to check the spread of Islamic fundamentalism.

Supporting Iraq

Consequently, when Iraq, led by Saddam Hussein, attacked Iran in 1980, the U.S. did not seriously protest the action. The U.S. saw the conflict as a way to keep Iran occupied. While the U.S. proclaimed neutrality in the eight-year Iran-Iraq War, its actions were increasingly aimed at helping Iraq, and relations between the two countries improved. As evidence of this improved relationship, diplomatic relations between the U.S. and Iraq were restored in 1984. In addition, U.S. intelligence agencies shared military intelligence with Iraq, and the U.S. extended the nation billions of dollars in credit to buy grain and other goods.

Iraq's invasion of Iran was also welcomed by other Persian Gulf states, including Saudi Arabia

and Kuwait. These countries' regimes also feared the spread of Islamic fundamentalism, and provided billions of dollars of financial aid to Iraq. Because of this international support, Saddam Hussein grew in importance and strength in the Persian Gulf. In fact, according to some analysts, this support may have even led Hussein to feel confident that he could later invade Kuwait with little fear of U.S. retaliation.

Some Americans objected to U.S. support of Iraq. These critics argued that Hussein was a repressive, militaristic dictator who had used chemical weapons against Iranians and his own people, was developing nuclear weapons, and was not to be trusted. "Our de facto alliance with Iraq makes little sense," argued history professor Nikki R. Keddie in 1987 during the war. Nevertheless, the U.S. government continued to view Iraq as a useful partner deserving of U.S. support. Under President George Bush, the U.S. government's policy toward Iraq was perhaps

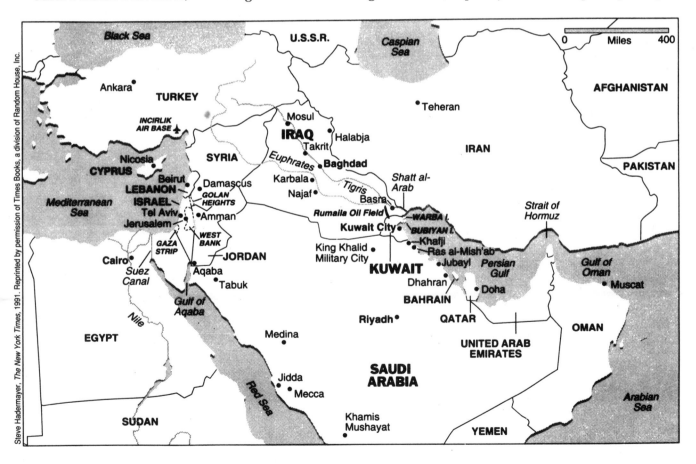

Steve Hademayer, *The New York Times*, 1991. Reprinted by permission of Times Books, a division of Random House, Inc.

best summed up by the assistant secretary of state for Near Eastern and South Asian Affairs John Kelly in an October 27, 1989 speech: "Iraq is an important state with great potential. We want to deepen and broaden our relationship." In spite of clear signs that Saddam Hussein was a potential military danger to his neighbors, the focus of U.S. policy remained, as Kelly testified in April 1990, "to attempt to develop gradually a mutually beneficial relationship in order to strengthen positive trends in Iraq's foreign and domestic policies."

When Iraq invaded Kuwait, however, the U.S. paid the price for not heeding Saddam Hussein's increased military buildup. The invasion clearly established that Hussein and his ambitions were a prime threat to U.S. interests in the Gulf. If Hussein could attack Kuwait, U.S. leaders reasoned, he may attack the other oil-producing, sparsely populated Arab states—especially Saudi Arabia. The threat that a militaristic dictator could control such a vast oil-rich region was deemed sufficient to warrant U.S. military intervention.

After Iraq's defeat, the U.S. still faces the dilemma of finding partners in the region while maintaining political stability and ensuring the availability of oil. *Iraq: Current Controversies* examines the issues raised by Iraq's invasion and retreat from Kuwait, and U.S. policy in the Persian Gulf. It examines the debates before, during, and after the 1991 conflict, and aims to give a better understanding of the war and whether future wars in the region are possible.

Chapter 1:

Prelude to the Gulf War: Is Military Action Justified?

Preface

The Iraqi invasion of Kuwait on August 2, 1990, sparked one of the most serious international crises of the late twentieth century. The response of the international community to the invasion was swift and harshly critical of Iraq's actions. The United Nations (UN) Security Council unanimously called for Iraq's complete and unconditional withdrawal from Kuwait, and sought to achieve that withdrawal through diplomatic pressure and economic sanctions imposed under UN Resolution 661 on August 6, 1990. UN diplomatic initiatives were backed up by a multinational armed force deployed to deter further Iraqi aggression in the Middle East. When diplomatic entreaties and economic sanctions failed to persuade Iraq to withdraw from Kuwait, the UN Security Council adopted Resolution 678 on November 29, 1990. This resolution authorized member states to "use all necessary means" to force Iraq out of Kuwait if it did not voluntarily withdraw by January 15, 1991. Ultimately, Iraq refused to comply with the deadline, and the international coalition forces commenced hostilities against Iraq on January 16, 1991.

One of the most important questions that was debated right up to the January 15 deadline was: Is military action justified? Supporters of the use of military force against Iraq, including U.S. president George Bush and other leaders of the international coalition, believed that military action was completely justified. They pointed out that Iraqi president Saddam Hussein had been given every opportunity to voluntarily withdraw from Kuwait and avoid war. Hussein, however, not only ignored twelve UN resolutions designed to obtain Iraqi withdrawal from Kuwait, he also rejected the international diplomatic efforts led by U.S. secretary of state James A. Baker III to resolve the conflict peacefully. While supporters of military action agreed that the UN sanctions were hurting the Iraqi economy, they believed that sanctions alone would not force Iraq to withdraw from Kuwait. Only military action, they concluded, could liberate Kuwait from Iraqi occupation.

The Importance of Kuwait

The liberation of Kuwait was seen as crucial to world peace and prosperity by those who supported military action against Iraq. Kuwait's importance rested on two main factors: its oil and its location in the unstable Middle East. Left unchecked, Hussein could potentially seize control of the oil fields in Saudi Arabia and other oil-rich Middle East nations. The Iraqi leader could thus exert a stranglehold on the U.S. and other Western nations dependent on Middle East oil by manipulating oil production and prices. As Baker argued, the Gulf issue concerns "a dictator who, acting alone and unchallenged, could strangle the global economic order, determining by fiat whether we all enter a recession or even the darkness of a depression."

Countering Iraqi aggression against Kuwait was also considered essential to preserve peace in the war-torn Middle East. The Iraqi threat to peace in the region was made even more ominous by the knowledge that Iraq possessed chemical weapons and a nuclear capability of undetermined power. Israel seemed particularly vulnerable to Iraqi attack because it was frequently threatened by Hussein. In April 1990, for example, the Iraqi president announced that Iraqi scientists had developed advanced chemical weapons, and added that, "We will make the fire eat up half of Israel, if it tries to do anything against Iraq." Similarly, on October 22, 1990, Hussein declared that the eight-year Iran-Iraq war, which Iraq started, was actually "a Zionist plot." The Iraqi leader also accused Kuwait of working for Israel in a "Zionist conspiracy" designed to bring the Iraqi economy to its knees.

A New World Order

Supporters of military action, however, believed that much more than the existence of Kuwait and the stability of the Middle East were threatened by Hussein. They also believed that the survival of a new international order was at risk. Many people had hoped that the demise of the cold war signaled a new era of peace and cooperation among nations. They further hoped that international law and diplomacy, conducted through institutions like a reinvigorated UN, would replace aggression and terror as the tools of foreign policy. To many observers, therefore, Iraq's aggression had to be stopped to preserve this new world order. As the *Times* of London editorialized on January 16, 1991, "The coalition ranged against Iraq represents a step towards the collective enforcement of international law.

This experiment must be made to work in the Gulf or countries must arm and ally themselves as best they can against the law of the jungle. This is a war about peace, not just in the Middle East, not just in our time, but in tomorrow's world."

Opponents' Arguments

The various arguments put forth by supporters of military action did not sway those people who remained vehemently opposed to the use of force against Iraq. For example, the argument that the liberation of Kuwait was justified by the need to defend world oil supplies was dismissed by critics like Doug Bandow, a former special assistant to President Reagan. Bandow conceded that should Hussein conquer the Persian Gulf and hold its oil off the market, he could trigger large price increases. However, this would defeat the purpose of the Kuwait invasion, which was to seize Kuwait's oil reserves and sell the oil for increased revenue. Furthermore, even if Hussein did stop his own production, other oil producers would step up their production, a search would begin for undiscovered and unrecovered supplies of oil, and reliance on alternative energy sources would increase. According to Bandow, therefore, Iraq's oil stranglehold was a "myth."

The argument that military action against Iraq was justified by the need to preserve peace in the Middle East was also assailed by critics. It seemed completely illogical to critics that war, the polar opposite of order and reason, could be used as a vehicle to restore stability to the volatile region. Indeed, Tom Bethell, Washington editor of the *American Spectator*, argued, "The whole notion of starting a war to restore stability is an Orwellian absurdity."

Many critics also rejected the idea that the war was justified to defend the new international order. They maintained that the Persian Gulf crisis was not a conflict between an aggressive dictator and a united world community trying to maintain international law, but a conflict between Hussein and the United States. When U.S. foreign policy was stripped of the legitimacy lent by UN involvement, critics argued, its unjustness was revealed. For example, while U.S. leaders frequently invoked the Iraqi atrocities in Kuwait as a justification for military intervention, critics were quick to point out that torture and mass murders have occurred in many countries but have been completely ignored by the U.S. As the *Washington Monthly* opined in April 1991, "The past decade is replete with cases in which the U.S. looked the other way. . . . The most notorious incident on Bush's watch was the murder of dissident students by the Chinese government in 1989. But while the U.S. chose to hunt down Manuel Noriega, other, more banal examples of evil went ignored: in El Salvador, Guatemala, South Africa, Liberia, Sri Lanka."

The Timing of Military Action

Finally, it should be understood that some people disagreed not necessarily with military action per se, but with the timing of military action. These people believed that the international economic sanctions imposed by the UN were having a devastating impact on the Iraqi economy. Supporters firmly believed that it was wrong to set such an early deadline as January 15, 1991, for Iraq to withdraw from Kuwait, and that the sanctions should have been given more of a chance to force a voluntary and peaceful Iraqi withdrawal. The debate over the timing of

military action was particularly vehement in the U.S. Congress, where the fight to continue sanctions and diplomacy was spearheaded by Sam Nunn, a Democratic senator from Georgia. The legislature's disagreement over whether to authorize war immediately after January 15, 1991, or to continue to rely on sanctions was evident in the congressional votes of January 12, 1991. The first Senate resolution, sponsored by Nunn and Senate majority leader George J. Mitchell, stated that the U.S. Constitution gives Congress sole power to declare war and called for continued economic sanctions against Iraq. It failed in a vote of 53-46. The second Senate resolution, approved by a vote of 52-47, authorized President Bush to use force against Iraq. In the House of Representatives, a resolution to continue economic sanctions was rejected by a vote of 250-183, while a resolution to authorize war was approved by a vote of 250-183.

Most of the viewpoints in the following chapter, which debate whether military action in the Persian Gulf was justified, were written prior to or immediately after the beginning of the Persian Gulf War. The editors' purpose in choosing viewpoints from this period is to acquaint readers with the heated public debates that took place under the threat of war and to place the subsequent hostilities in a historical and intellectual context.

Prelude to the Gulf War:
Is Military Action Justified?

Yes: Military Action Is Justified

Military Action Is Justified
Military Action Is Moral
Defending America's Oil Supply Justifies Military Action
Ending Iraqi Atrocities in Kuwait Justifies Military Action
Destroying Iraq's Nuclear Capability Justifies Military Action
The Failure of Economic Sanctions Justifies Military Action

Military Action Is Justified

Stephen J. Solarz

About the Author: *Stephen J. Solarz is a Democrat and a member of the U.S. House of Representatives from New York. The following article was written one week before the start of the Persian Gulf War.*

Ironies can sometimes be painful. I began my political career in 1966 as the campaign manager for one of the first anti-war congressional candidates in the country. Now, a quarter century later, I find myself supporting a policy in the Persian Gulf that might well lead to a war that many believe could become another Vietnam. Such a position is more and more anomalous, I know, in the Democratic Party. And yet I cannot accept, or be dissuaded by, the analogy with Vietnam.

In Vietnam no vital American interests were at stake. The crisis in the Gulf poses a challenge not only to fundamental American interests, but to essential American values. In Indochina the cost in blood and treasure was out of all proportion to the expected gains from a successful defense of South Vietnam. In the Gulf the potential costs of the American commitment are far outweighed by the benefits of a successful effort to implement the U.N. resolutions calling for the withdrawal of Iraq from Kuwait. The war in Vietnam dragged on for years and ended in an American defeat. A war in the Gulf, if it cannot be avoided, is likely to end with a decisive American victory in months, if not in weeks. Sometimes you are condemned to repeat the past if you *do* remember it—that is, if you draw the wrong lessons from it, and let the memory of the past distort your view of the present.

The United States clearly has a vital interest in preventing Saddam Hussein from getting away with his invasion and annexation of Kuwait. An aggressive Iraq bent on the absorption of its neighbors represents a serious economic threat to American interests. A hostile Iraq armed with chemical, biological, and eventually nuclear weapons represents a "clear and present danger" to American security. And a lawless Iraq represents a direct challenge to our hopes for a new and more peaceful world order. Any one of these reason would be sufficient to justify a firm American response to this brutal and unprovoked act of aggression. Together they make a compelling case for doing whatever needs to be done, in concert with our coalition partners, to secure the withdrawal of Iraqi forces from Kuwait and to establish a more stable balance of power in one of the most volatile and strategically important parts of the world.

There is, for a start, the question of oil. If Saddam succeeds in incorporating Kuwait into Iraq, he will be in a position to control, by intimidation or invasion, the oil resources of the entire Gulf. This would enable him, and him alone, to determine not only the price, but also the production levels, of up to half the proven oil reserves in the world. This is not simply a question of the price of gas at the pump. It is a matter of the availability of the essential energy that we and our friends around the world need to heat our homes, fuel our factories, and keep our economies vigorous.

> ## "The crisis in the Gulf poses a challenge not only to fundamental American interests, but to essential American values."

The United States needs a comprehensive energy policy that will reduce our dependence on Gulf oil. This was obvious at the time of the 1973 oil embargo, and it is obvious today. But regret at our failure to have diminished our dependence on Gulf oil, and our resolve to diminish

Stephen J. Solarz, "The Stakes in the Gulf," *The New Republic,* January 7-14, 1991. Reprinted by permission of *The New Republic,* © 1991, The New Republic, Inc.

that dependence in the future, will not solve our problem now. Even if we no longer needed to import oil, most other countries would still persist in their dependence; and to the extent that our economic well-being is linked to theirs, we cannot expect to insulate ourselves from the consequences of a cutoff in this essential source of supply.

"The Iraqi nuclear program is too far along to be stopped by an economic embargo."

Some have argued that Saddam's control of the oil resources of the Gulf would not pose an unacceptable threat to American interests, since he would presumably wish to sell the oil in order to raise revenues for his benign and malignant purposes. But Saddam would also be in a position to cut back dramatically on production, which would give him considerable leverage over the rest of the world, while assuring, through the inflated prices that his reduced production would command, an adequate level of revenue. It would be unthinkable for the United States to permit a rampaging dictator like Saddam to have his hands on the economic jugular of the world.

Far more important than the question of oil, however, is the extent to which, in American constitutional terms, Saddam is a "clear and present danger." This is a man who twice in the last decade has led his country into war, first against Iran in 1980, and then against Kuwait in 1990. Driven by an uncontrollable appetite for power, and by the ideological imperatives of the Baath party, which is committed to unifying the Arab nation under Iraqi control, he is determined to dominate the entire Middle East. President Bush's parallels between Saddam and Hitler are wildly overdrawn. But if there are fundamental differences between Saddam and Hitler, there are also instructive similarities. Like Hitler, Saddam has an unappeasable will to power com-

bined with a ruthless willingness to employ whatever means are necessary to achieve it.

Having stood up to the combined opposition of the superpowers, the Security Council, and the Arab League, Saddam's sense of invincibility will certainly swell—and the stage would be set for more campaigns of conquest and annexation. Moreover, if Saddam prevails in the current crisis, he might eventually pose a direct threat to the United States itself; it would be unacceptable to live in the shadow of an irrational man's nuclear arsenal, even if it is much smaller than our own. Iraq has remorselessly pursued a variety of long-range weapons programs that cannot be justified by any legitimate defensive needs. In addition to its nuclear program, Iraq is now working on an intercontinental ballistic missile system. Saddam is probably not in a position to produce a nuclear weapon within the next year, but he may well be able to do so in five to ten years. If we do not stop him now, we will almost certainly be obligated to confront him later, when he will be chillingly more formidable.

Political Reasons

How, in the context of a political resolution of the Gulf crisis, can we deal with the threat of Iraq's destabilizing weapons of mass destruction? Ironically, they will pose less of a problem if it should come to war, since Baghdad's chemical, biological, and nuclear facilities would be high-priority targets, and its capacity to use these instruments of demonic destruction would be crippled for a long time to come. There is a real danger, however, that a peaceful resolution of the crisis would leave Saddam with his terrible arsenal intact, and his efforts to acquire nuclear weapons proceeding apace. Such an outcome would be a Pyrrhic victory. The Bush administration has so far failed to accord this problem the priority it deserves.

Some will point out that we have lived for many decades with other countries possessing such weapons and have not felt compelled to insist upon their dismantlement. Why should we be any more concerned about the acquisition of nuclear weapons by Iraq than by Pakistan, India, Brazil, Argentina, or South Africa? The answer is that although the nuclear programs of these other countries are a source of legitimate concern, none of them has already used weapons of mass destruction. Apologists for Iraq have argued further that our anxieties are misplaced, inasmuch as Iraq is a signatory to the nuclear Nonproliferation Treaty; but Baghdad used chemical weapons in spite of its signature on the treaty prohibiting their use. In the matter of treaties, Iraq is not exactly to be trusted; and an accomplished sinner like Saddam will not be overly tormented by breaking his own word.

Sanctions Will Not Stop Saddam

Still others have suggested that Iraq will not be able to develop nuclear weapons without the type of assistance that has been cut off by the sanctions. This argument fails on a number of counts. First, it assumes that the sanctions will remain in effect in perpetuity. Second, it ignores the fact that our failure to prevent Pakistan from acquiring the components for its nuclear weapons program shows that a strategy of technological denial is not likely to succeed. Third, it turns a blind eye to the chemical weapons and biological agents already in Iraq's arsenal. Fourth, there is no doubt that Iraq has already obtained sufficient fissile material from both its operable reactor and the destroyed Osirak reactor to build several nuclear weapons, even without outside assistance, in the next ten years. The Iraqi nuclear program is too far along to be stopped by an economic embargo.

"Kuwait is being devoured before our eyes."

Had it not been for the Israeli attack on the Osirak reactor in 1981, Iraq would in all likelihood already have nuclear weapons. Indeed, many of those who criticized the Israeli raid at the time now recognize how fortunate it was for the entire region that the Israelis acted so decisively. If Israel had heeded the advice of the timid, Iraq would likely have used nuclear weapons in its war against Iran. Put starkly, there can be no prospect for long-term stability in the Gulf unless Iraq's weapons of mass destruction are dismantled or destroyed. The only question is one of means.

It is conceivable that Saddam can be persuaded to disarm himself of these weapons, if the United States and its coalition partners make it clear that this is an essential component of a diplomatic solution to the crisis. The international community should spell out its determination to maintain the sanctions in force—even if Iraq withdraws from Kuwait and complies with the other conditions of the various U.N. resolutions—until Baghdad agrees to dismantle the weapons. Still, we must recognize that this strategy may fail—in which case the United States must retain its option to use force to eliminate both the production centers for these weapons and their long-range delivery systems. This policy will enjoy the strong support of many of our partners, including a number of Arab countries. On two recent trips to the region I was struck by the great fear of Iraq's weapons of mass destruction and the recognition of the necessity of eliminating this nonconventional threat by whatever means are required.

Protecting the New World Order

The third reason for thwarting Saddam's ambitions lies in our hopes for the establishment of a new world order. How we resolve the first crisis of the post-cold war world will have profound historical consequences. Will this be a world in which relations among nations are governed by the rule of law, or will it be a Hobbesian world? Will it be a world in which the strong continue to dominate the weak, or will considerations of justice prevail over realities of force? Had the world responded with collective action when Japan invaded Manchuria, when Italy invaded Abyssinia, and when Hitler occupied the Rhineland, we might have been spared some of history's worst horrors. If we succeed in our efforts to secure the withdrawal of Iraqi forces and the restoration of the legitimate government of Kuwait through concerted international action, we will have created a powerful precedent for a much more peaceful world in the future. But if Saddam prevails, the word will have gone out to despots around the globe that the old rules still apply, that aggression still pays.

Kuwait's Agony

Kuwait is being devoured before our eyes. Newborn infants have been snatched out of incubators and left to die so the incubators can be carted back to hospitals in Baghdad. Thousands of Kuwaitis have been killed. Pregnant women have been bayoneted. Men have had their eyeballs burned out by cigarettes. Within a matter of months, Kuwait will have ceased to exist, the Kuwaitis having been murdered or exiled and the physical infrastructure of their country having been dismantled or destroyed. The failure of the United States and the international community to respond to previous acts of aggression is hardly a reason for not standing up to the man who is guilty of this one. The bitter fate that has befallen Kuwait should also lead the coalition of nations that has rallied to Kuwait's defense to require that Iraq pay full compensation for the havoc it has wrought. Baghdad's invasion was also the biggest bank heist in history; and if Iraq is not compelled to pay compensation, it will have been a handsome day's work for Saddam.

This crisis provides a rare opportunity, perhaps the first since the dawn of the modern age, to create a world order in which the international community upholds the sanctity of existing borders and the principle that nations should not be permitted to invade and to annex their weaker neighbors. The overwhelming votes in the U.N. Security Council demonstrate that there is, at last, an international consensus in favor of this objective. They also suggest that the dream of Franklin Roosevelt and the other founders of the United Nations, that the world organization could be used by the great powers as a mechanism for the preservation of peace, is being realized.

How shall we accomplish these essential objectives in a way that is consistent with our interests and compatible with our values? A national debate, stimulated by a series of hearings in the House and the Senate, has already begun. It would appear that there are, broadly speaking, three ways in which the withdrawal of Iraq from Kuwait, the restoration of the legitimate government in Kuwait, the payment of compensation to the victims of this aggression, and the establishment of a more stable balance of power in the region can be achieved.

"This man was willing to persist in his war against Iran despite a million Iraqi casualties."

The first is through the continued and perhaps protracted application of sanctions. Admiral William Crowe and General David Jones, former chairmen of the Joint Chiefs of Staff, among others, have argued that we should be willing to give sanctions a chance. If we wait another six, twelve, or eighteen months, they contend, the sanctions are likely to compel an Iraqi withdrawal from Kuwait. "What's the rush?" asks *The New York Times.* By waiting a little longer, these critics of the president's policy maintain, we can achieve our objectives without a war.

Of course it would be better to give sanctions more of a chance to work, if there is any reasonable possibility that they will bring about an Iraqi withdrawal, rather than take our troops to war. Nobody views with equanimity the loss of lives that an armed conflict would entail. And the supporters of a "go-slow" policy have rightly pointed out that the sanctions have received an unprecedented degree of support from the international community. All of Iraq's oil exports, which provided 90 percent of its foreign exchange earnings, have been cut off, and Iraq is clearly beginning to feel the economic consequences of its international isolation. Its factories are shutting down. Its productive capabilities have been impaired.

And yet it is difficult to be optimistic about the success of the sanctions. According to the detailed analysis by the International Institute for Economics of the likely impact of sanctions on Iraq, the embargo should bring about a reduction of approximately 40 percent in Iraq's gross national product. This will undoubtedly be a very serious blow to the Iraqi economy. But whether it will result in a withdrawal from Kuwait is another matter. Even Crowe, whose testimony before the Senate Armed Services Committee provided political legitimacy to the "go-slow" strategy, has said that his judgment on the efficacy of sanctions is "entirely speculative."

Iraq is a fertile country, and it will be able to feed itself. The smuggling of food and other essential items is already taking place across the Iranian, Jordanian, Turkish, and Syrian borders, and Iraq will be able to adjust as the economic pinch tightens. If the analysts are correct, the per capita income of Iraq will be reduced from approximately $2,600 to $1,600 a year. Even with its 40 percent reduction, however, Iraq will still have a per capita income more than twice that of Egypt, for instance, and substantially larger than that of Turkey, another of the front-line states. In any case, even if his people have to accept a less filling and nutritious diet, Saddam and his military will surely have enough to eat. This man was willing to persist in his war against Iran despite a million Iraqi casualties. It is hard to believe that he will be willing to withdraw from Kuwait simply because the Iraqi people will be forced to reduce their caloric intake or accept a diminution in their standard of living.

The Military Side

On the military side, there is no doubt that the sanctions are having an impact. As CIA Director William Webster told Congress, the international economic boycott is likely to affect seriously the Iraqi air force within ninety days, and to degrade to a somewhat lesser extent other

Iraqi forces over a period of nine to twelve months. Even so, the consensus among military experts is that even after a full year of sanctions, the capacity of the Iraqi forces in Kuwait to defend themselves will not be appreciably diminished. Most analysts believe that Saddam has written off his air force, given the vast air superiority enjoyed by the United States and its partners. The components of his military machine that constitute the core of his power—infantry, artillery, tanks, and armored vehicles already deployed in Kuwait—are precisely those that would be least affected by an extended embargo. The protracted application of sanctions will give the Iraqis time, moreover, to dig in and build up their defenses, to construct more roads and water-carrying pipelines from Iraq to Kuwait, thereby making an assault against them more costly in American lives.

"A 'go-slow' strategy . . . is more likely to play into the hands of Saddam."

Those who argue that sanctions without the use of force will be sufficient to compel an Iraqi withdrawal from Kuwait have never explained precisely how an embargo is likely to produce this result. They have failed to establish the connection between the undoubted economic impact of the sanctions and a political decision to quit Kuwait. There would appear to be only two ways in which sanctions can produce an Iraqi withdrawal from Kuwait and the other concessions necessary to end the crisis satisfactorily: either Saddam will decide to withdraw from Kuwait, or he will be overthrown by his own military and replaced by a leader (or a junta) that would make this decision.

But what are the chances, assuming the sanctions are maintained for another six to twelve months, or even longer, that Saddam will be willing to withdraw from Kuwait? He does not have to worry, after all, about running for re-election, or about a contentious Congress, or about a critical press, or about declining approval ratings in the polls. And no one can seriously believe that Saddam is more concerned about the well-being of his people than he is about the maximization of his power. This is not a sentimental man. Saddam is likely to calculate that it is a matter of time before the coalition crumbles and the sanctions erode. If all he has to worry about is the continued application of sanctions, he is much more likely to tough it out.

"A last resort is sometimes a necessary resort. Last is not the same as never."

This leaves the possibility of an overthrow of Saddam by his military. There must be many officers in the Iraqi army who understand that Saddam is leading them down the desert dunes to disaster and would dearly like to remove him. But Saddam has managed to stifle any stirring of discontent not only in his people, but especially in his military establishment. The armed forces are riddled with informers; and Saddam has demonstrated repeatedly that he will act with extraordinary ruthlessness against anyone whom he even suspects of plotting against him. Those who run afoul of his paranoia do not live to enjoy their own.

Thus it would appear that the prospects for the success of the sanctions are less likely than the prospects for the collapse of the coalition if we wait for the sanctions to be given more time to work. The coalition that President Bush has assembled with such skill is a fractious and fragile grouping, in which the Arab members in particular have different interests than we do. The incident on the Temple Mount in Jerusalem in fall 1990 was a clear warning about the flammability of this part of the world. The cultural repercussions of political events could easily destroy the coalition. And surely that is precisely what Saddam, a Machiavellian manipulator of

men and events, will attempt to achieve.

Nor will the pressures on the coalition come only from abroad. Once it becomes clear that Bush has opted for the prolonged application of sanctions, there will be strong demands to start bringing back many of the troops that we have sent to Saudi Arabia. Four hundred thousand soldiers are not necessary, if our sole purpose is to defend Saudi Arabia. And it will be very difficult to sustain such a massive presence in Saudi Arabia indefinitely, given the logistical requirements of such a deployment. Once we begin to withdraw forces from the Gulf, our coalition partners, most of whom believe that sanctions alone cannot induce Saddam to withdraw from Kuwait, are likely to conclude that it will be only a matter of time before Saddam prevails. At that point they will begin cutting their own deals, in anticipation of emerging regional realities.

Even if the coalition were to hold together while we waited for the sanctions to work, the chances are that by the time we concluded—say, a year or two from now—that they were not sufficient to induce Saddam to withdraw, we would have lost our will to use force. While some who have urged the president to give sanctions more of a chance to work have said that they would be prepared to support the use of force if the sanctions fail, the truth is that the great majority of those who favor waiting would still oppose a war against Iraq even if the sanctions failed to achieve an Iraqi withdrawal from Kuwait. And with the sanctions eroding, and the use of force no longer a politically viable option, Saddam would be well on his way to a victory. A "go-slow" strategy, then, is more likely to play into the hands of Saddam than to deliver him into the hands of the coalition arrayed against him.

A Negotiated Settlement?

For those who believe that there are no differences among nations that cannot be resolved diplomatically, there is always the hope of a negotiated settlement. But we must not generalize from our own fond norms. So far Saddam has not given any indication of a willingness to withdraw entirely and unconditionally from what his propaganda calls the nineteenth province of Iraq. An odd assortment of international itinerants, including Javier Pérez de Cuéllar and Kurt Waldheim, King Hussein of Jordan and Yasir Arafat, Yevgeny Primakov, Willy Brandt and Yasuhiro Nakasone, Muhammad Ali and Jesse Jackson have all beaten a path to Baghdad, only to return without anything to show for their efforts (except a handful of hostages who would have been released anyway when Saddam concluded that they were no longer valuable to him as a shield against attack). I strongly suspect that James Baker, even if he travels to Baghdad, is no more likely to come home with his pockets full of concessions.

"Just as we resisted the Finlandization of Europe, we must resist the Saddamization of the Middle East."

More to the point, what exactly is there to negotiate about? Some have suggested that we offer Bubiyan and Warbah, the two Kuwaiti islands that block Saddam's unfettered access to the Persian Gulf, as well as the Rumaillah oil fields, just south of the Iraqi border, in exchange for Saddam's withdrawal from the rest of Kuwait. But Kuwait, Saudi Arabia, a majority of the Arab League, the Security Council of the United Nations, and the Bush administration have all rightly rejected this idea, on the grounds that it would be a reward for aggression and set the stage for additional acts of banditry.

Saddam himself has attempted to link the question of an Iraqi withdrawal from Kuwait to an Israeli withdrawal from the West Bank and Gaza, or at least to the convening of an international conference to resolve the Palestinian problem. It should be obvious that this is simply an attempt to sow the seeds of discord among the countries arrayed against him. The two are entirely different issues. Iraq's invasion of Kuwait in 1990 was an unprovoked act of aggression, whereas Israel came into possession of the territories only after it was attacked by a coalition of Arab countries in 1967. Saddam did not invade Kuwait to help the Palestinians, but to maximize his own power. He is not moved by the plight of the Palestinians, or by anybody else's plight. He is merely exploiting it. And the Palestinians seem happy to assist in their own exploitation.

Paradoxically, if any real possibility of resolving this crisis peacefully exists, it lies not in negotiations leading to concessions that reward aggression, but in convincing Saddam that we are prepared to go to war if he does not comply with the terms of the Security Council resolutions. I suspect that it was a dawning realization that we are serious about opposing his grandiose ambitions, with force if necessary, that lay behind his recent release of the hostages. Surely it was not because he was suddenly filled with the holiday spirit.

In our joy over the reunion of the hostages with their families, however, we must not forget the threat Iraq still poses to vital American interests. Not until Saddam is finally persuaded that he has to make a choice between staying and dying or leaving and living will there be any real chance of inducing him to withdraw from Kuwait. Yet if such an ultimatum is delivered to him—and it is clearly implicit in the Security Council resolution authorizing the use of force—we have to be prepared to use force in the event he refuses to withdraw.

The Use of Force

This leads, then, to the third way of bringing the crisis to an end. The use of force, of course, raises profound political, moral, and constitutional questions. A war will undoubtedly bring many casualties—we should not delude ourselves with notions of surgical strikes—and no one can say with certainty what would happen in the wake of such a conflict. Force should be a last resort. But a last resort is sometimes a necessary resort. Last is not the same as never.

Some of those who oppose the use of armed

force have argued that war will increase instability and anti-Americanism in the Middle East. There is a measure of truth in this analysis. Still, a peacetime victory of Saddam over the coalition would surely represent a more considerable threat to the stability of the region than a wartime victory of the coalition over Saddam. It is important to note that the Middle East countries that are supposedly most vulnerable to Arab radicalization are precisely the countries that are supporting us most strongly, because their leaders need no lessons in the consequences of allowing Saddam to go unchecked.

"The crisis in the Gulf is not a Democratic issue or a Republican issue. It is an American issue."

Of course, there will be some expressions of hostility toward the United States in the Arab world if American weapons are used against Iraqi soldiers. But those expressions will surely be offset to the extent that other Arab countries are fighting alongside us in a war against Iraq, especially if we make it clear that our intention is not to occupy Iraq but to liberate Kuwait. Recent history demonstrates that the application of American force in the Middle East does not lead to a regional recoil from America: we were warned of the possibility of massive anti-American demonstrations if we attempted to punish Qaddafi for his role in a terrorist attack against American servicemen a few years ago, but our air strike against Libya in 1986 produced little negative response in the Arab world, and even seems to have resulted in enhanced respect for the United States.

Those who are anxious about the unanticipated consequences of a war have focused attention on the casualties that would result, even from a relatively brief and decisive campaign. I yield to nobody in my concern for American lives; but we must face the hard truth that what-

ever the casualties we might suffer, they are likely to be far smaller than those that would be inflicted upon us if we postpone the day of reckoning until Saddam has added nuclear weapons to his current arsenal of chemical and biological weapons. Forcefully denying Saddam the instruments of a nuclear war is itself an expression of concern for American lives. And if the maintenance of a large-scale American presence in the Gulf is a source of fiscal and political anxiety, surely we will be obliged to station a much larger deterrent force in the region if we permit Saddam and his army to remain in Kuwait than if we destroy much of his military machine and his weapons of mass destruction in the process of liberating Kuwait.

Others have suggested that even if we cannot force Saddam out of Kuwait, we can contain his expansionist tendencies and insulate the rest of the region from his marauding ambitions by permanently stationing American troops in the Gulf. They remind us that we contained Soviet and North Korean expansion for forty years and ask why a policy of containment cannot work in the Middle East. These critics are rather Panglossian about the realities of the Middle East. In Europe and on the Korean peninsula, the presence of American forces contributed to the stability of the countries we were trying to defend. In the Arab world, the long-term presence of many American troops would be almost certainly destabilizing.

Saudi Arabia's Position

It is doubtful, moreover, that Saudi Arabia, which is the most conservative Islamic society in the world, would permit us to maintain a sizable presence in the country for any appreciable period. The Saudis are right: if we keep our troops in the region, we may end up contributing unwittingly to the downfall of the very regimes that we set out to defend. And if we have brought 400,000 American troops to Saudi Arabia to force the Iraqis out of Kuwait, and then accept Baghdad's annexation of Kuwait as a fait accompli, the Saudis are unlikely to have much confidence in our willingness to defend them, and will be more likely to seek their security in a vassal relationship with Iraq. Just as we resisted the Finlandization of Europe, we must resist the Saddamization of the Middle East.

Supporting President Bush

If the president concludes that the sanctions are not likely to work, that there is no realistic prospect for an acceptable political settlement, and that we have no alternative but to use force, it will be essential for him to go to war multilaterally rather than unilaterally. The liberation of Kuwait and the elimination of the Iraqi threat is not only an American responsibility. Our Arab and European coalition partners have just as much—indeed, some of them have more—at stake than we do. It is one thing to be the head of an international posse attempting to deprive a criminal state of the rewards of its aggression. It is quite another for the United States to arrogate to itself the role of policeman of the world. The former is a task that the American people can understand and accept. The latter is an assignment that they do not seek.

Should it come to war, however, we will not be alone. Our Arab partners in this coalition (with the possible exception of Syria) are fully prepared to go to war along with us if that should prove necessary. The British have also been stalwart in their willingness to use force—and even Neil Kinnock, the Labour leader who once supported unilateral disarmament, has spoken up in favor of force should Saddam refuse to withdraw from Kuwait. President François Mitterrand has indicated that if the coalition should go to war, France will fight with it. And though it is true that the majority of the forces deployed in the Gulf are American, other countries have made sizable contributions as well. By the end of the year the British, the Egyptians, and the Syrians will have doubled their troop strength in Saudi Arabia, and the total number of foreign

forces available for combat will be 225,000. The armed units from twenty-eight countries lend the coalition not only legitimacy, but a substantial increase in military power. . . .

If the president does decide on the use of force, it will be important for him to have the support not only of our coalition partners, but also of Congress. There is no more fateful decision a nation can make than that of risking the lives of its men and women by going to war. It would be a serious constitutional and political mistake on the part of the president if he were to commit our forces to combat (in the absence of an unexpected provocation, such as a preemptive Iraqi attack) without congressional authorization. And there is another reason why the president should seek the support of Congress. If we go to war and if we win a quick and decisive victory, as is quite probable, the fact that the president did not seek the prior approval of Congress may become a source of debate among historians and columnists, but is not likely to hurt the president seriously with either Congress or the American people. But war is unpredictable, and we may get bogged down in a protracted conflict. Under those circumstances, with casualties beginning to mount, the president's ability to sustain support for the war will be gravely compromised if he fails to secure the authorization of Congress before hostilities begin.

A half century ago, when Hitler invaded Poland, the British House of Commons gathered to debate what course Britain should follow. After a halting defense of government policy by Neville Chamberlain, one of the opposition MPs [Members of Parliament] rose and began his remarks with the phrase, "Speaking for the Labour Party . . .". Instantly a voice thundered from the back benches: "Speak for England!" It is time to remember this advice. The crisis in the Gulf is not a Democratic issue or a Republican issue. It is an American issue.

Military Action Is Moral

George Bush

About the Author: *George Bush was elected president of the United States in 1988. He served as vice president under President Ronald Reagan between 1980 and 1988. The following viewpoint is taken from a speech delivered by President Bush to the National Religious Broadcasters Convention on January 28, 1991.*

The clergyman Richard Cecil once said, "There are two classes of the wise; the men who serve God because they have found Him, and the men who seek Him because they have not found Him yet." Abroad, as in America, our task is to serve and seek wisely through the policies we pursue.

Nowhere is this more true than in the Persian Gulf where, despite protestations of Saddam Hussein, it is not Iraq against the United States, it's the regime of Saddam Hussein against the rest of the world. Saddam tried to cast this conflict as a religious war. But it has nothing to do with religion per se. It has, on the other hand, everything to do with what religion embodies—good versus evil, right versus wrong, human dignity and freedom versus tyranny and oppression.

The war in the Gulf is not a Christian war, a Jewish war, or a Moslem war—it is a just war. And it is a war with which good will prevail. We're told that the principles of a just war originated with classical Greek and Roman philosophers like Plato and Cicero. And later they were expounded by such Christian theologians as Ambrose, Augustine, Thomas Aquinas.

The first principle of a just war is that it support a just cause. Our cause could not be more

George Bush, "Are We on God's Side?" Speech delivered to the National Religious Broadcasters Convention, January 28, 1991, Washington, D.C.

noble. We seek Iraq's withdrawal from Kuwait—completely, immediately and without condition; the restoration of Kuwait's legitimate government and the security and stability of the Gulf. We will see that Kuwait once again is free, that the nightmare of Iraq's occupation has ended, and that naked aggression will not be rewarded.

We seek nothing for ourselves. As I have said, U.S. forces will leave as soon as their mission is over, as soon as they are no longer needed or desired. And let me add, we do not seek the destruction of Iraq. We have respect for the people of Iraq, for the importance of Iraq in the region. We do not want a country so destabilized that Iraq itself could be a target for aggression.

"The war in the Gulf is not a Christian war, a Jewish war, or a Moslem war—it is a just war."

But a just war must also be declared by legitimate authority. Operation Desert Storm is supported by unprecedented United Nations' solidarity, the principle of collective self-defense, 12 Security Council resolutions and, in the Gulf, 28 nations from six continents united—resolute that we will not waver and that Saddam's aggression will not stand.

I salute the aid—economic and military—from countries who have joined in this unprecedented effort—whose courage and sacrifice have inspired the world. We're not going it alone—but believe me, we are going to see it through.

Every war—every war—is fought for a reason. But a just war is fought for the right reasons—for moral, not selfish reasons. Let me take a moment to tell you a story—a tragic story—about a family whose two sons, 18 and 19, reportedly refused to lower the Kuwaiti flag in front of their home. For this crime, they were executed by the Iraqis. Then, unbelievably, their parents were asked to pay the price of the bullets used to kill them.

Some ask whether it's moral to use force to stop the rape, the pillage, the plunder of Kuwait. And my answer: Extraordinary diplomatic efforts having been exhausted to resolve the matter peacefully, then the use of force is moral.

A just war must be a last resort. As I have often said, we did not want war. But you all know the verse from Ecclesiastes: There is "a time for peace, a time for war." From August 2, 1990—to January 15, 1991—166 days—we tried to resolve this conflict. Secretary of State Jim Baker made an extraordinary effort to achieve peace. More than 200 meetings with foreign dignitaries, 10 diplomatic missions, six congressional appearances. Over 103,000 miles traveled to talk with, among others, members of the United Nations, the Arab League, and the European Community. And sadly, Saddam Hussein rejected out of hand every overture made by the United States and by other countries as well. He made this just war an inevitable war.

We all know that war never comes easy or cheap. War is never without the loss of innocent life. And that is war's greatest tragedy. But when a war must be fought for the greater good, it is our gravest obligation to conduct a war in proportion to the threat. And that is why we must act reasonably, humanely, and make every effort possible to keep casualties to a minimum. And we've done so. I'm very proud of our military in achieving this end.

> ## "The price of war is always high. And so it must never, ever, be undertaken without total commitment to a successful outcome."

From the very first day of the war, the allies have waged war against Saddam's military. We are doing everything possible, believe me, to avoid hurting the innocent. Saddam's response? Wanton, barbaric bombing of civilian areas. America and her allies value life. We pray that Saddam Hussein will see reason. To date, his indiscriminate use of those Scud missiles—nothing more than weapons of terror; they have no military—they can offer no military advantage, weapons of terror—it outraged the world what he has done.

The Price of War

The price of war is always high. And so it must never, ever, be undertaken without total commitment to a successful outcome. It is only justified when victory can be achieved. I have pledged that this will not be another Vietnam. And let me reassure you here today, it won't be another Vietnam.

We are fortunate, we are very fortunate to have in this crisis the finest Armed Forces ever assembled. An all-volunteer force, joined by courageous allies. And we will prevail because we have the finest soldiers, sailors, airmen, Marines, and Coast Guardsmen that any nation has ever had.

But above all, we will prevail because of the support of the American people. Armed with a trust in God and in the principles that make men free. . . .

America has always been a religious nation—perhaps never more than now. . . . Churches, synagogues, mosques reporting record attendance at services. Chapels packed during working hours as Americans stop in for a moment or two. Why? To pray for peace. And I know—of course, I know—that some disagree with the course that I've taken, and I have no bitterness in my heart about that at all, no anger. I am convinced that we are doing the right thing. And tolerance is a virtue, not a vice.

But with the support and prayers of so many, there can be no question in the minds of our soldiers or in the minds of our enemy about what Americans think. We know that this is a just war. And we know that, God willing, this is a war we will win. But most of all, we know that ours would not be the land of the free if it were not also the home of the brave. No one wanted war less than I did. No one is more determined to seize from battle the real peace that can offer hope, that can create a new world order.

When this war is over, the United States, its credibility and its reliability restored, will have a key leadership role in helping to bring peace to the rest of the Middle East. And I have been honored to serve as President of this great nation for two years now, and believe more than ever that one cannot be America's President without trust in God. I cannot imagine a world, a life, without the presence of the one through whom all things are possible.

During the darkest days of the Civil War, a man we revere not merely for what he did, but what he was, was asked whether he thought the Lord was on his side. And said Abraham Lincoln, "My concern is not whether God is on our side, but whether we are on God's side." My fellow Americans, I firmly believe in my heart of hearts that times will soon be on the side of peace because the world is overwhelmingly on the side of God.

Defending America's Oil Supply Justifies Military Action

Karen Elliott House

About the Author: Karen Elliott House is vice president, international, of Dow Jones & Company, the publisher of the Wall Street Journal, *from which this viewpoint is taken. The article was written one week after Iraq invaded Kuwait.*

The world changed last week. A grandiose Middle East dictator took control—not just of a neighboring sheikdom, but of the West's economic destiny in the 1990s.

Saddam Hussein, an insular leader who has had almost no contact with the Western world, nonetheless appears to have read the West's aversion to military involvement with unerring accuracy. Indeed, President Bush took four days even to suggest forcing the eviction of Iraqi invaders from Kuwait—and to dispatch his secretary of defense to Saudi Arabia to seek "permission" to protect that country. The Iraqi leader effectively has what he wants, for now—the ability to dictate world oil prices through the occupation or intimidation of major Middle East oil producers.

The West is congratulating itself on a rare show of rhetorical unity, is pledging boycotts of Iraqi-Kuwaiti oil and is making feeble noises about resisting Iraqi aggression against "vital interests" in Saudi Arabia, the world's largest repository of oil. But it all looks to be too little too late.

Our vital interest is not merely some particu-

Karen Elliott House, "No Appeasement of Iraq," *The Wall Street Journal,* August 7, 1990. Reprinted by permission of The Wall Street Journal, © 1990 Dow Jones & Company, Inc. All Rights Reserved Worldwide.

lar piece of Middle East real estate. It is the free flow of oil at tolerable prices. And that already has been lost. Regaining it is entirely possible—but only with patience, persistence and, yes, military power. It is false comfort to believe that if Saddam Hussein stops at Kuwait, the problem has been contained. Saddam Hussein certainly is smart enough to know that he doesn't need to invade Saudi Arabia to dictate its oil policy; his invasion of Kuwait and the absence thus far of a serious Western response ensures that Saudi King Fahd meekly will follow Iraq's line on oil production and pricing. Saddam is the wolf and Fahd the sheep. But it is Western consumers who will wind up being slaughtered.

Just as Western leaders in the late 1930s deluded themselves in believing that Adolf Hitler's ambitions could be bought off with one more little piece of Central Europe, the West today deludes itself in believing that Saddam Hussein's ambitions end with Kuwait. Whether he chooses to gobble another oil sheikdom now or later, the Iraqi leader has an ambition: to rule the Middle East through military threat, political intimidation and economic might. Barring Western military action, little stands in his way. Saddam Hussein used $50 billion in Kuwaiti and Saudi loans over the past decade to buy weapons he now uses against Kuwait. In coming years he will use Western money extorted for oil to buy weapons he uses against future victims.

> ## "Our vital interest is not merely some particular piece of Middle East real estate. It is the free flow of oil at tolerable prices."

A West that can't seem to learn the military lessons of Munich now at least has the possibility of reordering its flabby political and economic priorities. To begin with, Americans ought to dispense with the illusion that we now live in a kinder, gentler world. A multi-polar world with regional aggressions unrestrained by super-

power influence is going to be a more dangerous and violent age. The end of the Cold War, in
short, will be the beginning of an era of Hot
Wars. One need only watch the Soviets flapping
in rhetorical chorus with the West over Iraq's aggression to realize that superpower amity has little effect on regional enmity.

"Dominating oil prices is but a means to dominating the Middle East."

As the president and Congress continue to argue over the degree to which the military budget should be slashed, all parties owe the American people a greater degree of honesty. Those
seeking to decimate the defense budget ought
to at least grant that it will make America's response to actions like Saddam Hussein's not just
improbable but impossible.

Those, like the president and the Pentagon,
who argue for maintaining military strength le-
gitimately can be asked the question: Under
what circumstances do you ever intend to use
military force? If the military's purpose is to protect America's vital national interests, surely
those amount to more than rescuing a few score
Americans in a Liberian coup.

Military analysts talk of the year it would take
to assemble a ground defense of Saudi Arabia.
What, one wonders, has the Pentagon been doing during the 1980s? If the proponents of maintaining military strength are correct—and they
are—then the U.S. response cannot be to wallow
in the experience of Vietnam. If $300 billion
buys us a military capability that truly cannot be
employed, then the U.S. would be better off following the Japanese example and using that sum
to "buy" friends and bribe adversaries.

That's no policy for a great power. But the sad
truth in today's Washington is that the distinction between doves and hawks comes down to a
choice between low-cost or high-cost appeasement.

In the end, the question is this: what, if not
the West's oil supplies, constitutes a vital national interest? Lest we forget, it was only 17
years ago that Americans fumed in long gas lines
and the country believed itself hostage to
Mideast oil producers' whims. In 1974, only
about 12.3% of America's oil imports came from
the OPEC [Organization of Petroleum Exporting Countries]. . . . That figure is now about
28%.

It may not be part of Saddam Hussein's
agenda to put Americans back in the gas lines.
But almost surely it is within his power. In a recent interview with this newspaper, the Iraqi
leader stated that it was his policy to raise the
price of oil in order to acquire funds to rebuild
his war-exhausted economy. He also said he
wanted to acquire sophisticated weaponry sufficient at least to equal Israel.

Noting that the price of oil was around $14 a
barrel, the president in late June 1990 said "this
does not represent half of the real value of the
oil price in 1971. Who is responsible for this injustice? They are some of the Western states and
some of my friends in the region who do not see
beyond their noses. . . . No one can rule out using the economy or the role of his economy to
defend himself."

Saddam Hussein's Grand Design

The West mustn't delude itself about Saddam
Hussein's grand design: dominating oil prices is
but a means to dominating the Middle East. He
is no Mideast madman to be cowed by threats,
bought off by bribes or grudgingly tolerated as a
Gadhafi-like nuisance. He is shrewd, calculating,
relentless and ruthless. Most important, he is
vain and amoral, unchecked by any internal or
external inhibitions. He is loyal only to himself.
For instance, his friend and supporter, Jordan's
King Hussein, who visited Baghdad less than 24
hours before the Kuwaiti invasion, was unwittingly dispatched home to call Mr. Bush and assure him Saddam Hussein had no intention of
military action against Kuwait.

Over the next days and weeks the world is

likely to see more evidence of Saddam Hussein's calculating character. Almost certainly, he and his new Kuwaiti puppets will continue to round up foreigners—Americans, British, French—and threaten their lives if the West seeks to retaliate. Saddam understands, far better than Americans, the degree to which Western policy can be made hostage to hostages.

Saddam may even eventually pull some substantial portion of his forces out of Kuwait. But the Iraqi leader plays for the long term. He survived an eight-year war with Iran because he cares nothing for the human costs to his people. He will count on outlasting any short-term show of Western resolve.

To a journalist who has spent substantial time in Saudi Arabia over the past decade, the Saudi reaction in coming months is fully predictable—as was Saudi unwillingness even to condemn strongly the invasion of a fraternal sheikdom. The Saudi royal family, which numbers some 4,000 princes, has presided over its vast oil reserves by having only one policy—an insurance policy that pays protective premiums to every tough-guy or terrorist in the region. It is a policy that hopes for the benefits of an American security blanket without paying the political price of allowing an American military presence in the kingdom. It is the same policy that the Kuwaitis pursued. If the Saudis persist, they almost surely will come to the same end.

"The U.S. will have to act for its own self-preservation."

The one safe assumption about Saudi reaction these days is that the princes are fueling their private planes and further feathering their overseas bank accounts, while whispering to Saddam Hussein that they will defer to him on oil prices.

For the U.S., the point is not to be deceived by Saddam Hussein's cunning, deterred by Saudi Arabia's cowardice or distracted by the in-

evitably vain search for unified Western action. America has simply to pursue its own interest—the free flow of oil at acceptable prices.

Saddam Hussein now controls oil prices. He must be forced out of Kuwait and the U.S. must demonstrate its staying power in the region to preclude future Iraqi intimidation of major Mideast oil producers. The U.S. must immediately institute a naval blockade of Iraq, which is the only way to enforce at least a partially effective boycott of Iraqi-Kuwaiti oil. A fully effective embargo would require disrupting pipelines that carry the flow of Iraqi oil through Saudi Arabia and Turkey. These nations should act immediately to stop those flows. Anticipating this, Iraq has already sharply reduced the flow of oil to Turkish pipelines. It is possible Saudi Arabia might be persuaded by Defense Secretary Richard Cheney to shut the flow through its country.

Issue an Ultimatum

Surely, given American air and naval dominance, this level of immediate military confrontation is feasible and sustainable. The U.S. is, after all, a nation that once was willing to institute a naval blockade of Cuba in the face of Soviet threats of nuclear Armageddon. It is a nation that was willing to maintain a 15-month military airlift to beleaguered Berlin. If the rest of the Western world wishes to assist the U.S. that is good—but America can't make its interests hostage to the absence of a Western consensus.

It is of course true that an effective blockade of Iraq would remove 20% of the world's oil production from the market, driving prices higher and making a recession more likely. So be it. American consumers are going to pay higher prices for their gasoline one way or another. Better to pay that price as a temporary by-product of stopping Saddam Hussein than to pay it in perpetual ransom to a tyrant holding the global economy hostage.

The time has come to present the Saudis with a simple and realistic ultimatum: Accept an American military presence immediately or an

Iraqi military domination down the road. Minimally, the Saudis ought to allow U.S. naval and air forces to use Saudi ports and airfields and to permit the propositioning of materiel for a possible land defense of the kingdom.

If the Saudis decline U.S. help now, it will make their own demise that much more likely. It also will make U.S. military intervention in the region that much more difficult—but in the end, no less inevitable. For all of today's flapping and dawdling, for all the concern over diplomatic niceties and military difficulties, the handwriting is on the wall. Whether this month, next year or somewhere in the 1990s, this country will conclude that the world's oil supplies and its own economic destiny simply cannot be subject to the whim of a single Middle East despot. The U.S. will have to act for its own self-preservation.

Ending Iraqi Atrocities in Kuwait Justifies Military Action

Dan Quayle

About the Author: *Dan Quayle is the vice president of the United States, and a former U.S. senator from Indiana. The following viewpoint is a speech delivered by Quayle to the Foreign Policy Research Institute conference in Washington, D.C. on December 18, 1990.*

The more we learn about Saddam Hussein's barbarism in Kuwait, the clearer it becomes that the crisis is not, as Neville Chamberlain once said of Czechoslovakia, "A quarrel in a far-away country between people of whom we know nothing." Rather, Kuwait's plight and the future security of the Gulf are vital issues that affect us all—strategically, economically, and morally. But before addressing some of the issues your conference poses, I would like to take just a moment to pay tribute to the valor of some of the Kuwaiti people.

When Saddam Hussein was trying to round up Americans in Kuwait to serve as his "human shields," the people of Kuwait hid many of our citizens in their homes and provided them with food, medicine, and desperately needed shelter. In doing so, they quite literally put their own lives, and the lives of their loved ones, in terrible danger. I know I speak for President Bush and all Americans in saying that the Kuwaiti people have upheld the true honor and good name of the Arabs. Their courage and humanity will always be remembered.

Dan Quayle, "The Gulf: In Defense of Moral Principle." Speech delivered to the Foreign Policy Research Institute, December 18, 1990, Washington, D.C.

Today, thanks to President Bush's firm policy, the nightmare has ended for Saddam's American hostages. The nightmare has also ended for those Americans who lived in hiding in Kuwait these past 4 months, dreading the knock on the door by Iraqi troops.

But for the people of Kuwait, the nightmare is not over. For them, the agony continues, and what an agony it is. Summary executions of scores of people in front of their families; public hangings; families being terrorized by midnight searches; arbitrary arrests of thousands of people, including children; detainees being tortured with electric shocks and prolonged beatings; hospitals being taken over by Iraqi military authorities; medical personnel being detained or killed; and an entire nation being systematically looted of its food, its equipment, and its supplies.

"Is it moral to prolong the agony of the Kuwaiti people indefinitely?"

The cruelty of the Iraqi forces occupying Kuwait is almost unbelievable. Listen to Deborah Hadi, an American woman married to a Kuwaiti:

> We took our cousin, who was in labor, to Sabah Maternity Hospital. Upon our arrival, we saw a Kuwaiti woman at the front door—in hysterics, because she was in labor and Iraqi troops would not allow her to enter. When she continued to scream they put a bayonet through her stomach, pinning her to the wall. We left the hospital immediately and delivered my cousin's baby at home.

Or listen to Abdulal, a Kuwaiti:

> While at the market buying food for a family, I saw two boys, 15 and 16 years old, in handcuffs escorted to a house by Iraqi soldiers. . . . The Iraqi soldiers then asked their mother to call all family members outside the house. . . . In full view of the mother, sister, and brother, as well as 15 men and women in the marketplace, the Iraqi soldiers shot and killed them.

As Congressman Tom Lantos, the Democratic

co-chairman of the congressional human rights caucus, put it back in October 1990,

> In the 8-year history of the . . . caucus, we have never had the degree of ghoulish and nightmarish horror stories coming from totally credible eye witnesses that we have had this time.

It seems to me that those who advocate endless patience with Saddam Hussein, those who say we should give him 12 months, or 18 months before contemplating the use of force, ought to think long and hard about what Congressman Lantos said.

And those who call for unlimited patience on moral grounds should ask themselves a few simple questions: Is it moral to prolong the agony of the Kuwaiti people indefinitely? If Kuwaitis refused to stand by as Americans were being hunted down by the Iraqis, is it right for Americans to stand by as Kuwaitis are being tortured and raped and brutalized? And will there even be a Kuwait left to save in a year or a year-and-a-half's time?

For our part, the Bush Administration's policy is clear and firm today, as it has been for the past 4 months. We are not going to budge one iota from the goals the President laid out at the start of this crisis, goals reaffirmed in 12 Security Council resolutions: achieving the complete and unconditional withdrawal of all Iraqi forces from Kuwait, restoring the legitimate government of Kuwait, releasing all the hostages, and maintaining the security and stability of the Gulf region. We must achieve all of these objectives.

Answering the Critics

Some critics of the Administration have questioned these goals. In particular, they have questioned the morality of coming to the defense of what they call a "feudal," "reactionary," and "repressive" regime.

Quite frankly, I am always astonished whenever I hear these charges made. First of all, the accusations against Kuwait are false. Secondly, since when has it become acceptable to loot and rape and torture people because they happen to live in a society whose customs differ from our own? And since when have Americans subscribed to a false, class-based morality that classifies some groups as "reactionary," and therefore expendable, and others as "progressive," and therefore beyond reproach?

"The United States and the world . . . have no reason to apologize for demanding that the legitimate government of Kuwait be restored."

This is precisely the warped and evil morality used by Stalin and his henchmen to justify their infamous campaign of terror during the 1930s. The people of the Soviet Union have turned their backs on the morally demented legacy of Stalinism. And so shall we.

The government of Kuwait is not the result of conspiracy and *coup d'etat*, and its rule is not enforced by terror and repression. The United States and the world, therefore, have no reason to apologize for demanding that the legitimate government of Kuwait be restored. Nor have we any reason to demand or accept anything less than the total and unconditional withdrawal of Iraqi forces from Kuwait. These are legitimate demands. These are moral demands. And these demands are not subject to negotiation.

In support of these demands, close to half a million troops are gathered in the Persian Gulf. Over one-third of the troop count is provided by our allies. But, some contributing nations are providing proportionately a greater percentage of their military forces than we are. Twenty-eight nations have committed military support to the allied Persian Gulf effort. This support comes from all quarters of the world, including members of the Warsaw Pact.

The majority of Muslim nations opposes the Iraqi invasion of Kuwait; 11 have committed military forces to the crisis. Egypt, Saudi Arabia, and Syria lead in terms of numbers of troops and equipment.

The UK [United Kingdom] has supported the allied effort in every way possible, including tens of thousands of troops, squadrons of fighter/bombers, and several navy vessels in the Gulf. The French have been supportive, with more than tens of thousands of committed troops and equipment. Turkey, which borders the much larger Iraq, from the outset courageously condemned the Iraqi invasion and pledged to send troops into combat in event of an Iraqi attack. The Germans and Japanese have pledged considerable sums of money.

The American people—like the international community as a whole—understand and support our objectives. A majority of the public approves of the President's decision to send troops to the Persian Gulf. And an equally large majority believes that the United States should, if need be, take all action necessary, including military force, to compel Iraq to withdraw from Kuwait.

The American People Understand

The American people understand that Saddam Hussein's Iraq poses a long-term threat not just to its neighbors but to us. They know that over the past decade, Saddam Hussein has bankrupted his people to bankroll his army. They know that he has launched two wars of aggression, against Iran and against Kuwait, at the cost of some 1 million lives—thus far. They know he is acquiring a sizable stockpile of chemical and biological weapons, and has used chemical weapons against both Iran and his own people. They know he has launched an ambitious campaign to acquire nuclear weapons. And they know that unless he is stopped today, a nuclear-armed Iraq will control the bulk of the world's energy supply tomorrow, thereby holding a gun to all our heads.

Because the President is determined to leave no stone unturned in the search for peace, he has offered to send Secretary of State James Baker to Baghdad, and has invited Iraq's Foreign Minister [Tariq Aziz] to Washington.

Unfortunately, Iraq's attempt to manipulate this process makes it far from certain that these meetings will take place. But one thing is certain. If Secretary Baker does go to Baghdad, his message to Saddam Hussein will be loud and clear: You may leave all of Kuwait peacefully, without conditions, or you will leave Kuwait by force.

Once Iraqi forces have left Kuwait, however, and once the legitimate Kuwaiti government has been restored, our job will still not be over. We will have to work to see that the President's final objective—maintaining security and stability in the region—is achieved. We cannot allow a situation in which an aggressive dictator has a million-man army, thousands of tanks and artillery pieces, hundreds of jets, and access to billions of petro-dollars.

We cannot allow such a dictator credibly to threaten any of his neighbors should they not meet his political and economic demands. Neither we nor our friends in the region are prepared to live with such a situation. Moreover, we cannot allow the development of new and more deadly chemical and biological weapons, and the long-range delivery systems to threaten every nation in the region. And we can't allow the acquisition of an indigenous nuclear weapons production capability—also deliverable at long ranges.

Saddam's record makes it clear that he would not hesitate to use these weapons, just as he has not hesitated to use chemical weapons against his own people. And we are not willing to let that happen.

"Having tried to erase an entire nation from the face of the earth, Saddam cannot simply walk away without penalty."

That is why we intend to see all the President's objectives attained, and all 12 UN [United Nations] Security Council resolutions carried out—including UN Security Council Resolution 674, which declares Iraq responsible for all damage resulting from its occupation of Kuwait.

Restoring the *status quo ante* would not be enough. Having tried to erase an entire nation from the face of the earth, Saddam cannot simply walk away without penalty and in a position to repeat his aggression.

"We will not fail. We will act decisively in defense of our moral principles and strategic interests."

As for the United States, we will continue to play a positive role in the region. Presidents Truman, Carter, and Reagan all recognized that the US has vital interests in the Middle East. And President Bush is fully determined to defend these interests.

As the President said in his September 11, 1990 speech to Congress:

> Our interest, our involvement in the Gulf is not transitory. It pre-dated Saddam Hussein's aggression and it will survive it. Long after our troops come home. . . there will be a lasting role for the United States in assisting the nations of the Persian Gulf. Our role then: To deter future aggression . . . to help our friends in their own self-defense . . . and to curb the proliferation of chemical, biological, ballistic missile, and above all nuclear technologies.

Of course, it won't be easy. Of course, we will all have our work cut out for us. But failure to achieve our objectives is unacceptable. Failure would mean that no future aggressor would be deterred by warnings from the United States or the United Nations. Failure would lead to a new, post-Cold War world more prone to anarchy, and more violent, than the world which preceded it.

We will not fail. We will act decisively in defense of our moral principles and strategic interests. And we will work together to ensure the security of all the states in the region. This is both the challenge and the opportunity facing us today.

Destroying Iraq's Nuclear Capability Justifies Military Action

Richard Perle

About the Author: *Richard Perle, a resident fellow at the American Enterprise Institute in Washington, D.C., served as assistant secretary of defense during the Reagan administration. The following article was written on August 22, 1990, three weeks after Iraq invaded Kuwait.*

In 1981, Israeli aircraft destroyed the Baghdad facility from which Saddam Hussein expected to obtain the plutonium for a nuclear weapon. The breathtaking accuracy of the Israeli air force was admired privately in defense ministries around the world. But most governments denounced the Israeli action.

Had Israel not sent its planes against the Osirak reactor, our world would be a different and far more dangerous one today. Saddam could have marched into Kuwait with the "try and stop me" swagger that would come from nuclear weapons added to his already formidable arsenal of nerve gas and hostages. Nuclear weapons, once thought of as the "great equalizer," must now be seen differently. They are one thing in the hands of governments animated by rational policies to protect national interests and a normal regard for human life. They are quite another in the hands of a brutal megalomaniac like Saddam who wouldn't blink at the mass destruction of his "enemies."

So nine years later we—this time it's our turn—had better be prepared to do it again.

The destruction of Iraq's nascent nuclear capability together with its capacity to build chemical weapons should be the first priority of American policy in the current crisis. The restoration of Kuwaiti sovereignty and the total withdrawal of Iraqi forces from Kuwait are important. But stopping Saddam from obtaining nuclear weapons is more important still. If this crisis ends with Iraq's nascent nuclear capabilities and chemical weapons production facilities and stockpiles intact, the Western world will have made a mistake of historic proportions.

It took the U.S. four days to decide that Iraq's brutal invasion of Kuwait was unacceptable. How long would it have taken the American president to respond—and who would have joined us—if Saddam had nuclear weapons? Would the U.S. have sent 100,000 troops within range of Iraqi nuclear missiles? With nuclear weapons Saddam would rule the Gulf and control the world's supply of oil.

> **"The destruction of Iraq's nascent nuclear capability . . . should be the first priority of American policy in the current crisis."**

In the years since Israel acted to enforce the nuclear non-proliferation treaty in the only way Saddam respects, Iraq, with help from America's allies, has rebuilt its nuclear facilities, burrowing deep underground and deploying massive air defenses to protect them. Meanwhile, Iraq is trying to obtain the ballistic missile technology that would enable a nuclear weapon to be delivered over great distances. One would think that there would be a concerted effort by Iraq's potential victims to thwart these nuclear missile ambitions.

Yet less than a month ago, at the last minute and over the strenuous objections of the Commerce Department (which had previously approved the deal), the U.S. stopped the shipment to Iraq of a $15 million sophisticated metallurgical furnace said to be for the manufacture of titanium alloy prosthetic devices. The furnace was actually intended to advance Saddam's nuclear and ballistic missile programs.

"The cohesion of the advanced industrial powers is essential to any effective administration of export controls."

Ariane, the French-led European space consortium, is now assisting Brazil in the development of a ballistic missile "for civilian space purposes." Brazil, in turn, has been supplying Saddam with missiles derived from earlier European-supported "civilian" programs. The U.S. is on the verge of authorizing the sale to a Brazilian company involved in missile development of a largely unsafeguarded supercomputer. It will almost certainly be put at the service of its missile development program. (At the same time, we have, for more than two years, refused licenses for Israeli universities to purchase supercomputers that they are willing to place under any set of restrictive safeguards the U.S. desires.)

Even the chemical weapons with which Saddam now threatens to destroy Israel, American forces in the Gulf or anyone else who stands in his way are derived, in large part, from Western suppliers of technology and precursor chemicals. The West Germans' lax regime of export controls and deliberately anemic enforcement has been most egregious. But they are not alone.

If American troops come under attack from Iraqi chemical weapons in 1990 (or Iraqi nuclear weapons later), myopic Western greed, nurtured by policy confusion and bureaucratic incompetence, will bear much of the blame.

When the current crisis is over, it should be a priority American policy to strengthen significantly controls over the export of sensitive technology to Iraq and to insist that our allies do the same. But even a strictly enforced, comprehen-

sive export control regime would be unlikely to stop Iraq's nuclear and chemical programs at this late stage in their development. That's why an air attack on the facilities is an essential first step to putting the Iraqi genie back in the bottle. The cork of export controls should follow.

If we are to destroy Iraq's nuclear and chemical weapons potential through military action and export controls, we need to organize our allies accordingly.

The NATO [North Atlantic Treaty Organization] allies (with the Soviet Union, Iraq's principal suppliers of military equipment and technology) have long insisted that the Gulf is outside NATO's "area" and thus not subject to coordinated NATO policies or actions. As the dire threat to the European economies of war and turbulence in the Gulf has long been obvious, the U.S. has long encouraged NATO to think about, and plan for, contingencies in the Gulf like the war and occupation now under way.

Until the Iraqi invasion of Kuwait, the American effort to broaden NATO's horizon had largely failed. Even as Iraqi occupation forces round up hostages and Saddam instigates a holy war against Western interests, West German Foreign Minister Hans-Dietrich Genscher, whose country is dependent on Middle East oil, cowers behind an interpretation of the German constitution that would preclude Germany joining its allies in the Gulf. And the French, whose cynical alliance with Iraq has helped to make Saddam a military power, were openly critical of the American blockade until joining it this week. (President Francois Mitterrand said that France would send ground forces to the United Arab Emirates in response to the Persian Gulf crisis.)

UN Sanctions

Britain, however, has behaved admirably in the current crisis. So have some others. Turkey gets half its oil through the Iraqi pipeline it closed in support of the U.N. [United Nations] sanctions and it trades extensively with Iraq. Although it has a great deal to lose, Turkey has courageously stood with the U.S., doing more for the security of the European Community than many of the community's own members.

The silver lining in the cloud of Saddam's invasion of Kuwait may be a long-overdue realization on the part of some NATO allies that they have important interests outside central Europe whose protection may require the exertion of military power. Defense Secretary Richard Cheney has been arguing this theme persuasively within NATO councils. He can now do so with the credibility that comes from demonstrated prescience.

> **"The most formidable threat to our well-being would be a Saddam in possession of true weapons of mass destruction."**

The cohesion of the advanced industrial powers is essential to any effective administration of export controls. This can be obtained only through a combination of argument and, where necessary, the sort of pressure that the world's largest market and principal supplier of technology can apply—when it has a mind to. What has been lacking is clarity and will on the part of the U.S. American ambivalence has been evident in the continuing differences between the departments of Commerce and Defense and the action of the Congress in pressuring a pliable and divided administration to decimate controls on the export of sensitive technologies to countries where they will be used for military purposes. In this situation it is hardly surprising that venal German and craven French exporters have elicited commercial envy at the Commerce Department and met acquiescence at the State Department.

For the more immediate task, the destruction of Iraq's present—as opposed to its future—weapons programs, the support of America's al-

lies, while desirable, is not essential. The U.S. has the air power to do the job alone. While some logistic support, like the use of European bases from which to stage air strikes, would be helpful, we should not be deterred by reluctance on the part of countries that, having been part of the problem, now wish to escape becoming part of the solution.

The True Threat

As for diplomatic support, it would be nice if we could get it—but not if we have to pay for it by ending the current crisis with a face-saving tactical retreat by Saddam that would enable him to fight another day. The opinion of Hans-Dietrich Genscher is a flyspeck alongside the Western interests that are at stake in toppling Saddam by destroying his military potential and, in so doing, making it plain that we will not allow nuclear weapons to fall into the hands of international thugs.

Saddam will not be the last menace to Western interests, and he is certainly not the most formidable. The most formidable threat to our well-being would be a Saddam in possession of true weapons of mass destruction and prepared to use them to extort power and wealth from those unable to defend against them or deter their use. In any contest in which one side is bound by the norms of civilized behavior and the other is not, history is, alas, on the side of the barbarians. This is a lesson to remember before we cancel the B-2 bomber and thereby give up the capability to destroy targets safely anywhere in the world without requiring foreign bases.

An attack on Iraq's nuclear and chemical facilities will not be cost-free. But in the long run, sparing them will prove even more costly. President Bush deserves to know that he will have bipartisan support for a policy that recognizes this.

We have a narrow choice: Fly now or pay later.

The Failure of Economic Sanctions Justifies Military Action

John C. Danforth and William Webster

About the Authors: *John C. Danforth, a Republican, is a U.S. senator from Missouri. He is a member of several Senate committees, including the Select Committee on Intelligence. William Webster is former director of the Central Intelligence Agency.*

Editor's Note: The following viewpoint is taken from a speech John C. Danforth delivered to the U.S. Senate on January 10, 1991. Danforth supported the Senate resolution authorizing President George Bush to use force to expel Iraq from Kuwait. During his speech, Danforth presented the testimony given by William Webster before a U.S. House of Representatives committee in December 1990. Webster concluded that sanctions would not force Iraq to withdraw from Kuwait.

Like all my colleagues, I have been engaged in intensive soul-searching on how I will vote on the question now before the Senate, whether to support the President if he determines force is necessary to expel Iraq from Kuwait. Throughout this soul-searching, two convictions have been foremost in my mind.

First, I am convinced beyond a doubt that the United States must not allow the status quo in Kuwait to stand. Some have argued that the President has not made a clear case for America's insistence that Iraq must withdraw from Kuwait, but for me the President's case is both crystal clear and overwhelmingly convincing.

John C. Danforth, address to the U.S. Senate, January 10, 1991. William Webster, testimony before the U.S. House of Representatives Armed Services Committee, December 4, 1990.

This is the first major test of the post-Cold-War world order. With the recent collapse of the Soviet Empire, the great threat we have feared since 1945 is no longer real. The likelihood is zero that the Soviet Union will precipitate war by invading Western Europe. But the events of August 2, 1990, have demonstrated to all that to be rid of one threat does not make the world safe. A growing list of countries now possess or soon will possess the instruments of mass destruction. One of those countries is Iraq. It is simply not sufficient to check the possibility of terrifying aggression at one of its sources. We must be prepared to check terrifying aggression at all of its sources.

In Kuwait, Iraq is the aggressor, and its actions cannot be tolerated. Nearly all of us agree on this point. Iraq attacked its neighbor, occupied its territory, and brutalized its people. It has fielded a massive army with chemical and biological warfare capability that it has no compunctions about using. It now controls 20 percent of the world's proven oil reserves, and, if undeterred, it could control an additional 25 percent of world reserves in Saudi Arabia by conquest or intimidation.

> ## "The United States must not allow the status quo in Kuwait to stand."

Some people have asked whether this conflict is not "just about" oil. To me, that is like asking whether it is not just about oxygen. Like it or not, our country, together with the rest of the world, is utterly dependent on oil. Our economy, our jobs, our ability to defend ourselves are dependent on our access to oil. To control the world's supply of oil is in a real sense to control the world. So what is involved in the Persian Gulf today is not only the preservation of the world order and the prevention of brutal aggression; it is the vital economic and security interests of the United States and the rest of the world as well.

For many years, commentators of various philosophical stripes, especially liberal commentators, have argued that the United States should not go it alone in the world. We should not take it upon ourselves to be the world's policeman. So the commentators have argued, with respect to Central America and elsewhere, that our country should not act unilaterally; we should work with other countries; we should address crises on a multilateral basis.

"Sanctions alone will cause suffering to the civilian population of Iraq but they will not force the Iraqi Army from Kuwait."

This is exactly what President Bush has done with respect to the present crisis. He has gone repeatedly to the United Nations Security Council for approval of concerted action. He and Secretary of State James Baker have consulted incessantly with countries throughout the world. He has asked for and received the military and economic support of more than 20 nations. He has been widely acclaimed, especially by the liberals, for this multilateral approach.

It is argued that while many nations have done something, few nations have done enough. I suppose this point would always be made no matter what the degree of commitment by our partners. But what are we to make of such an argument? That multilateralism was a mistake after all? That no matter how assiduously pursued, it never really works?

The advocates of multilateralism cannot have it both ways. They cannot applaud it one day, and jeer at it the next. Would that there were more leaders from the free world, but the fact is that the United States is the leader. We are the one remaining world power. And if the United States now retreats from its commitment for a joint effort on the ground that others are not as strong or as firm as we are, all the efforts to seek Security Council resolutions and to consult with other governments will have been an exercise of futility, recognized as such throughout the world.

The captain cannot abandon the ship. Having gained the approval of so many other governments, some of which are on the very border of Iraq and in great peril for their survival, it is unthinkable that our government would now lose its will. Having urged the world to approve combined action, it is not an option for the Congress of the United States to disapprove what we for months have asked others to support.

This then is my first conviction: We cannot accept Iraq's occupation of Kuwait.

My second conviction is that war with Iraq would be a disaster we should do everything to avoid. I have believed and I do believe that the negative consequences of war far outweigh the positive. These negatives have totally consumed my thinking and I have expressed them to the President and to key members of his administration.

I foresee many casualties, the use of chemical weapons by Iraq, terrorist strikes, Israel's involvement, and long-lasting turmoil in the Middle East. Repeatedly, I asked myself the same question: When we win the war, then what happens? What happens to the balance of power in the Middle East? To the governance of Iraq? To the stability of friendly governments in Egypt and Saudi Arabia? Repeatedly I have come to the same answers. While the status quo is unacceptable, the alternative of war is even worse.

Because of this conclusion I have for some time believed that if I had to vote on the matter, I would vote against authorizing the President to use military force. I have taken comfort in the proposition that we will soon be voting on it here in the Senate. Let us give sanctions a chance to work.

The Sanctions and the Status Quo

But after consulting with the best advice I can find, I have concluded that there is no comfort to be found in that proposition. It is clear to me that sanctions alone cannot reverse the status quo. Sanctions alone will cause suffering to the civilian population of Iraq but they will not force the Iraqi Army from Kuwait. And causing suffering to a civilian population without military results should never be the objective of a civilized nation.

I refer the Senate to the public testimony of Director of Central Intelligence William Webster before the House Armed Services Committee in December 1990. I ask unanimous consent, as others have, that a transcript of that testimony be printed in the Record at this point.

There being no objection, the material was ordered to be printed in the Record, as follows:

Sanctions in the Persian Gulf
Iraq, The Domestic Impact of Sanctions, December 1990

William Webster's Testimony

I appreciate the opportunity to address this committee on what the intelligence community believes the sanctions have already accomplished and what we believe the sanctions are likely to accomplish over time. Of course, sanctions are only one type of pressure being applied on Iraq, and their impact cannot be completely distinguished from the combined impact of military, diplomatic, and economic initiatives on Iraq.

At the technical level, economic sanctions and the embargo against Iraq have put Saddam Hussein on notice that he is isolated from the world community and have dealt a serious blow to the Iraqi economy. More than 100 countries are supporting the U.N. resolutions that impose economic sanctions on Iraq. Coupled with the U.S. government's increased ability to detect and follow up on attempts to circumvent the blockade, the sanctions have all but shut off Iraq's exports and reduced imports to less than 10 percent of their preinvasion level. All sectors of the Iraqi economy are feeling the pinch of sanctions and many industries have largely shut down. Most importantly, the blockade has eliminated any hope Baghdad had of cashing in on

higher oil prices or its seizure of Kuwait oilfields.

Despite mounting disruptions and hardships resulting from sanctions, Saddam apparently believes that he can outlast international resolve to maintain sanctions. We see no indication that Saddam is concerned, at this point, that domestic discontent is growing to levels that may threaten his regime or that problems resulting from the sanctions are causing him to rethink his policy on Kuwait. The Iraqi people have experienced considerable deprivation in the past. Given the brutal nature of the Iraqi security services, the population is not likely to oppose Saddam openly. Our judgment has been, and continues to be, that there is no assurance or guarantee that economic hardships will compel Saddam to change his policies or lead to internal unrest that would threaten his regime.

Let me take a few minutes to review briefly with you some of the information that led us to these conclusions, as well as to present our assessment of the likely impact of sanctions over the coming months.

The blockade and embargo have worked more effectively than Saddam probably expected. More than 90 percent of imports and 97 percent of exports have been shut off. Although there is smuggling across Iraq's borders, it is extremely small relative to Iraq's pre-crisis trade. Iraqi efforts to break sanctions have thus far been largely unsuccessful. What little leakage has occurred is due largely to a relatively small number of private firms acting independently. We believe most countries are actively enforcing the sanctions and plan to continue doing so.

"On balance, the embargo has increased the economic hardships facing the average Iraqi."

Industry appears to be the hardest hit sector so far. Many firms are finding it difficult to cope, with the departure of foreign workers and with the cutoff of imported industrial inputs—which comprised nearly 60 percent of Iraq's total imports prior to the invasion. These shortages have either shut down or severely curtailed production by a variety of industries, including many light industrial and assembly plants as well as the country's only tire-manufacturing plant. Despite these shutdowns, the most vital industries—including electric power generation and refining—do not yet appear threatened. We believe they will be able to function for some time because domestic consumption has been reduced, because Iraqi and Kuwaiti facilities have been cannibalized and because some stockpiles and surpluses already existed.

"Although sanctions are hurting Iraq's civilian economy, they are affecting the Iraqi military only at the margins."

The cutoff of Iraq's oil exports and the success of sanctions also have choked off Baghdad's financial resources. This too has been more effective and more complete than Saddam probably expected. In fact, we believe that a lack of foreign exchange will, in time, be Iraq's greatest economic difficulty. The embargo has deprived Baghdad of roughly $1.5 billion of foreign exchange earnings monthly. We have no evidence that Iraq has significantly augmented the limited foreign exchange reserves to which it still has access. As a result, Baghdad is working to conserve foreign exchange and to devise alternative methods to finance imports.

We believe Baghdad's actions to forestall shortages of food stocks—including rationing, encouraging smuggling, and promoting agricultural production—are adequate for the next several months. The fall harvest of fruits and vegetables is injecting new supplies into the market and will provide a psychological as well as tangible respite from mounting pressures. The Iraqi population, in general, has access to sufficient staple foods. Other foodstuffs—still not rationed—also remain available. However, the variety is diminishing and prices are sharply inflated. For example, sugar purchased on the open market at the official exchange rate went from $32 per 50-kilogram bag in August 1990 to $580 per bag in December 1990. Baghdad remains concerned about its food stocks and, increasingly, diverts supplies to the military. In late November 1990, Baghdad cut civilian rations for the second time since the rationing program began, while announcing increases in rations for military personnel and their families.

On balance, the embargo has increased the economic hardships facing the average Iraqi. In order to supplement their rations, Iraqis must turn to the black market, where most goods can be purchased but at highly inflated prices. They are forced to spend considerable amounts of time searching for reasonably priced food or waiting in lines for bread and other rationed items. In addition, services ranging from medical care to sanitation have been curtailed. But these hardships are easier for Iraqis to endure than the combination of economic distress, high casualty rates, and repeated missile and air attacks that Iraqis lived with during the eight-year Iran-Iraq war. During this war, incidentally, there was not a single significant public disturbance even though casualties hit 2.3 percent of the total Iraqi population—about the same as the percentage of U.S. casualties during the Civil War.

Looking Ahead

Looking ahead, the economic picture changes somewhat. We expect Baghdad's foreign exchange reserves to become extremely tight, leaving it little cash left with which to entice potential sanctions busters. At current rates of depletion, we estimate Iraq will have nearly depleted its available foreign exchange reserves by Spring 1991. Able to obtain even fewer key imports, Iraq's economic problems will begin to multiply as Baghdad is forced to gradually shut down growing numbers of facilities in order to keep critical activities functioning as long as possible. Economic conditions will be noticeably worse, and Baghdad will find allocating scarce resources a significantly more difficult task.

Functioning Industries

Probably only energy-related and some military industries will still be fully functioning by spring 1991. This will almost certainly be the case by summer 1991. Baghdad will try to keep basic services such as electric power from deteriorating. The regime also will try to insulate critical military industries to prevent an erosion of military preparedness. Nonetheless, reduced rations, coupled with rapid inflation and little additional support from the government will compound the economic pressures facing most Iraqis.

By Spring 1991, Iraqis will have made major changes in their diets. Poultry, a staple of the Iraqi diet, will not be available. Unless Iraq receives humanitarian food aid or unless smuggling increases, some critical commodities, such as sugar and edible oils, will be in short supply. Distribution problems are likely to create localized shortages. But we expect that Baghdad will be able to maintain grain consumption—mainly wheat, barley, and rice—at about two-thirds of 1989's level until the next harvest in May 1991.

The spring grain and vegetable harvest will again augment food stocks, although only temporarily. To boost 1991's food production, Baghdad has raised prices paid to farmers for their produce and decreed that farmers must cultivate all available land. Nonetheless, Iraq does not have the capability to become self-sufficient in food production by 1991. Weather is the critical variable in grain production and even if it is good, Iraqis will be able to produce less than half the grain they need. In addition, Iraq's vegetable production in 1991 may be less than normal because of its inability to obtain seed stock from abroad. Iraq had obtained seed from the United States, the Netherlands, and France.

Although sanctions are hurting Iraq's civilian economy, they are affecting the Iraqi military only at the margins. Iraq's fairly static, defensive posture will reduce wear and tear on military equipment and, as a result, extend the life of its inventory of spare parts and maintenance items. Under now-combat conditions, Iraqi ground and air forces can probably maintain near-current levels of readiness for as long as nine months.

We expect the Iraqi Air Force to feel the effects of the sanctions more quickly and to a greater degree than the Iraqi ground forces because of its greater reliance on high technology and foreign equipment and technicians. Major repairs to sophisticated aircraft like the F-1 will be achieved with significant difficulty, if at all, because of the exodus of foreign technicians. Iraqi technicians, however, should be able to maintain current levels of aircraft sorties for three to six months.

"Standing by themselves and without the credible threat of military force, sanctions have no chance of expelling Iraq from Kuwait."

The Iraqi ground forces are more immune to sanctions. Before the invasion, Baghdad maintained large inventories of basic military supplies, such as ammunition, and supplies probably remain adequate. The embargo will eventually hurt Iraqi armor by preventing the replacement of old fire-control systems and creating shortages of additives for various critical lubricants. Shortages will also affect Iraqi cargo trucks over time.

While we can look ahead several months and predict the gradual deterioration of the Iraqi economy, it is more difficult to assess how or when these conditions will cause Saddam to modify his behavior. At present, Saddam almost certainly assumes that he is coping effectively with the sanctions. He appears confident in the ability of his security services to contain potential discontent, and we do not believe he is troubled by the hardships Iraqis will be forced to endure. Saddam's willingness to sit tight and try to outlast the sanctions or, in the alternative, to avoid war by withdrawing from Kuwait will be determined by his total assessment of the political, economic, and military pressures arrayed against him.

Danforth's Commentary

The conclusion of Director Webster is that sanctions in themselves will not lead to the overthrow of Saddam Hussein, and that they will not lead him to change his policy toward Kuwait. The Director states that if Saddam Hussein decides to withdraw from Kuwait, that decision, and I quote,

> will be determined by his total assessment of the political, economic, and military pressures arrayed against him.

It is my privilege to serve on the Select Committee on Intelligence. I am precluded, of course, from divulging classified information I have received in briefings in that committee. However, I am free to state my own conclusions on the basis of my total understanding. My conclusion is this. Standing by themselves and without the credible threat of military force, sanctions have no chance of expelling Iraq from Kuwait.

"To wait for sanctions to work is to wait while we get weaker and Iraq bides its time."

Some have argued that sanctions would over time weaken Iraq's military position and make an eventual conflict less costly to American forces. But this assumption is not borne out by the best available advice, including Director Webster's public testimony. The Director states that "under known combat conditions, Iraqi ground and air forces can probably maintain near current levels of readiness for as long as 9 months." He further states that the Iraqi Air Force would feel the effects of sanctions to a greater degree than ground forces, which are more immune to sanctions, but it is ground forces that dug into Kuwait in massive numbers and it has been said that ground forces have never been defeated by air superiority alone.

I know that there have been various interpretations offered in the Senate about exactly what Director Webster said in his testimony on December 5, 1990. It could be said that he testified that sanctions work. If the meaning of "work" is to inflict pain on civilians, that conclusion is absolutely correct. But there is no way to read the testimony of Director Webster on December 5 and come out with a conclusion that the sanctions offer any possibility of removing Iraq from Kuwait in the foreseeable future.

I would like to quote just a few excerpts from the letter that Director Webster has written today to Chairman Les Aspin, of the House Armed Services Committee. These are the words of William Webster. First, characterizing his testimony of December 5, he said:

> I also testified that there was no evidence that sanctions would mandate a change in Saddam Hussein's behavior and that there was no evidence when or even if they would force him out of Kuwait.

And then the Director goes on and says this:

> The ability of the Iraqi ground forces to defend Kuwait and southern Iraq is unlikely to be substantially eroded over the next 6 to 12 months even if effective sanctions can be maintained. This is especially true if Iraq does not believe a coalition attack is likely during this period. Iraq's infantry and artillery forces—the key elements of Iraq's initial defense—probably would not suffer significantly as a result of sanctions. Iraq could easily maintain the relatively simple Soviet-style weaponry of its infantry and artillery units and can produce virtually all of the ammunition for these forces domestically. Moreover, these forces will have additional opportunity to extend and reinforce their fortifications along the Saudi border, thereby increasing their defensive strength.

The Director then says:

> On balance, the marginal decline of combat power in Baghdad's armored units probably

would be offset by the simultaneous improvement of its defensive fortifications.

Iraq's Air Force and air defenses are more likely to be hit far more severely than its army, if effective sanctions are maintained for another 6 to 12 months. This degradation will diminish Iraq's ability to defend its strategic assets from air attack and reduce its ability to conduct similar attacks on its neighbors. It would have only a marginal impact on Saddam's ability to hold Kuwait and southern Iraq. The Iraqi Air Force is not likely to play a major role in any battle for Kuwait.

Our judgment remains that even if sanctions continue to be enforced for an additional 6 to 12 months, economic hardship alone is unlikely to compel Saddam to retreat from Kuwait or cause regime-threatening popular discontent in Iraq.

So is time on our side, as I have long wanted to believe? I cannot persuade myself that this was any more than wishful thinking on my part.

"The key to peace is maintaining a credible military threat."

What happens for the next 9 months or a year, or more than a year, as we vainly wait for the Iraqis to leave their fortifications? Do we keep more than 400,000 troops in place through Ramadan, through the Hadj, through the summer? And if so, what happens to their readiness, their support by the American people, their acceptance by the Muslim masses? To ask these questions is to answer them.

Waiting Makes No Sense

To wait for sanctions to work is to wait while we get weaker and Iraq bides its time. The one and only chance to accomplish our objectives without war is to maintain sanctions accompanied by a credible military threat. Without a credible military threat, our alternative is sanctions followed by nothing at all.

The key to peace is maintaining a credible military threat, and this is precisely the point our pending votes will address. Those who would give sanctions a chance before military action is even possible would decouple the two components which must be kept linked, if we have any chance of getting Iraq out of Kuwait without a fight. They would foreclose any possibility of a just peace.

This is why I cannot vote for sanctions alone. This is why I cannot vote to deprive the President of the credible threat of force. It is indeed a supreme irony that it is only through the threat of force that a stable world can be maintained. But that is an irony we have recognized ever since World War II.

Prelude to the Gulf War: Is Military Action Justified?

No: Military Action Is Not Justified

Military Action Is Not Justified
Military Action Is Immoral
Defending America's Oil Supply Does Not Justify Military Action
Liberating Kuwait Does Not Justify Military Action
Destroying Iraq's Nuclear Capability Does Not Justify Military Action
Maintaining Economic Sanctions May Prevent the Need for Military Action

Military Action Is Not Justified

Robert Brenner

About the Author: Robert Brenner is a professor of history at the University of California, Los Angeles. The following article was written shortly after the outbreak of hostilities in the Persian Gulf.

Why is the United States at war with Iraq? It is a lot easier to say what are *not* the reasons for US intervention in the Gulf than to provide a fully satisfactory account of its presence there. According to the Bush administration, the USA is fighting Iraq because Saddam Hussein is a ruthless tyrant who has carried out an unjust invasion of Kuwait. In the pompous rhetoric of the President's State of the Union address, 'What is at stake is . . . a new world order—where diverse nations are drawn together in common cause to achieve the universal aspirations of mankind: peace and security, freedom and the rule of law . . . Saddam Hussein's unprovoked invasion . . . will not stand.' It is important to take the administration's rhetoric seriously, because what might be called its empirical premises are, in one respect, obviously correct. Saddam Hussein *is* a ruthless tyrant and his invasion of Kuwait must be condemned. Popular support in the USA for the administration's war is based, to an important degree, on the perceived nature of the Iraqi regime and, above all, the injustice of his invasion. For this reason, the peace movement has the task of showing that, although the public's perception and judgment of the Iraqi regime and its invasion is not in error, nevertheless the US intervention could not be more wrong. This is, most relevantly, because US action is in no way motivated by Saddam's awful regime or his

Robert Brenner, "Why Is the United States at War with Iraq?" *New Left Review,* January/February 1991. Reprinted with permission.

violation of democratic rights, and will only make things much worse for the people of the region and of the United States itself. . . .

That the US intervention has nothing to do with its stated aims of opposing tyranny and expansionism is most obvious from the very recent history of the USA's relationship with Iraq itself. Right up to the day of its invasion of Kuwait, Iraq was a close ally of the United States. When Iraq first invaded Iran, the USA symptomatically failed to denounce its aggression, and simply called for negotiations to settle the outstanding differences between the parties. Somewhat later Ronald Reagan ordered the 'tilt' in the Middle East toward Iraq, and as a result the USA, as well as the other Western powers—along with the Soviet Union—gave Iraq massive material, especially military, aid throughout the 1980s. This aid was proffered despite the repressiveness of Saddam's domestic rule, well-documented in the reports of international human-rights organizations. It was given, what's more, despite the widely accepted fact that during this period the Iraqi regime was carrying out the mass murder of some 45,000 Kurds, a non-Arab national minority within its territory. Indeed, the US administration opposed the effort to pass an international resolution condemning Iraq for deploying chemical weapons against the Kurds, as well as against its external enemies. At the same time, the US State Department made sure to have Iraq removed from its list of 'terrorist nations'.

"The US intervention could not be more wrong."

The reason for this support for Iraq is obvious, and directly undercuts the argument that the USA is today fighting Iraq because it has carried out an unjust invasion. The United States backed Iraq precisely to support its unprovoked invasion of, and war against, the USA's (then) hated enemy, Iran. The Iran-Iraq war dragged on for eight years, ending only in 1988. It involved Iraq's extensive use of poison gas and vicious attacks against civilians. In total, the war brought over one million Iranian and Iraqi deaths. In its later stages the US Navy directly intervened in support of Iraq in the Persian Gulf. Meanwhile, US experts, while supplying Iraq with satellite intelligence photographs of Iran, were directly working with Saddam to implement the military strategy that allowed Iraq to stave off defeat in the war's final stages. In addition, the US government went to great lengths to help Iraq secure private credit, notably by guaranteeing a loan of some $3 billion from the Banca Nazionale de Lavoro in Atlanta. Right up to the night of 2 August 1990, US arms dealers were sending the most modern and lethal weaponry to Saddam, sanctioned and encouraged to do so by the US government.

U.S. Hypocrisy

The idea that the United States is worried about invasions, or stands in any vaguely principled way against authoritarian regimes and for human rights, or for the right of nations to self-determination, is a cruel joke, belied by the unending succession of direct armed interventions by the USA since World War II—in Greece, Korea, Guatemala, Iran, Lebanon, Cuba, Santo Domingo, Vietnam, Southern Africa, Grenada, Panama and so on. There is no point in discussing the recent history of US intervention in Central America; US support for death-squad regimes, which over the decade have killed some 50,000 in El Salvador, and perhaps 150,000 in Guatemala, as well as its 'low intensity' Contra war against Nicaragua, is all too notorious. . . .

In his State of the Union address, George Bush had the audacity to state that 'the cost of closing our eyes to aggression is beyond mankind's power to imagine'. Unfortunately the United States has for years been closing its eyes not only to its own ghastly invasions and atrocities, but to those of its allies; and the costs are there for all to see. . . .

[For example], East Timor secured its independence from the Portuguese in the summer of 1975, but was given little time to enjoy it. After a brief but violent conflict among Timorese political groupings fighting for control, FRE-ITILIN secured a victory and governed the country until 7 December. On that day, Indonesia—one of the USA's staunchest allies—launched an invasion of East Timor, obviously having received a go-ahead from the United States, for Gerald Ford and Henry Kissinger had departed the country only a few hours before the invasion started. The Indonesian regime had initially endeared itself to the United States in 1965 when, on coming to power in a bloody coup, it had killed between 500,000 and 1,000,000 of its leftist opponents. In the course of taking over East Timor in the following years, the Indonesians slaughtered between 100,000 and 200,000 people, one sixth to one third of the population—a clear case of genocide. However, the United States has not only shielded Indonesia from attack whenever the East Timor question has been raised in the UN [United Nations], but it has continued to make Indonesia a major beneficiary of US aid. . . .

"The United States has for years been closing its eyes not only to its own ghastly invasions . . . but to those of its allies."

Perhaps most cynical of all is the US government's sanction of aggression and the suppression of human rights directly pursuant to its attack upon Iraq. Above all, and in the face of successive highly critical United Nations resolutions, the USA persists in defending continued Israeli control of the occupied territories—secured through Israel's ruthless repression of the Palestinians' struggle for self-determination, the Intifada.

In the recent period, one has witnessed, close-up on television, the tragedy of the deaths of several Israeli civilians as a result of Iraq's missile attacks. But the fact is that other tragedies have not received any such coverage in the media. Over the course of the three years of the Intifada, between Winter 1987 and Winter 1990, some 890 Palestinians have been killed, and fewer than 30 Israelis. A further 12,000 Palestinians are in administrative detention. In Spring 1982 Israel invaded Lebanon, supposedly in response to attacks by Palestinians just over the border, but in reality in response to a situation in which the Palestinians' observation of a cease-fire for an extended period had put Israel under increasing pressure to negotiate a settlement. In any case, far from confining themselves to securing Israel's frontiers—the ostensible reason for the invasion—Israel bombarded Beirut, killing some 20,000 civilians in the process, and did nothing to prevent the massacres of many hundreds of Palestinians in refugee camps at Sabra and Shatila. Israel today still controls a substantial part of Lebanon.

Not only has US support for Israel continued undiminished despite its aggressions and repressions; it could hardly be clearer that the defence of the Israeli positions vis-à-vis the Palestinians is a central objective of the USA's Gulf policy itself. As recently as early January 1991 *Newsday* reported that Iraq was willing to withdraw from Kuwait in exchange for a US promise not to attack; the withdrawal of foreign troops from the region; and moves toward a solution to the Palestinian problem. It is obvious that, had he so wished, Bush could have interpreted such a settlement—requiring no more than an international conference that would consider (not necessarily resolve) the Israeli-Palestinian question among other Middle East conflicts—as the unqualified victory he demanded. That he did not do so is indicative of the lengths to which the US government will go to prevent even the possibility of a weakening of the Israeli position. . . .

Economic and Geopolitical Interests

It is fairly easy to specify the imperial goals—economic and political—that the USA wants to achieve through its current policy in the Gulf. However, what ultimately makes that policy difficult to understand is that the means the United States is pursuing to secure its goals are either unnecessary for their achievement or are destined to have the effect of preventing their realization, or will likely involve costs far out of proportion to the benefits to be derived. One is therefore forced to the conclusion that while these goals form the necessary background to an explanation of US military intervention in the Gulf, there is actually more here—or perhaps less—than meets the eye.

"Perhaps most cynical of all is the US government's sanction of aggression . . . directly pursuant to its attack upon Iraq."

Oil is obviously, in a general way, the key issue. Because of oil the Middle East constitutes the region perhaps most pivotal for US policy. If what was at stake was an unfriendly invasion in Sub-Saharan Africa, the response would likely be very different. A central goal of US, and Western, policy in the region has been to keep oil in the hands of states of a very particular sort, and out of the hands of other sorts of states. A major part of the Middle East oil is under the control of dictatorial rulers who are the direct clients and creations of the West, and who rule over sparsely populated nations that can in no way constitute a real alternative source of political power in the region. This is no accident and is, of course, the way the USA and the Western powers like it, for it means that the region's oil will flow smoothly and will, to a large extent, be kept from nationalist regimes with the potential to 'destabilize' the area (perhaps by threatening to use the wealth of the region to the benefit of the people who live there). Saudi Arabia and Kuwait are creatures of imperialism and of the oil companies ARAMCO and BP respectively. They are, in every sense, puppet states and, because of their sparse populations, can hardly become much more. They have the additional advantage—precisely because they represent little more than extended families closely attached to the West—of having little desire to spend too much of their money in developing their domestic economies, and are therefore quite pleased to place their gigantic incomes in Western banks or businesses, vastly improving the liquidity of the capitalist economy. This is especially advantageous today, with the world's financial system stretched to breaking point. In contrast, Iraq and Iran are large, densely populated nations, which—especially with the help of oil—can develop their economies and, on that basis, constitute states with the capacity to upset the tranquility of the region. There can be no doubt that US policy in the region, especially since the time of the Iranian revolution, has been about controlling both Iraq and Iran. Since this remains a priority, it helps explain US discomfiture with Saddam's invasion and the desire to stop him.

Oil Supply Not Really Threatened

Nevertheless, to say that the United States and the West would prefer the status quo in the Middle East—and especially the status quo ante, the Iranian revolution—does not amount to demonstrating that the Iraqi invasion constituted a really serious threat to US and Western oil interests. It is obvious that the USA, and the West more generally, would not countenance a hostile state monopolizing the region's oil. For such a monopoly would constitute a powerful political weapon. The fact is, though, that there is no evidence that Iraq planned to take over Saudi Arabia; in any case, once the US troops were sent there any putative threat to the region's oil supply from Iraq was dissolved.

So long as no nation monopolizes Middle East oil, it does not much matter to oil consumers whether the oil of Kuwait is in Iraqi or Kuwaiti hands. Whoever owns the oil must sell it at the world-market price. OPEC [Organization of Petroleum Exporting Countries] can of course try to set prices, but can do so only within strict limits or for the very short term. Attempts to set prices above a certain level simply provoke

the opening up of wells that had hitherto operated at too high a cost, thereby raising supply and forcing down the price level. It meant a great deal to Iraq as a seller of oil to be able to have the price set at $25 per barrel, as opposed to the $20 per barrel at which Kuwait was selling it. But the difference at the pump amounted to only five cents. . . .

"It is fairly easy to specify the imperial goals . . . that the USA wants to achieve through its current policy in the Gulf."

What about geopolitics in the Middle East? There is no doubt that the United States places a very high priority on international stability within the Middle East, and sees Saddam's Iraq as a serious threat to that stability. But it is very hard to believe that Bush and the US State Department went to war because they thought that they could, in this way, pacify the region. For it had been very widely concluded that war against Iraq—especially the defeat of Iraq—would actually lead to the destabilization of the region.

The reason the USA had supported Iraq in recent years was, in large part, to balance the other two major regional powers, Iran and Syria, both of which were fairly hostile to the USA. If Iraq is really crushed, there will be an enormous vacuum of power and a huge shock to the regional balance of power. Syria has already benefited by virtue of its increased power over Lebanon. It is hard to see why Iran would not also vastly improve its power within the region as a consequence of an Iraqi defeat.

Equally to the point, as it becomes ever more clear that the USA's supposed 'surgical strikes' in Iraq are in fact killing large numbers of Iraqi civilians, there is likely to be an enormous upsurge of Arab nationalism, Islamic fundamentalism, and anti-American feeling among the masses of the region. . . .

With the sudden end of the Cold War, the

United States undoubtedly saw a golden opportunity to make a massive show of force so as to enhance the potential for political stability on a world scale. No doubt, too, the target was the Third World: both nationalist regimes that sought to act without the approval of the United States, and domestic revolutionary movements. The expulsion of Iraq from Kuwait was therefore sought for its discouraging impact on potential disturbers of the peace, external or internal. Nevertheless, although one attractive aspect, in the eyes of the administration, of an attack on Iraq was obviously its demonstration effect, it is hard to believe that the war was actually conceived for that purpose. It is not easy to think of many extant nationalist regimes with the desire or potential to defy the USA. Indeed, it is doubtful if Iraq itself would have acted as it did, had it known that the US was likely to disapprove. At the same time, there can be little doubt that proponents of revolution by armed struggle, dependent on territorial bases in the countryside, have been more than satisfactorily discouraged by the terrible toll taken by US interventions in Central America and beyond over the past decade. A war against Iraq was hardly necessary to deter them further. On the other hand, it is far from clear that mass urban-based revolutions—either of secular, social or religious sort—could in any simple or direct way be short-circuited by the threat of external intervention. To put the same point another way: with the total collapse of the Soviet Union, the United States had probably achieved as close to a Pax Americana, conceived in purely military terms, as was feasible. The additional costs of a full-scale war could only secure marginal gains toward this goal.

Bush's Decisions

One caveat must be made here. Had Bush been certain he could win the war quickly, and entirely by means of air power, he might reasonably have concluded that that price was low enough to be worth the outcome. This possibility cannot be entirely ruled out. Still, in view of the fact that Bush certainly had heard from many advisers, including the CIA [Central Intelligence Agency], the State Department, and his military chief of staff, that a ground war was difficult or impossible to avoid, it is hard to see how he could have *counted* on avoiding the costs of such a conflict. But if a ground war does develop, there is a real likelihood, as many commentators have warned, that the major cost in American lives will precipitate powerful political opposition at home, and that the cost in dollars will very much exacerbate an already serious recession. In this light, the Iraq war as a means to deter potential disturbers of the 'new world order' seems an incomprehensibly risky proposition for the American government.

"It had been very widely concluded that war against Iraq would actually lead to the destabilization of the region."

It is possible to state an initial conclusion: the USA has major economic, regional geopolitical and world-imperial interests in stopping Saddam Hussein. However, two questions remain unanswered: first, how will the war secure these interests, rather than actually preventing their achievement? and second, in what way can the goals that it may be feasible to achieve possibly be considered worth the likely cost of their realization? That these questions are far from academic is obvious from the fact that the USA's allies among the advanced capitalist states, with the exception only of Britain and France, have assessed the threat posed to their fundamental economic and political interests by the Iraqi invasion very differently from the way the USA has. Indeed, they have viewed the war as unnecessary at best and counterproductive at worst. Except for England and France they are sending only token troop contingents—ranging in size from the 1,800 (0.26 per cent of the total) sent by Canada, to the 300 (0.04 per cent of the total) sent by Denmark—and offering little financially. Most indicatively, both Japan and Germany are notably unenthusiastic about, if not actually disapproving of, the US policy, and have needed to have their arms twisted to give even the meagre support so far proffered. . . .

"The United States went to war with Iraq because it placed such a high value on projecting US power/force on a world scale."

There has rarely been a war with such purely imperialist roots; but, like other imperialist wars, this one appears almost certain to bring counterproductive consequences for capitalist interests, most notably those of the USA. It is this likelihood—because it appeared so evident so early to so many, notably among the leading allied capitalist powers—that makes explanations of the war more difficult than might at first appear.

U.S. Power

It is difficult to avoid the conclusion that the United States went to war with Iraq because it placed such a high value on projecting US power/force on a world scale in the aftermath of the Cold War that mundane cost calculations seemed beside the point. The key to the emergence of this rather puzzling perspective was the extremely paradoxical position in which the USA found itself, internationally and domestically, in the summer of 1990. At that point, the United States had, in purely military-political terms, reached a position of power on an international scale perhaps greater than it had enjoyed at any time since the end of World War II. On the other hand, its economic position, ultimately based on manufacturing competitiveness was in profound relative decline, with little prospect of reversal. Meanwhile, with the end of the Reagan 'boom', Bush faced an impasse on domestic policy that seemed virtually insoluble and therefore likely to end his presidency in 1992.

By the summer of 1990 the crisis and overturnings in the East, and the Soviet Union's virtual abdication of its former international role, appeared to have opened up almost unlimited horizons for the United States. US policymakers appear to have been overtaken by euphoria, hatching plans for aggressive action to display US power so as to secure a now-perfectable Pax Americana. From this perspective the attack on Iraq makes sense. But, again, the question immediately imposes itself: aggression and power for what? . . .

In a bygone era of classical imperialism, military power could, at least in many cases, be directly translatable into material advantage. It might secure colonies and land, exclusive control of valuable raw materials, monopolies of export markets, privileged access to financial opportunities, and so forth. There was, in other words, a way in which military power and military action constituted a valuable tool for the redistribution of the world's wealth; the ability to redistribute wealth might, moreover, be just as valuable as—or able to compensate for—the ability to produce and sell on the market. But it is difficult to see that situation as one that persists today to any great extent. What wars have recently paid dividends in these ways? For this reason the role of world cop is pretty much a *faux frais* of capitalism, as well as individual capitalists, and a very expensive one at that. In consequence, one might expect the disagreement over who is to bear the cost and responsibility for the role of world policeman to be a major source of conflict among the advanced capitalist states. There has, in fact, been some evidence of this. But the overwhelming trend, as all can see, has been for the United States enthusiastically and obsessively to assume the role. As George Bush himself modestly put it to *Time* magazine: 'I would not call the United States the world's policeman, because there are certain areas where we wouldn't be in a position to act or want to act. But we have a disproportionate responsibility for the freedom and the security of various countries'. The question remains, why?

It is difficult to avoid the conclusion that those in charge of the American state see the build-up and assertion of military strength as the only way of maintaining the appearance of American power and hegemony. But, in the light of what I have just argued, this is a paradoxical goal. If you can't gain much directly from military might, and it imposes such a tremendous drain on your resources, why do you want it so much? The resolution of the paradox, from the standpoint of the American state, would seem to be that there is simply no alternative. This is not the place for a systematic discussion of US economic decline; but the fact is that across the manufacturing economy—from high technology, to mainstream manufacturing, to low-skill/cheap wage production—US-based producers are losing out to Japan, to Germany, to some extent to other European producers, and to the East Asian economies. At the same time, as part and parcel of this trend, the most powerful sections of US capital, based in finance and multinational corporations, are pursuing their interests on a world scale and have, to an important degree, unhinged their fate from that of US-based manufacturing. This is not the result of whim, but reflects the fact that, generally speaking—for a variety of economic, institutional, social and political reasons—the best opportunities for profitable investment no longer lie within the United States. It is far from evident that even an enormous state commitment could reverse this situation; moreover, it appears quite obvious that sufficient political pressure to secure such a commitment will not be forthcoming, precisely (in part) because strong support for it is lacking among the leading US banks and manufacturing corporations. In this context, it is not surprising that little interest exists within the political establishment for seeking to re-strengthen US power through restrengthening the underlying economy. The American state is thus obsessed with directly building up and projecting military-political power, because power, and its expression, is available to it in no other manner or form. The US state builds its military strength, in a way, to compensate for its loss of economic power—and because it cannot rebuild this power—even though so doing will undoubtedly contribute to further relative economic decline and, in the end, political-military disintegration. . . .

> ## "Those in charge of the American state see the . . . assertion of military strength as the only way of maintaining the appearance of American power."

Bush's attack on Iraq thus appears to be designed to establish, and make clear to all, that the United States remains the world's hegemon. Because that is valued for its own sake, mere considerations of cost, human and economic, have been thrown out of the window to the detriment of US power in the long term, and to the detriment of the people of the Middle East, and the United States, in the short term.

The Political Impasse at Home

Although in the summer of 1990 the Bush government appeared to face a limitless vista of freedom of action abroad, it confronted the most profound, and politically depressing, constraints at home. Not only was the S&L [savings and loan] scandal discrediting the political establishment, but, more to the point, the economic crisis of the S&L banks was showing itself to be only the tip of the iceberg: a profound financial crisis was extending itself virtually across the entire economy. Commercial banks, real-estate companies, investment houses, consumers, state and local governments all faced record indebtedness at a point when returns on investment—especially in such mainstay sectors as real estate—were falling precipitately. What made this indebtedness so frightening was that the long Reagan boom had obviously come to an end, and a new recession, which promised to be as bad as that of 1979-82 if not much worse, had already begun to envelop the economy, with many states already fiercely gripped by depression.

At this point, to head off a crash, Bush was compelled to take the politically disastrous step of going back on his pivotal campaign promise not to raise taxes. This was the only way to prevent a rising budget deficit from pushing interest rates through the ceiling and precipitating a crash. However, this action brought about a sharp division in the Republican Party and a momentary reprieve for the Democrats. Bush's popularity ratings had soon fallen to their lowest point since his election. More to the point, there was no prospect for improvement. . . .

In this situation Iraq's rather reckless invasion of Kuwait appeared as a godsend to the Bush administration—a chance to kill several birds with one stone. The administration could, first of all, organize the massive show of US power that policymakers were already itching to stage. By this means, Bush could also distract attention from the domestic political impasse and absorb the citizenry in a patriotic crusade, justified in the name of the defence of democracy and opposition to aggression. The result would be a tremendous victory, internationally and domestically, that would not only assure triumph in the next election, but also a world-shaking celebration of US might. Best of all, there appeared the opportunity of securing these goals very cheaply, for it was undoubtedly assumed that Iraq would not wish to risk war, and would meekly and quickly evacuate.

"Bush's attack on Iraq thus appears to be designed to establish . . . that the United States remains the world's hegemon."

What is most revealing about the run-up to the war is that, while Bush undoubtedly hoped to dislodge Iraq from Kuwait without resort to force, he was—essentially from the start—quite set on going to war in order to impose a total US victory, were that to be necessary. The USA's insistence not merely on Iraqi withdrawal but on unconditional Iraqi surrender makes shockingly clear the obsession of the administration to have its show of American power, no matter what the cost. As soon became evident, the Bush administration had absolutely no interest in negotiations or sanctions. To negotiate would have been to forego the opportunity of imposing the humiliating defeat that was required to display America's strength and will; for negotiations would obviously have required at least a certain recognition of Saddam Hussein and the consideration of some sort of compromise, however one-sided, for securing Iraq's withdrawal. . . .

Military Justification

As to sanctions, we now know that these were, virtually from the start, merely a tactic of the administration, designed to provide a cover and (thin) justification for the military build-up. The administration could not rely on sanctions because, were these to work, they would eventuate in those messy negotiations and compromise the administration most hoped to avoid. By mid October 1990, Bush's Chief of Staff, Colin Powell, had requested and been granted the doubling of US troops in the Gulf, from around 225,000 to 450,000 (this was formally announced immediately after the November election). Since it would have been prohibitively expensive to maintain this number of troops for the time required for sanctions to be effective, it is obvious that Bush decided to depend solely on the military option—scaring Iraq from Kuwait or dislodging it through actual combat—fewer than three months into the crisis, at the very latest. . . .

As the administration itself has admitted, Bush moved quickly to avoid what his government has termed 'the nightmare scenario'—the start of an Iraqi troop withdrawal just after the deadline. Such a move might very well have forced the opening of negotiations . . . and, while securing Kuwait, deprived the USA of unconditional victory through unbridled power.

Military Action Is Immoral

Robert F. Drinan

About the Author: *Robert F. Drinan is a Jesuit priest and a professor of law at Georgetown University in Washington, D.C. This article was written on February 8, 1991, three weeks after the start of the Gulf War.*

Four of the traditional seven conditions established in Catholic teaching for a just war cannot, in my judgment, be fulfilled in the Persian Gulf war.

The seven norms for a just war originated by St. Augustine, defined by St. Thomas Aquinas and synthesized by Suarez and others require:

1. The war must be declared by a legitimate public authority possessing the power to do so. The action of the U.N. [United Nations] Security Council with regard to the invasion of Kuwait may have fulfilled this requirement.

2. A real injury must have been suffered. The injury done by the invasion of Iraq to the nation of Kuwait inhabited by 400,000 people was real.

3. There must be a reasonable hope of success. The allied strength of 27 nations should be able to vanquish Iraq in a military engagement.

While these three conditions may be verified, the four others are not and cannot be satisfied.

The four conditions that are not met are:

1. The traditional definition of a just war, in Catholic doctrine, requires that every possible means of settlement must have been exhausted. The commentators go to great length to point out that war can be tolerated only after there have been comprehensive efforts to exploit every possible method of obtaining a peaceful settlement.

Robert F. Drinan, "Persian Gulf War Fails to Qualify as Just," *The National Catholic Reporter*, February 8, 1991. Reprinted by permission, National Catholic Reporter, PO Box 419281, Kansas City, MO 64141.

There was abundant evidence, before Jan. 15, 1991, that the economic sanctions against Iraq were working. There are mounting signs that the economic sanctions, coupled with diplomatic measures that were never fully exhausted, might well have brought about circumstances that would force Saddam Hussein to capitulate.

2. A second condition is moral intention. Jurists and moral theologians indicate that a nation must be waging a war not for some selfish reason, but for a humanitarian objective. The threat to about 50 percent of America's oil supply has to be one of the principal motivations for the initiative of the White House. Lofty rhetoric can be employed to suggest the United States is fighting to deter aggression, to bring about a "new world order" and to make the Gulf safe for smaller countries. But if Kuwait grew bananas instead of pumping oil, the United States would, in all probability, not be its self-appointed liberator.

> ## "Four of the traditional seven conditions established in Catholic teaching for a just war cannot . . . be fulfilled in the Persian Gulf war."

There is, therefore, at least a serious doubt that the cause is morally desirable.

3. A third requirement that is difficult, or impossible, to fulfill, is that only legitimate and moral means be used in prosecuting the war. In their 2,500-word statement on war, the 3,300 bishops at Vatican II proscribed "any act aimed indiscriminately" at the destruction of "entire cities or extensive areas." The word Vatican II used is *condemnation*—a term seldom used in the 16 constitutions running to 103,000 words issued by Vatican II.

The council, apparently, desired to absolutize the preexisting principle of the immunity of noncombatants from direct attack. The words of Vatican II are vehement: The bombing of "extensive areas along with their population is a crime against God and man himself."

Those leading the war in the Gulf repeatedly seek to explain they are bombing only military targets. But one has to wonder whether it is not inevitable that almost countless civilians are hit by the 1,000 sorties every day that drop their bombs on Iraq and Kuwait.

One is reminded of the piercing conclusions reached by the bishops at Vatican II in their statement on war—contained in sections 79-82 of the *Pastoral Constitution on the Church in the Modern World*. In talking of the abomination used in modern war, the council fathers note that war "through a certain inexorable chain of events . . . can urge man on to the most atrocious decisions."

The objectives of war become so imperious that they overwhelm and obliterate the carefully crafted ban on bombing civilians, which is not only a part of Catholic morality but is also a highly developed part of the modern legal rules governing the conduct of war.

4. The fourth requirement for a just war is proportionality, that is, the good to be achieved must outweigh the harm done.

Let us assume, for a moment, that the good to be achieved in this war is accomplished. Iraq leaves Kuwait, and the emir and his government return. President Bush insists this is all he wants. A desirable objective—although there has never been an election in Kuwait and the status of human rights in that very wealthy country, the size of New Jersey, is extremely low.

"The evils and suffering entailed to bring about the restoration of a dictator to his throne in Kuwait are incalculable."

The Kuwaitis, with the highest average income of any nation of the earth, including the United States, presumably can restore their dev-astated nation to its former conditions. Other good developments are possible but by no means certain.

The evils and suffering entailed to bring about the restoration of a dictator to his throne in Kuwait are incalculable. Their immensity grows every day.

How many citizens, of all the nations, will eventually be killed? And how do we justify the immense sufferings of thousands of migrant workers from the Philippines and Pakistan who fled Iraq and Kuwait? And how does one justify the loss of Israeli lives and the severe impact on the economy of that nation by a sharp decline in tourism?

Good Must Outweigh Harm

The definition of a just war is not very explicit in its definition of proportionality. But it is very clear that the good to be achieved has to outweigh the harm caused. At the moment, it is difficult to see how the isolated political good of restoring one government outweighs the evils of countless lives lost, thousands of persons wounded, property destroyed, an economic system severely damaged in the Gulf and at least $200 billion spent by the United States to achieve the restoration of the government of a tiny nation.

The massive expenditures might alone be a reason it is easy to say the evils that result from the war in the Gulf outweigh whatever good might eventually happen. The staggering cost of the war—estimated at perhaps $1 billion a day—will be added to the already mind-boggling deficit of more than $3 trillion.

Bush, who pledged no new taxes, will almost certainly add the expenditures of the war to the debt that is already choking the economic growth of America and making it impossible to give adequate social services to the poor in the United States. President Lyndon Johnson did the same thing with the cost of the Vietnam War—thus beginning the economic downfall of the United States.

Even the one small good sought from the

war—the return of the government of Kuwait—may not happen without new forms of instability in the Middle East. If the government of Iraq is weakened or destroyed, Iran and Syria—no friends of the United States—will seek to move into the vacuum. New animosities against Israel may be aroused, thus adding fuel to the chronic political turmoil in the Middle East.

Of all of the foregoing conditions required for a just war, perhaps the most important is the requirement of proportionality. In an excellent article on the morality of war in the *Catholic Encyclopedia*, Jesuit theologian Father Richard McCormick states firmly that "it is immoral directly to take innocent human life." McCormick goes on to state that "if no other principles were violated by total warfare (they are), the immunity of noncombatants would be sufficient in itself to proscribe such warfare."

All Seven Conditions

For a war to be just, it must fulfill all seven conditions the Catholic church has imposed and elaborated for 1,500 years.

Vatican II proclaimed Catholics and the world must look on war "with an entirely new attitude." Pope John XXIII was even more direct in *Pacem in Terris*, issued on Easter Sunday 1963, a few days before he died. He stated that in the modern era "it is hardly possible to imagine that . . . war could be used as an instrument of peace."

More and more voices in America are saying that since we entered the war we should finish it. That does not square with the Catholic view of warfare. If a war cannot be justified before it begins, it cannot be justified after it has commenced.

If the United States stopped making war immediately, more good would be done than harm. It would be possible, of course, for the United States and its allies to remain in Saudi Arabia to deter Saddam Hussein from invading that nation.

The people of America are now taken up with the dream or delusion that the United States is acting nobly in spending massive sums of money to extinguish the lives of thousands to "liberate Kuwait."

Many countries have been taken over by dictators. All of Eastern Europe and China fell to the communists. Tibet, Afghanistan and East Timor were captured by outside forces. The United States did not race to war over those tragedies, because it realized that war seldom, if ever, can drive out a dictator without adverse consequences that outweigh whatever good is done.

Why has that sensible policy been abandoned now that minuscule Kuwait has been invaded? The Catholic doctrine on a just war teaches us, it seems to me, that Operation Desert Storm cannot be morally justified.

Defending America's Oil Supply Does Not Justify Military Action

David R. Henderson

About the Author: *David R. Henderson, an associate professor of economics at the Naval Postgraduate School in Monterey, California, was a senior energy economist during the Reagan administration. This article was written in October 1990.*

President Saddam Hussein of Iraq has no qualms about torturing or even murdering innocent people. If he should manage to hold on to Kuwait and to capture Saudi Arabia, he would have access to even greater wealth than he has in Iraq. No doubt, he would attempt to use that wealth to strengthen his military, maybe even to speed up development of nuclear weapons. Saddam could then be an even bigger menace to peace in the Middle East than he was before he invaded Kuwait.

But many Americans—including President George Bush, Secretary of State James A. Baker III, and former secretary of state Henry Kissinger—believe that if Saddam succeeds in extending his control to a large part of the Arab world, he could pose a direct threat to the United States by severely damaging our oil-dependent economy. President Bush has stated that his military action in the Persian Gulf is about "access to energy resources that are key . . . to the entire world." Bush claims that if Saddam gets greater control of oil reserves in the Middle

David R. Henderson, "Do We Need to Go to War for Oil?" Cato Institute *Foreign Policy Briefing*, October 24, 1990. Reprinted with permission.

East, he can threaten "our jobs" and "our way of life." Baker claimed that Saddam, by controlling much of the world's oil, "could strangle the global economic order, determining by fiat whether we all enter a recession, or even the darkness of a depression." And Kissinger wrote that an unchecked Saddam would be able to "cause a worldwide economic crisis."

Bush, Baker, and Kissinger are mistaken. The annual cost to the U.S. economy of doing nothing in the Persian Gulf would [have been] at most half of 1 percent of our gross national product, and probably much less. Saddam's vaunted "oil weapon" is a dud.

> ## "Saddam's vaunted 'oil weapon' is a dud."

Saddam cannot single-handedly cause shortages and gasoline lines. Only the U.S. government can do that. As long as our government avoids imposing price controls, any cutback in supplies that Saddam causes will result in higher prices, not shortages. That is the lesson to be learned from the 1970s. Countries, including the United States, that imposed price controls experienced shortages, and many Americans were angry because they had to line up, Soviet style, for gasoline. Countries, such as West Germany, that avoided price controls made it through the 1970s with no gasoline lines. That is no surprise. If governments let oil prices rise, people cut down on marginal uses of oil but continue to use it where it is most valuable. They take fewer trips to stores and fewer driving vacations, for example, but continue to drive to work. People insulate their houses and close off unused rooms. Airlines drop marginal flights. Utilities switch from oil to coal and natural gas when oil becomes too expensive. In 1973, the last year of low oil prices, utilities in the United States used 3.515 quadrillion Btu [British thermal units] of oil. By 1983 they had reduced their use of oil to 1.544 quadrillion Btu, a reduction of 56 percent. Oil users make literally thousands of adjustments that—voilà—cause the amount they consume to just equal the amount supplied. The market works.

Of course, Saddam does not have to create gasoline lines to hurt us. Simply by raising the price of oil, a good we import in large quantities, he can hurt the U.S. economy. But how much would a price increase hurt us? Let's look at the numbers.

Take the worst case that has any plausibility whatsoever. Assume that Iraq not only holds on to Kuwait but also is able to grab and keep Saudi Arabia and the United Arab Emirates. Iraq would then control virtually all Middle Eastern oil production except that of Iran. Those fields had been producing about 12.3 million barrels per day (mbd) before the price run-up in late July 1990. But, although Saddam may be evil, he is not stupid. He does not want to grab the oil fields only to let them sit idle. He wants them so that he can sell their oil. Saddam would surely continue to produce and sell oil from those fields if the U.S. government and other governments let him. If he continued to sell 12.3 mbd, the effect of his actions on the world price of oil would be zero. Oil would sell for the pre-crisis price of about $20 per barrel.

However, Saddam would not necessarily sell the same amount of oil. He would have a much tighter grip on the OPEC [Organization of Petroleum Exporting Countries] cartel, whose members have kept oil prices low by producing more than their agreed quotas. By controlling the output of the four major cartel members, Saddam would gain some degree of monopoly power and could use that power to cut the combined production of the four members and drive up the world price.

Little Effect on Price of Oil

How much monopoly power would Saddam have? More than he had, but not necessarily a lot. Remember that Saddam is operating in a market in which world output is about 60 mbd. A reasonable estimate, therefore, is that he would use his newly acquired monopoly power to cut output from 12.3 mbd to a minimum of 8.3 mbd, which is probably the profit-maximizing level of output. That would amount to a 6.7 percent cut in world output. Because, in the short run, demand for oil is fairly inelastic, small cuts in production can cause large increases in world prices. According to an estimate by Derriel Cato of the U.S. Department of Energy's Energy Information Administration, the short-run elasticity of demand for oil is about -0.15. In other words, a 10 percent increase in price causes a 1.5 percent decrease in the quantity of oil demanded. Conversely, a 1.5 percent decrease in supply causes a 10 percent increase in price. With an elasticity of -0.15, a 6.7 percent cut in world production causes about a 50 percent increase in price. The pre-crisis price was $20 per barrel, so we can conclude that, absent U.S. military intervention, the price of oil would have risen to only about $30 per barrel.

"How much monopoly power would Saddam have? More than he had, but not necessarily a lot."

How much would such a price increase cost the United States? Before the crisis, we imported about 8 mbd. A price increase would lead us to cut our imports as well as our consumption and to increase our production. But assume pessimistically—and contrary to common sense and evidence—that we would continue to import 8 mbd. The cost of those imports would then rise by $80 million per day, or $29.2 billion per year.

Twenty-nine billion dollars is not small change, but it is only about half of 1 percent of our $5.4 trillion GNP [gross national product]. A loss of half of 1 percent of GNP is surely not what Kissinger had in mind when he referred to an "economic crisis." The cost per American would be only about $112 per year. At the gasoline pump, the cost would show up as an additional 24 cents per gallon. And that's on top of the old price of about $1.09 per gallon, for a total of about $1.33, a bit less than we're paying now.

"Added military spending does not guarantee success. All it guarantees is our continued presence in the gulf."

Consider, by contrast, the costs of war. Sending troops to the Persian Gulf has not been cheap. Secretary of Defense Richard Cheney estimates that the cost of sending extra troops to the gulf and keeping them there will total $17.7 billion by the end of September 1991. That is in addition to our regular spending to protect the gulf, Southwest Asia, and Northwest Africa, which one expert has estimated at $46 billion in fiscal year 1990. . . . Some experts believe those costs could reach $1 billion a day. Remember also that added military spending does not guarantee success. All it guarantees is our continued presence in the gulf.

Moreover, we can be sure that as a result of the U.S. intervention, less oil will be produced—because the UN [United Nations] embargo, enforced mainly by the United States, assures that no Iraqi or Kuwaiti oil can be sold. With the embargo, President Bush is keeping about 5 mbd of Iraqi and Kuwaiti oil off the world market. Note the irony here. The alleged purpose of U.S. intervention in the gulf was to preserve "our jobs" and "our way of life" by keeping oil prices low. But the one sure result of U.S. intervention is to keep them high. President Bush is doing as a matter of policy what he feared Saddam might do.

War Brings Higher Prices

Oil production in the Middle East is very likely to fall even further, sending prices even higher. Bringing oil to the surface is difficult when guns are being fired all around. In fact, the rise in oil prices to $38 per barrel could well have been due to the mere anticipation of an even smaller supply of oil. . . . So a cost-benefit analysis that considers only some of the costs of military action shows that military action in the gulf is more expensive than inaction. . . .

Finally, all my estimates of the damage that Saddam can do are for the short run. The annual damage he could inflict on us would get smaller the longer he restricted oil production. As the price of oil increases, other oil producers will produce more; indeed, that is already happening. Moreover, according to energy economists Arlon R. Tussing and Samuel A. Van Vactor, when the price of oil goes above $20 per barrel, substitutes for oil—particularly natural gas—become economically feasible. That is not just idle speculation. According to Tussing and Van Vactor, there is no large-scale use of petroleum liquids or of any other primary fuel that cannot also be served by natural gas or methane or other derivatives that can be produced at a comparable cost. Even automobiles can run on alternative fuels. For instance, a substantial portion of the taxicabs in Vancouver and Calgary run on liquid fuel derived from methane, and a large fraction of cars in New Zealand run on compressed natural gas—and their owners receive no special subsidies or tax breaks. A conversion kit for an automobile costs about $1,600, but the alternative fuel costs are equivalent to 70 cents a gallon for gasoline.

Moreover, according to the *Oil and Gas Journal*, reserves of natural gas outside the United States and Canada were equivalent to 80 years of production at the end of 1989. Throughout the 1980s, additions to natural gas reserves were three times annual production. In short, natural gas is a good substitute for oil, is already being used as such, and is in abundant supply. Those facts are presumably what have prevented the OPEC cartel from raising the price of oil above $20 per barrel for more than short periods of time in recent years. And none of those facts change if Saddam replaces the Saudis as the dominant actor in the OPEC cartel.

Liberating Kuwait Does Not Justify Military Action

Murray N. Rothbard

About the Author: *Murray N. Rothbard is editor of the* Rothbard-Rockwell Report, *a publication of the Center for Libertarian Studies in Burlingame, California. The following article was written in October 1990.*

Let's examine the arguments for the U.S. march into Arabia and its war against Iraq.

"He's Another Hitler!" Oh come on, knock off the Hitler analogy already. What are you saying, for God's sake? That "if we don't stop him on the Euphrates, we'll have to fight him in the streets of New York"?

Wouldn't it be great, by the way, if everyone observed a moratorium on Hitler for at least a year? No more "another Hitler" every time someone starts a war someplace, no more bellyaching about Hitler in general. There is more hysteria now, 45 years after his death, than when he was still alive. Isn't this the only case in history where the hysteria against the loser in a war continues, not only unabated but intensified, 45 years *after* the war is over? And consider too, the guy was only in power for 12 years! In a sense, Hitler will achieve his "1,000-year Reich" after all, because it looks as if we'll be hearing about him for another 900 years or so.

"Saddam's a megalomaniac, he's crazy." Yeah, crazy like a fox. He looks pretty shrewd to me: knocking off Kuwait quickly, and not trying to take on the U.S. frontally. "He's 'unpredictable.'" A code word for crazy. But look, George Bush and all his apologists keep saying that Bush

should always "keep his options open" so as to keep the Enemy guessing and off-base. But how come when Saddam does that it's "crazy" whereas when Bush does it it's the height of sound strategy? Double standard fellas?

"He's BAD." Very bad, no question about it. [As Dana Carvey, ace Bush imitator, would put it: "Saddam: B-A-A-A-A-D."] But Marshal Kim Il-Sung, Maximum Leader of the still-Stalinist regime of North Korea, is even WORSE. So? Why aren't we launching a big propaganda campaign against Marshal Kim, to be followed by sending army, navy, air force, and U.N. [United Nations] stooges on North Korea's border, itching for a fight?

And furthermore, the WORST guy, by far the worst guy of the post-World War II era, worse than Saddam, worse even than the Ayatollah (or is he kinda good now?), is the genocidal monster Pol Pot, Maximum Leader of the Khmer Rouge, who, as head of the Democratic Republic (Communist) of Kampuchea (Cambodia) genocidally slaughtered something like one-third of the Cambodian population. (His own people! As the media have correctly charged Saddam did in dropping poison gas during his war with Iran. Although it wasn't "his own," it was against the poor, hapless Kurds, who have yearned for their own country for 1,000 years, and have experienced nothing but oppression from Iraq, Iran, and Turkey.)

"If we're supposed to go to war against Bad Rulers, why are we allied with . . . the mass murderer Pol Pot?"

Not only that: the punch line is that the Reagan-Bush administration has been allied with the monster Pol Pot in his guerrilla war against the Vietnamese Communist-puppet regime in Cambodia (Gorbyish Commies as against the ultra-Maoist Pol Pot), shipping Pol Pot weapons, so that he is just about to take over Cambodia

Murray N. Rothbard, "Mr. Bush's War," *Rothbard-Rockwell Report*, October 1990. Reprinted with permission of the Center for Libertarian Studies, Burlingame, California.

once again! (Very recently, the Bush Administration has, in response, pulled back slightly from that commitment to Pol Pot.)

So if we're supposed to go to war against Bad Rulers, why are we allied with—or certainly not hostile to—the mass murderer Pol Pot? To say nothing of a host of other dictators, despots, etc. who have been dubbed "pro-West" by the U.S.?

Iraqi Wars

But let us return to Saddam. Saddam is definitely BAD. But—and here's the point—he was just as bad a few short years ago when he was the heroic "defender of the free world" against the BAD fanatical mullah-run Shiite Iranians (Remember them?). Remember how, in the extremely bloody eight-year war between Iraq and Iran (which, by the way, Saddam launched, shortly after the Iranian Revolution, to grab a key waterway), the U.S. "tilted toward" (in plain English: sided with) Iraq? Well, the current Butcher of Baghdad was the same Butcher of Baghdad then. He was the same totalitarian despot; and he was also the aggressor. So how come the lightning-fast change? And not only that: does anyone remember, not long ago, when two Iraqi fighter planes crippled an American warship in the Persian Gulf, and the U.S. immediately blamed it on Iran? After which we shot down an Iranian civilian airliner, killing hundreds?

But, you see, Iran was ruled by fanatical theocratic Shiite mullahs, and pro-Iranian Shiites constituted a subversive threat, at the beck and call of evil Iran, to . . . Saudi Arabia, Kuwait, and the other Gulf States! So whatever happened to those Bad Guys, and that threat? Answer: they're still there. But the U.S. government, and its kept sheep in the media, have decided to forget them, and so, presto changeo! They just disappear in the public press. A couple of years ago, the U.S. government gave the signal: Iran Bad, Iraq Pretty Good, and the media and the politicians all jumped into line. And now, bingo, with no conditions changed, the Administration gives the signal to reverse course—Iraq Bad, Iran Pretty Good, and everyone shifts. And we used to ridicule the Commies for changing their line (on war and peace, Hitler, etc.) with lightning speed!

But, "he invaded a small country." Yes, indeed he did. But, are we ungracious for bringing up the undoubted fact that none other than George Bush, not long ago, invaded a very small country: Panama? And to the unanimous huzzahs of the same U.S. media and politicians now denouncing Saddam? But Manuel Noriega, so Bush and the media told us, was intolerable: he was untrustworthy and thuggish, he used and even sold drugs, and, moreover, he was pockmarked ("Pineapple-Face," as he was elegantly called by the U.S. media), and he was odiously short. (George Bush, we are told, has an intense aversion to uppity short guys.) Gee, in his dislike of short, pock-marked guys, it's Bush who sounds thuggish to me. Besides, Noriega's attributes as thug, drug-dealer, and even short and pockmarked, never kept him from being a pet of Bush's so long as he continued to take orders from the CIA [Central Intelligence Agency]; it was Noriega's infidelity to the CIA that got him into deep trouble.

> ## "Are we ungracious for bringing up the undoubted fact that . . . George Bush, not long ago, invaded a very small country: Panama?"

And another invader of a small country not universally condemned in the U.S. media was Israel, invader of Lebanon, and invader and occupier for over two decades of the Arab lands of the West Bank and Gaza Strip. Why don't the U.S. and the U.N. band together to drive Israel out of these occupied areas? Double standards, anyone? "But Noriega was opposed to 'democracy.'" Ah, come on, don't give me that one. Of course, if the goal of the U.S. action was, as the Bush Administration claimed, to "restore democracy to Panama" (when did they ever have it?), then how come Bush angrily refused the pleas of Panamanians after the invasion to hold free elections? Why did we insist on foisting the Guillermo Endara clique upon them for years?

By the way, the one refreshing aspect of the U.S. war against Iraq is that no one has yet had the gall to refer to Kuwait as a "gallant little democracy" or to Saudi Arabia in the same terms.

"But Saddam's short-lived 'people's revolutionary' regime in Kuwait was a puppet-government of Iraq's". Absolutely. But so was the Endara government in Panama, sworn in on a U.S. army base a few minutes after the U.S. invasion began. So?

Repeat query: Does anyone really think that we would ever have to fight Saddam in the streets of New York?

Don't Cry for Kuwait

Before we get all weepy about gallant little Kuwait, about the obliteration of the Kuwaiti nation by an unprovoked bullying attack, etc., let's look at some history.

In the first place, there is no "Kuwaiti nation" in any proper sense. The Middle East is very much like Africa, where the existing "nations" are simply geographical expressions resulting from the arbitrary carving up of the continent by Western imperialism. Kuwait, Saudi Arabia, et al. were simply carved out as mere geographical expressions by Great Britain after the British Empire conquered and sliced up the Ottoman Empire during World War I. Moreover, Britain shamelessly betrayed its promises that it made (through T.E. Lawrence) to give the Arabs independence after the war. Winston Churchill, the quintessential British imperialist, used to boast that he created "Jordan" one Sunday afternoon at the stroke of a pen.

Furthermore, before Great Britain finally granted independence to its Kuwait colony in 1961, it was so little respectful of the "historic borders" of this alleged nation that it carved away one-half of old Kuwait and granted about a half each to the states of Iraq and Saudi Arabia.

And what about historic Kuwait? During the pre-World War I days of the Ottoman Empire, Kuwait was simply a part of the Ottoman district whose capital was Basra, a city in southern Iraq. Iraq has had border struggles with Kuwait since 1961, and it once invaded and conquered Kuwait, which "ransomed" restoration of its independence by paying a huge amount of oil money to Iraq. More recently, the major Iraqi grievance is that Kuwait has been literally stealing Iraqi oil. The oil field straddles the Iraq-Kuwait border, and Iraq charges that Kuwait has been drilling diagonally from its side of the border to tap reserves from Iraqi territory. An article in the *Wall Street Journal* admits that "U.S. officials say there is reason to think the Iraqi claim may be true."

Another reason not to cry for Kuwait: its rotten social system. Has anyone wondered why the neocons and the rest of the Establishment haven't referred to Kuwait as a "gallant little democracy?" Because it might be little, but it sure ain't no democracy. Little Kuwait (a bit smaller than New Jersey), has a population of 1.9 million; of this only one million are Kuwaitis. The rest are immigrants; including 400,000 Palestinians (who are all pro-Iraq and anti-Kuwait); and several hundred thousand once-dreaded Shiites. These immigrants are not citizens.

"There is no 'Kuwaiti nation' in any proper sense."

Of the three classes of Kuwaiti citizens, however, only the "first-class" citizens are allowed to vote. Second- and third-class citizens are latecomers who "only" emigrated to Kuwait during the 20th century. They don't count. The "first-class" citizens are limited to those Kuwaiti tribesmen who have been residents in Kuwait since the mid-eighteenth century, when these Arab tribes settled there. They constitute 12% of the

Kuwaiti population (about 230,000). Of these, women—of course—can't vote, reducing the ruling elite to 6% of the total.

The 6% elite are allowed to vote for a National Assembly, the Kuwaiti rulers' feeble concession to representative government. The National Assembly, when allowed to meet, often calls for more powers to itself, and more democratic rule. Two weeks before the Iraqi invasion, in an important action not mentioned in the U.S. media, the Emir of Kuwait angrily dissolved the National Assembly. So much for that!

When you get right down to it, then, the ruling elite of Kuwait consists of one royal family, the al-Sabahs, who staff all the top government positions from the ruling Emir on down, and of course run its oil. The al-Sabah family consists of 1,000 males, a family of tribal chieftains. Kuwait, in short, is a ruling Emirocracy or Sabahklatura, who have all become multimillionaires because the land they unjustly rule happens to contain an enormous amount of oil. This is the "legitimate government" of Kuwait that George Bush has pledged himself to restore! The crucial questions: Why must any American die for the Sabahklatura of Kuwait? Why are American taxpayers being plundered to keep that crummy family in their ill-gotten gains? Why die for Kuwait?

Destroying Iraq's Nuclear Capability Does Not Justify Military Action

David Albright and Mark Hibbs

About the Authors: *David Albright is a senior scientist at Friends of the Earth, an environmental organization in Washington, D.C. Mark Hibbs is European editor of* Nuclear Fuel *and* Nucleonics Week *in Bonn, Germany. The following article was written in March 1991.*

Just two hours after U.S. warplanes began attacking Iraq on January 16, 1991, President George Bush went on national television to report the goals of the assault. "As I report to you, air attacks are under way against military targets in Iraq. We are determined to knock out Saddam Hussein's nuclear bomb potential," the president said, before ticking off other objectives. The prominence Bush gave to Iraq's nuclear "potential" repeated a theme that the administration began pushing vigorously in November 1990 as a rationale for the use of military force against that country. But after a months-long investigation of the requirements any country would need to build nuclear weapons, and an assessment of Iraq's ability to meet those requirements, we conclude that Saddam Hussein was many years away from developing usable nuclear weapons.

Indeed, the Iraqi nuclear bomb-making capability was so primitive that the international

David Albright and Mark Hibbs, "Iraq and the Bomb: Were They Even Close?" *Bulletin of the Atomic Scientists,* March 1991. Reprinted with permission from the *Bulletin of the Atomic Scientists.* Copyright © 1991 by the Educational Foundation for Nuclear Science, 6042 S. Kimbark, Chicago, IL 60637, USA. A one-year subscription is $30.

sanctions put in place after the August 2, 1990, invasion may have had more substantive effect than the tons of bombs dropped by U.S. and allied planes five months later. "There may be good reasons to go to war with Iraq," one U.S. government official said before January 16, 1991, "but Iraq's nuclear program isn't one of them."

Immediately after Saddam Hussein invaded Kuwait, the German Foreign Office issued an internal memo to its export control officials. The document ordered an end to a training program three German firms had been conducting for Iraqi engineers, "in the light of newest evidence of German involvement in the nuclear weapons field in Iraq, and threatening political complications [arising from] such a suspicion."

The training program was part of a concerted Iraqi effort to overcome what Western experts believe was its nuclear Achilles' heel, lack of skilled personnel. The three firms—one of which was Interatom GmbH, which supplied staff from its advanced reactor department—had been training the engineers for nearly a year before the export control office was informed of the full scope of the training program. The Iraqis were on the staff of a Baghdad organization known as Industrial Project Company (IPC), which the Mossad, Israel's intelligence agency, believes is at the pinnacle of Iraq's entire military procurement effort.

> ## "There may be good reasons to go to war with Iraq, but Iraq's nuclear program isn't one of them."

Although Interatom officials told German export authorities that the transfer of nuclear know-how was forbidden, customs agents emphasized that IPC staff expressed a keen desire to get specific and extensive nuclear-related information. IPC is also behind a company called Al Fao General Establishment, in Baghdad. According to U.S. and Israeli intelligence reports, Al Fao has been active in procuring missile technology for Iraq. A U.S. government expert said that Al Fao wanted laboratory equipment from Interatom which could be used as a clean room for manufacturing missile guidance systems, or centrifuge components needed to enrich uranium for use in nuclear weapons. A work room, German investigators said, was the first dual-use (civilian-military) export to Iraq that was stopped after Kuwait was overrun.

"For a country such as Iraq, constructing a nuclear weapon is a formidable task."

In July 1990, President Saddam Hussein of Iraq said on French television, "We do not have nuclear weapons, but we would see no problem in a Western nation helping us to develop nuclear arms to help compensate for those owned by Israel." But because Iraq's quest still depended heavily on foreign help, as these incidents illustrate, the U.N. [United Nations] boycott imposed after the invasion may have been the most effective way to delay Iraq's quest for the bomb. The embargo stopped several significant technology transfers which might have advanced Saddam Hussein's drive to make nuclear explosive material. Based on numerous interviews with U.S., European, and Israeli government officials and a December 1990 conversation with a former German centrifuge expert who met with Iraqi centrifuge designers in Baghdad two years ago, we conclude that even before war broke out Iraq was five to ten years or more from having the ability to make the highly enriched uranium it would need for a nuclear arsenal.

On Thanksgiving Day 1990, President George Bush told U.S. troops in Saudi Arabia that "those who would measure the timetable for Saddam's atomic program in years may be seriously underestimating . . . the gravity of the threat." But that warning and others were based on sketchy information and improbable assumptions. Most evidence supported the view that Iraq remained far from possessing the infrastructure needed to produce nuclear weapons, and worst-case assessments such as the president's seriously overstated the risk that Iraq would soon detonate a nuclear explosive.

It is true that Iraq had more than one path to possessing nuclear weapons. The first method was to seize the small amount of highly enriched uranium in its possession, which was under international inspection, and fabricate it into a single nuclear weapon. Another was to acquire more fissile material clandestinely from other nations.

The surest route to a nuclear arsenal, however, depends on developing the indigenous capability to produce nuclear explosive material and fabricate it into deliverable nuclear weapons. Iraq appeared committed to doing this, even though it signed the Nuclear Non-Proliferation Treaty. According to intelligence collected by Western governments in 1990, Saddam Hussein got serious about acquiring technology and equipment for nuclear weapons in 1987. Two different organizations were involved in the procurement and development tasks for his clandestine nuclear program: The first, Al Qaqaa State Establishment, located in Iskandariya near Baghdad, was thought to be in charge of developing the non-nuclear components for a nuclear weapon, German intelligence documents say. The second, Nassr State Enterprise in Taji, also near Baghdad, was said to be responsible for Iraq's uranium enrichment effort. Independently of these organizations, IPC agents in Europe actively sought weapon and uranium enrichment technology and equipment as well.

The Quest for a Workable Weapon

The biggest immediate concern was that Iraq would construct one nuclear explosive out of a small amount of highly enriched uranium which remained in its civilian nuclear program. This material was committed to peaceful uses and inspected every six months by the International Atomic Energy Agency (IAEA), which last checked in November 1990 and found the material intact. But the possibility existed that Iraq would snatch the material between inspections and use it in a bomb. Even now it is impossible to say where this material might be.

A Nuclear Weapon

A nuclear weapon, even a crude one, has thousands of parts. Los Alamos National Laboratory has produced a secret document detailing what is needed to make a nuclear weapon and where to buy it; the document is 500 pages long. For a country such as Iraq, which has little electronic, chemical, or metallurgical manufacturing capability, constructing a nuclear weapon is a formidable task.

An Iraqi nuclear explosive device would have to be a fission device (as opposed to a thermonuclear, or hydrogen, bomb), presumably based on an implosion design. Such designs, one of which was the basis for the bomb dropped on Nagasaki, are well known. . . . An implosion bomb contains a mass of nuclear material—in this case, highly enriched uranium—in its center. The conventional high explosives around the central mass detonate simultaneously, imploding and compressing the fissile material to a supercritical mass. At that instant, neutrons must be injected into the material to initiate the chain reaction and explosion. An alternative fission bomb design, the "gun" type, was used to destroy Hiroshima. But because it requires more fissile material, Iraq was unlikely to pursue that design.

Many aspects of the design and development of an implosion fission device present special problems:

Iraq might not have enough highly enriched uranium for a "crude" nuclear device, that is, one containing just slightly less fissile material than necessary to achieve criticality when the device is assembled. To make a crude implosion device using weapon-grade uranium (enriched to over 90 percent uranium 235), one would have to start out with at least 15 kilograms. This assumes that the design would incorporate a thick reflector/tamper and that little fissile material would be lost in processing—although such losses can under many circumstances reach 10-20 percent. But Iraq has only 12.3 kilograms of 93 percent enriched uranium, some of which might fuel the Tammuz II research reactor at Tuwaitha Nuclear Research Center near Baghdad. The material was intended for the 40-megawatt Osiraq reactor, destroyed by Israel in 1981 just before it was scheduled to begin operating.

> ### "A U.S. government official said in December 1990 that he would be surprised if Iraq had been able . . . to develop confidence in a nuclear design."

Iraq also has about 10 kilograms of 80 percent enriched uranium at the 5-megawatt IRT-5000 reactor supplied by the Soviet Union. Up to two-thirds of the enriched uranium has been irradiated in the reactor and would require remotely operated chemical processing to extract the highly enriched uranium, a step that would have been difficult for Iraq to accomplish quickly, even before the bombing of Tuwaitha. The unirradiated highly enriched uranium, however, could be added to the 93 percent material, possibly providing Iraq with just enough material for a crude bomb. . . .

Before a nuclear device could be assembled, the designers would have to complete certain steps in order to have confidence that it would work. They would have to perform theoretical calculations, then a significant number of experiments, including non-nuclear explosions, to confirm the theoretical calculations. These would require a steady supply of electronic components, conventional explosive charges, and fabricated nuclear components, probably made from natural uranium.

Carson Mark, former head of the Theoretical Division at Los Alamos National Laboratory, thinks Iraq would have needed at least a year of hard work to make one nuclear explosive device out of about 12 kilograms of weapon-grade uranium. Most of this time would be spent developing confidence that the device would work. Mark said that accomplishing this goal would require an appreciable commitment of resources and skilled personnel, including physicists, chemists, metallurgists, electrical engineers, and persons capable of precision machining. Even then, he said, the designers would probably be unable to predict the device's nuclear yield.

A U.S. government official said in December 1990 that he would be surprised if Iraq had been able to conduct the large numbers of implosion tests necessary to develop confidence in a nuclear design. He said that it took the Pakistanis several years to master an implosion system, even though they were working from a proven design provided by an "external source." Press reports have often identified China as the source of Pakistan's weapons design.

Building a more sophisticated design places a premium on acquiring advanced electronics and high-explosive capabilities from industrialized nations, which Iraq was aggressively pursuing. Between 1986 and 1991 the U.S. government approved the sale to Iraq of $1.5 billion worth of computers, electronic equipment, and machine tools which could be used in its nuclear, chemical, and ballistic missile programs.

Smuggling Technology

Iraq was caught in March 1990 trying to smuggle military-standard and -specification detonation capacitors from CSI Technologies of San Marcos, California. The capacitors' many applications include nuclear weapons as well as conventional warheads and military laser systems. An implosion system can use this type of detonation capacitor, which stores large amounts of electrical energy, with a high-speed electronic switch, called a "krytron." This assembly can supply within a fraction of a microsecond a burst of electrical energy to the detonator or blasting cap which sets off the conventional high explosives. Following an 18-month undercover investigation by the U.S. Customs Service in collaboration with the British government, five persons were arrested in London and the capacitors they were carrying—they had been given dummies instead of real ones—were confiscated.

> ## "Eventually, Iraq will probably be able to design a deliverable nuclear weapon, if it is still determined to do so."

Customs officials identified the end-users for the capacitors as the Al Qaqaa State Establishment, the top-secret facility involved in developing missiles and explosives for Iraq's Ministry of Industry and Military Industrialization. German intelligence believes that Al Qaqaa, which has experience with modern conventional high-explosive and high-speed measurement technologies, was given responsibility to develop the nonnuclear components of a nuclear explosive device. . . .

Soon after the March arrests, Saddam Hussein asserted that his Ministry of Industry and Military Industrialization had succeeded in producing similar capacitors. While this claim cannot be verified, in 1989 Iraq was able to buy about 150 lower-quality capacitors from Maxwell Electronics, a California-based firm. The head of that company speculated that Iraq may have upgraded these capacitors.

William Higinbotham, who headed the electronics group at Los Alamos during the Manhattan Project, thinks that is possible. "It is not a question of know-how, which is now widespread," he said in a December 1990 interview, "but a matter of whether Iraq has the highly developed skills and trained operating personnel necessary to make these types of capacitors and high-speed switches." He believes, however, that Iraq could easily have taken six months or longer to make them, even if they had blueprints.

To initiate the chain reaction in the highly enriched uranium after it is sufficiently compressed, neutrons must be injected into the material. One type of initiator, located at the very center of the device, could be made from alternating spheres of polonium 210 and beryllium, separated by a thin layer of material able to shield the beryllium from the alpha particles produced by the radioactive decay of polonium 210. When the shock wave from the high explosives hit the initiator, it would crush the beryllium and polonium together, producing copious numbers of neutrons. Polonium 210, a decay product of uranium 238, is relatively easy to obtain in sufficient quantities for a nuclear explosive device.

Another type of initiator would be a timed neutron generator, located outside the high explosives, which would inject neutrons into the core at the right moment. One common type is a vacuum tube that produces neutrons by accelerating deuterium into a tritium target. Iraq acquired neutron generators of this type, used in oil exploration. But, according to Higinbotham, this particular kind of generator is probably unsuitable for nuclear explosives, which require extremely precise timing.

None of these problems presents an insurmountable obstacle to a determined and well-funded research, development, and procurement effort. Eventually, Iraq will probably be able to design a deliverable nuclear weapon, if it is still determined to do so. But an effective embargo could still inhibit its ability to obtain high-technology components that would make the task easier.

Iraq's Program

Because the status of Iraq's program to design and make nuclear explosives is not well known, speculation ranges widely on how long it would take Iraq to make a single weapon. Direct confirmation of the relevant activities is lacking, as is information about all the types of helpful equipment and technology Iraq obtained before the embargo.

In a National Intelligence Estimate completed in fall 1990, the U.S. intelligence community estimated that Iraq could build a nuclear explosive device in "six months to a year, and probably longer." This estimate assumed that Iraq would mount a crash program to build an explosive out of its safeguarded material, and that it possessed advanced bomb-making technology. Even so, the assessment noted that the device would have a low nuclear yield, would be too bulky to deliver by missile or even by aircraft, and might not detonate.

> "Although Iraq may still be able to design and build a bomb, building a sizable arsenal . . . is a challenge of a much higher order."

A recent German intelligence assessment concluded that Iraq would need considerable help from abroad to complete a successful nuclear weapons program. That assessment pointed out that, up to now, there are no indications of direct foreign assistance to Iraq in the development of nuclear weapons.

Although Iraq may still be able to design and build a bomb, building a sizable arsenal that would present a meaningful threat to its enemies is a challenge of a much higher order, because it depends on acquiring additional nuclear explosive materials. Iraq has three main ways to do this:

• *Enlarge its own safeguarded stock.* If the embargo remains after the war on shipments of safeguarded highly enriched uranium, Iraq will be unable to acquire more highly enriched fuel for its IRT-5000 reactor—if it can be operated after the bombing of Tuwaitha. It would therefore have to use the 80 percent enriched fuel it has in stock, further reducing its inventory of weapon-usable material.

If the embargo is lifted, the Soviets may resume their sales of highly enriched fuel to Iraq. An alternative would be to supply lower-enriched fuels that could not be used in weapons, but this may present problems. France once tried to substitute low-enriched uranium fuels for the highly enriched fuels that were to run the Osiraq reactor, but Saddam Hussein objected. Furthermore, the Soviets probably have not yet developed the kind of low-enriched fuel the reactor would require. To do this they could expect help from Western countries, including the United States, which have successfully converted many of the world's research reactors from highly enriched uranium to 20 percent enriched uranium fuels.

• *Obtain materials clandestinely.* A possible clandestine source of both highly enriched uranium and plutonium is civilian or military nuclear programs in other parts of the world. The civilian plutonium programs in Europe and Japan handle large quantities of nuclear explosive materials, making them targets for theft or diversion.

In the early 1980s, senior Iraqi military figures were interested in buying more than 30 kilograms of plutonium from an Italian arms smuggling ring that claimed to have such material for sale. The deal fell through when the smugglers were unable to produce any plutonium. As the amounts of plutonium in international and national commerce increase, security will need to tighten to prevent these materials from being stolen.

• *Produce its own material.* To assure its supply of nuclear material, Iraq would have to develop the ability to produce such material. The bombing of the Osiraq reactor closed off one potential plutonium route to the bomb. According to a U.S. official, Iraq might still have been pursuing a plutonium route to the bomb before the war, but this was secondary. Instead, Iraq was concentrating its efforts on the difficult task of making highly enriched uranium.

The embargo was, and may continue to be, the most effective way to prevent Iraq from succeeding in this effort. The actions of German export officials, followed by the economic embargo cutting off access to foreign technology, had already hampered Iraq's uranium enrichment program before war broke out.

Gas Centrifuges

For several years Iraq had been pursuing the development of gas centrifuges, which use rapidly spinning rotors to separate the more desirable uranium 235 isotope from the more plentiful uranium 238 isotope. Any country intent on mastering the gas centrifuge process must go through several time-consuming steps before it can expect to build a pilot plant containing a few thousand relatively unsophisticated machines —the minimum number necessary to produce enough weapon-grade uranium each year for one nuclear explosive.

First Iraq would have to develop and test the gas centrifuge itself. And since each centrifuge can enrich uranium only slightly, engineers would have to learn how to connect centrifuges together by pipes into "cascades" that cumulatively produce significant quantities of enriched uranium.

"The embargo was, and may continue to be, the most effective way to prevent Iraq from succeeding in this effort."

Bruno Stemmler, a former centrifuge expert at the German firm MAN Technologien GmbH, met secretly with Iraqi centrifuge design engineers in 1988. Stemmler said in a December 1990 interview that Iraq appeared to be at an early stage in the development of the centrifuge itself. He described a visit to a secret laboratory on the southeast edge of Baghdad, still under construction, in which he was shown a bench centrifuge apparatus, or a "test stand." He said that the building had only one test stand, and he saw no testing equipment such as would be used to check the rotor bearings or the balancing of the rotor. He saw no inlets or outlets in the casing other than for the vacuum system, implying that uranium hexafluoride was not being used, and thus that the apparatus was unable to enrich uranium. Stemmler said he helped Iraqi experts solve problems in the test stand's vacuum system and was asked where the Iraqis could obtain more vacuum equipment. He concluded that the test stand could only be used for elementary mechanical tests of the rotor.

"Iraq tried, with limited success, to acquire technologies and components for the entire enrichment program."

Stemmler estimated that Iraq would need five years of testing and many additional test stands to get an operating centrifuge, and at least another year or two of testing with uranium hexafluoride to get a machine operating at a capacity of roughly one "separative work unit" (a standard measure) per year. He said that he met with up to 15 excellent Iraqi centrifuge design engineers, but he did not think that Iraq had enough technical support personnel or facilities to back up the complex testing program needed to develop gas centrifuges. According to an official at Urenco, Europe's commercial enrichment consortium, several dozen technicians are needed to provide support to each test stand, as it goes from initial tests to "hot" testing using uranium hexafluoride.

Other Evidence

But other evidence makes it clear that Iraq tried, with limited success, to acquire technologies and components for the entire enrichment program, including the manufacture of centrifuges. More than a year after an undercover investigation failed to substantiate allegations,

the German government still believes that German centrifuge design officials who had been involved in Urenco's enrichment effort in Germany tried to recruit other centrifuge experts to work for Iraq. Iraq also was given blueprints for several German centrifuge designs. Stemmler said that Iraqi engineers showed him designs for the Gl-type centrifuge, which Germans developed in the 1960s and early 1970s, with a separative capacity of less than two separative work units.

A Nassr State Enterprise official, Safa Al Haboobi, was appointed director of Technology Development Group (TDG), an Iraqi procurement firm based in London. Intelligence sources say that through Haboobi, TDG acquired an 18 percent share of the firm Schmiedemeccanica AG, in Biasca, Switzerland. Intelligence sources say Schmiedemeccanica, which manufactured centrifuge endcaps and baffles for Iraq, also agreed in 1990 to supply preformed maraging steel cylinders ("preforms") to Iraq for centrifuge rotors. According to a U.S. nuclear proliferation expert, the order was not filled before the U.N. embargo started. Before 1988 the German firm H&H Metalform Ltd. sold Iraq flow-forming machines, which could shape the preforms into thin centrifuge rotor tubes or outer missile casings.

The U.S. official also said that Iraq ordered spin-forming machines, which can shape centrifuge endcaps, from another Swiss firm, Schäublin. But the machines were confiscated in July 1990, before they could be shipped to Iraq. The same official said that Iraq acquired seven machine tools, which he described as simple computer-controlled lathes.

Iraq also ordered about 50 metric tons of low-grade maraging steel from the German firm Export-Union GmbH. The material is only marginally usable for centrifuge rotors, but it could be used for missile applications. According to a company official, only a "test shipment" of 3-millimeter steel sheets actually went to Iraq, although the original order included maraging steel rings with a diameter of about 800 millimeters, used in the manufacture of missile casings.

On December 16, 1990, the London *Sunday Times* claimed that Iraq had a cascade operating at Tuwaitha, the location of Iraq's known nuclear facilities, which are inspected by the IAEA. Stemmler called this assertion ridiculous. He said that developing a cascade would be "far, far more difficult" than balancing a rotor in a single centrifuge. Iraq would need large quantities of uranium hexafluoride, computerized control equipment to maintain precise pressures and temperatures throughout the cascade, autoclaves for inserting uranium hexafluoride into the cascade, and desublimers for withdrawing it. Although Stemmler thought that Iraq would have little trouble obtaining a power supply (frequency inverter) for a single rotor assembly, getting the power supply for an entire cascade would prove "extraordinarily difficult."

A Western enrichment expert said that the biggest obstacle to operating a cascade is developing equipment that will run for years without failing. "Infant mortality," the crashing of a centrifuge during startup, is a major problem that must be addressed in the development stage, since the failure of one centrifuge can cause the entire cascade to fail. The expert said that Iraq would probably concentrate on building one reliable centrifuge, then test and prove a cascade of 10 centrifuges before moving on to cascades of 100-150 machines. . . .

How Long?

To gauge the amount of time Iraq might have needed to build a pilot enrichment plant, it is useful to consider Brazil's unsafeguarded enrichment program, which has benefitted from a more sophisticated industrial and nuclear infrastructure than Iraq's. Brazil decided to develop centrifuges in the late 1970s and still has not reached its goal of 1,000 operating centrifuges. In September 1982, Brazil succeeded in producing slightly enriched uranium in its own centrifuges. In 1984 it operated its first cascade of nine machines. In 1988 Brazil inaugurated a new gas centrifuge enrichment plant at Ipero, in the state of São Paulo, with 50-100 machines.

Brazil now plans to expand the Ipero plant to about 1,000 machines, each with a capacity of about two separative work units per year. About 1,600 people, including about 800 engineers, are working on the enrichment program at Ipero and an experimental center on the campus of São Paulo University. About 40 Brazilian companies are under direct contract to the enrichment program, working on steel, alloys, welding, vacuum technology, and synthetic materials. Another 160 companies are indirectly linked to the program.

"[Iraq's] nuclear effort was at such an early stage that there was little to destroy."

After all this effort, and assuming it operates 1,000 machines, Brazil would still need about two to three years to produce enough weapon-grade uranium for one crude nuclear explosive. It seems safe to assume that what has taken Brazil over a decade would have taken Iraq at least that long.

Meantime, Iraq's "nuclear sites" were prime targets in the early raids by U.S. and allied warplanes. But the effect of air attack on the Iraqi weapons program, such as it was, is highly questionable. The research reactors at Tuwaitha, which may have been destroyed, were unconnected to the bomb program. The highly enriched uranium fuel left over from the Osiraq reactor, or not yet irradiated in the IRT-5000, could easily have been moved before war broke out—as could any key pieces of laboratory equipment. Nuclear scientists and engineers have presumably stayed out of harm's way. The war may put a damper on any future program by damaging Iraq's industrial capacity, but the nuclear effort was at such an early stage that there was little to destroy. If Iraq is determined to pursue nuclear weapons after the war, outside help will still be the key to its success.

Maintaining Economic Sanctions May Prevent the Need for Military Action

Sam Nunn

About the Author: *Sam Nunn, a Democrat, is a U.S. senator from Georgia, and chairman of the Senate Armed Services Committee.*

Editor's Note: The following viewpoint is taken from Sam Nunn's speech before the U.S. Senate on January 10, 1991. Nunn opposed the Senate resolution (passed on January 12) authorizing President George Bush "to use all necessary means" to force Iraq out of Kuwait unless it ended its occupation by January 15, 1991. Nunn co-sponsored an alternate resolution calling for continued economic sanctions against Iraq, which the Senate rejected.

It is regrettable that because of Iraqi intransigence, the meeting in Geneva with Secretary James Baker produced no diplomatic breakthrough and very little that was encouraging. I noted with interest—and I must say with almost complete amazement—that the Iraqi Foreign Minister refused to accept President Bush's letter to Saddam Hussein because the letter, according to the Foreign Minister, was supposedly not polite. I have not seen President Bush's letter. But I find that Iraqi protest both ironic and, indeed, repulsive.

Was it polite when Saddam Hussein used chemical weapons against his own people? And

Sam Nunn, address to the U.S. Senate, January 10, 1991.

then, again, against Iran? Was it polite when Iraqi forces launched a brutal, unprovoked invasion of Kuwait? Was it polite when Iraqi forces used savage violence against innocent Kuwaiti civilians and took hostage innocent foreigners residing in that country?

Saddam Hussein and his top spokesmen do not have the standing in the court of world opinion to raise the issue of politeness.

I still believe there is room for some hope that diplomacy can succeed in avoiding war. But as January 15th approaches, as so many of my colleagues have already observed, the Congress must act. Article 1, section 8 of the Constitution provides that the Congress clearly has the authority and the duty to decide whether the Nation should go to war. In many past instances it is true that military actions have occurred without congressional authorization. Pursuant to the authority assumed by the President in his constitutional capacity as Commander-in-Chief in today's fast-moving, interconnected world with instant communications, a world plagued with nuclear weapons and international terrorism, there are certainly instances when United States military force must be used without congressional authorization.

"Sanctions and diplomacy combined with a threat . . . should be given more time."

There are many gray areas where the Congress, by necessity, has permitted and even encouraged and supported military action by the Commander-in-Chief without specific authorization and without a declaration of war. I do not deem every military action taken as war. I think there is always room for debate on definitions. But a war against Iraq to liberate Kuwait initiated by the United States and involving over 400,000 American forces is not a gray area.

In this case, I believe the Constitution of the United States is absolutely clear. It is essential, to comply with the Constitution and to commit the Nation, that Congress give its consent before the President initiates a large-scale military offensive against Iraq. I think the founding Fathers had a great deal of wisdom when they put this provision in the Constitution. One of the main reasons, of course, was to prevent one person from being King. They did not want that. But I also believe that there was another purpose, and that is to make sure that when this Nation goes to war and asks its young men and, increasingly, young women also to put their lives on the line, the Nation must commit itself before we ask them to lay down their lives.

"We have an obligation as leaders to distinguish between important interests . . . and interests that are vital."

The President's January 8, 1991 request that Congress approve the use of military force presents Congress with an issue, simply stated, but profound in its consequences; not simply short term but also long term. Many of us strongly believe a war to liberate Kuwait should be the last resort and that sanctions and diplomacy combined with a threat—a continuing threat of force—should be given more time. Should we give the President—after all of these debates when the die is cast—should we give him blanket authority to go to war against Iraq to liberate Kuwait? This is the question we face. There are numerous questions that will have to be answered in the minds of each of us before casting our vote.

The first question I try to ask when it comes to matters of war and peace is the question of whether a particular situation is vital to our Nation's security. In this case, *is the liberation of Kuwait vital to our Nation's security?* We all agree with the goal of restoring Kuwaiti sovereignty; no doubt about that. But have we concluded here that the liberation of Kuwait in the next

few weeks is so *vital* to our Nation's security that we must take military action *now* instead of waiting a few months—waiting a period of time to allow the economic embargo and blockage to take its toll?

Sanctions' Effects

Back in August and September 1990 when the embargo was successfully—and I'd say very skillfully brought about by President Bush, through what I think was his superb leadership—no one thought or predicted the embargo was going to be over by January 1991. No one predicted we were going to be able to bring about the termination of Iraqi presence in Kuwait by January. None of the intelligence experts or other experts who testified felt the embargo was really going to have much effect before April or May of 1991 and almost all of them said it would take at least a year. There was no surprise about that. I'm absolutely amazed when people say well, we've waited four months and five months and the embargo is not working. They must not have been there at the beginning or they must not have talked to anybody at the beginning about how long it was going to take. It's very puzzling to me how someone could give up on the embargo after five months when nobody that I know of predicted that it was going to last less than nine months to a year, and most people said a year to eighteen months from the time of inception, which was August of 1990.

When we talk about the question of vital—a lot of times we in Washington throw that word around as if it's just another word. Sometimes we use so many words in the course of debate that we don't think carefully about what we mean. I recall very clearly President Reagan's 1982 declaration that Lebanon was vital to the *security* of the United States. Shortly thereafter, following the tragic death of more than 200 Marines, we pulled out of Lebanon, we pulled out of a country that only a few weeks before had been declared vital. Today, as we debate this, eight years later, [we are] pursuing our newly proclaimed vital interest in Kuwait. It was not vital before August 2, 1990. Nobody had said it was vital then. There was no treaty. In fact, when we were protecting Kuwaiti vessels coming out of the Gulf for several years during the Iran/Iraq war, the Kuwaitis didn't even let us refuel, as I recall. I'd have to be checked on that one but that's my recollection.

All of a sudden it's vital—vital. And while this embargo has been undertaken since August 2nd, and while we all seem to take for granted that the liberation of Kuwait is vital, not just in general but in the next 2 or 3 or 4 weeks—while that's been going on, our Government has watched passively, said very little if anything, while our former enemy, a nation on the terrorist list for years and years and I believe it still is—Syria—used its military power to consolidate its control over Lebanon, the same country that was our vital interest in 1982. So one of our so-called vital interests, Lebanon, eight years ago, is now under the control of Syria, while we have pursued another vital interest.

The point is, not all these things are simple. The point is we ought to be careful about defining vital. A lot of things are important, very important, that aren't vital. Vital in the sense of young men and young women being called to put their lives on the line.

Panama and Nicaragua

In more recent history, we defined Panama and Nicaragua as vital, and we used force in the case of Panama directly. In the case of Nicaragua, we supported force. I supported both of those decisions. But after achieving our short-term goals in both these countries—we arrested Manuel Noriega and we cheered the election of President Violetta Chamorro—we seem to have forgotten their on-going economic and political agony. These were countries in which we used or supported force for one reason or the other. Again I supported it in both cases. And now, while we're pursuing another vital interest, they are going through economic and political wrenching experiences with the outcome being

very uncertain. Both the Bush Administration and the Congress have unfulfilled responsibilities regarding those two countries.

My point is, we throw around the word "vital" very carelessly. When politicians declare an interest to be vital, our men and women in uniform are expected to put their lives at risk to defend that interest. They train for years to be able to go out and, if necessary, give their lives to protect what we declare to be vital. Sometimes when you see how quickly we come to use that term, it makes you wonder whether we are fulfilling our responsibility to those men and women in uniform. We have an obligation as leaders to distinguish between important interests which are worthy of economic, political, and diplomatic efforts and interests that are vital, that are worth the calling by the leaders of this Nation on our young men and women in uniform to sacrifice, if necessary, their lives.

"The international sanctions are . . . having a devastating effect on Iraq's economy."

Former Secretary of Defense and former CIA [Central Intelligence Agency] Director James Schlesinger spoke to this very point when he testified before our Committee. He testified that he did not think liberation of Kuwait "was a vital interest on the 2nd day of August, 1990." Dr. Schlesinger, however, went on to say, quoting him again:

> . . . the investment of the prestige of the President of the United States now makes it vital (he does not use the word "vital" lightly) for Iraq to withdraw from Kuwait. I do not think that it is necessary, to achieve that objective, for us to turn to war. I think that we can avoid war and still achieve the objective of Iraqi withdrawal from Kuwait.

This brings up the next question.

Are there reasonable alternatives to war? What is the likelihood that sanctions will work? In testimony before the Congress, and in public and private statements as recently as January 3, 1991, the Bush Administration stopped short of saying that sanctions cannot get Iraq out of Kuwait. The Administration acknowledges the significant economic impact sanctions have had on Iraq but now says there is "no guarantee" whether or not they will bring about an Iraqi decision to withdraw from Kuwait. In August 1990, President Bush asserted himself, saying, quoting him, "Economic sanctions, in this instance, if fully enforced, can be very, very effective . . . and nobody can stand up forever to total economic deprivation." That is from President Bush.

Sanctions Having a Devastating Impact

The international sanctions are, indeed, having a devastating effect on Iraq's economy, for two basic reasons. The Iraqi economy is based on oil, which accounts for about 50 percent of the country's GNP [gross national product] and almost 100 percent of the country's hard currency earnings. Iraq is essentially landlocked, dependent upon oil pipelines, foreign ports, and international highways for its imports and exports. As Georgetown University specialist on economic sanctions Dr. Gary Hufbauer testifies before the Senate:

> On no previous occasion have sanctions attracted the degree of support they have in the Iraqi case. Never have they been so comprehensive in their coverage. Never have they imposed such enormous costs on the target country. Moreover, Iraq's economy, geographically isolated and skewed as it is toward oil, is far more vulnerable to economic coercion than other economies that have been the target of sanctions.

The net result to date is that the international sanctions have cut off more than 90 percent of Iraq's imports, almost 100 percent of Iraq's exports, including virtually all of Iraqi oil exports. Iraqi industrial and military plants are receiving from abroad virtually no raw materials, no spare parts, no new equipment, no munitions, no lubricants. Moreover, Iraq now has no way to earn hard currency to purchase desperately needed imports, even if they can be smuggled in spite of the embargo. "Amstel Light" beer may be available in Baghdad, but it is a very poor substitute for such essentials as motor oil and transmission fluid.

"The Administration's position is that if we wait for sanctions to work, Kuwait . . . will be further victimized. Tragically, this is no doubt true."

The key to a meaningful embargo is oil: so long as Iraq's oil exports are shut down—and no one disputes that they are shut down, no one; that is not in dispute—Saddam Hussein will be deprived of at least half of his country's GNP and essentially all of his hard currency income. So long as oil exports are shut down, he will become progressively weaker—there is no doubt about that. We worry about recession in the United States—we worry right now about a recession—we're talking about whether the economy of the United States is going down 3-5 percent of our GNP, and it's of great and legitimate concern. Saddam Hussein has to worry about a devastating reduction of approximately 70 percent of his GNP by the summer of 1991. By the end of summer 1991, the country will be an economic basket case, and I mean Iraq and Saddam Hussein may be in jeopardy with his own people.

The question is: can anyone guarantee that Iraq will abandon Kuwait when their GNP goes down 70 percent? Can anybody guarantee that? The answer is no. We can't guarantee that. But the other options we have also must be held to the same standard. A sanctions policy is not perfect. There are no guarantees here. But it has to be weighed against the alternatives. The Bush Administration is correct when they point out that sanctions do not guarantee that Iraq will leave Kuwait. But the story does not end there. What guarantees do we have that the war will be brief and that American casualties will be light? No one can say whether a war will last five days, five weeks, or five months. We know we can win, and we will win. There is no doubt about that. There is no doubt about who wins this war. Our policy and our military planning, however, cannot be based on an expectation that the war will be concluded quickly and easily. In large measure, the scope and scale of the hostilities, once begun, will be determined by Iraq's willingness to absorb massive punishment and to fight on. A quick Iraqi military collapse is possible in days. We hope it will happen if war comes. But it cannot be assured.

The Administration argues that the coalition may crumble before Iraq withdraws from Kuwait. . . . Admiral William Crowe, the former Chairman of the Joint Chiefs of Staff, took this issue head-on during his testimony before the Armed Services Committee in November 1990. Quoting Admiral Crowe, the immediate past Chairman of the Joint Chiefs, "It is hard to understand," he said, "why some consider our international alliance strong enough to conduct intense hostilities, but too fragile to hold together while we attempt a peaceful solution."

"The risks associated with continued emphasis on sanctions are *considerably less* than the very real risks associated with war."

The Administration's position is that if we wait for sanctions to work, Kuwait and its citizens will be further victimized. Tragically, this is no doubt true. But to quote Admiral Crowe again: "War is not neat, not tidy; once you resort to it, war is uncertain and a mess." The additional cost to Kuwait of letting sanctions work must be weighed against the cost to Kuwait in terms of human lives, human suffering, as well as national resources, if the United States-led coalition launches a military offensive to liberate a country, which is heavily fortified.

Those who support prompt military action argue that delay will allow Iraq to strengthen its defensive positions in Kuwait, thereby adding to the eventual cost of forcing Iraq out of Kuwait. A couple of observations on this point. This would have been a better argument in September and October of 1990 than it is today. Iraq already has had five months to dig in and to fortify and they have done so in a major way. Kuwait has fortifications reminiscent of World War I. This argument also overlooks the costs to the Iraqi military of sitting in Kuwait with a 500,000-man force while logistical support degrades because of the sanctions.

The Webster Letter

I am aware [CIA] Director William Webster sent Congressman Les Aspin a letter on January 10, 1991 that addressed this issue. I read the Webster letter as confirming that the sanctions, if kept in place for six to twelve months, will severely degrade Iraq's armored forces, air force and air defenses. I consider that good news. For some unexplained reason, and I'm sure people will have a reason, but I find it puzzling now because I don't understand what it is, Judge Webster implies that Iraq's tanks, its air defenses, and its over 700 combat aircraft will not play an important role in Iraq's defense of Kuwait. I would certainly hate to try to explain this to several hundred American pilots that are out there, the Air Force and Navy pilots, who have the job of putting their lives in their aircraft at risk to knock out these very targets at the beginning stage of any conflict. I don't understand the Webster letter, frankly. Perhaps we will get more from that later. But it's incredible to me that he seems to write off the importance of the tanks, the aircraft, and the air defenses. Everything I've heard is that we are going to have to make those the priority targets, among others. And to write those off and say that degrading them is really not going to play a big role to me is bewildering. But we'll wait and hear from Director Webster at a later point.

Supporters of prompt military action argue that our offensive military capability will degrade if our huge force sits for months in the

Saudi desert. This is also true, and for several months I have suggested that we should institute a policy of unit rotation, commencing with quick reaction forces, such as the 82nd Airborne, that might be needed on short notice elsewhere in the world. We should take full advantage of the coalition's superiority in air and sea power, while establishing the capability of deploying additional ground forces to the region quickly if needed.

I find it puzzling, however, that proponents of our early military option voice concern about the degradation of our 400,000-strong force, fully backed by the United States and supported by numerous allies, yet at the same time, those favoring authorization of an early military offensive minimize the degradation of Iraq's 500,000-man force in the Kuwaiti theater, a force essentially supported only by Iraq, totally lacking significant allies and subjected to a remarkably effective international embargo.

In weighing the costs of the military option, one must also consider our long-term interests in the region. Has there been any in-depth analysis in the Administration about what happens in the Middle East after we win? And we will win. The President's declared goals include establishing stability in the Persian Gulf and protecting U.S. citizens abroad. Considering the wave of Islamic reaction, anti-Americanism and terrorism that is likely to be unleashed by a highly destructive war with many Arab casualties, it is difficult to conceive of the Middle East as a more stable region where Americans will be safe.

No Guarantees

Finally, the Administration has argued there is no guarantee economic hardships will in the end compel Saddam Hussein to withdraw from Kuwait. I have attended Intelligence Community as well as Defense and State Department briefings for 18 years. I have been thinking back. I cannot recall one instance where I ever came out of those briefings with any guarantee of anything. For the Intelligence Community to say they can't guarantee that Iraq is going to get out of Kuwait because of the sanctions which is going to reduce his GNP by 70 percent and cut off all the hard currency, for them to say that is true. Nobody can guarantee it. But what else have they guaranteed? I haven't seen any guarantees on any subject from the Intelligence Community. It's not their fault. They're not in the business of guaranteeing. The CIA is not the FDIC [Federal Deposit Insurance Corporation]. They give you the facts, then you use common sense to come to conclusions.

In summary, I believe that on balance there is a reasonable expectation that continued economic sanctions, backed up by the threat of military force and international isolation, can bring about Iraqi withdrawal from Kuwait. I believe that the risks associated with continued emphasis on sanctions are *considerably less* than the very real risks associated with war and, most importantly, the aftermath of war in a very volatile region of the world. . . .

"Continued economic sanctions, backed up by the threat of military force and international isolation, can bring about Iraqi withdrawal from Kuwait."

In conclusion, a message to Saddam Hussein: You are hearing an impassioned debate emanating from the U.S. Capitol, both the House and the Senate. These are the voices of Democracy. Don't misread the debate. If war occurs, the Constitutional and policy debates will be suspended and Congress will provide the American troops in the field whatever they need to prevail. There will be no cutoff of funds for our troops while they engage Iraq in battle. President Bush, the Congress, and the American people are united that you must leave Kuwait. We differ on whether these goals can best be accomplished by administering pain slowly with an economic blockade or by dishing it out in large doses with military power. Either way, Saddam Hussein, you lose.

In concluding, and in closing, I can think of no better person to quote than General Norman Schwarzkopf, Commander of U.S. forces in the Gulf, who will bear the heavy responsibility of leading American forces into combat, if war should occur.

On the question of patience, General Schwarzkopf said in mid-November 1990 in an interview, quoting him:

> If the alternative to dying is sitting out in the sun for another summer, then that's not a bad alternative.

On the question of cost of waiting for sanctions to work, General Schwarzkopf also said in an interview in November, quoting him:

> I really don't think there's ever going to come a time when time is on the side of Iraq, as long as the sanctions are in effect, and so long as the United Nations coalition is in effect.

On the question of effect of sanctions, General Schwarzkopf said in October 1990—and this is immediately prior to a major switch in the Administration's policy—immediately prior to it—quoting General Schwarzkopf:

> Right now, we have people saying, "OK, enough of this business; let's get on with it." Golly, the sanctions have only been in effect about a couple of months. . . . And now we are starting to see evidence that the sanctions are pinching. So why should we say "OK, we gave them two months, they didn't work. Let's get on with it and kill a whole bunch of people." That's crazy. That's crazy.

End quote, from the Commander in the field.

In closing, I believe that before this Nation is committed to what may be a large-scale war, each of us in the Senate of the United States in reaching a decision which will be very personal and very difficult for all of us, we should ask ourselves a fundamental question: will I be able to look at the parents, the wives, the husbands, and children in the eye and say their loved ones sacrificed their lives for a cause vital to the United States, and that there was no other reasonable alternative? At this time, I cannot.

Chapter 2:
Did the Persian Gulf War Strengthen the U.S.?

Preface

The U.S. deployed 541,000 soldiers to the Persian Gulf during the 1990-1991 Iraq crisis. The last time American troops were deployed in such numbers was in the Vietnam War. In examining how the Persian Gulf War affected the U.S. domestically and internationally, both supporters and critics of the war have made comparisons to the Vietnam experience.

After more than a decade of fighting, the Vietnam War ended in American defeat and divisiveness. For years afterward people referred to the "Vietnam syndrome" to describe a lack of public unity and confidence in the United States. *Newsweek* reporter Charles Lane writes: "For half a generation, the memory of defeat in Vietnam—and the deep national divisions exposed and fed by that defeat—haunted the United States. A 'can't-do' spirit seemed to dog the government's efforts."

Many people argued that the lopsided victory in the Persian Gulf, coupled with the relatively low loss of American lives, finally removed any lingering aftereffects of Vietnam. President George Bush proclaimed that "we've kicked the Vietnam syndrome once and for all." *Time* reporter Stanley W. Cloud wrote, "When the U.S.-led forces raced across Kuwait and Iraq. . . they . . . defeated not just the Iraqi army but also the more virulent of the ghosts from the Vietnam era: self-doubt, fear of power, divisiveness, a fundamental uncertainty about America's purpose in the world."

One part of the Persian Gulf War's positive effects, according to its supporters, was that it reestablished the U.S. as the world's leading military power. The crisis, writes *Newsweek* reporter Kenneth Auchincloss, "was an emphatic reminder of what almost everyone has known since at least 1989: that there is only one superpower in the world and the United States is it. Given all the recent moans about America's economic troubles, the reminder couldn't have been more timely."

Auchincloss and others argue that the victory led to new respect among other countries for American power and resolve, restoring whatever respect had been lost after the Vietnam defeat.

In addition to changing how the world viewed America, the Persian Gulf War changed how Americans viewed themselves. In the time between October 1990 and February 22, 1991, the percentage of polled Americans who believed that America is moving in the "right direction" rose from 19 to 58 percent, while those who believed America is "seriously off course" fell from 78 to 39 percent. This change in public attitudes, as well as the many parades held after the war for American veterans, reflected an increased patriotism and pride. "If there is a long-lasting effect of the war, it is the tremendous confidence that Americans have rediscovered in themselves, in their industries and in their country," states Sheldon Kamieniecki, a specialist in political opinion at the University of Southern California in Los Angeles.

Easy Success

Whether this increase in pride is beneficial is a matter of some controversy, however. Some people opine that the easy success against Iraq could tempt the U.S. into other military adventures abroad and ultimately lead to another Vietnam. Others argue that the military victory in Iraq has distracted Americans from dealing with U.S. problems. Government analyst John Herbers writes: "The engagement has meant a grave setback for America's efforts to deal with many of our most pressing domestic difficulties." Herbers and others argue that the military effort consumed energy and resources that could have been better used to improve U.S. education or health care, or to decrease poverty. Much as the Vietnam War diverted resources from President Lyndon Johnson's Great Society programs of the 1960s, the Persian Gulf War could weaken the U.S. by distracting Americans from fundamental problems at home.

The Persian Gulf War, much like the Vietnam War, may affect the U.S. for years to come. The viewpoints in this chapter examine the question of whether America's victory in the gulf will strengthen or weaken the U.S. in the future.

Did the Persian Gulf War Strengthen the U.S.?

Yes: The War Strengthened the U.S.

The War Revitalized the U.S.
The War Proved the U.S. Is the World's Sole Superpower
The War Ended the Nation's Trauma over Vietnam

The War Revitalized the U.S.

William J. Bennett

About the Author: *William J. Bennett is senior editor of the* National Review, *a biweekly conservative magazine. He previously served as U.S. secretary of education and later headed the Office of National Drug Control Policy.*

A recent episode of *Saturday Night Live* opened with a skit parodying the Pentagon's press briefings on the Gulf War. It featured a [defense secretary] Dick Cheney look-alike and a Marine general. Nothing new there, of course; the government has always been fair game for spoofs. But what made this sketch different—and in some ways significant—was that the object of ridicule was not Cheney or the military, but the press, presented as a pack of baying wolves. The defense secretary, infinitely patient, explained that they would be happy to answer any questions that did not endanger military operations, whereupon the press badgered him with such questions as, "Could you tell us the date the ground war will begin?" or "Which of America's half-million troops in the region are most vulnerable to an Iraqi attack?"

When *Saturday Night Live*, the counterculture comedy show par excellence, prefers the military to the media, a major cultural shift is taking place. Charles Krauthammer has written that, except for revolution, nothing changes a country more than war. And in the reaction to war with Iraq the contours of a new and more confident America can be seen. A successful prosecution of the Gulf War may replace Vietnam as one

of the defining events in the American psyche.

It was a long time in coming. Ronald Reagan began us on this road to recovery with his firm leadership in the Eighties. The prudent use of force—by President Reagan in Grenada and Libya, by President Bush in Panama—moved us further along the road to recovery. But these were victories in miniature. We still could not claim a military victory on the magnitude of the Vietnam defeat. Doubts remained.

> ## "In the reaction to war with Iraq the contours of a new and more confident America can be seen."

An American-led Allied victory in the Gulf, against a malevolent dictator with the fourth-largest standing army in the world, will put such doubts to rest. We will remember the right lessons from Vietnam, but more important, we will at long last let go of the wrong ones.

We are already seeing a healthy reassessment of our fundamental institutions. The military, so unjustly maligned by the elites these past 25 years, is the war's big winner. When we called on our armed forces at a critical hour, they were there. A commercial republic needs to be reminded about the importance of things like duty, honor, virtue, and the hitching up of one's purposes to larger purposes beyond the self. The military is teaching us a civics lesson.

In the popular culture, we may finally move beyond the spate of Vietnam movies like *Born on the Fourth of July, Platoon,* and *Apocalypse Now,* where we were instructed on morality and national security by the Oliver Stones of the world. By this time next year, I wouldn't be at all surprised to see some new titles: *Day of the Patriot? Combat Ready: The Story of Colin Powell?* perhaps even *The Bridge over the River Tigris?*

In sharp contrast to the military's performance is that of the mainline churches. Their leaders have demonstrated, once again, that on matters of profound moral importance, they have virtually nothing useful, significant, or specifically religious to say. Their marked inability to make the classic distinctions between the use of force in a just manner for right purposes and the use of violence to advance evil is a sign of sheer moral exhaustion. That we can no longer look to the spokesmen of most of the mainline American religious institutions on important moral issues is bad news indeed. That they have become increasingly irrelevant to the public debate is, alas, the good news.

The press has also lost ground. In reporting the war, many journalists are doing what they do best: informing the American people. But some of the press act as if they were also our moral and intellectual guardians. There is the claim, for example, by Marvin Kalb (formerly of NBC, now of Harvard), that "in a war the primeval patriotic instincts of the American people rise to the surface . . . and any institution that seems to be critical of the troops and those who command them will be regarded with deep suspicion."

"The events in the Gulf remind the world . . . that America is usually on the right side of a war."

Kalb seems to be saying: The American people need the press to protect them from their own worst instincts. That sounds a little wide (and maybe a little left) of the mark. It omits the conclusion that the press may have some instincts of its own. Indeed, the public's concern about the press arises from the fact that some reporters seem concerned that the Reagan defense buildup is being vindicated to excess, or that the military is looking a little too good and the course of the war is going a little too well. So when the press offers itself to the American people as protection against the charms of the military, Americans are skeptical.

We recognize that those doing the fighting have the graver responsibility than those sitting on the sidelines, giving the play-by-play. We want the press there, but not in the way. And I wouldn't be surprised that, as the *Saturday Night Live* skit illustrates, the people would like to see reporters exhibit a bit more civility and common sense when asking our military leaders questions. Skepticism is one thing; prosecutorial zeal quite another.

Sweeping Reappraisals

The events in the Gulf remind the world (and should remind elite opinion) that America is usually on the right side of a war—indeed, on the right side of history. That was true in Vietnam as well. The Vietnamese boat people who fled Ho Chi Minh's paradise—some to America, others, tragically, to their unknown graves beneath the South China Sea—attest to that. Notwithstanding, in today's history books a great many pages are devoted to the "lessons" of Vietnam that point to the opposite moral. In his history of the United States, Henry Steele Commager argued that Vietnam showed America's vulnerability and raised doubts about its supremacy and intentions. As the *Wall Street Journal* put it recently, "In the years that passed from Vietnam into Watergate and through the reflexive opposition to the Reagan presidency, an intellectual fascination with failure, limits, and the contrary seemed to develop." If President Bush is successful in his prosecution of this war, and all signs point to this, he will in effect force a sweeping reappraisal of these assumptions. Historians will have to write about an American success rather than a failure.

This in turn might lead people to ask how such a nation came to be, to ask about the philosophy behind our success, "the canon behind the cannons." The impressive performance of our technology in the Gulf might even entice a few more students to pursue math and science, to be on the cutting edge of the next generation of technology, may be to gain a new appreciation for modern weapons themselves.

The philosophy is moral as well as technical, and as such, quintessentially American. The air war in Iraq and Kuwait has demonstrated that weapons also save lives, quite apart from saving countries. When you can shoot Patriot missiles up to shoot Scud missiles down, you're saving lives. When you can shoot other weapons from a distance, without exposing your troops to close fire, you're saving lives. When you can use laser beams to guide a bomb into the front door of a defense ministry building without taking down its neighbor, you're saving lives. Ask the Israelis. Ask the Saudis.

The political implications of these questions ought to be enormous. Those who voted against authorizing the president to use force ought to explain their vote. I am not accusing them of voting in bad faith or of a lack of patriotism. I am accusing them of being wrong on a fundamental issue. Their vote ought to be a matter they are called on to defend.

"America will lead, for no other country can make the moral and military difference."

That is after all what politics is supposed to be about in a free society. Important acts, important votes, should have important political consequences. Senators and House members should be asked to explain how it was that they voted to the left of the United Nations on this one—and then to convince the American people that they are ready for prime time in international affairs. Let them also explain exactly what, short of another Pearl Harbor, might constitute a justifiable use of American military might. My guess is that the politicians who voted against the president will want to change the subject. We owe it to our system to make sure that we hold them accountable for their actions, so that future politicians will be taken with the seriousness they deserve.

With a victory in the Gulf, critics will say that we should now have as vigorous an effort at home as we had abroad. That is true, provided we recognize the limitations of government power. There is no Patriot missile for the social and domestic problems of welfare, education, poverty, unwed mothers, and child abuse—with the possible exception of a massive infusion of sound moral values. Federal involvement in these matters is simply not a sufficient solution—in many cases, it is exacerbating the problems it was to address. We need to relearn that these problems require not a program launched from Washington, but matters of the heart and soul: of family, church, neighborhood, and school; of habit and character; of personal aspiration, self-discipline, and hard work. . . .

The Gulf War has triggered an important debate about America's role in the world. To that debate I would add that there is a large middle ground between de facto isolationism and an all-embracing interventionism. It is that large middle ground, known as responsible, selective engagement, that we should occupy. That we cannot be the world's "policeman" is a truism. But the *reductio ad absurdum* of this is that we cannot act *anywhere*. For America to pick up the sword in some circumstances is a moral imperative. And not to pick up the sword in some places—where evil is on the march, where innocent people are being massacred, where vital interests and allies are under attack—is moral abdication. Sometimes crises arise which do not fall clearly into either category. But such are the uneasy burdens of a great, and good, power.

America's Leadership

Upon his departure from America, Lech Walesa left us with these words: "Take care of this country. If you do not lead us, who will?" We are now demonstrating that there is an answer. America will lead, for no other country can make the moral and military difference. This will make a few people, here and elsewhere, unhappy. But it will make countless others happy—and encouraged. They've been waiting a long time.

The War Proved the U.S. Is the World's Sole Superpower

Jonas Bernstein

About the Author: *Jonas Bernstein is a staff writer for* Insight, *a conservative weekly magazine of news and analysis.*

While it may be true that, as Victor Hugo said, an invasion by an idea is more inexorable than an invasion by an army, it is also true that an idea is taken more seriously when backed by superior firepower. The image of dazed Iraqis crawling out of their battlefield bunkers to surrender to anything remotely American—even, according to one report, a pilotless aircraft—has given George Bush's idea of a new world order a certain vigor it previously lacked.

Just how far the U.S. president is willing and able to reorder the world will become easier to assess once the smoke from the Persian Gulf war finally clears. But what already is clear, many analysts say, is that the United States has emerged from this war in a position of undisputed military power and with an international prestige similar to what it enjoyed immediately after World War II. It may even be in a stronger position than 45 years ago, given that Soviet power is in decline.

The U.S.-led victory over Iraq—the result of dazzling high technology and less flamboyant but equally impressive logistical feats—was as much a demonstration of democratic capitalism's resiliency as the fall of the Berlin Wall was of communism's bankruptcy. "For a long time,

people believed that democracies were inherently weaker militarily than more authoritarian or totalitarian societies," says Patrick Glynn, a resident scholar at the American Enterprise Institute in Washington. "But in this technological age, we may have arrived at the point where democratic societies, by their nature, presuming they pay attention to it, have an inherent military advantage."

"We hear so often about our young people in turmoil, how our children fall short, how our schools fail us, how American products and American workers are second-class," said President Bush in his March 6, 1991 victory address to Congress. "Well, don't you believe it. The America we saw in Desert Storm was first-class talent."

It was enough to convince Margaret Thatcher, for one, that the United States is the world's only megapower. "After victory in the Cold War and in the Gulf, we face a still nobler, still more challenging task—to advance the reign of freedom and free enterprise throughout the world. It is now, more than ever, America's destiny, supported by her faithful friends—and no friends are truer than her friends in Britain—to press ahead with that endeavor," said the former British prime minister in a speech March 8, 1991.

"The U.S. has emerged from this war in a position of undisputed military power."

The Soviet Union, once universally accorded superpower status, has been beset by precipitous decline at home and the collapse of its empire abroad. Moreover, Soviet economists newly unfettered by the age of *glasnost* have said that the West has long grossly exaggerated the size of the Soviet economy. And its arms, when tested against state-of-the-art U.S. equipment, have been defeated.

Some have looked to Germany and Japan as

potential contenders for superpower status. They would seem to have the means: Their economies are enormous and robust. But both nations maintained a low profile in the Gulf, showing themselves content to be bound by constitutions that deliberately discourage an active international role. In Germany, attention remains focused on the problems of reunification, and bold moves on the international scene now seem at least decades away. Japan's economic nationalism has so far been unaccompanied by a desire to pursue diplomacy with comparable vigor. Only the United States seems to meet all the tests of superpowerdom; in the absence of serious competition, that makes America the megapower on the world scene.

"Undoubtedly, the Gulf war's other big loser was the Soviet Union."

What was new in the war against Iraq was that, in contrast to the incrementalism of the Vietnam War, this time the U.S. military set out to achieve a victory in the shortest possible time. Their approach was the "don't-screw-around school of military strategy," as Secretary of Defense Dick Cheney called it in September 1990, a.k.a. "the doctrine of invincible force." To achieve this goal, U.S. Gen. H. Norman Schwarzkopf and his advisers rewrote Carl von Clausewitz. The ground campaign, for instance, was not simply the "orchestration of individual campaigns" as the Prussian military strategist defined the art of war, but rather a coordinated set of actions launched simultaneously and all occurring—by historical standards—at lightning speed.

"What you're talking about, really, is a different kind of warfare," says Glynn. "It's not really strategy or tactics anymore. It's the level between strategy and tactics, where you have combined armed operations, employing a vast variety of forces in different locales, many of them deep in

the enemy's territory. It happens all at once, on a massive scale, highly coordinated, with a great variety of forces."

The success of all the technological wizardry, of course, depends on the people who use it. "Hardware is only part of the picture," says Ray Cline, a former deputy director of the CIA [Central Intelligence Agency] and current president of the Washington-based U.S. Global Strategy Council. "It's the skill, the organization, the training, particularly the logistical support and so on, that make a difference." Glynn agrees: "The advantage is not simply in being able to have the computers, but also obviously it depends heavily on smart personnel, capable of taking initiative."

Technology also has allowed the Pentagon to devise a military strategy that employs overwhelming force while preserving the distinction between civilian and military targets and minimizing American losses. Ironically, this leap in fighting capability has made war a more moral enterprise. This in turn may account for a part of Desert Storm's overwhelming domestic popularity.

"The moral factor also turns out to be important for democracy, because democracies have trouble, as we learned in Vietnam, waging war where there are a lot of civilian casualties on the enemy side," says Glynn. "Sympathy crosses borders." This moral component, predicts Cline, will be enshrined in a new Pentagon strategic doctrine. "Of course you have to use lethal weapons to kill lethal targets, but we don't want to be Attila the Hun," he says. "In World War II, we were killing innocent people all the time. We bombed Baghdad and we didn't kill many people, and that's great. I think the new strategic doctrine is going to stress what I call 'nonlethality': minimizing the loss of life."

Soviet Loss of Influence

Undoubtedly, the Gulf war's other big loser was the Soviet Union, or more specifically, its military hardware and doctrine, which it had imparted to Saddam Hussein over the past decade or more. Not surprisingly, the Soviet brass has rushed retroactively to put some distance between themselves and their erstwhile ally. "As concerns the quality of Soviet military technology that happened to be in the Iraqi arsenal, it was the least of the causes," Defense Minister Dmitri Yazov told the military newspaper Red Star. Nikolai Kutsenko, a deputy director of the Soviet army's Center for Operational-Strategic Research, concurred, adding that "Iraq's weaponry, including that which is Soviet-made, was mainly produced in the 1960s and 1970s and is a generation or two behind the corresponding weaponry of the multinational forces."

"The allied success in the war is the final nail in the coffin of the Soviet Union's superpower status."

Other Soviet officials additionally argued that the war saw no real face-to-face contest between the top-of-the-line U.S. tanks and planes and their Soviet counterparts. The Iraqis, they noted, possessed a limited number of MiG-29s and T-72s, and flew a number of the former to Iran, while abandoning a number of the latter on the battlefield.

The problem was more with the professional training of the Iraqi army, said one official, who went on to downplay Red Army responsibility for that training. This despite the fact that thousands of Soviet military advisers were in Iraq from 1972 until recently, and large numbers of Iraqi officers have passed through Soviet military academies.

Defense Minister Yazov, however, did allow that "what happened in Kuwait and Iraq necessitates a review of the attitude to army air defense and the country's entire air defense system." He also announced that the Soviet military will hold a conference to discuss the advanced technologies used by the U.S.-led coalition in the war. "The echo of missile thunder in the desert must put us on our guard," he told the official news agency Tass.

Even with such admissions, some say, the Soviet reaction is a brave front, masking the realization that it has suffered a loss of face, perhaps the worst to date. What both Washington and Moscow now know is that a war between the United States and the Soviet Union "would have been a more even match, but we still probably would have won," says Glynn. "That is, accept all the caveats about the fact that it's Iraqis, and it wasn't in every case first-line equipment.

"Nonetheless, the result has been so disproportionate that it's hard to see how Soviet soldiers operating under similar doctrine could have won. You know, they have many of the same kinds of cultural handicaps as the Iraqis: A good part of the Soviet army is not from the well-educated Russian populace; there are all kinds of people from fairly backward parts of the Soviet Union that compose this army, whose loyalty may be in doubt, whose fighting will may be in doubt. So my sense is that no matter how you look at it, it suggests that we have the edge in conventional weaponry."

Others see the damage done by the Gulf war to Soviet prestige in even starker terms. Edward Atkeson, author of "The Final Argument of Kings: Reflections on the Art of War," who was chief of Army intelligence for Europe until 1980, says that the allied success in the war is the final nail in the coffin of the Soviet Union's superpower status.

U.S. Sole Superpower

"I would say that this amounts to a reversal of the 1965 Glassboro meeting between Brezhnev and LBJ [Lyndon B. Johnson], when we agreed to the first SALT [Strategic Arms Limitation Talks] treaty, which essentially blessed the achievement of the Soviet Union in gaining parity with the United States," he says. "And it's from that point until now that we have talked about two superpowers. I would argue that what this campaign demonstrates is that the United States is the sole surviving superpower in the world." Atkeson says that if previous victories over Soviet weaponry and doctrine—such as Israel's destruction of Egypt's Soviet-supplied air defenses in 1973 and of Syria's in 1982—were inconclusive, this time there is little room for doubt. "Now we have confirmed that the enormous superiority of Western weaponry and integration of systems has catapulted us very obviously way ahead of anything they ever even thought about being capable of."

"A diminished Soviet role does not automatically mean a *Pax Americana*."

Moscow's successive attempts to arrange a cease-fire that would allow Saddam to withdraw his forces from Kuwait and prevent their destruction by allied ground forces—this despite their rhetorical support for U.S. and allied objectives—may have been more a desperate bid by the Kremlin to limit the humiliation than a move to reassert itself. "I think a lot of the motivation behind [Mikhail] Gorbachev's successive attempts to get a cease-fire was pressure from the general staff to bring things to a halt," says Atkeson, "because it did so clearly portray them in a second-class status."

And even if part of the Soviet motive was to try to retain some influence in the Middle East, Bush's polite but total dismissal of the initiatives merely underscored the Soviet Union's growing international irrelevance. "What in effect Bush did is he treated Gorbachev as if he was [the U.N.'s] Perez de Cuellar," says Joshua Muravchik, a resident scholar at the American Enterprise Institute. "And the Soviet reaction was really quite remarkable: Once Bush did that, in the context of the way the world used to be, you'd expect that they would raise some hell and bluster. Instead, the Soviet reaction was, 'Please understand we didn't mean any harm.'"

There reportedly is disagreement within the Bush administration over postwar relations with the Soviets in general and how much to include them in any new arrangements for the Middle East. The debate reportedly has Vice President Dan Quayle, national security adviser Brent Scowcroft and Cheney on the side of keeping the Soviet role to a minimum, while Secretary of State James A. Baker III reportedly remains determined to keep relations with the Soviets on a steady course, and even to involve them in negotiations over the future of the Middle East. Baker was scheduled to meet with Gorbachev to exchange ideas on a post-Persian Gulf war settlement.

Norman Podhoretz, editor of *Commentary* magazine, sides with the former camp. "The Soviets' own view has always been that there's an objective balance of power that has to be respected," he says. "In other words, to the extent that they were our equal in power, they had to be treated as an equal in any negotiation in any region. Well, by their own lights they don't deserve to play much of a role in the postwar settlement, both because they don't appear to have the power and because they also assume no responsibility."

Despite Baker's meeting with Gorbachev, it may be that this view has won out: In his March 6, 1991 speech about the postwar Middle East, Bush did not once mention the Soviets. And, given its dire domestic situation, it is unlikely that Moscow will try to sabotage any U.S.-led plan for the region. "The reason that they've been as restrained as they've been is that they're still trying to keep the door open on Western aids and credits," says Podhoretz. "I can't imagine that they would reverse course, unless they decided that there were no hope for help anyway, which doesn't seem to be the case. So I don't see them as playing any kind of spoiler role in the immediate future."

America's Role

But a diminished Soviet role does not automatically mean a *Pax Americana*. With Saddam Hussein's rule increasingly shaky, Iraq's minority Kurds and majority Shiites are in revolt, both with apparent Iranian backing. The Baathist regime's long-term prospects for survival are questionable. The country could ultimately split up into Kurdish, Sunni and Shiite spheres, with the latter even declaring a pro-Iranian Islamic republic.

"We're going to have to recognize that there's a great deal of old-fashioned disorder in the new world order and that we are going to have to contend with the traditional means," says former Secretary of Defense James Schlesinger. "Either we are going to have to help create a balance of power in the region, or we will have to participate in the region to sustain a balance of power. What we have done by smashing up Iraq is to make Iran the guardian of the Gulf. And in the '80s we spent our time trying to prevent their dominating the Gulf, and now that the counterweight of Iraq is removed, if we withdraw there is no counterweight. Now that doesn't sound much like a new world order to me."

Indeed, President Bush's view of the Middle East, as outlined in his March 6 speech, stopped well short of a Middle East reshaped in America's image. It stressed joint military exercises with the allies, a renewed diplomatic effort to end the Arab-Israeli conflict, a continuation of the arms embargo on Iraq and a vague call for "economic development for the sake of peace and progress."

A More Modest Vision

And while Kuwait, having been turned upside down by the recent upheaval and remaining under heavy U.S. political influence, may go some distance toward democracy and modernity, the Bush administration is not, it appears, setting such high goals for the rest of the region.

Beyond employing U.S. military force to reverse acts of aggression in strategic areas, the president may have a more modest vision for his new world order. Perhaps it was best summed up by his point man on Capitol Hill, Indiana Sen. Richard G. Lugar: "With all these situations, we have to be confident enough in our ideals that, where applicable and where there are opportunities, we are prepared to say, 'We think this might be a better idea.'"

The War Ended the Nation's Trauma over Vietnam

Ben Knapen

About the Author: *Ben Knapen, editor-in-chief of* the NRC Handelsblad, *a Dutch newspaper, previously served as its Washington, D.C. correspondent.*

The most beautiful war monument is in Washington, near Lincoln's Roman temple where, on the eve of his inauguration, George Bush was presented to the people in a heavenly ray of light, to the echoing falsetto of the Beach Boys. The most beautiful monument was concealed from view, in the dark just beyond the reach of the floodlights. You could only feel your way around it, which just one or two people did.

The Vietnam war memorial stands in a small, man-size excavation. The names of nearly 59,000 soldiers killed in action are engraved on the black granite stone, a worthy, modest reminder of the last great war. People visiting the Vietnam memorial tend to be in sombre mood. It is not a place for spotlights.

Maybe America had to lose a war before it could allow itself such an impressive monument. In any case, it was thanks to the super patriot Ronald Reagan that the monument was created and placed here, near the shrines of national glory that dot the Washington Mall.

The overwhelming American victory in the Gulf has far-reaching consequences both for America and the rest of the world. A page has been turned, although nobody knows what the next chapter will bring or how it will evolve. One

Ben Knapen, "The Remedial War," *European Affairs*, April/May 1991. Reprinted with permission.

thing is for sure: America is tearing itself loose from Vietnam, thus releasing renewed energy. Of course, Vietnam has gradually been digested in literature and, for a larger audience, film, but the episode has never become actual history, i.e. a closed chapter. This was not possible since Vietnam was not a total defeat and the downfall ran counter to the whole state concept called America, whereas in weary Europe, after two world wars and an escape into all sorts of 'isms' and ideologies, disenchantment and resignation finally set in as a practical basis for illusion-free reconstruction. Resignation and disenchantment are not American escape routes.

After Jimmy Carter's hopeless penance, there appeared Ronald Reagan who, by lulling the country into a mood of collective self-adulation, instilled renewed confidence and blocked the harsh light of reality. But Vietnam was still there. Although the neo-conservative thinkers in America reduced the trauma to a problem of long-haired, unpatriotic pot-smokers and an overly critical press, every politician knew this was a sham. Any political-military complication in the world was scrupulously avoided by the anxious post-war president. In 1983, the Americans quickly packed their bags in Lebanon when 241 marines were killed there. The invasion of Grenada was so futile that it completely defeated its purpose, i.e. deleting any trace of Vietnam. The fact that during the operation so many things went wrong and that afterwards Reagan handed out 100 more combat medals than the actual number of participants, made everything all the more painful.

> ## "America is tearing itself loose from Vietnam, thus releasing renewed energy."

Despite all the pep talks against communism and in favour of a free world, the so-called overall unilateralism of the Reagan years was simply an excuse to reinforce the concept of America as a bastion. The Star Wars defence plan could have been the crowning glory of this new line of thinking if it had been taken seriously. 'Stop the world, we want to get off'.

"The United States has regained its self-respect."

All this is now well and truly in the past. The bland 'wimp' (according to a *Newsweek* cover in October 1987 referring to George Bush) has given his country an overwhelming victory. The entire concept of war, as commonly perceived following the pointless deaths in the trenches during the first World War, has been turned on its head. Allied troops marched through the Iraqi trenches in southern Kuwait at a price of nine casualties. On the allied side, the total number of soldiers killed in action was 139, which is quite remarkable when one considers that the conflict took place between two military forces totalling over half a million troops each. Future chronicles will somehow have to make sense of these figures.

For the first time since Eisenhower and MacArthur, America has found itself a new general as hero and, if the fear of marksmen has waned since Dallas '63, Norman Schwarzkopf might well parade his triumph in an open vehicle on Broadway. The most senior general, Colin Powell, has already been discussed as a possible vice presidential running mate for Bush's re-election bid in 1992, and after the 1996 election, as the first black President of the United States. In view of the current state of euphoria, it looks as if the Republicans will stay in the White House until the year 2000.

There is no doubt that the taste of victory has affected all Americans involved. Superiority on all fronts, the absence of any howlers which in Grenada incurred ridicule, and the humiliation of the big bad man from Baghdad—'a great military man', said Schwarzkopf in jest—all this illustrated every minute on TV what Reagan had been claiming for eight years: 'Morning again in America'.

The United States has regained its self-respect. This may be a hollow observation, for little has actually changed since the seventh of August 1990 when Bush, opting for the largest post-war air lift, took the risky option, which on 30 April 1975 in Vietnam had been scornfully dismissed. Yet America no longer has sole supremacy, as it did following the glorious victory in 1945. In those days, America accounted for almost 50% of the gross world product, as against just over 20% at present. Then, America was by far the world's biggest money-lender; now it is the largest debtor. Then, America could count on allies and bases throughout the world to keep communism in check, but this togetherness has been lacking for some years.

Historical facts, however, have only a relative value since they can be categorised according to cause and effect. In other words: Was this bleak image of a superpower-in-decay not just what the rather cautious establishment surrounding Bush needed to hoist the flag and jeopardise the entire national prestige for some far-flung country such as Kuwait? At any rate, the fact is that America won a real war, that it was a war which did not leave behind any traumas other than those of individual grief and that the technical, organisational and strategic superiority of American warfare will constitute a point of reference for US intervention in world events for a generation of Americans. Vietnam is over, 'coming home' at long last has become an event which is no longer associated with images of bitter reality, and this can only release new energy.

A New World Order

Where could this lead?

Over the past months, Pax Americana has been mentioned repeatedly, or, with reference to the text on the dollar bill, the *novus ordo seclorum*—a new world order. Nearly everyone has made observations about Bush's reference to a new world order and has warned against optimism and the danger of placing too much confidence in establishing good relations between nations and states. It is easier to win a war than to win peace, according to a worldly saying.

Henry Kissinger recently wrote that a world order is not feasible because the United States lacks the necessary supremacy. Peace without supremacy can exist only if there is a balance of power, according to this American who has always remained too much of a European to completely detach himself from the concept of balance as enshrined by the Vienna Congress.

"The fact is that America won a real war."

According to Kissinger, the American administration ought to draw up a list of priorities in terms of regions and disputes. There are certain disputes and regions which are of such vital importance to America that if the need arose, the country would have to secure its interests in a unilateral, military way. Other regions are sufficiently important to justify presence with the help of allied forces. Finally, there are areas which are simply of no concern to America. In any case, America should refuse to act as an army of mercenaries ever again, since this proves that there is no vested interest at stake.

This is typical Kissinger reasoning, based on a national interest which can evidently be defined and the sort of *Realpolitik* of which even Kissinger, in his heyday as tamer of the world spirit, was not capable in Washington. And that was no coincidence: Kissinger was unable to do this because the US stubbornly refused to adapt to European terms. Time and again, Kissinger complained about the American inability to formulate a consistent, national interest and establish constant values in its foreign policy. Objectives oscillated depending on the national mood, swinging from active battling against communism to détente, from an active human rights policy to isolationism, from collective security to America First—all within less than 40

years. 'We are our own worst enemy', said Kissinger many years ago.

America and the rest of the world are on different wavelengths. It is quite easy to prove, for example, that America understands oh so little about the Middle East. In American history, the Judaic-Christian heritage is dominant, while Islam is absent. But there is more. 'The nation's fate is not to have an ideology but to be one', Richard Hofstadter, the wise historian, said four decades ago about America. During his first visit to US troops in the desert in August 1990, the Secretary of State, James A. Baker, said: 'America is where our ideals are'. In other words: America is everywhere.

The United States of America was the first country to be established as an idealistic promise. The promise originates from Enlightenment-era ideals and can thus claim to be universally applicable: 'One nation, under God, with liberty and justice for all', as recited every morning by millions of American school children, hand on heart, facing the Stars and Stripes. The universal applicability of the US Constitution is learnt at mother's knee: suffrage, division of powers, freedom of speech and the right to the pursuit of happiness. Anyone who appreciates the fact that these rights are self-evident will understand why, without any hesitation, the Americans imposed a democratic model on Japan in 1945 without worrying too much about specific Japanese traditions. Why worry, why doubt? The American model was so self-explanatory. What else?

The American Idea

The foreign policy of a powerful country cannot function without power, resources, trade, oil and arms, but the driving force is that of ideas. Americans believe in universality, the general applicability of their ideas. This is evident in the international use of the language, which, due to the omnipresence of American media has an American slant. Take, for example, the uprising staged by a young prophet and his disciples on 20 November 1979 in the al-Haram Mosque in

Mecca. The puritan orthodoxy of the prophet and his disciples was soon branded 'Islamic fundamentalism.' The prophet from Mecca, followed by the Ayatollah from Iran, were symbols of reaction against progress and were often considered to be medieval. This interpretation implies that education and progress will undoubtedly solve this problem one day. Progress replaces fundamentalism with a modern way of living. Wars and crises are mere convulsions in the inevitable process of modernisation.

"Thanks to military power and political willpower, America can act as a regulating factor in the Arab world."

Regional experts are absolutely baffled by what they refer to as American naivety. Japanwatchers find it hard to accept that Americans have displayed so little empathy regarding Japanese idiosyncrasies. Europeans look upon the indomitable optimism on the other side of the ocean with something approaching pity. And over the past few months, the Arabs have had to explain why the Americans mismanaged the world of the desert and Islam. It is quite true that Americans invariably fail to appreciate the special circumstances in specific regions. Not so long ago, William Fulbright, the powerful senator from the Vietnam era, said: 'When we started in Vietnam, I commissioned the translation [of Ho Chi Minh] by the Frenchman, Lacouture, because nobody knew a single thing about the country'. This proves the inextirpable babel surrounding 'Pax Americana' and the role of the United States in the world. For many countries throughout the world, Pax Americana is a situation of foreign, i.e. American, supremacy, either as a military superpower or as an economic-imperialistic ruler or patron of a certain government. Other countries view Pax Americana as a model of civilisation to be sneered at because, as an enormous cultural steamroller, it flattens every-

thing which is different from Coca-Cola and CNN [Cable News Network]. As such, fear of change has been continually projected on America for over a century, and no European intellectual will deny the mixed feelings of admiration and contempt prompted by his first visit to those shores.

This, however, is only one side of Pax Americana. To the Americans, it looks quite different. At the risk of over-generalising, the situation is more or less as follows: An orderly relationship between states and nations is only possible once dictators and robber barons have been replaced by democracies and, since time and progress are generally valid, America can lend a helping hand to speed up this process. This is *novus ordo seclorum.* Recently, a traditional representative of this line of thought, the conservative and brilliant columnist George Will, wrote frankly: 'There are 21 Arab nations and not one Arab democracy. Let's not be cruel but let's say to Kuwait: Congratulations! You will be the first'. Pax Americana not only entails a free flow of oil but ideally, a Douglas MacArthur-type person in Baghdad, telling all the ladies to take off their veils, use their right to vote and join in, just like in the US. Why not? . . .

A Regulating Factor

Thanks to military power and political willpower, America can act as a regulating factor in the Arab world. Disappointments are, just like former American victories, preprogrammed. Objections, difficulties or incongruities can be produced by anyone who cares to take a closer look at the hornet's nest of the Arab world. If America had been sufficiently cynical and committed to *Realpolitik*, it would have steered clear of all the intrigues in the region. But it didn't. Conclusion: Vietnam and what followed failed to equip America with this armour.

'America is where our ideals are'—something along these lines will be engraved on the Kuwait monuments in a couple of years' time in Washington. It will not be a particularly attractive monument. Vietnam is over.

Did the Persian Gulf War Strengthen the U.S.?

No: The War Weakened the U.S.

The War Weakened the U.S.
The War Cost the U.S. Its Peace Dividend
The War Distracted the U.S. from Its Domestic Problems
The War Exposed America's Weaknesses

The War Weakened the U.S.

Richard Barnet

About the Author: *Richard Barnet is a founder of the Institute for Policy Studies, a Washington, D.C.-based think tank, and has written twelve books on foreign policy. His most recent book is* The Rocket's Red Glare: War, Politics, and the American Presidency.

When Operation Desert Storm ended in the triumphal hundred-hour ground war, George Bush's mysterious slogan "New World Order" suddenly took on meaning. The United States is now the only global military superpower, and the new political arrangements in the Middle East, whether formally negotiated or not, will be in large measure a Pax Americana. The United States will be more assertive in pressing for an Is-raeli-Arab settlement, and, with the realignment of forces in the region, some progress may well be made. Saudi Arabia is now firmly in the American camp. Syria has been accorded the status of an honorary former terrorist state and is using its new financial support from coalition partners to build up its military forces. Iran is biding its time. Cheap oil is here to stay until the next crisis, and the quick and efficient destruction of much of Iraq and Kuwait may well lift the United States out of recession.

What sort of New World Order will be built on all this? The war in the Gulf has already changed the political culture of the United States. "By God, we've kicked the Vietnam syndrome once and for all," President Bush exulted at a White House appearance. The United States finally fought a big war against a plausible, if in-flated, enemy; won decisively; and the public ap-

plauded. The Pentagon's reticence about fighting wars that risk estranging the military forces from the civil society has given way to justifiable pride in a war well fought, and to new confidence that the administration will stop the budget cuts and borrow enough money to finance the permanent preparation for an endless series of high-tech wars across the planet.

Last January 1991 the country was divided about the risks of the war and, to a lesser extent, the morality of resolving the crisis by killing tens of thousands of Iraqis who themselves are the victims of Saddam's crimes. The stunning victory has blown away all thought of risk, and, for all but a tiny minority, success has settled the moral questions, too. It will be easier now to convince the public that the escalating misery in the poor countries of Asia, Africa, and Latin America is essentially a continuing military problem.

"Will the war that worked bring about a fundamental change in the U.S. role in the world? I think not."

Does this mean that the United States is now embarked on a worldwide military crusade for the New World Order? Is our top export now to be high-tech war, our slogan "Have smart bombs, will travel"? In his remarks to the Economic Club of New York, before the ground war began, President Bush suggested that American leadership in fighting the Gulf War would result in "vastly restored credibility" for the United States that could be translated into more "harmonious" relations with its major industrial competitors. In other words, the leverage over the allies that the United States enjoyed during the Cold War but lost when the Soviet Union dropped out of the global conflict can now be restored by the United States' becoming the policeman in strategic areas of the Third World. This notion of America's role in the world is re-

Richard Barnet, "An Illusion," *Harper's Magazine,* May 1991. Reprinted with permission.

flected in high-level Pentagon statements about the missions of the armed forces published several months before Iraq invaded Kuwait. General A. M. Gray, commandant of the Marine Corps, wrote, three months before the invasion of Kuwait, that the United States must maintain "a credible military power projection capability with the flexibility to respond to conflicts across the spectrum of violence throughout the globe."

This shift in the political culture will have an effect on the U.S. budget. The "peace dividend" lies buried in the desert. But will the war that worked bring about a fundamental change in the U.S. role in the world? I think not. It is hard to think of sites for future wars that feature all the essential conditions that made the Gulf War, despite the numbers of troops and the financial cost, the most splendid of little wars: Saddam's brutal aggression against a small, defenseless country without even a shred of a plausible legal claim; a villain out of central casting, with nuclear ambitions and a weakness for poison gas, who at both the negotiating table and on the battlefield revealed an unerring instinct for his own jugular; in the absence of Soviet opposition; a treeless battlefield ideal for high-tech slaughter; shared oil anxieties stronger than the economic rivalries dividing the United States, Japan, and Europe; countries rich enough to pay the warriors not only to fight a "free" war but also to rebuild what they destroyed.

"The afterglow of victory is not enough to restore the sinews of nationhood."

The politically sophisticated generals who crafted the Gulf operation, having restored the reputation of the armed forces, are in no hurry to risk it again. They understand that other political crises will not offer such promising terrain and that long, inconclusive, and disappointing wars are just as dangerous to the health of the United States' military now as they were before President

Bush exorcised the demons of Vietnam.

Nor are Germany and Japan, the principal beneficiaries and reluctant financiers of the U.S. war effort, willing to support the United States in a crusade against evil regimes around the globe. Once the real economic costs, the disastrous environmental effects, and the long-term political fallout of the war are assessed, the United States' major industrial competitors are likely to be more restrained in supporting future crusades for world order orchestrated by this nation—even to the limited extent that they have cooperated in this one. The more the United States assumes the posture of the Lone Ranger and continues to treat the United Nations as a flag of convenience, the more guarded they will be.

Economic Constraints

For all the bravado in Washington about the dawn of the second American century, making war will not be the primary basis of national power in this new century. Having neglected its technological and industrial base, the United States is now extremely dependent on short-term foreign capital. If the United States, Europe, and Japan continue to move toward competitive trading blocs, such an economic world order cannot be policed by American military power.

The American role in the New World Order will ultimately be determined by economic constraints. The growing vulnerability of the U.S. economy, its dependence on foreign capital, its failure to invest in roads, bridges, schools, and civilian technology are now taking such a dramatic toll on civil society that unless the investment priorities are radically changed, American influence will inevitably decline. The Soviet Union, it should be remembered, disappeared as a global political actor at the very moment when it was at the pinnacle of its military power. Despite the promilitary sentiment sweeping the United States, it may not be politically possible for an American president to lead the American people into the next century as the new Sparta:

The United States is the only advanced industrial nation without national health insurance. It is number one in the percentage of the population behind bars. And it has a murder rate unequaled anywhere in the world that keeps statistics. As the President himself noted in his victory speech to Congress, during the one hundred hours of the ground war more Americans were killed by gunfire on our city streets than in the Kuwait-Iraq theater of operations. The afterglow of victory is not enough to restore the sinews of nationhood, and as these weaken so does the real power of the United States to influence the New World Order. For the crucial battles of the new century, our industrial competitors concentrate on their economic bases, while the United States, seemingly unable to understand the shifting foundations of national power, risks being caught in a time warp of an American century that is long gone.

The War Cost the U.S. Its Peace Dividend

Robert L. Borosage

About the Author: *Robert L. Borosage is a senior fellow at the Institute for Policy Studies, a foreign and public policy research institute based in Washington, D.C.*

"Thank you, Saddam Hussein."

The people in the Grand Milwaukee Hotel who laugh and applaud the chair's opening words aren't a gang of fanatics lusting for jihad against the infidel. They are the well-creased agents of 247 Wisconsin companies doing business at a September 1990 Defense Contracting Workshop set up by the House Armed Services Committee chairman, Les Aspin, to bring Pentagon money to the Dairy State. Hussein has turned what might have been a wake into a festive orgy of deal making.

Across town, in the Northlawn housing complex, sixty-five-year-old Ronnie Land doesn't share in the gratitude for Hussein. Her son and her grandson are among the reserves who've been called to duty. The nineteen-year-old grandson, who joined the military to learn a trade, is now in the Saudi desert, separated from his pregnant young wife. Land, "worried sick" about them, wishes the United States weren't in the Persian Gulf. She looks out her window at a Milwaukee that has just set a new murder record and that has the country's highest teenage-pregnancy rate. "We have people dying here on the streets, families in trouble," Land says. "We should be putting our money to work here at home where we need it."

George Bush has called the crisis in the gulf

the "defining moment" for the "post-cold-war world." "In the life of a nation," Bush said, "there comes a moment when we are called to define who we are and what we believe." Of the fusillade of sound bites unleashed by the president over Iraq, this one lands closest to the mark. The desert face-off comes at a time when the United States must decide anew its priorities and role in the world. As this is written, the country is on the verge of war, but whether or not war takes place, Americans will have to choose between the cost of policing the president's "new world order" and the chance of addressing the disorder in Ronnie Land's world.

The end of the cold war is an epochal event of the kind that comes rarely in a nation's history. For forty-five years, the global struggle against communism had first claim on American resources. When Mikhail Gorbachev sued for peace and popular rebellions toppled Eastern European regimes, the war that was thought to be permanent came to an abrupt and unexpected end.

> ## "The end of the cold war offers a desperately needed . . . chance for domestic and international renewal."

For the United States, this blessing could not be more opportune. The forty-five-year war was exacting an ever more burdensome toll in debts incurred and investments not made. In less than a decade, the United States went from being the world's leading creditor nation to its greatest debtor. Money-center banks now teeter on the edge of collapse. Murder rates in cities are so high that Ronnie Land's grandson is probably safer in the Saudi desert than in his own neighborhood. Schools have a hard time providing safety, much less education. The gulf between rich and poor is growing. All this at the height of the "Reagan recovery"; it will get worse in the recession that has already begun.

The end of the cold war offers a desperately

needed, serendipitous chance for domestic and international renewal. The best historical parallel is the reconstruction that took place after World War II. The military budget was slashed by ninety percent in three years. A GI bill sent returning soldiers to college; veterans' benefits helped them buy homes in new suburbs; government subsidies aided the conversion of military industry to civilian production.

"As communism collapses across the globe, the Pentagon is mobilizing against the threat of peace."

The United Nations was founded to keep peace worldwide. A dollar-based monetary system was created, with the International Monetary Fund and the World Bank to superintend it. The Marshall Plan provided billions to rebuild allies and enemies alike in Europe, creating markets for American goods at the same time. The foundations for an era of unprecedented economic growth were put in place.

Programs of similar scope could attend the end of the cold war. At home, attention could be turned from the Communist menace to real security concerns: making our economy competitive, cleaning up our environment, reviving our educational system. Military spending accounts for as much as twenty percent of the country's manufacturing production. Conversion of the garrison economy will require planning and subsidies for displaced workers and disrupted communities, but the benefits could be immeasurable.

Some of the funding for conversion could come from the "peace dividend." The military spends almost $300 billion a year, over half of it to defend Europe from the Red Army. Now the Germans are paying room and board for Soviet soldiers while building housing for them back in the U.S.S.R. Even the cautious editorialists of the *New York Times* agree that the military budget could be cut in half with ease. We could retain

the most powerful military in the world and still free nearly $150 billion a year to invest in rebuilding our country at home.

Without raising taxes, dramatic new initiatives could be launched. For example, sixty-six percent of all federal research and development funds and almost seventy percent of the Energy Department's budget now go directly to the military. The country could invest a significant portion of that on developing environmentally sustainable technologies: solar and other renewable energy sources, new forms of production, public transportation. With environmental despoliation a growing threat, these technologies are an investment in survival. They are also good business: The country that develops them will gain the edge in the markets of the future.

The peace dividend offers more than new money. As Senator Daniel Moynihan has written, the end of the cold war also provides the opportunity to get "our government back in order," to begin dismantling the national-security state created to run the permanent war. For example, in 1989 the government created 6,796,501 new secrets. Secrecy masks the Pentagon's multibillion-dollar "black budget," the global and domestic activities of the intelligence agencies and the initiatives of the president.

The Post-Cold War Era

Abroad, the way is open to address the fundamental challenges of the post-cold-war era. The promise of collective security—lost in the cold war—can now be revived. The collapse of the Warsaw Pact is already transforming security arrangements in Europe. The United Nations can be revitalized—freed from its cold-war shackles—but not if it is used merely as a fig leaf for punitive American expeditions, as it has been in the gulf. The Soviet Union is urging joint efforts to end all testing of nuclear weapons and to end the proliferation of all weapons of mass destruction—nuclear, biological and chemical.

The end of the cold war makes change inescapable, but the new priorities that Ronnie Land wants and the country needs will not come easily. No one is as tenacious and imaginative as a bureaucrat whose budget is threatened. As communism collapses across the globe, the Pentagon is mobilizing against the threat of peace.

At first, the Bush administration simply refused to admit that the cold war was over. In 1989, the administration was still intent on deploying new tactical nuclear weapons in Germany. In 1990, the White House press secretary dismissed Gorbachev as a fraudulent "drugstore cowboy."

"The gulf crisis has virtually ended all discussion of a post-cold-war reconstruction."

At the same time, the Pentagon began to dress to fit the fashion of the day. Want a war on drugs? The military copped almost $2 billion for drug patrols and carried out the costliest drug bust ever, the $164-million collar of Panama's Manuel Noriega. Ecology in vogue? Sam Nunn, head of the Senate Armed Services Committee, suggested that military satellites and labs be enlisted in the fight for clean air.

However trendy, these "be all that you can be" operations aren't very compelling. American forces in the Andes helped poison about one percent of Peru's coca crop in 1989; insects ate twenty times as much. Rock music and 27,000 troops bagged Noriega, but money laundering and the drug trade still flourish in Panama. Even army green can't camouflage the fact that the military is the nation's worst polluter. Cleaning up its wastes alone will cost an estimated $150 billion.

Only after revolution swept Eastern Europe and the Soviet Union imploded did the administration finally concede that we were entering the post-cold-war world. One of its first priorities was to campaign against deep cuts in military spending. The post-cold-war world was "a dangerous place," Bush explained. The global threat was no longer communism but "instability." "We need forces able to respond to threats in whatever corner of the globe they may appear," said Bush. "Terrorism. Hostage taking. Renegade regimes and unpredictable rulers." For these we required a "lean, mean military." The Pentagon put forth a five-year plan calling for cutting its forces by about twenty-five percent but its spending by only ten to fifteen percent.

If instability is the new threat, there will be no shortage of enemies. But the world has been unstable for a long time without requiring the United States to police it. Although splendid little raids on Grenada and Libya gain popular approval, Americans have little taste for imperial policing after Vietnam. Thus by 1990, voices across the political spectrum—from reborn isolationists, corporate leaders, mayors and educators to environmentalists and populists—began to call for deep cuts in military forces and budgets.

Enter Saddam Hussein. The gulf crisis has virtually ended all discussion of a post-cold-war reconstruction.

With the exception of Senator Moynihan, no political leader of either party has spoken in any depth about the opportunity that beckons at the end of the cold war.

Reliving Korea

For the national-security elite, the crisis is a journey back to the future—not to Vietnam but to Korea. After World War II, as the society turned to peace, cold warriors around President Truman wanted to sustain a costly, standing military to wage a global struggle against communism. Truman, Roosevelt's belittled successor, faced a contentious Congress and a flagging economy, and increases in military spending seemed impossible to contemplate. Then Communist forces attacked in Korea. The United States led a UN-sanctioned "police action" but mobilized for a global cold war. Military spending went up, never to return to prewar levels.

Today it's *déjà vu* all over again. The crisis, the president has argued, justifies "giving the military the tools to do its job—the Peacekeeper [the MX missile on rails], the Midgetman, the B-2 [the Stealth bomber at $860 million a plane] and the Strategic Defense Initiative." Of course, with the Pentagon's ruling out the use of nuclear and chemical weapons in the gulf, none of the "tools" the president mentioned has any role in the gulf crisis.

"Lives and resources will be expended abroad, while the country continues its decline at home."

Lawrence Korb, former assistant secretary of defense under Reagan, argues that the mobilization itself "seems driven more by upcoming budget battles on Capitol Hill than a potential battle against Saddam Hussein." All five services—even the Coast Guard—have sent forces to the gulf. The navy sent six carriers and eight nuclear subs to the Arabian Sea south of Saudi Arabia. From there only a few of the carriers' planes can actually reach a target (the carriers move into the Persian Gulf at great risk). The subs serve no essential purpose. But carriers and subs are dear to the hearts of navy brass. Similarly, the air force has sent Stealth fighters and bombers; the marines will no doubt launch an amphibious landing somewhere. Whether this impresses Hussein remains to be seen; it has already worked on Congress.

Costs of the War

When the president and Congress finally agreed on a budget in 1990, less than $10 billion was cut from the military's spending, which didn't include the cost of the gulf effort. With the gulf crisis costing an estimated $30 billion a year without a war, spending on the military will actually go up, not down, in the first year after the end of the cold war.

Whether or not a war takes place, the national-security planners are already aiming for a "permanent presence in the gulf" that will provide a central argument for sustaining military spending in future years. Military planners have been seeking permanent bases in the gulf since the late Seventies. In 1980, twenty percent of all the activities of the Army Corps of Engineers were devoted to construction of Saudi military bases. (Since 1950, the Saudis have been the recipients of an astounding ninety-five percent of all of America's foreign military-construction sales.)

The gulf crisis provides a golden opportunity to gain long-sought-after bases while helping to fend off future budget cuts. In September 1990, Pentagon officials hinted that even after Iraq is out of Kuwait, they would seek to maintain 10,000 troops in the region. Secretary of State James Baker retreated, under political fire, from his suggestion for a NATO [North Atlantic Treaty Organization]-like structure in the gulf, but he still asserts the United States' role as guarantor of "long-term stability" in the region. Now the Pentagon has begun to float the argument that the crisis will delay the force reductions called for in its own plan.

In addition, the budget agreement contains a protection scheme for the military. For three years [until 1994], Congress is barred from transferring money from the military to domestic programs. Military spending cuts can only be used for deficit reduction. In a time of economic decline, this will curb any enthusiasm for deep cuts. After three years, if Bush and the Pentagon have their way, a new bipartisan consensus will have formed to support a global American military role in the post-cold-war era.

The White House hails this global role as an expression of America's prowess in the world, but it is surely a recipe for decline. Engaged in martial expeditions across the world, the United States will be even less able to compete with other industrial nations than we are today. Lives and resources will be expended abroad, while the country continues its decline at home. The best chance since the Forties to renew American society and the economy upon which it rests will be lost as the country goes abroad in search of monsters to destroy.

The War Distracted the U.S. from Its Domestic Problems

Steve Tesich

About the Author: *Steve Tesich is a playwright, screenwriter, and novelist whose works include the movie* Breaking Away.

The Holy Roman Empire, it's been said, was neither holy nor Roman nor an empire. By the same token, the New World Order of George Bush is neither new nor orderly nor concerned with the long-term welfare of the world. It is the same old world order reasserting itself in a violent way. Our motives for being engaged in the war in the Persian Gulf had as much to do with what we are fleeing as they do with the invasion of Kuwait.

We are fleeing, as we have for decades, from the unfulfilled pledge that we are one nation, under God, with liberty and justice for all. The hopeless despair of our millions, the Third World poverty in the heart of our cities, the resulting tidal wave of crime—this social rot at our very heart has become as dangerous as any nuclear waste dump. Lacking the resolve to confront those problems, we are fleeing from them in all directions: to the suburbs, to cities in other parts of the country, to other countries, to other wars.

But we have been doing this for a long time. The social diseases of racism, poverty, drug addiction and crime, never fully addressed, were allowed to fester and grow while we devoted our energies, lives and resources to containing communism.

And then came Vietnam. While the war raged over there, another one exploded over here. The Third World nation within our nation rose up, demanding to be included in our pledge. It was a pivotal moment in our history. It was the first time we were engaged in two wars. We lost both, and we learned nothing from our defeats.

The war in Vietnam and its outcome have, over a period of time, been reduced to one simple lesson: It was too long. The implicit assumption is that the lives lost, the napalm, the burning children, My Lai, our government lying to us—all of these and other horrors of that war would have been acceptable had they only taken less time.

This war in the gulf, we were reassured, would be a lot quicker. Polls suggested that a large majority of our population supported it—if it didn't last too long. The implications of that view are alarming. It seems to follow that if the wrong thing can be done quickly it becomes right, and if the right thing cannot be accomplished quickly it becomes wrong and should, therefore, be abandoned.

> **"The war in Vietnam and its outcome have . . . been reduced to one simple lesson: It was too long."**

Our social problems cannot be solved in this way. Neither poverty nor the crime it breeds can be quickly blasted out of existence. Still, we tried the quick fix. Before he launched the war in the gulf, George Bush launched the War on Crime. Remember that war? Already it seems long ago. There were other wars. A war on poverty. A war on drugs. The very names of those campaigns signify impatience and anticipation of quick results. The problems that took generations of neglect to create require the patient dedication of generations to undo, but we have become a nation that no longer has the will, the vision or the deep-seated conviction to measure its endeavors by generations. We not only want results in our lifetime, we want them next weekend. The false lesson of Vietnam has come back to haunt us. The social "wars" at home, we have now come to realize, can never be won quickly, and therefore we have abandoned them.

"We have come to rely on external enemies for comfort and confirmation of our identity as a people."

The Reagan social doctrine proclaimed that our identity as a nation lies not in how our most disadvantaged live but in the diverting spectacle of the affluent. For a whole decade we watched or participated in the greedy rampage of the rich. In their pursuit of hourly fixes of huge profits and overnight wealth, they plundered our resources and our financial institutions. They wreaked havoc on an already indebted nation and they pushed millions of hard-working men and women into poverty. They mocked the very work ethic we used to celebrate as one of our virtues. They traded in influence as if some of the most respected offices in our land were commodities to be bought and sold like pork bellies. These Wall Street warriors were applying the lesson of Vietnam. If quick, profitable victories can be achieved, they become right. What we must not forget, now that they've sent us the bill for their rampage, is that we considered them heroes at the time. We cheered them on as the very embodiment of what's right about our country.

During the 80s, in a very violent way, the rich got richer, and, in an even more violent way, the poor got poorer. Crime didn't just grow; it grew so vast that in many neighborhoods it became the only effective form of government, recruiting to its ranks more and more members from the despair and poverty of inner cities. Since we know that what would be required to solve this problem is a "war" much longer and much costlier than the war in Vietnam, we have abandoned it. We have even abandoned all efforts to contain it. As it spreads and as we flee from it, we'll go anywhere in search of the solace of quick victories in quick wars.

We have now become that most worrisome of superpowers: isolationists in regard to problems at home and interventionists in regard to the problems of other nations. It is a very disturbing combination. We have come to rely on external enemies for comfort and confirmation of our identity as a people. In our desperate flight from ourselves, we have gone a step further. We no longer merely look for enemies; we invest in their development. Neither Saddam Hussein nor Manuel Noriega, as despicable as these men are, achieved their full potential by themselves. We helped them along. We nurtured them.

Smaller Enemies

Hafez al-Assad of Syria, our ally now, waits in the wings, the next Saddam. We'll need others. The loss of one huge and reliable enemy, the Soviet Union, will require the creation of many smaller enemies.

The moment was there for Bush when Iraq invaded Kuwait. Saddam's invasion demanded a response, but the choice was ours. The sanctions were put in place; they could have worked. But sanctions required patience and deep-seated convictions, and patience is a virtue we no longer have or trust. We all want quick results now, from our corporate leaders, who have abandoned long-term investment in their enterprises for the sake of quick results during their term of office; to our political leaders, who behave in the same way; to the person in the street, whose hopes rise and fall with the results of state-sanctioned lotteries.

The speed with which Bush went from Desert Shield to Desert Sword to Desert Storm suggests a moody and impatient President of a moody and impatient nation. It suggests that neither we as a people nor he as our President has strong beliefs. What we have now, all we have now, is temporary moods. How else to explain the incessant, daily and sometimes hourly updates measuring the mood of the nation and the mood of the President as the war went on? We're keeping an anxious eye on one another for signs of slippage. A policy and a people whose actions are motivated by longstanding, profound convictions would have no such anxiety. But neither the President nor the country can ever acquire those convictions if it is fleeing from itself for yet another temporary confirmation elsewhere, this time in the desert of Saudi Arabia.

As a result, the war raged on. We watched it on television, spellbound. It has brought out the worst in us. In the initial, uninterrupted, commercial-free coverage there was only one sponsor: war. Our TV anchors were pitching weapons, enthusiastically explaining their specifications, range and payloads, using computer graphics to demonstrate their virtues. The names of these weapons quickly achieved the jargon status of brand names. Technophiliacs were speaking to us, and in their orgy of delight in sophisticated hardware, war and violence became as banal as the regular programming that the war had replaced. And it served as a preview to various members of our coalition—to Assad and other like-minded consumers—of the weapons they will need if they want to become competitive participants in the next war in that region.

"The temporary sense of unity we feel in our support for 'our boys' will be short-lived."

This banal acceptance of violence reached its apogee a few days into the war. President Bush appeared on television to warn the nation against premature euphoria. His presumption that the destruction and the violence that had been unleashed could actually induce euphoria seems to me the true definition of political pornography. What could have prompted this man we elected as our President to think us so lacking in basic human decency that we could actually experience euphoria over one of the most violent episodes in our recent history? Either he knows us all too well or he has slandered us as a people.

A Moody Nation

The temporary sense of unity we feel in our support for "our boys" will be short-lived. We must not forget that we have become a moody nation and that moods can change. But even if it does not change, the support we extend to our troops is not a true measure of the worth of a great country. That worth lies in the way we support all our boys and girls, all our children, all our people at home. Eventually, very soon I hope, "our boys" will return from abroad. And where then will we find our source of unity as a nation?

It can only be found if we try to realize the unfulfilled pledge to all of our people. We cannot keep fleeing from that pledge. We must disenchant ourselves of the notion that our destiny lies in the detours we take to avoid it. We must either redistribute and share the blessings of this land or those growing millions will share their violent despair with us and make the possibility of peace a memory.

In order to achieve that union we will need the patience of the tillers of the soil. We will need to recommit ourselves to the virtue of planting trees in whose shade we will never sit. If we are to have peace, all must share in it. All must bear the burdens and all must share the blessings of whatever we do. Then and only then will we have the strength, derived from moral authority, to be a powerful and respected voice in the affairs of the world.

The War Exposed America's Weaknesses

Gar Alperovitz

About the Author: *Gar Alperovitz is president of the National Center for Economic Alternatives, a research and policy institute in Washington, D.C. He is the author of* Atomic Diplomacy: Hiroshima and Potsdam.

The Gulf war cut to the heart of America's political-economic system, brutally laying bare some ugly truths about our leadership and our very nature as a people.

The war revealed George Bush to be a "true believer," ideologically committed to a particular global perspective for which he is willing to kill. The President's conviction that he is creating a New World Order through war is, in fact, a radical idea—quite different from the judgment of almost half the members of the U.S. Senate who (before timidly rallying 'round the flag) voted against the use of force as unwise and unnecessary. Most likely the outcome will be profound *dis*order.

At the same time, the Gulf crisis exposed a deeply unprincipled, dishonest, and undemocratic side of the President's character: Having initially obtained Congressional and public support for an embargo and a defensive strategy against an attack on Saudi Arabia, Bush violated even minimal standards of public trust. He prepared his plans in secret and waited until only forty hours after the 1990 election to announce a unilateral decision to double America's troop commitment—and then proclaimed the offensive goal of ousting Saddam Hussein from

Gar Alperovitz, "What the War Says About Us," *The Progressive,* April 1991. Reprinted by permission from *The Progressive,* 409 E. Main St., Madison, WI 53703.

Kuwait by force of arms.

As Sam Nunn, the indignant chairman of the Senate Armed Services Committee, realized, both the Congress and the American people were crudely manipulated in a matter involving life and death: With the nation's prestige on the line around the world, many felt trapped into supporting the President's announced position, whatever the consequences.

Bush's own impulse was also evident. He would gladly have taken the nation to war without Congressional approval—and the Constitution be damned!—had he not been forced to recognize the political costs.

Nevertheless, the people—*we*—have no one to blame but ourselves for permitting this travesty of democratic practice. Nor should we be surprised. The crisis revealed us to be extraordinarily naive. Bush, after all, was Ronald Reagan's hand-picked ideological successor. Bush's intervention in Panama, in violation of international law and without Congressional authorization, was a foretaste of the Gulf war. And long before he was elected, Bush showed his ruthless, unprincipled side in his racist exploitation of the Willie Horton issue in the 1988 Presidential campaign. (Even former Republican National Committee Chairman Lee Atwater, at death's door, has apologized for his part in this viciousness.)

> ## "The Gulf war . . . [revealed] some ugly truths about our leadership and our very nature as a people."

Bush also illuminates America's deep commitment to violence—especially the use of air power—in foreign policy. Since World War II, our nation has accepted the massive aerial bombardment of other societies, although such attacks commonly strengthen the morale of the opposition even as they murder innocent civilians by the thousands.

The use of the atomic bomb against the largely civilian "targets" of Hiroshima and Nagasaki symbolizes this tradition, but civilian deaths from conventional air attacks in World War II were extraordinary, as they were in Korea and Vietnam (and, illegally, in Cambodia). Bush is a World War II fighter pilot; his national-security adviser, Brent Scowcroft, is an Air Force general.

This is not simply an "ideological" or "personal" matter: Our national-security institutions—the CIA [Central Intelligence Agency], the Pentagon, the State Department, the military-industrial complex—initiate the policies and strategies which give reality to abstract ideology. Bush, a former director of the CIA and ambassador to the United Nations and China, is both symbol and product of these entrenched institutions.

"We are only beginning to confront the deeper issues illuminated by the Gulf crisis."

Our system gives national-security elites enormous unaccountable power. The President and his tiny group of close advisers can focus international and national attention on issues, over-dramatizing some, ignoring others. Bush might just as easily have presented the invasion of Kuwait—like many postwar border conflicts and invasions in the Middle East and Africa (including Syria in Lebanon and Israel on the West Bank)—as a "very serious problem" rather than as a cause of war. He could have characterized it as one among many difficulties this sad world must contemplate, and relegated it to the middle pages of the press while a diplomatic solution was developed.

Saddam Hussein's regime was brutal and totalitarian. But so are those (for instance) of China and Syria. The White House chose to put *this* issue on the front page, inflated it to the level of a national and international "crisis" of historic proportions, and systematically shaped public opinion to the point of war.

And Congress, though not without power, is revealed to be at a severe and fundamental disadvantage in our "system." There simply are not many forceful constitutional, legislative, or practical mechanisms which force the President to be accountable when he is hell-bent on a chosen initiative.

No Honest Debate

With the media easily focused by the White House and national-security elites, and bolstered by Congressional insiders, it became extremely difficult to conduct an honest debate about real options. Still, the decision to go to war was "democratic" as that term is usually understood in the West: The people's representatives authorized the killings. If it was wrong in the most fundamental sense, it is a mistake to blame our predicament on dishonest leadership: The source of our difficulties lies deeper—both with our system and with us.

As a people, we commonly accept violence as policy. We have allowed or endorsed the continuous buildup of armaments in the Middle East for decades. We have regularly accepted (and voted for) leaders who defined America's interests largely in military terms, authorizing an accelerating nuclear arms race and $300 billion military budgets. We applauded (the polls tell us) the bombing of Libya, the invasions of Grenada and Panama.

We also commonly salute the idea that America is—and must remain—"Number One," and that our fiat must set the terms of reference for the world as a whole. We, too, are prisoners of a dangerous and obsolete ideology.

And we must face the reality of our violent domestic culture—child-abuse and wife-beating, murder in the inner cities, the assassination of leaders from Lincoln to Kennedy, from Malcolm X to Martin Luther King Jr. Our television and films encourage us to regard crime and violence as "entertainment." A systematic emphasis on death and destruction is presented as "normal" or, at least, inevitable.

We are largely indifferent to the homeless and the poor. We put more people in prison, per capita, than any other advanced industrial nation. We define those who violate our norms as "criminals" rather than as people in severe trouble. (Malcolm X once said, "I have no mercy or compassion in me for a society that will crush people and then penalize them for not being able to stand up under the weight.")

Is it any wonder, then, that we so easily support leaders who proclaim "evil empires," demand more weapons, and tell us we must intervene with force around the world to support a theory they are convinced is the unchallengeable truth?

American Materialism

Our own love affair with materialism and consumption exacerbates the problem. True, corporate interests have done their best to persuade us, through advertising and other strategies, that we must have gas-guzzlers and every energy-consuming appliance imaginable. But we as individuals and as a society have bought the message, defining success as money and luxury. We cannot duck our own responsibility: Had *we* wanted to force Congress and the Executive to enact a serious energy policy, and had we done what we could on a purely personal, voluntary basis, the oil companies could not have prevailed.

The American people were late to react to the Korean war, and they took a great deal of time to restrain the elites who took them to war in Vietnam. In this crisis, the people initially were on the move much faster. Over time, increasing numbers may demand that our Government deal with international crises without resorting to death and destruction.

In the meantime, however, we have failed. Those who believed all along that this war was unnecessary should have forcefully demanded from the beginning that there be no killing. We let the elites get ahead of the game. We cannot ignore our own reluctance to act, our slowness, our complicity.

We are only beginning to confront the deeper issues illuminated by the Gulf crisis—the feeble nature of America's structure of constitutional accountability, the power of our national-security institutions and the military-industrial complex, the dangerous influence of corporate interest-groups, the expansionist commercial dynamic of our capitalist system, our society's extraordinary commitment to materialism, and the profound violence at the very core of our culture.

Chapter 3:

What Are the Military Lessons of the Persian Gulf War?

Preface

The Persian Gulf War took place when the United States was engaging in fundamental debates over the purpose of its military. The cold war with the Soviet Union, which had lasted for more than forty years and had helped define U.S. military and defense objectives, seemed all but over. Many analysts argued that the reduced Soviet threat eliminated the need for an extensive U.S. military. As of August 2, 1990, the U.S. Congress and the Pentagon had agreed to a five-year plan to reduce America's armed forces in the wake of U.S. budget deficits and the fading cold war. This "peace dividend" budget would cut annual military spending by 34 percent compared to the 1985 budget and reduce active U.S. military personnel by 24 percent between 1991 and 1996.

Ironically, August 2 was also the day Iraq's Saddam Hussein invaded Kuwait. The crisis launched by that invasion, which culminated in the Persian Gulf War, rekindled the debate over America's military. Analysts now tried to evaluate U.S. military performance during the war and answer the question: Did the Persian Gulf War make the arguments for cutting America's military capabilities obsolete?

Those who oppose significant reductions in U.S. military power argue that the Persian Gulf War proved that the U.S. should not cut its defense budget. Saddam Hussein's Iraq is but one example of a Third World country with a dictatorship, unsettled relations with its neighbors, and money to buy and develop modern weapons, these people argue. North Korea, Libya, Iran, and Pakistan are mentioned by columnist Charles Krauthammer and others as potential new Iraqs with the power to greatly disrupt the world. America needs a strong military, Krauthammer and others maintain, to protect itself, its interests, and its allies from these unstable nations.

The general success of America's armed forces in the Persian Gulf, including the performance of high-tech weaponry and equipment, also caused analysts to question the wisdom of cutting defense spending. They pointed out that if plans for a reduced military budget are enacted, the production of many weapons shown to be effective in the war, including the M-1 Abrams tank and the F-15 Eagle aircraft, would be phased out. Defense analyst Frank Gaffney Jr. says, "If planned Pentagon cuts are fully implemented, by 1995 the United States would not be able to mount a Desert Storm operation." Gaffney and others conclude that the success of the Persian Gulf War proves that America must maintain its large military capabilities.

Military Solutions

Critics of military spending vehemently disagree with this logic. They contend that maintaining high levels of military spending will only increase the chances of military solutions to future conflicts. These critics point out that the military "victory" in Iraq fell short. UN forces did not remove Saddam Hussein from power, nor did they protect the Kurds from torture and extermination. Social critic Michael Lerner writes: "In almost every area, the Gulf War has not produced the results its champions promised."

Instead of increasing military spending and thus a reliance on military solutions, these critics argue that the U.S. should work harder to develop nonmilitary solutions. Such options could include banning arms sales to aggressor countries or developing strong economic sanctions or other diplomatic options to war.

The viewpoints in this chapter examine what military lessons the Persian Gulf War holds for the U.S. and whether the U.S. can rely on military power in the future.

What Are the Military Lessons of the Persian Gulf War?

The War Proves the Need for a Strong Military

The War Proves the Need for a Strong Military
The War Proves the Importance of International Military Cooperation
The War Proves the Need for United Nations' Involvement in World Conflicts
The War Proves the Need for a U.S. Military Presence in the Gulf

The War Proves the Need for a Strong Military

Kenneth L. Adelman

About the Author: *Kenneth L. Adelman was director of the U.S. Arms Control and Disarmament Agency under President Ronald Reagan. He is the coauthor of the book* The Defense Revolution.

"You saw some action once, too, didn't you?" a young CIA [Central Intelligence Agency] analyst asked an intelligence veteran in the movie *Three Days of the Condor.*

"Do you miss the action?"

The experienced hand answered slowly and carefully, "It's not the action I miss. It's the clarity."

In the post-Gulf War world, Americans will miss the clarity of that conflict. Foreign confrontations do not come any clearer:

• The triggering act, the conquest of another nation, was unmistakable and wholly unjustifiable.

• Our foe looked like, and *was*, the devil incarnate.

• The enemy state was repressive and totalitarian, brimming with armaments and striving for weapons of mass destruction (but luckily not yet attaining nuclear capability).

• The world community, incensed, lent its support to a UN [United Nations] resolution authorizing the use of force.

• The Allied coalition was wide and included all the key Arab and European states.

• Congress, less incensed, went along with the president's strong leadership after the diplomatic track proved fruitless.

• The timing was ideal—our first post-Cold War was when we still retained a Cold War arsenal.

• The military victory was quick and decisive, with far fewer Allied casualties than anticipated.

That degree of clarity was unique. The outlook for America at the crossroads—standing somewhere between the Cold War era and the awaited New World Order—is necessarily murky.

For decades, we knew who our enemies were—the octogenarians atop Lenin's tomb during the October Revolution parade. We knew that, while aggressive abroad and repressive within, they nonetheless proceeded rationally and within some bounds (no matter how wide) of morality. And we knew they controlled their own forces.

Much of that has changed. We no longer know who may be our main enemy next, how irrational our adversaries may be, or how much control they can maintain over their own forces. Though plagued by uncertainty, we will still be guided by lessons learned over the years—especially lessons learned (or reinforced) by the Gulf War.

President Bush launched a moral crusade against Saddam Hussein and his aggressive apparatus. Pitched as a moral battle, it was widely supported. Yet after the Allied victory, the president reverted to his more comfortable ground of realpolitik by evoking regional balances of power and noninterference in internal affairs, weighing this geopolitical factor against that, and so on. As he proceeded along these lines, he severed his connection with American sensitivities.

> ## "Without a moral component, most Americans dismiss foreign affairs."

Americans want to do good abroad, more than they want to do well among foreigners. Without a moral component, most Americans dismiss foreign affairs as best left to others. We foreign policy aficionados may lament this and dismiss it as remnants of Wilsonian idealism, but such is embedded in the American psyche. The type of foreign policy "realism" practiced by President Richard Nixon and Secretary of State Henry Kissinger, and shared within the Bush administration, remains unconvincing to the American people. Unconvinced, they will be unsupportive.

A Triumph of Leadership

Skepticism about presidential competence has been prevalent since Vietnam, CIA revelations, Watergate, and Iran-Contra. The Gulf experience showed the presidency at its best.

"Mr. Lincoln astonished us all," said his personal secretary, John Hay, after the Civil War ended and Lincoln lay dying. So did Mr. Bush astonish us all with his decisiveness and effectiveness. Following the Iraqi invasion in August, he marched the world toward battle—not through soaring rhetoric, as do most wartime leaders—but through a series of crisp actions, each of which moved toward his goal yet none of which was too unsettling.

Above all, Bush succeeded because he reduced myriad intricate issues to bare-bone truths. Most successful presidents keep things simple in times of complexity. The erudite ex-Secretary of State Dean Acheson called Harry Truman "simple" as a man and "great" as a president, correctly considering the two compatible. On this issue Bush, like Truman, seemed singularly devoid of indecision or doubts. To quote again from Acheson's memoirs, *Present at the Creation:* "No one can decide and act who is beset by second thoughts, self-doubt, and that most enfeebling of emotions, regret. With the President, a decision made was done with and he went on to another." Again, ditto for President Bush.

Historians have long known that there are only a few critical occasions in any term that demand decisive leadership by the president. Otherwise, the office can be handled routinely. Bush handled his first, and perhaps his most treacherous, such occasion masterfully.

Similarly, the chain of command beneath the president worked splendidly. As a lesson of Vietnam, we learned that a local commander should be given responsibility for local command decisions, while a president and secretary of defense must make the most momentous decisions.

After the war, commentators all chimed about how major military decisions were left to the military. This is only partly true, and should be only partly true. Indeed, the biggest decision of all—whether to go to war to liberate Kuwait, or instead to muster forces merely to protect Saudi Arabia and wait for international sanctions to expel Iraq from Kuwait—was made by the President. It appears that U.S. chairman of the joint chiefs of staff Gen. Colin Powell preferred the latter (and longer) option.

The timing of the war's start was also driven by political as much as military factors. The president's key military personnel advised that they would need a year to prepare for an assault against the Iraqi troops dug into Kuwait. Later, most top field commanders felt that mid-February would prove best for our attack; yet mid-January was chosen instead. And the dogged Allied pursuit of SCUD launchers was more driven by political than military considerations, as that concentrated effort kept Israel out of the war (thus eliminating an unwanted complication to Arab coalition members).

"Among the greatest lessons of the Gulf War was how well our high-tech arsenal operates."

While other examples can be given, the main point remains: War is fought for political goals, which politicians are best able to realize and pursue. Realizing this, the Founding Fathers named the president as commander in chief. So presidents should decide key politico-military issues, as did Lincoln, who understood political goals and forces during the Civil War better than did his generals.

As a lesson of Vietnam, the Bush team learned that Americans prefer their wars to be snappy and decisive. Once an air campaign begins, it should be waged vigorously, yet morally. Leveling Baghdad, or inflicting horrendous civilian casualties among its four million inhabitants, was both unconscionable and unnecessary.

Moral Campaigns

Fortunately, the march of weaponry makes moral campaigns more possible, not (as the literature has had it for years) less so. Advanced defense systems were shown to work and to save lives: both *ours*—by dramatically reducing Iraqi hits of coalition pilots in aircraft, and of Israelis and Saudis in their homes—and *theirs*—by limiting peripheral Iraqi civilian casualties.

Among the greatest lessons of the Gulf War was how well our high-tech arsenal operates. And among the greatest ironies was how the most maligned weapons of the 1980s became the most valuable weapons of 1991. What defense skeptics and arms control advocates most sought to scrap or curb throughout the 1980s became the technological wonders of the first war of the 1990s. These consist of the four S's—Stealth, Sea-launched cruise missiles, SDI [Strategic Defense Initiative]-like defenses, and Space systems. Each depends upon the fifth S, semiconductors.

Advances in military wizardry have been awesome, altering the arithmetic of armed assault. Norman Augustine, chairman of Martin Marietta (and coauthor with me of a new book), calculated that from the Civil War through the Vietnam War, it took anywhere between 10,000 and 100,000 rounds of rifle fire to produce a single enemy casualty. And it took some five tons of air munitions, or three tons of artillery, to destroy a single tactical target—be it a truck, tank, or a bunker.

In the Gulf, precision munitions enabled our troops, really for the first time ever, to both identify *and* hit the right target in just a few tries. Initially came "smart weapons," which soldiers need to keep aimed during their entire flight. Later came a generation of "brilliant weapons," which soldiers need only shoot in the right general direction. The sensors and minicomputers of a "brilliant weapon" can tell whether it is spotting a tank, tree, or bridge and then guide it to the pre-selected target.

Although each of the four S's was previously deemed wasteful, or even venal, all were life-saving in the Gulf War. The first air assaults were conducted by two of our most maligned military merchandise—*Stealth aircraft*, which evaded enemy radar and enabled our pilots to hit Iraqi antiaircraft systems quick and hard, without being detected and shot down by enemy arms, and *sea-launched cruise missiles* (SLCMs), which went precisely where desired, also without endangering pilots.

SDI—President Reagan's much-mocked if not maligned "Star Wars" program of defenses against ballistic missiles—was once considered unworkable, even irresponsible. Unworkable, so critics claimed, since it was virtually impossible to knock down ballistic missiles in flight. Irresponsible because having the capability to do so challenged the traditional notion that defenses are destabilizing, that vulnerability is somehow stabilizing.

"Arguments over our All-Volunteer Force can now be buried."

Our fiery domestic debate over SDI in the 1980s seems ludicrous since defenses against ballistic missiles proved so valuable in the 1990s. Iraqi SCUD attacks have transformed the Patriot missile from yet another arms control woe into a cherished military system. Any lingering doubts can be settled by asking any Israeli or Saudi whether he would rather be protected by the *theory* of mutually assured destruction or by the *reality* of an antiballistic missile system.

The last S—*space systems*—has been sneeringly called "spy satellites" each time an unexplained craft is launched from the Kennedy Space Center. Such dastardly sounding devices helped furnish superb tactical intelligence on Iraqi nuclear, chemical, and other military sites that American aircraft then destroyed.

The Gulf War displayed an impressive American (and coalition) fighting force. Arguments over our All-Volunteer Force can now be buried. With volunteers we had plenty of soldiers—indeed, during the war, recruitment shot up—and highly capable troops at that. Nearly all enrollees had earned a high school degree or its equivalent, which is the best single indicator of success as a soldier. With volunteers we had fine teamwork, which is pivotal to military effectiveness, since so many maneuvers require so much precision. A Vietnam-like conscripted army means a rapid turnover in personnel, which does not permit the same soldiers to work and live together as a team.

Peering Ahead

What now? We face a world in which America is seen (and felt) as increasingly powerful militarily and increasingly vulnerable economically. Politically we stand supreme. For the values America embodies—free enterprise and freedom—have now penetrated the darkest recesses of the world. Even the few lingering dictatorships must now adorn their rule with words about democracy and people's choice.

While our values have triumphed, their implementation will be problematic in various regions. There will be ups and downs in the fate of democracy, especially in Latin America and Africa, though the overall trend will move upward.

And there will be continued security threats. The immediate post-Cold War wish, that conflict has finally ended for the human species, is as misguided in the century's last decade as it was in its first decade. For it was also believed then that "modern" conditions made conflict inconceivable, a view young Winston Churchill summarized before demolishing:

> War is too foolish, too fantastic to be thought of in the Twentieth Century. Civilization has climbed above such perils. The interdependence of nations in trade and traffic, the sense of public law, the Hague Convention, and lib-

eral principles have rendered such nightmares impossible.

After presenting the conventional wisdom—jarring to read now, after the wholesale carnage of World Wars I and II—young Churchill pointedly asked, "Are you quite sure? It would be a pity to be wrong."

It would be a pity now too. While there is little doubt that the Soviet threat is declining, the Soviet strategic buildup continues as perhaps the element *least* affected by Gorbachev's reforms. Moreover, Moscow keeps building conventional arms. The hemorrhaging of its Warsaw Pact allies does, nonetheless, hollow the overall threat, especially since Soviet troops will be gone from Czechoslovakia and Hungary in 1991, and from Germany and Poland by the summer of 1994.

Less of a concentrated threat, the Soviet Union may become more of a diffuse threat. The Soviet crack-up could crank up more violence within....

"New threats [come] from Third World nations with First World weaponry."

New threats [come] from Third World nations with First World weaponry. Saddam Hussein stands as a prototype of irresponsible, resentful leaders who already (or will) possess ballistic missiles that are (or will be) equipped with chemical, biological, or nuclear weapons.

Columnist Charles Krauthammer put it best. In the year-end issue of *Foreign Affairs* journal, he wrote how "the post-Cold War era is thus perhaps better called the era of weapons of mass destruction. The proliferation of weapons of mass destruction and their means of delivery will constitute the greatest single threat to world security for the rest of our lives."

The same concern grips leaders in government. Defense Secretary Dick Cheney emphasized how, by the turn of the century,

> more than two dozen developing nations will

have ballistic missiles; 15 of those countries will have the scientific skills to make their own, and half of them either have or are near to getting nuclear capability, as well. Thirty countries will have chemical weapons, and ten will be able to deploy biological weapons.

The composition of those countries makes Cheney's scenario even scarier. For among those soon making ballistic missiles are such "bad guys" as Libya, Iran, and North Korea, besides Argentina, Brazil, Israel, Pakistan, India, and South Africa. . . .

Possible Solutions

Recognizing that threats still exist—a point made more convincing by Saddam Hussein . . . we can take several steps to address if not redress security problems we face ahead.

Protective diplomacy is always best. Crisis prevention is far preferable to crisis management but requires active American involvement in the world.

Of course, active involvement need not mean that America must become the world's policeman. As the lessons of Vietnam were learned, so should be the lessons of Iraq. It is important to get them right. The main lesson is that the United States can, with wide international and sufficient domestic support, employ military force effectively to counter an aggressive act in a region critical to our national security.

Learning the wrong lessons of Iraq can cause as many woes to future U.S. foreign policy as the Munich syndrome and the Vietnam syndrome caused to our past foreign policy. The main lesson *not* to learn is that all the conditions existing in Iraq—those listed in the paragraphs above—need be met before American forces can be deployed. Demanding such conditions would have precluded such beneficial uses of U.S. military power as those against Grenada in October 1983, Libya in April 1986, and Panama in December 1989. None received much support from regional or key European states, even those most cordial to us, but all three deployments were wise—even in retrospect. For they liberated Grenada while saving American students, reduced Libyan terrorism, and freed Panama from the drug-infested clutches of Gen. Manuel Noriega.

To help the Soviets retain tight control over their weapons of mass destruction, the Bush administration should open a quiet dialogue with top Soviet chiefs on this sole topic. . . .

As to threats from Third World leaders, the United States would be wise to expand the bilateral INF (Intermediate Nuclear Force) Treaty, which Presidents Reagan and Gorbachev signed in 1987, into a multilateral treaty. We could thereby move to ban all land-based ballistic missiles with ranges between 300 and 3,400 miles.

The present situation is ludicrous, as Iraq or North Korea can legally have SCUD missiles while the United States and the Soviet Union cannot. That incongruity would end if U.S. and Soviet envoys introduced a joint treaty at the 39-nation Conference on Disarmament in Geneva.

"As the lessons of Vietnam were learned, so should be the lessons of Iraq."

Americans and Soviets could thereby cooperate on stopping missile proliferation, just as we have cooperated on stopping nuclear proliferation over the years. But unlike that situation, this accord would not be discriminatory, for we would not be asking any country to give up anything we and the Soviets had not already foregone. The have-nots would not resent the haves. Ideally, everyone would become a have-not.

Such an approach would be timely now, when memories of SCUD attacks remain fresh and when ballistic missiles are beginning to spread like wildfire. The effort might even succeed. Some states would sign up out of sheer superpower sway, others, out of moral suasion (it is, after all, the right thing to do). But most would sign up out of pure fright that otherwise their archenemies would get these bloody things.

The War Proves the Importance of International Military Cooperation

Michael Howard

About the Author: *Michael Howard is the Robert Lovett Professor of Military and Naval History at Yale University in New Haven, Connecticut.*

The Duke of Wellington remarked glumly on the morrow of Waterloo that there was only one thing worse than winning a battle, and that was to lose it. We are beginning to see what he meant. From the Baltic to the Caspian, there now stretches a huge arc of confusion bordering at times on anarchy. In Central and Eastern Europe, inexperienced leaders face the problem of reconstituting not only economies but entire societies poisoned by 40 years of Marxist totalitarianism. Farther east, the collapse of Soviet political and economic leadership has encouraged every group with any experience of national autonomy to demand independence from a center that has nothing left to offer them. The center itself is paralyzed by factional fights. It is 1918 again—though 1918 mercifully without Lenin.

The analogy with 1918 is strengthened by the second victory of the United States and its allies; the defeat of Saddam Hussein has extended the arc of confusion from the Caspian Sea to the Persian Gulf. Once again, military victory has made the West the arbiter of the destinies of the Middle East. President Bush is confronted with the same ominous challenge that Andrew Marvell defined for Oliver Cromwell after the latter had bloodily pacified Ireland in 1651:

The same arts that did gain
A Power, must it sustain.

The trouble is that the American people do not want that power. That is one of the features that distinguishes Pax Americana from the Pax Britannica of the 19th century. In 1898, the British Army under Horatio Herbert Kitchener defeated the Mahdi of the Sudan as completely as Gen. Norman Schwarzkopf has defeated the Iraqis. British rifle and machine-gun fire mowed down 11,000 Sudanese; 29 Europeans were killed. London went wild with joy. General Kitchener was made an earl, and the Sudan was effectively annexed to the British Empire. An elite branch of the British civil service was created to run it and did so with commendable efficiency for 50 years.

"Once again, military victory has made the West the arbiter of the destinies of the Middle East."

This was the example that Rudyard Kipling urged his American cousins to follow a year later in the Philippines, and which some nostalgic imperialists urge on them still.

Take up the White Man's burden
Send forth the best ye breed—
Go bind your sons to exile
To serve your captives' need
To wait in heavy harness
On fluttered folk and wild
Your new-caught, sullen peoples
Half devil and half child.

But the sun has set on the days of empire. The global growth of nationalist sentiments—itself a spore of European culture, disseminated worldwide by Western technology— hugely multiplied the costs of even the most benevolent imperial rule. As Kipling bluntly pointed out, good intentions do not make imperial rulers more popular.

Take up the White Man's burden

Michael Howard, "The Burdens of Victory," *U.S. News & World Report,* May 13, 1991. Copyright © 1991 U.S. News & World Report. Reprinted with permission.

And reap his old reward;
The blame of those ye better
The hate of those ye guard.

For another, the growth of democracy has made those costs unacceptable at home. In the 20th century, even the British were prepared to spend little money and even less blood on retaining their imperial possessions: When serious disorders threatened their control of India and Palestine, they swallowed their pride and left. The United States has never shown much enthusiasm for going down the same path; at least not since the golden years of Teddy Roosevelt. America has been tempted to tread it mostly by the fear that if it does not, others will. But now there is less fear that an American withdrawal will create a vacuum that will be filled by Soviet power, and the popular demand to bring the boys home from the Middle East is overwhelming.

The appalling consequences of the war, mercilessly displayed on television, have led liberal and conservative columnists to join forces and urge Bush to take up the white man's burden in the Middle East and fight:

The savage wars of peace
Fill full the mouth of Famine
And bid the sickness cease.

But the president knows very well that this is possible only if the American people are prepared to roll up their sleeves, accept political responsibilities and stick around for quite a long time. He no doubt knows equally well that the same columnists would be the first to complain if he did.

Sympathy or Support?

The West has now to contemplate the unintended consequences of both its bloodless and its bloody victories. The first essential is to not feel guilty. The chaos that we are witnessing results from the downfall or the death throes of tyrannies whose continuation meant continuing misery for their own people and danger for the world. The Communists in Moscow and the Ba'athists in Baghdad provided stability of a kind, but it was the stability of a prison. Those liber-

ated or still struggling for liberation, whether they be Poles or Lithuanians, Georgians or Kurds, naturally turn to us for help and lament bitterly if they do not get it. Humanitarian aid should certainly be given whenever and wherever possible, and on the largest practicable scale; but political support is another matter. It is easy to feel and express sympathy for liberation struggles, but sympathy is too often interpreted as a promise of support.

"Any armed intervention should take place with the broadest possible international consensus."

Historians are likely to give President Bush more credit for resisting the pressure to rush into Iraq than do his political adversaries. It is true that during the war he made a number of statements he now may regret. Elevating Saddam Hussein, who was no more than a nasty and dangerous local despot, to the stature of Hitler was demeaning to the president and misleading to the American people. Bush's appeal to the Iraqi people to rise against the tyrant was unwise, but whether it had been made or not, Hussein's enemies would have tried to overthrow him. Yet the stated object of the war was clear: It was the implementation of the United Nations resolution to liberate Kuwait and exact reparations from Iraq for the damage done. In going beyond that objective the United States would have been on its own. As it is, the United States has established itself as the dominant force in the region, even though it has made clear its reluctance to stay there.

The American people, however, would undoubtedly have supported Hussein's overthrow. Even if the president had not demonized him, the media did, with the enthusiastic cooperation of Hussein himself. But insistent and nagging questions still arise. How should Hussein be overthrown: by a march on Baghdad? And after that, what? An American occupation of Iraq, with General Schwarzkopf in the role of Douglas MacArthur? Support for a succession of native military leaders, on the model of Vietnam? Immediate withdrawal, leaving Iraq at the mercy of Syria and Iran? Nevertheless, so long as Saddam Hussein remains in power there will remain a sense of frustration and incompleteness, for which the president must bear much of the blame.

Regardless of how matters turn out in Iraq, the war has furnished the United States and its partners with a paradigm of the problems likely to arise under "the new world order," and President Bush has provided a model of how to deal with them. A local despot tried to take advantage of regional disorder to annex a defenseless neighbor. The act was clearly identified as both a threat to American interests and an outrage against international law. The widest possible consensus was obtained for an action carried out under the aegis of the United Nations but one in which the United States called the shots. A military force was assembled in sufficient strength to achieve its stated objectives with astonishing speed and completeness.

"The United States . . . must define its interests and maintain the military capacity needed to defend them."

Those who are unhappy with the results need only contemplate the alternatives. One was of Hussein continuing to bargain, mobilizing Third World opinion on his side while support for the United Nations action slowly dribbled away and Kuwait was systematically destroyed. Another is of a drawn-out military confrontation, inconclusive because of insufficient application of force, in which the United States and its partners gradually lost heart and prestige.

The lessons for future American policy seem clear. First, the United States should retain the

capacity and the will to use military force when its vital interests are threatened—interests that need to be clearly defined and understood. These do not and cannot extend to the promotion of "democracy" throughout the world, and aspirants to statehood or self-government should be left with no illusion about this. The sympathies of American citizens must not be confused with the interests of the United States. There are many means short of armed force by which a power as rich and influential as America can make its preferences felt. The fact that the use of force carries fewer risks than it did during the years of the cold war should not be an incentive to employ it.

Moscow's Importance

Secondly, to the extent feasible, any armed intervention should take place with the broadest possible international consensus. The importance of Soviet cooperation cannot be overstated. If the Soviets had pursued their traditional policy of blocking agreements at the United Nations and defending their protégés in the Middle East, not only would united action have been impossible but fear of provoking a superpower confrontation might well have deterred the United States from acting. Yet the Soviet Union retains great negative power, even if it no longer poses an active challenge to Western interests. Friendly relations with Moscow and the survival there of a government interested in maintaining friendly relations thus remain a fundamental Western interest.

At the same time, we must realize how precarious are the prospects of any such government and be prepared for a change of course. A total reversal of Soviet policy is unlikely: Even an authoritarian Soviet regime will see little profit in reassuming its thankless responsibilities in Eastern Europe, let alone posing a renewed threat to the West. But one cannot be sure. Even if the Soviet Union disintegrates, Russia will remain a nuclear superpower. So American interests in Europe still need to be explicitly defined, and if they are to be extended to include Poland, Hungary and Czechoslovakia, that needs to be made clear as well.

If the United States is not going to bear the white man's burden all over a world that will continue, new order or no new order, to be stubbornly disorderly, it will need to follow a two-track policy. First, it must define its interests and maintain the military capacity needed to defend them. This means a drastic curtailment of the requirements for nuclear deterrence and careful attention to those for projecting conventional military power.

International Cooperation

But if that projection of power is not to leave the United States stuck with further responsibilities that its people are unwilling to accept, the second track is equally important. That is the cultivation of international consensus and international cooperation, especially the maintenance of close relations with the emerging European Community and with Japan. So long as this triad remains stable and prosperous, the external disorders will gradually abate. Even when they do not, their impact is likely to remain regional. Only if it operates from this secure base can the United States effectively intervene in the affairs of the confused world beyond its borders, and even then it should do so with great care. Rescuing damsels in distress is all very well; but the damsels all too often expect their rescuers to marry them.

The War Proves the Need for United Nations' Involvement in World Conflicts

Brian Urquhart

About the Author: *Brian Urquhart is a former undersecretary general of the United Nations. He has written several books on international relations, including* Decolonization and World Peace.

Within the UN [United Nations], the end of the cold war has had its most immediate effect on the work of the Security Council. The Council has been able to make notable progress in peacemaking and peace-keeping tasks that had languished during the cold war—for example, in Namibia, Afghanistan, the Iran-Iraq War, Cambodia, Central America, and Western Sahara. Now the Iraq-Kuwait crisis, to which the UN has made an unprecedentedly firm and united response, is putting to the test, as well as raising questions about, the concept of collective security itself.

The United Nations has so far not provided a *system* for peace and security so much as a last resort, or safety net. Sometimes it was able to mount a peace-keeping force as a kind of sheriff's posse when things had already got out of hand. The question is whether, in the new international climate, the nations of the world are capable of the effort—and expenditure—to create and maintain a system based on vigilance, consensus, common interest, collective action, and international law. Ideally such a system would keep a permanent watch on international peace

Brian Urquhart, "Learning from the Gulf," *The New York Review of Books,* March 7, 1991. Reprinted with permission from *The New York Review of Books.* Copyright © 1991 Nyrev, Inc.

and security around the world, preempt or prevent conflict, mediate disputes, assure the protection of the weak, and deal authoritatively with aggressors or would-be aggressors.

This is a very large order. It requires, first of all, a return to the provisions of the UN Charter that were the distillation of the terrible lessons of the Second World War and of the events that led up to it, including the failure of the League of Nations.

But the creation of a reliable system for international peace and security involves more than reacting, however forcefully, to a crisis that has already happened. It requires both the creation of conditions in which peace can be maintained, and the capacity to anticipate and to prevent breaches of the peace. It requires respect for, confidence in, and, if necessary, the capacity to enforce, the decisions of the Security Council and the findings of international law. That respect and confidence were eroded in the forty years of the cold war, as has become very clear in Iraq's response to the Security Council in the present crisis. It will take time and effort to restore respect and to make sure that confidence in the Security Council is shared by the UN members generally. Governments will also have to be prepared to support and put adequate resources behind both global and regional security systems. Peace-keeping, particularly, has until now had to be run on a shoestring.

"The outcome of the Gulf crisis . . . will have an immense impact on the international system."

Apart from dynamic diplomatic action, and an increasing effort to apply legal norms where these are relevant, two kinds of operational activities are required to give reality to the Security Council's decisions. They are peace-keeping, which may be compared to the work of the police in a nation-state, and enforcement, which corresponds to the work of the military. Until recently, popular emphasis and interest lay mainly in peace-keeping, an original creation of the United Nations. The Iraq crisis has highlighted the necessity of also maintaining the capacity for enforcement and of linking the two activities.

Obviously the outcome of the Gulf crisis, whatever it is, will have an immense impact on the international system, and especially on the future of the Security Council and the UN. Even before we know that outcome, the crisis provides some useful lessons for the future.

"In the Iraq-Kuwait case collective security has turned out to mean war on a large scale."

Between August 2 and November 29, 1990, the Security Council adopted twelve resolutions on a variety of aspects of the Kuwait crisis. It imposed sanctions and an embargo, and finally authorized the use of force if Iraq did not comply with its resolutions by January 15, 1991. This decisiveness and sense of urgency were unique in the Council's history.

Already on August 25, in Resolution 665, however, the Council, in asking states with maritime forces in the Gulf area to monitor shipping, had begun to depart from the letter of Chapter VII of the Charter (Action with Respect to Threats to the Peace, Breaches of the Peace and Acts of Aggression). Articles 46 and 47 clearly imply that enforcement measures under Chapter VII would be under the control of the Council and its Military Staff Committee (the Chiefs of Staff of the five permanent members), but no such control was provided for. On November 29, in Resolution 678, the Council went further down this divergent road in authorizing "member states cooperating with the Government of Kuwait . . . to use all necessary means"—i.e., the use of force—after January 15, 1991.

This tendency to diverge from the procedures of Chapter VII was inherent from the beginning of the crisis. While the Council acted quickly and forcefully in early August, it was not in a position to assure the security of other states in the region against possible Iraqi attack. Thus a parallel operation, under Article 51 of the Charter—which provides for the inherent right of individual or collective self-defense—and independent of Security Council decisions, was mounted under the leadership of the United States to protect Saudi Arabia. When this deployment of forces began it was the accepted wisdom among the Security Council members that sanctions and the embargo were to be the means of securing Iraq's withdrawal from Kuwait, and that it might well be six months or longer before they began to have a serious impact on Iraq. Later, however, when the defensive buildup in Saudi Arabia was so great as to acquire offensive capacity—particularly after the decision of the US administration on November 9 to deploy larger numbers of American forces—it began to be said that sanctions were too slow, and that if Iraq did not speedily withdraw, force would have to be used to drive Iraq out of Kuwait. This tendency culminated in Resolution 678 of November 29, setting the January 15, 1991, deadline.

Offensive Buildup

The wisdom of moving from a defensive action to an offensive buildup, with a stated deadline, as opposed to relying on sanctions for a longer period, will certainly remain a matter of debate. But there were practical reasons for the divergence from the course of action set out in the UN Charter. Forty years of cold war have meant, among many other things, that the steps outlined in the Charter for providing the Security Council with standby forces to enforce its decisions have never been taken. No agreements have been concluded with member states under Article 43 to make assistance and facilities available to the Council armed forces. The Military Staff Committee, which was to assist the Council in the application of armed force, has conducted purely token meetings throughout the cold war period, and, despite recent Soviet suggestions for its revival, it is still a largely inactive body.

The very idea of a United Nations command under the Security Council, though traditionally accepted for peace keeping operations, was never seriously considered for enforcement operations in the Gulf. Suggestions that naval or military forces in the Gulf should come under the Security Council and the Military Staff Committee were apparently regarded as unrealistic or unacceptable by the main participants in the military buildup in Saudi Arabia—even though Article 47, Section 3 of the Charter states,

> The Military Staff Committee shall be responsible under the Security Council for the strategic direction of any armed forces placed at the disposal of the Security Council.

These same powers apparently never considered the possibility that the Security Council should work out arrangements for the command of forces in the Gulf, as Article 47.3 also suggests. Although in Korea in 1950 the Security Council, during the brief absence of the Soviet Union, designated the United States as the Unified Command, the Council members evidently believed that in the Gulf the designation of a command structure by the Security Council, or even the discussion of such a thing, would impede the effectiveness of the operation.

"We are entering a period of great instability."

The goal of Chapter VII is action short of force, if possible. The Charter therefore places an important condition on the ultimate use of force. Article 42 states,

> Should the Security Council consider that measures provided for in Article 41 [sanctions] would be inadequate or have proved to be inadequate, it may take such action by air, sea or land forces as may be necessary to maintain or restore international peace and security.

No determination about the inadequacy of sanctions has ever been made by the Council.

On November 29, 1990, the Council authorized the use, after January 15, 1991, of "all necessary means" by "member states cooperating with the government of Kuwait" to enforce its previous decisions. The Council thus married the resolutions it had adopted on the Gulf crisis and the forces that were gathered in Saudi Arabia under Article 51, for a future enforcement action under the political and military leadership of the United States. A main, if unspoken, objective of the Council's authorization of November 29 was, in legitimizing forceful action, to preserve the coalition represented by military contingents to Saudi Arabia. It remains to be seen how effectively this objective will be achieved if the war is long and becomes highly destructive.

Options to War

In the Iraq-Kuwait case collective security has turned out to mean war on a large scale. In the present state of military technology, this is a sobering phenomenon which points urgently to the need to develop other effective methods for rolling back, or preferably preventing or preempting, aggression.

The Gulf crisis also raises many broad issues which are becoming a part of the wider concept of international security. These issues will have to be faced squarely if the present generation of international organizations is to evolve into a reliable and effective system of international security.

The most obvious of these broader issues is the urgent need for progress on arms control, on the flow of arms to sensitive regions, and on the proliferation of weapons of mass destruction. With the world's annual arms bill running at about one trillion dollars a year, and with vast accretions of the most sophisticated weapons in regions as volatile as the Middle East, and elsewhere, the sudden indignation in the West about Saddam Hussein's buildup of arms seems, at best, naive. In fact several of the industrial nations now arrayed against him were his suppliers only months ago. Will the Gulf crisis be enough to put serious and urgent purpose into some of the most important objectives of the Charter—into multilateral arms control and restraint on the world trade in arms—as well as into regional security arrangements that provide equitable security for all states? If it does not, talk about a "new world order" will remain largely rhetorical.

The most vivid image of the Gulf crisis at the moment is the picture it conveys of the face of modern war. Perhaps what we are able to see on television is misleading, for it naturally concentrates the eye on the efficiency of the coalition's tanks, infantry, aircraft, and sea power—which attest to the wonders of modern high technology. Because the cameras do not show what happens when the bombs and missiles fall, television gives a far less vivid idea of the range, horror, and destructiveness of missiles or bombs. Nor does television give much idea of the likely ecological, political, economic, social, or other consequences of an all-out war.

One of the consequences of World War II was the general conviction, reflected in the United Nations Charter, that disarmament was essential for a peaceful and stable world. Perhaps the Gulf War will serve to remind us of the need for arms control and the dangers of the proliferation and the flow of arms, especially to the more volatile regions of the world. The war also obviously points to the urgent need for far better considered, long-term, worldwide energy strategies, including the future of oil.

"The methods, the financing, and the logistical support for peace-keeping all need to be much strengthened."

The Gulf crisis is a reminder, moreover, that throughout the world there are borders, largely a legacy of the age of colonialism, that are still controversial and may well be major sources of conflict in the years to come. This is particularly true in regions where the borders do not correspond to ethnic, economic, or social realities. The nature of this widespread problem must be an important element in our thinking about ways to strengthen and develop mechanisms for anticipating and mediating future threats to peace.

Rich and Poor

The persistent gulf between rich and poor is already being claimed, speciously, as one justification for Iraq's aggression against Kuwait. It is undeniable, however, that widespread poverty, especially when juxtaposed with enormous wealth, is a breeding ground for extremist movements, instability, and conflict. Rapidly increasing migrations of people from poorer to richer economies are now a worldwide phenomenon, and an urgent problem for virtually all the successfully industrialized states. The political, social, and economic implications of these migrations are vast and have contributed a poignant element to the Gulf crisis. When the present conflict is over, the disparity between rich and poor, along with the pressures of an ever expanding population, will remain potentially our biggest and most explosive long-term problem.

With the collapse of Marxism there is a rush of nations to join the industrialized, so-called "North." These include the Soviet Union, the countries of Eastern Europe, and, to some degree, China. In present circumstances, this can only mean a widening of the gulf between rich and poor. The residual "South," holding more of the world's population and with little immediate hope of overcoming poverty and despair, will command less and less attention. The new buzzword "marginalization" is unfortunately all too appropriate to these poorer parts of the world. The concentration of international attention on the Gulf crisis has tended to heighten this feeling of being marginal in many regions of the world.

The world's population has doubled since 1945 and will probably double again in the next fifty years. In large parts of the developing world poverty is endemic and growing worse. A vast economic migration is pressing into the industrialized world. Matters are further complicated by more immediate global problems—natural disasters, drugs, mortal diseases such as AIDS, and terrorism.

Our technological precocity, moreover, combined with the population explosion, has inadvertently produced a terrifying assault on our natural environment, and for the first time in history the life-support system of the planet itself is threatened. Sustainable development, in the words of Gro Harlem Brundtland, chairman of the World Commission on Environment and Development, is "development that meets the needs of the present without compromising the ability of future generations to meet their own needs." One of the most important questions of our time is whether sustainable development on a worldwide scale is attainable. That in turn will depend on our success in achieving a reasonable degree of international peace and security.

Future Challenges

It is not only the end of the cold war, but the unusual clarity of the Iraqi aggression against Kuwait, that has made possible the speed and unanimity of Security Council action in the current crisis. Future challenges are unlikely to present such clear grounds for the Council's action. It is therefore urgently necessary to consider what system of collective security will be best suited to the conflicts and forms of dangerous instability that are likely to arise in the future, especially since the removal of the constraints of the cold war.

We are entering a period of great instability, characterized by longstanding international rivalries and resentments, intense ethnic and religious turmoil, a vast flow of arms and military technology, domestic disintegration, poverty and deep economic inequities, instantaneous communication throughout the world, population pressures, natural and ecological disasters, the scarcity of vital resources, and huge movements of population.

In such a situation, no one nation, or even a partnership of two or three powerful nations, is going to be able to assume the role of world arbitrator and policeman, even if we suppose the

other nations would accept it, which they are most unlikely to do. The United Nations, therefore, must be brought to maturity to take that role.

"The aim in the future should be to prevent as many disputes as possible from degenerating into actual violence."

If we are to talk seriously of a "new world order," the world's disputes and conflicts should all be a concern of the United Nations, daunting as the prospect may seem. In the current crisis in the Gulf, we have seen the tremendous effort and resources required to mount a convincing response to just one situation of conflict, admittedly a particularly flagrant act of aggression in a particularly sensitive part of the world. A credible international security system, or "new world order," will have to respond with appropriate collective action, through either regional or global organizations, to the vast range of disputes, threats to, or breaches of the peace, or even acts of aggression, which are likely to occur in the aftermath of the cold war. It is no longer acceptable that international action is taken only when a situation threatens the interests of the most powerful nations. Indeed this is one of the main criticisms now being made of the action in the Gulf. A system of international peace and security must be comprehensive and universal, and it must protect the interests of the weak as well as the strong. All nations should participate according to their means. Is this a dream, or is it practical and political common sense?

Basic Principles

The basic principles of such a system are already set out in the Charter. Its necessary elements are also clear.

• The mechanism for political coordination and consultation among governments needs to be far more effective and inclusive than any previous arrangement. The Security Council, the General Assembly, the secretary-general, and the corps of permanent national representatives to the United Nations provide a working basis for such a mechanism. Their procedures and functioning will have to become far better informed, more active, more consistent, and more universal.

• If the word "security" is to acquire real significance, the UN must find a way to keep a continuing, systematic watch on destabilizing developments all over the world, socioeconomic as well as political and military. Special attention must be given to dangerous buildups of armaments beyond what Mr. Eduard Shevardnadze has called "criteria of defense sufficiency," and to potential threats, especially to the weaker nations.

"More countries should create standby units available for international service."

• Necessary action to anticipate, preempt, or correct dangerous situations should be taken as a matter of course by the Security Council. Again this should include a far more dynamic approach to the flow of arms and military technology, to proliferation, and to means of regulating the sale and supply of arms.

• The mechanisms for carrying out the decisions of the Security Council need to be developed and made more systematic. These include:

Pacific Settlement (sometimes called peace-making), including mediation, concerted diplomatic activity, conciliation, good offices, etc., and legal recourse on matters of a justiciable nature. Here the secretary-general and his senior colleagues should continue to play a central role. The International Court of Justice should be used more often and more imaginatively. (It might have considered, for example, some of the matters in dispute between Kuwait and Iraq.) The activities of regional arrangements and agencies should be strengthened, and coordinated with the work of the Security Council. (The Arab League might have shared its preoccupations over tension between Iraq and Kuwait with the Security Council.)

Conflict Control

Conflict Control (sometimes called peace-keeping). The methods, the financing, and the logistical support for peace-keeping all need to be much strengthened. Training in peace-keeping should be incorporated into military establishments throughout the world as part of their regular responsibilities. (More countries should create standby units available for international service.) Different methods of financing peace-keeping forces—including subventions by large multinational corporations and other interests that benefit from peace-keeping—should be urgently studied. Peace-keeping units should be regarded not as an abnormal expense but as a routine and indispensable feature of the "new world order." They should be deployed in dangerous areas, if possible in advance of crisis. (Iraq's claims on Kuwait and Saddam Hussein's propensity for invading his neighbors had been well known for many years. Some international peace-keeping presence on the Kuwait-Iraq border would at least have served as a warning and a tripwire.)

Enforcement Capacity and Collective Security. Although Chapter VII was originally considered to be the most innovative part of the Charter, largely because of the effects of the cold war less attention has been given to its implementation than to any other part of the Charter. This has become glaringly obvious during the Gulf crisis. The Security Council should be far better prepared to meet the next threat to the peace or act of aggression. There should be, among other things, far better analysis of how sanctions can be applied more effectively and what their impact is.

In case enforcement measures again become necessary, the Military Staff Committee of the Security Council should as soon as possible work out possible agreements both for the provision of forces under Article 43 of the Charter and for their strategic direction and command. The committee should be required to study and report on the extent to which the provision of forces under Article 43 is still a practical option in present conditions.

The Charter envisaged the gradual conversion of the existing military setup into a worldwide system of common and collective security. The Military Staff Committee was also supposed to advise and assist the Security Council on "the regulation of armaments, and possible disarmament" (Article 47.1), a task closely related to the basic task of conversion. The Military Staff Committee should now be instructed to embark on an extensive study of how to convert modern military technology, including the various means of deterrence, to the needs of an international system of common security in this highly unstable world.

The present composition of the Military Staff Committee is, to some extent, an anachronism. To achieve wider confidence and cooperation, the Security Council should invite other strategically and politically important states to take part in the MSC's planning and work. . . .

Future Effectiveness

The key to the effectiveness of a future system of peace and security will be the combination and interaction of all these elements. Thus the Security Council should be informed as a basis for action by a stronger UN mechanism that will keep a constant watch on threats to peace. (The tensions between Iraq and Kuwait in the summer of 1990 were exactly the kind of situation, in a sensitive part of the world, that should have been closely monitored by the Security Council.)

The Council should meet regularly to survey the condition of international peace and security throughout the world, not, as in the past, just to deal with particular crises or to react to a conflict which has already started. It should provide the center for a new process of continuous political and diplomatic consultation on the problems of regional and global security. Regional arrangements should be more closely linked to the Security Council, and should in principle (according to Article 52 of the Charter) be the first resort in regional disputes.

The aim in the future should be to prevent as many disputes as possible from degenerating into actual violence. In places where the danger of conflict is imminent, such as parts of the Middle East today, the Council should deploy peace-keeping missions to report on the situation and try to contain it while diplomatic and pacific solutions are being sought. If these peace-keeping efforts fail, they should have the function of a tripwire which would set in motion, after suitable warnings, preplanned enforcement action under Chapter VII of the Charter. The actual existence, through the preparatory work of the Security Council and the MSC, of a system of enforcement or deterrence, and a general agreement that in certain prescribed circumstances enforcement measures would come into play, would provide a strong deterrent to aggression.

Such a system would be a giant step forward from the belated and improvised efforts to which the United Nations has so far been limited. It entails a new degree of commitment to the United Nations. It can only work if governments, especially the more powerful ones, genuinely accept, and cooperate in, the basic aim of converting both the present diplomatic and the military system into a system of common security. Governments, if they want the United Nations to be respected and taken seriously, will also have to respect its decisions and make decisions that can if necessary be enforced. Such changes in attitude would be the best practical test of a commitment to a "new world order."

The War Proves the Need for a U.S. Military Presence in the Gulf

David O. Smith

About the Author: *David O. Smith is a U.S. Army lieutenant colonel and a senior fellow at the U.S. State Department's Institute Center for the Study of Foreign Affairs in Arlington, Virginia. He previously commanded a battalion in South Korea.*

Operation Desert Storm, the military campaign that liberated Kuwait, constitutes a watershed in Middle East politics comparable in magnitude to the founding of Israel in 1948. Political, social, and economic forces have been set into motion which will profoundly influence the region for decades. As leader of the 28-nation coalition victorious against Iraq, the United States will be viewed as responsible both for the success of military operations and for shaping the postwar environment. A common danger of war is that military victory often contains the seeds of future conflict. Therefore, the United States must implement a postwar regional strategy recognizing that the existing security structure has been shattered beyond repair, and that it must be replaced with a sturdier framework capable of protecting the Gulf from future threats.

Every US President since World War II has recognized vital American interests in the Gulf, but we have tended to rely on others to protect those interests while concentrating ourselves on the global Soviet threat. Until its 1971 withdrawal

David O. Smith, "The Postwar Gulf: Return to Twin Pillars?" *Parameters,* Summer 1991. Reprinted with permission.

from "east of Suez," Britain policed the area. Afterward, to fill the resulting void, the Nixon Administration promulgated what came to be known as the "Twin Pillar" policy of relying on two moderate regional states—Iran and Saudi Arabia—to do the job. The Iranian Revolution effectively eliminated the stronger pillar, Iran; now, a decade later, the Iraqi invasion demonstrated the inability of the other, Saudi Arabia, to deter regional aggression. The present postwar flux affords an opportunity to implement a new regional strategy firmly rooted in emerging political reality and based on two sturdier pillars: an increased US military presence in the Gulf and the creation of a new regional balance of power.

"A common danger of war is that military victory often contains the seeds of future conflict."

The Gulf War has highlighted several lessons relevant to formulating a new regional strategy. The first concerns the singular importance of US political and military leadership in what President Bush has characterized as the New World Order. The post-Cold War era may be multipolar in an economic sense, but the response to Iraq's invasion of Kuwait demonstrated that the United States was the only power with the will and the ability to project massive military power rapidly to the Gulf. The key to building and sustaining the global consensus to confront Iraqi aggression was American resolve, patience, and, above all, the willingness to exercise political leadership. Militarily, we can expect a number of our allies to maintain large, modern military establishments, but none will have more than a modest capability to deploy forces rapidly and sustain them. Therefore, while some allies may contribute small forces and others may assist financially, the United States must be expected to bear the burden of political and military leadership should deterrence fail once again.

The second lesson concerns the role of the Soviet Union. Despite its economic and domestic political problems, we can expect the Soviet Union to remain a military superpower with the will and ability to project strong military forces anywhere in Asia well into the foreseeable future. However, despite occasional expressions of Soviet concern over the extent of US bombing of Iraq, the Cold War may be essentially over in the Gulf. Mikhail Gorbachev seems to have decided very early in this crisis that Soviet economic and security interests dictated support for US policy objectives. Accordingly, he abandoned his patron-client relationship with Iraq, revised his regional security assistance policy, and voiced support for US diplomacy and military actions, including war. The Bush-Gorbachev summit in Helsinki in September 1990 further suggested that an opportunity may now exist to achieve a true commonality of superpower interests in other areas as well.

"What goes on in the Gulf affects not only us but all members of the interdependent global economy."

Similarly surprising has been the positive role played by the United Nations. In the first international crisis of the post-Cold War era, this formerly moribund organization demonstrated that it was no longer hostage to superpower politics or radical rhetoric. Faced with a clear-cut case of aggression, and not hamstrung by Soviet vetoes in the Security Council, it acted quickly and decisively to throw a mantle of legitimacy over US actions. Given the glowing success of the war, the UN can be expected to be a prominent diplomatic player in any future crisis.

Finally, the always fragile Arab consensus on regional issues has been weakened severely, if not destroyed altogether. Although nearly every Arab state opposed the Iraqi invasion of Kuwait, many of them believed that the subsequent internationalization of what they saw as a purely intra-

Arab dispute was worse. The prolonged bombing campaign against Iraq seemed to heighten such sentiments. Those who oppose future US policy in the region will be able to exacerbate this split in three ways: first, by inciting poorer Arab states to unite against the wealthy Gulf monarchies which, they will maintain, have sold out to the West in a frenzied effort to retain their undeserved oil wealth; second, by portraying Operations Desert Shield and Desert Storm as American neo-colonial interventions at Israeli behest; and third, by linking the crisis to the Palestine issue. All three themes already resonate strongly in the Arab world. Even states that support us now may find themselves constrained in the future by their domestic popular opinion.

Not all the lessons are new; some already known have been reinforced. For example, despite the massive Reagan military buildup, Operation Desert Shield demonstrated graphically that the United States still has insufficient strategic air and sea lift to move forces quickly to the Gulf. Because of this, the bulk of the ground forces initially deployed—airborne and light infantry—were not properly equipped to confront a well-armed regional opponent. The first American units in Saudi Arabia were at great risk from Iraqi armor and mechanized forces for several weeks until the first heavy units arrived from the continental United States. Also relearned was the lesson of the 1973 and 1979 oil crises—that what goes on in the Gulf affects not only us but all members of the interdependent global economy. Even in the unlikely event that we substantially reduce our oil imports, either through conservation or by embracing alternative energy strategies, our economic health and that of the rest of the world will likely remain tied directly to Gulf oil production well into the next century.

Things We Have Yet to Learn

Having learned this much, there is still much we need to know. The first major question mark is Israel. How can we insulate our commitment to Israel from the relationship we seek to build with moderate Arab states? Our past relationship was based in large measure on the perception that Israel would be a strategic asset in a global confrontation with the Soviet Union. In the post-Cold War era, this may no longer be a relevant consideration. As the Gulf War amply illustrated, Israel will continue to be a minor hindrance at best, a major impediment at worst, to closer relations with the Arab world. Of course, if Israel is provoked into taking unilateral military action against an Arab state, any regional framework we seek to build may quickly come apart.

"The exact nature of the future Iraqi threat is only speculative."

A second major question is what role the Western allies and Japan will play in the postwar Gulf. In the war itself, with the exception of Britain and France, they played relatively minor military roles, though the financial contributions pledged by Japan and Germany are quite substantial. Should the allies prove unwilling to shoulder what the American people perceive to be a fair share of the burden or prove reluctant to become fully engaged in the region, a strong potential will exist for strains in other, perhaps more vital, aspects of the alliance.

Next, how will we finance our future strategy? The war diverted attention from what may well be our most important long-term security interest—the economic health of the nation. As President Bush has already observed in another context, we may have more will than wallet. We have already forgiven a $7 billion military debt for Egypt. Although we have not yet done the same for Israel, we can expect continued pressure to do so. The final monetary cost of Desert Storm appears to be in the neighborhood of $70 billion, possibly less. If the wealthy Gulf states and our allies fail to pay a reasonable share of this staggering financial burden, the budget may become the chief obstacle to building a viable regional framework regardless of the risk to vital national interests.

Will we be constrained by membership in international organizations in the future? In the past, the UN and other international organizations have been little more than forums for public diplomacy. However, the UN has played a positive role in this crisis and we have stressed repeatedly the importance we attach to compliance with its resolutions. In so doing, we may have created a precedent that could tie our hands in the future. With the Gulf War now behind us, we will be under intense pressure in the UN from Arab members of the international coalition to resolve the issue of Palestine. There might also be resolutions concerning other issues which, if we choose to ignore them, could rekindle Cold War passions, provoke alliance controversy, or create domestic discontent.

Finally, why did deterrence fail for Kuwait and succeed for Saudi Arabia? From a military standpoint, there was little reason for the Iraqi army to halt at the Saudi border. We must carefully examine both our pre-crisis diplomacy and deterrent responses. While it's clear that Saddam Hussein made an error of the first magnitude, we must find out why he was not deterred. The last thing we need is a witch hunt over "Who lost Kuwait?" However, past errors of either omission or commission must be analyzed to ensure that future aggressors do not again misperceive our regional commitment.

Long-term Interests and Threats

To be successful, a regional strategy must be based upon correctly identified interests and a realistic threat assessment. Our interests in the Gulf in the next decade generally will remain unchanged and can be summarized as threefold: Western access to a reliable source of oil; overall stability in the region and particularly within the moderate Arab states; and security for Israel. Historically, our greatest challenge has been to reconcile the contradiction between the first two objectives and the last while maintaining our credibility in the region. This will be no easier in the postwar environment where four major threats will continue to exist. Of these, two are direct military threats while two are longer-term political threats.

Iraq. The exact nature of the future Iraqi threat is only speculative. Will Saddam Hussein continue to survive? Will he be able to eventually reconstitute his military capability? Will he regain a nuclear weapons capability? We have certainly diminished his position in the Arab world and swept away much of his potential to attack the legitimacy of the Gulf states, support terrorism, threaten Israel, or intimidate OPEC [Organization of Petroleum Exporting Countries]. Yet Saddam remains on the Middle East stage. And even his fall from rule would not necessarily clarify Iraq's future role. An irredentist successor state might well seek revenge and redressment of perceived wrongs, and, as a minimum, retain the ability to commit terrorist acts.

"Our future [military] presence will be dictated by the . . . threat which the Gulf monarchies perceive."

Iran. Though weakened militarily and economically by eight years of war, Iran may pose the greater long-term threat. It has gained much from the Gulf War. Having received unexpectedly from Saddam a favorable war settlement, and benefiting economically from the upward fluctuation in oil prices, Iran may recover much faster than anticipated and seek to regain a dominant position in the Gulf. Iran also may have the capability to develop a nuclear and chemical arsenal within a decade.

The Palestinian Problem and Israel. This issue will dominate the postwar Gulf political agenda. Our habitual tendency has been to put Palestinian and Gulf problems into separate compartments and act as if they are not related. Arabs make no such distinction. Most fail to see the difference between Iraqi aggression in Kuwait, which we condemned and confronted, and what they perceive as Israeli aggression against the Palestinian

people, which we continue to excuse or ignore. A cardinal tenet of US policy in the prelude to Desert Storm was to deny any such linkage. Now, however, the pressure from other parties in the international coalition to deal with it more forthrightly will be enormous. Successful long-term regional political and military cooperation with the Gulf Arab states may well be held hostage to positive movement on this issue.

Instability in the Arab Monarchies. We cannot yet gauge the long-term political and social impact on the Arab world of the massive Desert Shield deployment and the use of US military force against Iraq. Resentment in certain sectors of the population of these states can be expected to persist and be susceptible to Iraqi or Iranian manipulation, particularly if our postwar military presence is intrusive or perceived as inordinately large for the threat. While the Gulf monarchies are at risk in the longer term, Jordan, though not a coalition member, is especially vulnerable now. Hitherto a staunchly moderate regime, King Hussein's actions have already resulted in reduced remittances from his expatriate workers in the Gulf and a cut-off of economic aid from Saudi Arabia and Kuwait. His survival may depend on a much closer accommodation with the political aspirations of Jordan's Palestinian majority, which appears to remain even now pro-Saddam, and on distancing himself from US objectives in the region. In formulating policy for dealing with King Hussein, we should remember that fallen moderate Arab regimes tend to be replaced by more radical successors hostile to Western policies.

Postwar Political Framework

Our postwar regional strategy must therefore be designed to offset the political vulnerabilities of the Gulf states while deterring military threats to the region. We must forestall further development of weapons of mass destruction in the region, fully engage our allies in regional security matters, and resolve those issues which have in the past greatly complicated relations with Arab states. These goals can be accomplished first by continuing an embargo on arms, spares, and high-technology exports as well as trade and credit restrictions pending Iraqi acceptance of international controls on nuclear and chemical technology. This measure eventually could be expanded to include other states which do not adhere to adequate international inspection and controls. Next, we should encourage NATO [North Atlantic Treaty Organization] to address the need to undertake out-of-area missions when necessary to protect vital alliance interests such as access to Gulf oil. Even if this is not possible, allies such as Germany and Japan can do more within their constitutional limits—for example, building and maintaining dedicated sealift, contributing to regional development initiatives, or providing in-transit support for US forces in future contingencies. The Gulf monarchies should be encouraged to set up a regional "Marshall Plan" for poorer Arab states.

Palestinian Issues

Above all, we must make a genuine, concerted effort to resolve Palestinian and West Bank issues. Failure to do so may, in the long term, destroy the political foundation necessary to build a stable regional framework. If we believe that our interests in the Gulf are truly vital, we must summon the political will to persuade Israel to participate in a meaningful dialogue with representatives of the Palestinian people. We must likewise be sensitive to Israel's concern for security and be prepared to meet its anticipated defense requests. While expensive in the short term, it will be cheaper than another war. At best, Israel will continue to be the unknown variable in our regional calculus, and failure either to consult closely with its leaders or to address its perceived security needs may lead to unilateral action destructive of our policy objectives.

Undoubtedly the most controversial element of our postwar regional strategy will be the scope and nature of US military presence in the region. Historically the Gulf has been an "economy of force" region for the United States. First Britain, then the Shah, and finally the Saudis have borne the major military burden to safeguard our (and their) interests. Clearly this policy has failed, and an expanded US military presence—the first pillar of our postwar strategy—is the price we must pay. The Gulf monarchies traditionally have desired only a minimal US presence, and in the past we have been limited to a small naval presence in Bahrain, a relatively large training establishment in Saudi Arabia, periodic ship visits and aircraft deployments, shared surveillance and intelligence assets, and consultations during the periodic crises of the Iran-Iraq war. Our future presence will be dictated by the type and magnitude of the threat which the Gulf monarchies perceive. At the very minimum we should be able to make modest increases over past levels. With the Iraqi military devastated, our military task will be simplified greatly. Initiatives we should pursue are these:

• A CENTCOM [Central Command] Forward Headquarters in the Gulf, possibly within the present composition of our naval task force in Bahrain.

"Regional states can be expected to be more accommodating to an increased US presence."

• In conjunction with our allies, a greatly enhanced security assistance effort aimed at improving the military capability, training, and interoperability of the Gulf Cooperation Council states. Coupled with this could be a robust effort to expand maintenance facilities, operating bases, and warehouses for spare parts to facilitate future contingency deployments. Israel will of course view such steps as a security threat, and we must be prepared to increase its military capability proportionally.

• Periodic short-term deployments of US and other allied or Arab forces within the Gulf Cooperation Council Peninsula Shield or CENTCOM Bright Star framework to utilize the facilities and equipment referred to above.

If Iraq seeks to reconstitute an offensive military capability, regional states can be expected to be more accommodating to an increased US presence. We should then be prepared to do the above plus:

• Stock afloat in maritime pre-positioning ships sufficient equipment for at least two armor or mechanized brigades. One could be stationed in the Indian Ocean and the other in the Mediterranean to permit rapid reinforcement in the Gulf with both if necessary or reinforcement of Israel with one.

"The second pillar of our post-war strategy . . . should be a strategic partnership between Egypt and Saudi Arabia."

• Pre-position two heavy division sets of equipment in Italy or Turkey. Should this not be possible because of CFE [conventional forces in Europe] considerations, one set could be pre-positioned either in locations controlled by our allies—Djibouti or Akrotiri in Cyprus for example—and the other on the Arabian peninsula in a facility financed and maintained by the Saudis. The final possibility would be to pre-position them at East Coast ports in the United States, ready for immediate sea-loading.

• Seek Saudi approval and funding to construct a regional training center for Arab or GCC [Gulf Cooperation Council] forces to use in conjunction with Peninsula Shield exercises.

• Build motorized ground forces that have more anti-armor capability than light forces, and more and heavier artillery, but which are more rapidly deployable than heavy forces. As an absolute minimum, we must buy more strategic air and sea lift.

• Maintain a surface action group in the Gulf and a carrier group in the North Arabian Sea at all times, even at the risk of reductions elsewhere.

A number of other initiatives may be desirable from a military point of view, but may threaten the Gulf monarchies in the long term and therefore should *not* be considered. These include:

• Attempting to build a formal treaty organization along the lines of NATO or an invigorated CENTO [Central Treaty Organization]. This action would play directly to Iraq's accusation that the Gulf monarchies are illegitimate governments existing only at the sufferance of Western masters. We have already demonstrated forcefully our commitment to the Gulf states. An Arab collective security arrangement without a formal US role is far more palatable to regional public opinion.

• Forward-basing large air or ground forces on the peninsula. It is difficult to conceive of any Gulf state, with the possible exception of Kuwait, wishing to host a long-term US military presence in the future. And even if Kuwait would invite us, a US ground presence should be as small as possible consistent with the threat so as to avoid becoming the focus of regional animosity.

• Pre-positioning a massive amount of equipment on the peninsula. While useful in a Gulf contingency, it would be unavailable for an Israeli or non-Gulf contingency.

A New Regional Partnership

Since the foregoing will result in a US military presence in the region that remains more over-the-horizon than forward-based, the second element of our strategy should be a more credible regional military counterweight to Iran and Iraq. It should aim to deter future aggression and, should deterrence fail, be capable of defending long enough to allow US military force to be brought to bear. In the past, three states have comprised the Gulf balance: Iran, Iraq, and Saudi Arabia. Even though Iraq emerges tremendously weakened from the Gulf War, Saudi Arabia alone, with its vast territory to defend and small population, cannot cope with the worst-case threat, a combination of Iraq and Iran. Neither can the Gulf Cooperation Council states together match them; their population is too small, and their military forces are too weak, nonstandard, and likely to remain so for years.

The second pillar of our postwar strategy, therefore, should be a strategic partnership between Egypt and Saudi Arabia. This would be a symbiotic relationship with Saudi Arabia providing money, basing, and armaments, while Egypt provides the bulk of Arab military forces defending the peninsula. The GCC and other Islamic states could also participate in this defense, but Egypt with its large population and modern armed forces would play the paramount role. Since Egypt is a noncontiguous Arab state, such an arrangement would be preferable from the Saudi point of view to an increased US military presence in the Kingdom.

Why not Syria instead? Syria has played a positive role so far, both diplomatically and by its decision to commit troops to the multinational ground force in Saudi Arabia. We should be very cautious, however, about rushing headlong into a closer relationship with Syria. In many ways Hafez Assad is a mirror image of Saddam Hussein: a harborer of terrorists, a ruthless dictator who eschews democratic principles, and a human rights abuser. We should refrain from repeating the mistake we originally made with Iraq, adopting the cynical and expedient policy—so common to the region—of believing that the enemy of my enemy is my friend.

"In the post-Cold War era, the Gulf will be the most . . . dangerous point on the globe."

The benefits of the concept outlined above are many. It would permit a nearly complete withdrawal of US military forces from the Arabian peninsula and therefore would be far less costly in dollars, domestic public opinion, and re-gional consequences. The Gulf states could offset hostile propaganda by portraying the new regional balance of power as an Arab solution to an Arab problem. It would preserve US freedom of action and military flexibility in a contingency involving Israel; it would contribute to solving Egypt's massive economic problems; and, perhaps most important, its reliance on regional Arab states would be less destabilizing to the Gulf monarchies. . . .

To Conclude

None of these objectives will be gained easily. Maintaining peace and stability in the Gulf will be extremely problematic, but we can no longer afford the risk of relying on regional surrogates to protect vital US interests. At the same time, we must be sensitive to the realities of regional politics. We cannot impose either a military presence or a security framework; whatever structure we seek to build must have strong regional support. In the short term and from a strictly military standpoint, it may be more desirable to deter aggression in the Gulf ourselves than to depend on regional allies; however, to do so risks a long-term catastrophe if our presence serves only as a catalyst to topple the feudal monarchies which now own and protect the oil.

We do not necessarily need to aim for symmetry as we construct our pillars. We must be both patient and flexible. Ideally, a strong regional counterweight with only a relatively slight increase in US military presence would best serve our interests. However, should the regional pillar prove to be weak, we must then build a larger US deterrent capability in spite of the risks outlined above. In the post-Cold War era, the Gulf will be the most vulnerable, and therefore the most dangerous, point on the globe. Our future strategy must reflect this basic fact.

What Are the Military Lessons of the Persian Gulf War?

The War Does Not Prove the Need for a Strong Military

The War Does Not Prove the Need for a Strong Military
The War Proves the Need to End Arms Sales to the Middle East
The War Proves the Need to Seek Political Alternatives to Military Force
The War Proves Military Force Cannot Solve International Problems

The War Does Not Prove the Need for a Strong Military

Michael T. Klare

About the Author: *Michael T. Klare is an associate professor of peace and world-security studies of Hampshire College in Amherst, Massachusetts. He is the author of* American Arms Supermarket *and other books on U.S. military policy.*

Whatever the final outcome of events in the Persian Gulf, Operation Desert Storm has inaugurated a new paradigm for the U.S. military. While prior models for combat assumed that U.S. forces would fight the Warsaw Pact in Europe or guerrillas in Central America, this model envisions periodic battles with well-armed regional powers like Syria or Iraq. To distinguish these clashes from European "high-intensity combat" or a Central American "low-intensity war," Pentagon officials categorize them as "mid-intensity conflict" (MIC).

Like Desert Storm, future mid-intensity conflicts are likely to be rapid-paced and high-tech, entailing unrestrained use of the most sophisticated weapons. In essence, the United States will fight rising Third World powers by wielding weapons designed for a war with the Soviet Union.

Although there is no obvious candidate for the "next Iraq," the perceived risk of mid-intensity conflict will likely persist for years. Other Third World nations such as Syria, Pakistan, and Brazil harbor ambitions that could eventually lead to a collision with the United States, and some of these aspiring powers possess large and modern arsenals, including weapons of mass de-struction—chemical, nuclear, and biological munitions.

"There was a time when conflict in developing countries conjured up a vision of simple, low-tech warfare that would not require sophisticated weapons," Adm. Carlisle Trost told Congress early in 1990, but "that time has passed." Today, "developing countries are armed with 'First World' weapons. Proliferation of chemical weapons, growing access to nuclear weapons capability, and proliferation of cruise and ballistic missiles, submarines, and high-performance tactical aircraft mean that virtually any nation . . . can bring capable and deadly weapons to bear." This being the case, Trost argued, "the fundamental defense issue for the United States in the foreseeable future is to maintain a military posture that protects our interests and those of our allies from a diversity of regional threats."

A national security posture based on MIC has many obvious attractions for the U.S. military—not least of which is that it provides a rationale for retaining large high-tech forces in the Pentagon lineup. The Warsaw Pact's rapid dissolution leaves little need for such forces in Europe, and the Green Berets and other lightly armed infantry forces can conduct anti-narcotics and counterinsurgency operations in Latin America. By contrast, the threat posed by emerging Third World powers arouses much anxiety in Congress, so the Defense Department can justify retaining armored and mechanized units like those it is withdrawing from Europe.

"Operation Desert Storm has inaugurated a new paradigm for the U.S. military."

Adopting MIC as the central thrust in strategy has another major attraction: it invests the United States with a mission that appears worthy of a superpower. Knocking off Manuel Noriega can't compare as a cause to containing Soviet expansion over 40 years. With the Cold War's end,

Michael T. Klare, "Behind Desert Storm," *Technology Review,* May/June 1991. Reprinted with permission from *Technology Review,* © 1991.

many U.S. leaders perceived a "mission gap"—the lack of a military mission comparable in scale and importance to the policy of containment. And American leaders clearly crave such a mission: "We have to put a shingle outside our door saying 'Superpower Lives Here,' no matter what the Soviets do, even if they evacuate from Eastern Europe," Gen. Colin Powell of the Joint Chiefs of Staff has suggested.

No one embraces this global mission more enthusiastically than George Bush. When Iraq is vanquished, he declared in his 1991 State of the Union address, we "will have sent an enduring warning to any dictator or despot, present or future, who contemplates outlaw aggression." Yes, he said, America will bear a disproportionate share of the burden of delivering this message. But that is our calling: "Among the nations of the world, only the United States has had both the moral standing and the means to back it up. We are the only nation on earth that could assemble the forces of peace."

"As the 1980s ended, many military analysts began to worry about the threat posed by emerging Third World powers."

So the United States has again found a global mission. And while this new posture comes wrapped in moralistic finery, it carries important geopolitical advantages that U.S. policymakers have not ignored. Many of the regions most significant from an MIC perspective are sources of critical raw materials—especially oil—that unquestionably provide vast strategic benefits to those nations who possess or control them. As the self-appointed guardian of these critical assets, the United States can assume a dominant role in world affairs. By providing a capacity for military intervention, Sen. John McCain (R-Ariz.) suggested in 1990, U.S. forces "will remain the free world's insurance policy."

Nevertheless, the MIC posture carries pro-found dangers for the United States. This country will have to maintain a mammoth military establishment, keep military budgets at peak Cold War levels, and eliminate hope that a significant "peace dividend" can be garnered from the Cold War's end.

America's World Role

An MIC-dominated strategy also raises deep questions about America's world role. A belief in the efficacy of force to keep belligerent local regimes in check could diminish efforts to implement non-proliferation treaties and other such measures to curb the spread of sophisticated weapons. And although President Bush speaks frequently of a "new world order" based on cooperation, Washington's concomitant desire to serve as the preeminent superpower could result in interventions that will alienate friends and divide the world community.

For all its potential significance, the focus on mid-intensity warfare is recent. Throughout the 1980s, the proliferation of low-intensity conflict in Central America and a hypothetical high-intensity conflict in Europe dominated U.S. military planning. To prepare for combat in Europe, the nation spent billions of dollars on modernizing U.S. nuclear and non-nuclear forces. To fight low-intensity wars, the Pentagon conducted a huge buildup of "power-projection" forces that could be deployed around the world—aircraft carriers, amphibious assault groups, light infantry units, and special operations forces. Officials either considered mid-sized conflicts insignificant or assumed that their arsenal would suffice for any eventuality.

As the 1980s ended, many military analysts began to worry about the threat posed by emerging Third World powers. Although Pentagon rhetoric continued to stress the Warsaw Pact and guerrilla warfare, it was evident that a war in Europe was the least plausible contingency and that the lightly armed forces intended for low-intensity wars would be cut to ribbons by a heavily armed regional power.

These analysts began to reassess U.S. strategic

assumptions and press for a military doctrine for full-scale combat with emerging powers. Essential to their arguments is the view that MIC is not just a Central American military action writ large but a new ballgame. Compare, for instance, Operation Just Cause (the December 1989 invasion of Panama) and Operation Desert Storm. In Panama, the United States faced a glorified police force of perhaps 10,000 troops equipped with zero tanks and missiles and four propeller-driven planes. In response, Washington committed 25,000 infantry troops. In Iraq, the United States faced a battle-tested army of 1 million equipped with some 5,500 tanks, 700 modern planes, and a vast supply of guided missiles. To overpower this force, Washington deployed 500,000 combat troops backed by some 1,800 aircraft and 150 warships.

"Running through [U.S. military] documents is the conviction that . . . the United States alone can stop aggressive regional powers."

The clear distinction between the encounters reflects a growing differentiation between smaller and poorer Third World countries like Panama and a dozen or so regional powers that have acquired modern arsenals and the ability to produce nuclear or chemical munitions. That select group includes Argentina, Brazil, Egypt, India, Iran, Iraq, Israel, Pakistan, South Africa, Syria, Taiwan, Turkey, and the two Koreas. Such nations stand out as military leviathans in the Third World.

So long as the Soviet Union was seen as the overwhelming threat to U.S. security, policymakers largely ignored this potential threat. Indeed, to secure allies against the Soviet bloc, U.S. officials established formal or informal alliances with many of these countries—often providing them modern arms and war-making technology. And while the bulk of aid went to close allies like Is-

rael and South Korea, Washington provided sophisticated scientific and technical gear to Iraq and other Soviet allies in the hope of diminishing their dependence on Moscow.

Superpowers and the Third World

"In the years ahead, many lesser powers will have sizable arsenals," observed the influential Commission on Integrated Long-Term Strategy, a high-level study group formed by the Department of Defense and the National Security Council in 1988. Growing supplies of chemical weapons, ballistic missiles, and nuclear arms in the arsenals of these lesser powers, the commission warned, "will make it much riskier and more difficult for the superpowers to intervene in regional wars." As a result, "the U.S. ability to support its allies around the world will increasingly be called into question."

Because any impediment to intervening in the Third World was anathema to Henry Kissinger and the other former security officials who participated in this study, the commission called for significantly expanding America's capacity to conduct intensive, high-tech wars in non-NATO [North Atlantic Treaty Organization] areas. "We must diversify and strengthen our ability to bring discriminating, non-nuclear force to bear where needed in time to defeat aggression," the commission argued.

This perspective seems to have had a decisive influence on the strategic outlook of the new administration. Speaking at the Coast Guard Academy in May 1989, Bush introduced the theme in his first major address on national security. "The security challenges we face today do not come from the East alone. The emergence of regional powers is rapidly changing the strategic landscape." In response, we must both intensify efforts to curb the spread of advanced weapons, and, if necessary, "we must check the aggressive ambitions of renegade regimes."

The notion of well-armed renegades became a major theme in administration rhetoric especially after the collapse of communist regimes in Eastern Europe. Bush continued to stress the Soviet threat through 1989, but early in 1990, with the Warsaw Pact in disarray and the Soviet economy in shambles, he came to portray adversaries like Iraq and Syria as the preeminent threats to U.S. security.

Thus, the perception that mid-intensity engagements would dominate the current era was widespread among military leaders even before Iraq invaded Kuwait, and the Department of Defense had already begun reshaping its forces for the MIC mission. In January 1990, in his first annual report to Congress, Secretary of Defense Dick Cheney warned that the United States must "recognize the challenges beyond Europe that may place significant demands on our defense capabilities." The United States must adopt strategies "that rely more heavily on mobile, highly ready, well-equipped forces and solid power-projection capabilities."

"Central to the notion of winning quickly is the belief that every advantage in technology should be employed."

In the ensuing months, Cheney and his associates began converting this precept into formal policy. In February, he approved a top-secret Defense Policy Guidance statement for the years 1992-97 that orders the services to deemphasize the Soviet threat and prepare for clashes with Third World powers. Details remain secret, but reporters briefed on the document indicate that it calls for reducing U.S. forces in Europe and simultaneously creating a multi-division strike force based in the United States. This force would be intended for rapid deployment to Third World trouble spots—the sort of force that was rushed to the gulf after the invasion of Kuwait.

The chiefs of staff of the Army and Air Force, the chief of naval operations, and the commandant of the Marine Corps issued similar guidance to their cadres. Thence, in statements, documents, and position papers, senior military leaders hammered out a strategy for U.S. military forces in the 1990s—a doctrine built around the concept of mid-intensity conflict. While rough in places, this doctrine was well developed as of August 7, when President Bush ordered U.S. forces to prepare to confront Iraq.

A Post-Vietnam Doctrine

At the heart of MIC doctrine is a belief that protecting vital U.S. interests will inevitably provoke clashes with the emerging powers of the Third World. "Changes in Europe and the Soviet Union do not promise a tranquil world nor an end to threats to American interests around the globe," an Air Force "white paper" affirmed in June 1990. Of particular concern are regional powers "working their own agenda" and equipped with modern weapons. This combination of "emerging threats to national security interests [and the] proliferation of sophisticated weapons . . . presents new challenges for U.S. military forces," the Air Force noted. "*The likelihood that U.S. military forces will be called upon to defend U.S. interests in a lethal environment is high.*" (Emphasis added.)

Army chief of staff Gen. Carl Vuono had given the same outlook two months earlier: "The United States is a global power with vital interests that must be protected throughout an increasingly turbulent world. . . . The proliferation of military power in what is often called the 'Third World' presents a troubling picture." The United States "cannot ignore the expanding military power of these countries," he said, and thus "the Army must retain the capability to defeat potential threats wherever they occur." Ultimately, "*this could mean confronting a well-equipped army in the Third World.*" (Emphasis added.)

Running through the documents is the conviction that the United States—and the United States alone—can stop aggressive regional powers. "There will be no substitute for the leadership that the United States has provided to the West," Vuono affirmed in January 1990. "No other allied or friendly nation has, or is likely to develop, the necessary economic, political, and military power to replace the United States in that role."

This theme was given even more prominence after the outbreak of fighting in the Persian Gulf. "There is absolutely no substitute for decisive, clearheaded American leadership," former Assistant Secretary of Defense Richard Armitage told the *Washington Times* in August. "Those who so recently predicted America's imminent decline must now acknowledge that the United States alone possesses sufficient moral, economic, political, and military horsepower to jump-start and drive international efforts to curb international lawlessness."

"The Pentagon is . . . using the Persian Gulf conflict to test and refine even more advanced standoff missiles."

The MIC paradigm further holds that the United States should use decisive force when a hostile Third World power provokes it to battle. To prevail in these clashes, the Air Force noted two months before Iraq invaded Kuwait, "U.S. forces must be able to provide a rapid, tailored response with a capability to intervene against a well-equipped foe, hit hard, and terminate quickly."

It is apparent from such statements that MIC is consciously intended to overcome what U.S. military officers see as the mistakes of Vietnam. From their perspective, the principal error was to apply firepower gradually in the belief that the enemy would sue for peace at a low level of escalation, whereas, in fact, North Vietnam took advantage of "gradualism" to build up its own military. The new doctrine calls for the fast, concentrated firepower to destroy an enemy and crush its will to fight.

One can, of course, draw other lessons from Vietnam—for instance, lessons about the need for political clarity and cohesion when commit-

ting a democracy to a conflict abroad. It would be a mistake, moreover, to view Vietnam as a "limited" conflict, given the years of steady bombing by B-52s and other aircraft of North Vietnam, Laos, and Viet Cong positions in the South. Still, the aversion to gradualism governs the thinking of current Pentagon leaders. "Many of us here who are in this position now were in Vietnam, and that has left a profound impact on our feelings about how our nation ought to conduct its business," explains Gen. Charles Horner, commander of U.S. Air Force units in Saudi Arabia. "We think that war is a very serious business and it should not be dragged out in an effort to achieve some political objective."

Central to the notion of winning quickly is the belief that every advantage in technology should be employed to stun, cripple, and defeat an enemy. The army of the future "must be lethal," Gen. Vuono wrote in 1990. "Lethality results from quality soldiers . . . equipped with weapons that are superior to those of any adversary and available in numbers adequate to defeat potential enemies." Gen. Norman Schwarzkopf accentuated the point in September when discussing U.S. plans for a war with Iraq: "We would be using capabilities that are far more lethal, far more accurate, and far more effective than anything we've ever used."

The implication is clear: there will be no gradualism, no restraint on firepower. The president underlined the precept in November: "Should military action be required, this will not be another Vietnam; this will not be a protracted, drawn-out war. . . . If one American soldier has to go into battle, that soldier will have enough force behind him to win, and then get out as soon as possible."

A Military Wish List

From these maxims came the U.S. battle plan in the gulf, and from them is emerging the military doctrine of the 1990s. If fully adopted, this doctrine will have an enormous impact on U.S. foreign policy, inviting a military response to disagreements that will inevitably arise with emerging regional powers in the Third World. The MIC doctrine has already begun to govern the organization of U.S. forces and the development of hardware for the years ahead.

"Paying for the Persian Gulf conflict . . . will encumber the U.S. Treasury for years to come."

Although their plans had proceeded only slightly by August 2, senior officers had begun in early 1990 to hammer out a blueprint for combining arms and combat forces to serve U.S needs in future mid-intensity conflicts. Since August, while improvising in Saudi Arabia, Pentagon officials have stepped up development of an MIC master plan. Operation Desert Storm, combined with what is known of the Pentagon's still-incomplete plans for MIC, suggests what weapons and forces are likely to dominate the military's funding "wish list" for the 1990s.

• *Strategic mobility:* U.S. forces would have to arrive quickly and in enough strength to overcome formidable foes. This means possessing ships and aircraft to transport hundreds of thousands of troops to distant areas and sustain them there for months or years. "Even the most combat-ready land force cannot protect our national interests if it cannot deploy sufficient combat power to the fight in time to make a difference," Gen. Vuono observed in April 1990. Arguing that U.S. mobility is inadequate, he called for investing more in airlift and sealift equipment.

Faced with the task of rapidly moving troops to the gulf, the Defense Department has emphasized this point even more since August. While the Pentagon has generally scored well for the speed and efficiency of the deployment, a number of logistical shortcomings have appeared, particularly with moving heavy items like tanks. A likely beneficiary of this assessment is the C-17 long-range cargo plane, a frequent target for congressional budget-cutting in the past.

• *Mobile firepower:* Against well-equipped, pro-fessional armies, U.S. forces must wield potent weapons that can be moved quickly to a distant battle. In the view of many military experts, the highest priority is for a light tank-killing vehicle that can be air-lifted to where it is needed. To this end, the Marine Corps recently contracted with Cadillac Gage Textron to place a 105-millimeter assault gun on its Light Armored Vehicle; the Army is looking at similar options.

Other ground combat systems likely to figure prominently in a mid-intensity conflict are advanced missiles, rockets, and artillery. For destroying tanks, the Army is counting on the Advanced Antitank Weapons System-Medium (AAWSM), a shoulder-fired missile to replace the Dragon antitank missile, along with an upgraded version of the venerable TOW antitank missile. In development is the Kinetic Energy Missile, an anti-tank weapon that uses high speed to punch through heavy tank armor, and "smart" submunitions for antitank bombs and missiles.

• *Advanced tactical aircraft:* To back up ground forces, the Pentagon will continue to rely on tactical airpower. As in Operation Desert Storm, air support will be provided by late-model F-14s, F-15s, and F-16s, plus the F-117A stealth fighter.

New Weapons

Since combat planes must overcome modern fighters and air defense systems of Soviet or Western European manufacture, Air Force officials insist they will need a host of more capable aircraft. Thus the Pentagon is developing the Advanced Tactical Fighter (ATF). To select the final ATF design, the Air Force is financing two experimental models: the YF-22A (designed by a joint Lockheed-Boeing-General Dynamics team), and the YF-23A (designed by Northrop and McDonnell Douglas). The Air Force will soon select one of these designs for production in the late 1990s.

• *Advanced "standoff" missiles:* Given the growing effectiveness of enemy artillery and defenses, U.S. forces must be able to fire highly accurate missiles at air bases, command centers, military factories, tank formations, and so on from distant locations. Thus, the Pentagon is rushing forward with an assortment of standoff missiles—so called because they are launched from a helicopter, ship, or other platform well beyond the range of standard defenses. The weapons—many of which were first used in the gulf conflict—employ sensors and microcomputers to locate, track, and strike targets.

Heading the list of new and experimental standoff weapons are systems with names like Tomahawk, Paveway-III, SLAM, and HARM—names that are becoming familiar as a result of the gulf war. Most conspicuous so far is the Tomahawk sea-launched cruise missile (SLCM), a Navy weapon used for attacks on such targets as heavily defended command posts, factories, and nuclear reactors. Paveway-III, also known as the GBU-24, is a laser-guided bomb, apparently the one featured in some of the most dramatic TV footage of the war. The SLAM (Standoff Land-Attack Missile) has been used by carrier-based aircraft to attack Iraqi ports and other targets. The HARM (High-Speed Anti-Radiation Missile) rides the electronic signal given off by tracking radars to home in on and destroy air defense installations.

The Pentagon is also using the Persian Gulf conflict to test and refine even more advanced standoff missiles. Tacit Rainbow, now in final development, is a loitering cruise missile that, like HARM, homes in on electronic signals. The Air Force is developing an advanced cruise missile as well as AGM-130, a television-guided, rocket-powered bomb. And the Army is proceeding with development of its new Tactical Missile System (ATACMS) following its initial combat firings in the Persian Gulf.

Missile Defense

• *Anti-tactical ballistic missile systems:* Because potential adversaries have their own cruise and ballistic missiles—notably the Scud—Pentagon officials avidly seek defensive systems. Generically known as anti-tactical ballistic missiles (ATBMs), such weapons are often described as the tactical version of the Star Wars system proposed as a shield against Soviet ICBMs. Making the link explicit, the Strategic Defense Initiative Organization (SDIO) has given Israel $158 million to develop the Arrow, an experimental ATBM to intercept the Scud and other intermediate-range ballistic missiles. And while allied forces now rely on the Patriot missile, the SDIO is also developing a U.S. ATBM, the ERINT (Extended-Range Interceptor) for shooting down missiles more advanced than the Scud.

"It is essential to seek alternatives to intervening against aggressive regional powers."

• *Command, control, communications, and intelligence:* In high-tech battles, U.S. forces would need to rapidly detect enemy movements, communicate intelligence data, and pass battle orders through the chain of command. Thus, "C^{3}I" systems (for command, control, communications, and intelligence), are considered especially vital for fighting unfamiliar adversaries in unknown and forbidding terrain. By enabling commanders to initiate lightning offensives and counterattacks, C^{3}I will provide a critical advantage against superior numbers.

U.S. C^{3}I will rely on satellites more and more. Key links are the Defense Satellite Communications System and the NAVSTAR Global Positioning System, along with assorted spy satellites of the Central Intelligence Agency and the Defense Intelligence Agency. At least six such satellites were used to pinpoint the location of Iraqi missile sites and other key military installations for attacks by U.S. bombers.

For precise, immediate data on enemy movements, U.S. commanders have J-STARS (Joint Surveillance, Target Attack Radar System), a radar-equipped plane that locates tanks, helicopters, and low-flying aircraft. Also for spotting ground targets is the just-deployed LANTIRN (Low-Altitude Navigation and Targeting Infrared System for Night), an electronic pod attached to F-15 and F-16 fighters. Closer to the battle, troops might use small pilotless planes to fly over enemy formations and send back images.

- *"Middleweight" combat formations:* MIC operations will require new types of combat brigades and divisions. So far, all the Army has is heavy divisions for massive tank battles in Europe and light divisions for Third World police operations. As Desert Shield soon proved, neither is ideal for MIC—heavy divisions can't be moved quickly, and light divisions are essentially defenseless against armor and artillery. What is needed, in the view of many strategists, are middleweight forces tailored to mid-intensity conflict. Such forces, according to military analysts at the Center for Strategic and International Studies in Washington, D.C., should possess "the firepower, mobility, and survivability of heavy divisions, but [be] as rapidly deployable as light infantry divisions."

Although strategists are just beginning to think about the shape of these forces, presumably they will be bigger than the existing 10,000-troop light infantry divisions and have fewer tanks and armored fighting vehicles (AFVs) than existing armored and mechanized divisions. One proposal circulating in Pentagon corridors calls for mobile armored forces equipped with some combination of AFVs, light armored vehicles, and missile-armed HMMWVs (High Mobility Multipurpose Wheeled Vehicles, as the Army calls its jeep replacement).

Road Not Taken

Fully implementing this blueprint would undoubtedly provide the Pentagon with strong and versatile forces for mid-intensity conflicts. The unequivocal U.S. military success in the Persian Gulf appears to lend considerable legitimacy to this model. Moreover, many analysts will say this is unassailable confirmation of the lessons learned from the Vietnam War. And for some policymakers—certainly senior Bush Administration officials and many members of Congress—the threat from emerging powers justifies whatever investment is required for these capabilities.

Still, the costs will be staggering. Procuring new systems and replacing the equipment expended or destroyed in the Persian Gulf will cost hundreds of billions of dollars. The same billions of dollars might otherwise be available for reducing U.S. budget shortfalls. Investing so much technological talent in weapons also diminishes the resources available for developing civilian products that might enhance U.S. competitiveness.

"Israel, and possibly other friendly nations, will demand a cornucopia of new weapons to defend against their neighbors."

Paying for the Persian Gulf conflict and all the new weapons the Department of Defense seeks will encumber the U.S. Treasury for years to come, consuming resources desperately needed to rebuild cities, rehabilitate industries, and restore damaged ecosystems. These costs will not be shouldered with equal equanimity by all Americans. The drain on resources, which might erode the long-term health of the economy, could provoke widespread dissent and disorder.

An MIC-oriented military posture will also likely result in repeated U.S. involvement in conflicts of the gulf variety and could produce a tidal wave of anti-Americanism. Many Arab and Moslem communities—including those opposing Saddam Hussein—are dismayed by the massive destruction in Iraq and are likely to resent the United States and its allies for years to come. Rather than departing the gulf as soon as the fighting ends, U.S. troops are likely to remain indefinitely to maintain Mideast stability and protect pro-U.S. Arab governments against the internal unrest that could ensue from their complicity in destroying Iraq. What's more, Israel, and possibly other friendly nations, will demand a cornucopia of new weapons to defend against their neighbors, further boosting the U.S. military bill.

Added to all this is the risk of recurring involvement in Third World power struggles that could escalate into major conflagrations. If the premise of U.S. strategy is that we will probably come into conflict with emerging powers intent on "working their own agenda" (as the Air Force has put it), and that therefore we may wind up "confronting a well-equipped army in the Third World" (as suggested by Gen. Vuono), then just that is likely to happen—as it did four months after Vuono uttered his prophetic words.

This is not to say that the military offensive against Iraq was planned before the invasion of Kuwait, or that U.S. forces were spoiling for a fight. Rather, it is to suggest that an MIC-oriented doctrine encourages a militant response to overseas developments. That, in turn, could lead to quick military action.

Because U.S. forces are likely to be permanently stationed in remote and inhospitable locales, we can expect a decline in voluntary military enlistment—prompting vigorous calls from Congress and the Pentagon for reinstituting a draft. This, too, could provoke understandable opposition from those unfairly burdened by the steady erosian of domestic programs.

"The world community could have imposed rigorous non-proliferation measures on Iraq years earlier."

Finally, despite the president's fervent dreams for a new world order, a policy designed to demonstrate our superpower status while advancing America's geopolitical and economic interests is unlikely to result in international cooperation. Rather, it will produce a new *Pax Americana* in which U.S. soldiers are the principal instrument of regional stability. We may receive benefits from this policy, but we could also pay a heavy price in blood and in the continued decline of our cities, civilian industries, and natural environment.

Alternatives

Given this assessment, it is essential to seek alternatives to intervening against aggressive regional powers. To give just one example: the world community could have imposed rigorous non-proliferation measures on Iraq years earlier. Instead, from 1985 to the spring of 1990, presidents Reagan and Bush approved the sale to Iraq of $1.5 billion worth of advanced scientific gear, much of it of obvious military utility. They endorsed massive arms sales to Iraq by France, Brazil, and other Western nations as well. The Soviet Union and China also contributed to Baghdad's military potential, and many nations participated in the flow of advanced military technology to Iraq—including technology for developing nuclear and chemical weapons. Had these military transfers been blocked, Hussein would not command the massive arsenals now at his disposal and probably would have been much more wary of military adventurism.

Strengthened international efforts are needed to curb the spread of advanced military technology and discourage adventuristic potentates. Such measures may not be foolproof, but they provide a substitute to intervention and should be thoroughly tested before the United States commits itself to a strategy that will lead to recurring military involvement in regional conflicts around the world.

The War Proves the Need to End Arms Sales to the Middle East

Anthony Sampson

About the Author: *Anthony Sampson is the author of several books on international affairs, including* The Arms Bazaar, *a book on the international arms trade.*

It didn't take long. At the Singapore arms fair in March 1991 European arms manufacturers were boasting that their systems had been "combat-tested" in the gulf war. But this was a war that provided a caricature of the danger of the international arms trade: it was the Soviets and the West who sold Saddam Hussein the weapons which enabled him to build up the world's fourth biggest fighting force. Will the West ever stop selling weapons to potential foreign enemies?

Arms-control experts insist that we now have a unique chance—perhaps a last chance—to stop the reckless selling of weapons. There is a lesson in the history of the last 20 years in the Middle East. Ever since oil prices quadrupled in 1973, arms sellers have been turning oil into arms, with little sign of any consistent diplomatic objective on the part of the buyers. In the 1970s they equipped the Shah of Iran with the most sophisticated tanks and planes, supposedly to defend him against the Russians; but the shah's arsenal was then taken over by the Ayatollah Khomeini, who used it against Iraq. Saddam was armed to defend Iraq against Khomeini, and then turned his weapons against Kuwait and

Saudi Arabia. In the meantime the Saudis and Kuwaitis were spending billions of dollars on planes, tanks and high-tech systems which proved almost useless when they faced a real danger. In the words of Adnan Khashoggi, the arms middleman for the Saudis in the '70s: "The Arabs have learned that it's no good buying arms if you can't use them."

The gulf war has certainly produced some agonized rethinking among arms buyers. The Kuwaitis were humiliated by their defenselessness against the Iraqis. The Saudis made little effective use of their own costly weaponry. Soviet exports also suffered; the Scud missile was a clumsy instrument compared with the pinpoint-accurate Patriot and Tomahawk systems.

It is the effectiveness of computerized missiles that provides both a new danger and a new opportunity for arms control. Nearly every country in the Middle East now wants Patriots or their successors, and the United States is for the time being the only supplier. The French and the British are lagging behind the Americans in most sophisticated weaponry, and the Soviets are still more backward. The old excuse for selling weaponry—that if we don't, the Russians will—is now less persuasive.

"The Americans . . . have a clear opportunity, and responsibility, to take a new initiative to control arms sales."

The Americans thus have a clear opportunity, and responsibility, to take a new initiative to control arms sales. There are some hopeful signs. The Missile Technology Control Regime (MTCR), set up by seven nations in 1987, has already had some effect, particularly in stopping the Condor 2 missile which Iraq was developing with Argentina and Egypt. There is also a new opportunity to restrain competition among manufacturers in NATO [North Atlantic Treaty Organization] countries. If Europe had a more integrated arms industry, there would be less pressure to find markets abroad.

"The United States' missile superiority gives it the power to extend and enforce missile-technology control."

The most effective way to cut back on arms buying is to stop the flow of money financing it. The most startling fact about the arming of Iraq was the willingness of the West to provide not only the finances but also the subterranean channels, including the Italian Banca Nazionale del Lavoro, currently under investigation in Washington. And the most worrying development since the gulf war has been the decision of President George Bush to revive report credits for American arms companies, to enable them to compete more effectively with European arms exporters. The president's motive is clear:

"Maintenance of a viable U.S. defense is critical," as presidential spokesman Marlin Fitzwater explained it. It is an old justification. But in the past the providers of aid to the developing world, including the World Bank, have been far too little concerned with the linkage with arms. Now at last the World Bank and the IMF are insisting on restrictions on military spending—strongly backed by the former president of the World Bank, Robert McNamara. And donor countries, particularly Japan, are watching their clients' military aspirations more carefully.

Controlling arms sales today is mainly a question of political will. The five permanent members of the U.N. Security Council—the Russians, Americans, French, Chinese and British—between them sold 87 percent of the weapons bought by developing countries in the late 1980s. Having acted in unison over the gulf war, they should be able to confront the mistakes which helped to cause the war. The United Nations, with its enhanced prestige, should be able to monitor sales more effectively, perhaps with the help of a register of arms sales, as advocated by Norway's former prime minister Gro Brundtland. The United States' missile superiority gives it the power to extend and enforce missile-technology control. And the Japanese, who do not export weapons but who supply critical components, could become important participants in new plans for the control and monitoring of arms sales. It will not be easy to withstand national pressure to sell weapons for short-term economic advantage. But if we cannot face up to the danger and the opportunity this time, we may not have another chance.

The War Proves the Need to Seek Political Alternatives to Military Force

Harold H. Saunders

About the Author: *Harold H. Saunders is a visiting fellow at the Brookings Institution, a Washington, D.C. think tank that performs research and analysis on foreign and domestic policies and events. Saunders has served on the National Security Council Staff for thirteen years, and later held several posts in the U.S. State Department, including director of intelligence and research and assistant secretary for Near Eastern and South Asian affairs.*

This policy essay examines the concept of political settlement in the context of the crisis that began when Iraq invaded Kuwait on 2 August 1990. Its purpose is not to second-guess policymakers, although I do not hide my views. Its purpose is rather to reflect on the political alternatives to war and on the foundations for building peaceful relationships in our changing world.

Soviet and U.S. leaders and citizens have concluded that nuclear war is not a usable instrument of policy. However, the next crisis that occurs may pose the real possibility that nuclear or chemical weapons could be used. If war with weapons that are increasingly prevalent cannot be fought, we need to give at least as much attention to developing and honing political instruments for blocking or turning back aggression as we do to military planning.

Harold H. Saunders, "Political Settlement and the Gulf Crisis," *Mediterranean Quarterly,* Spring 1991. Reprinted with the permission of *Mediterranean Quarterly,* published by Duke University Press under the editorial direction of Mediterranean Affairs, Inc. Copyright © 1991, Mediterranean Affairs, Inc.

When Iraq invaded Kuwait, policymakers had a choice between two possible approaches. They became the focus of debate in the United States until war began on 16 January 1991.

The first option can be described initially by recounting what the United States and other key members of the United Nations did in August and September 1990, with some exceptions. That course included the initial action of the UN Security Council condemning Iraq's invasion and calling for Iraqi withdrawal. It further included the prompt deployment of military forces at the request of the government of Saudi Arabia to bolster its defenses against a continued Iraqi advance. This approach included UN-approved and militarily enforced economic sanctions against Iraq, blocking both imports and the exports on which most of Iraq's income depended. Underlying these actions was an intensive political effort to build a broad international coalition to support them, both militarily and financially.

Some Arab friends complained that the U.S. moved too quickly and foreclosed the possibility of an "Arab solution." President George Bush had to weigh the possibility that the world would be confronted with dislodging Iraqi forces not only from Kuwait but from the key oil centers of Saudi Arabia as well. He felt this was an unacceptable risk.

> ## "When Iraq invaded Kuwait, policymakers had a choice between two possible approaches."

Carried to its logical end, this approach would have differed from what was done—even before November—in several important respects. It would have established a longer time frame—twelve to twenty-four months—to allow time for economic and international pressures to take their full toll. It would have avoided deadlines. It would have maintained a more flexible military posture for developing an offensive military capability at any time without locking leaders into the self-imposed irreversibility of an early buildup.

Most relevant to the concept of political settlement, this approach would have given priority to creating a climate in which mediators could work by avoiding personalized confrontation and name-calling, while firmly opposing aggression. It would have addressed aggressively the political issues—such as the Israeli-Palestinian conflict—that Saddam Hussein exploited to strengthen his political constituency across the Arab world.

In short, not creating a short time frame and the self-constructed trap of irreversible military deployment and a deadline, and avoiding an atmosphere of personal confrontation, would have worked actively to develop a political climate in which third parties could try to work toward a political settlement.

The Bush Approach

The second approach—building from but altering the first—is what the United States eventually did. When by the end of October the combination of UN resolutions, economic sanctions, and military deployments did not produce a change in Iraqi policy, President Bush began to express personal impatience and announced a near doubling of American forces without rotation to create an offensive military option. Coupled with this move was U.S. pressure in the UN Security Council to pass a resolution in effect authorizing the use of military force to liberate Kuwait if Iraqi forces did not withdraw by 15 January 1991. The military buildup then focused on that deadline.

Although experience indicated that economic sanctions take time to work, this approach set a short time frame eventually defined by the 15 January deadline. It came to rely mainly on the threat of force to produce Iraqi withdrawal. Its attitude toward attempts at mediation and political settlement was voiced by the White House press spokesman before Iraqi for-

eign minister Tariq Aziz and U.S. Secretary of State James Baker met in Geneva in early January when he said: ". . . no negotiation, no compromises, no face-saving measures."

Although the war began on 16 January, analysis of these two approaches remained as relevant for the postwar as for the prewar period. Before the war, political settlement was posed as an alternative to war. In the wake of war, political settlement must be central to building the peace. While circumstances changed, the elements of the political agenda remained the same—although perhaps even more compelling.

"Old concepts such as state and power . . . do not fully explain what we see going on around us."

The purpose here is not to argue what would have worked. That debate is highly relevant, and there are cogent arguments on both sides. The purpose here is to use this experience to understand what the elements of a workable political option are. If the judgment in a future crisis is that the military option is too costly, policymakers must have a political alternative. In addition, how we deal with political settlement of the issues raised during this conflict will determine the course of the Middle East and the U.S. position there.

Explaining the U.S. interests in turning back Iraq's aggression, President Bush told the Congress and the American people that a principal U.S. interest lay in using the crisis to establish a new world order. The Congress in giving qualified support to the president's use of force stated that he must report to them that he had exhausted all peaceful means before launching military action.

It was not apparent that President Bush—working from World War II experience—clearly pictured how our profoundly changing world works when he spoke of the new world order. Nor was it clear, given the political instruments available to him, that he had indeed exhausted all peaceful means before going to war. Whether the war was just because it was truly a last resort is a subject for honest discussion and difference, but working effectively for political settlement in the postwar Middle East requires understanding the implications of how the world is changing.

Developing a new world order—and we need a better term—depends on a new understanding of our changing world. In a historic perspective, we are in the midst of a paradigm shift—a shift from explaining how nations relate as power politics to new ways of comprehending international relationships in a highly interdependent world.

In the traditional paradigm, leaders of nation-states amass economic and military power for pursuing objectively defined interests in zero-sum contests with other nation-states. They rely heavily on institutions of state. Power is defined in economic and military terms, and leaders use it either to achieve their objective by the use of force or to force others to concede what they want at the negotiating table. This is the worldview that seemed to underlie the course the U.S. took in 1990-91.

Today, old concepts such as state and power—as we have normally defined them—do not fully explain what we see going on around us. Familiar instruments of statecraft such as military force and negotiation do not reliably produce the results we expect of them.

International Relations

Relationships among nations are rather a political process of continuous interaction among significant elements of whole bodies politic. States still exist, and force is still used. Governments are authoritative representatives of bodies politic, but they are only one of many actors that influence the course of events. Change does not occur only through a linear progression of actions and reactions by governments. Change occurs in a continuously shifting kaleidoscope of interactions among many participants. Nations face problems that no one of them can deal with outside relationships with other nations. The in-

struments they use in building and sustaining those relationships are political because political environments must be changed before many problems can be dealt with.

Learning to work effectively in our changing world requires us not just to give lip service to the old notion that war is a last resort. We have to devote all creative energy to imagining new ways of producing results by political means, since military action is becoming intolerably costly.

"Saddam Hussein appealed to a vast population whose memory is shaped by a deep sense of foreign . . . abuse."

Before anyone dismisses that statement by reminding us that Saddam Hussein is a dictator so there is no Iraqi body politic, please remember one point. Saddam Hussein is a charismatic leader who appealed to a constituency of 100 million Arabs and a much larger number of Muslims. While President Bush seemed to be fighting with Hitler and World War II in his mind, Saddam Hussein's model seemed to be the Suez crisis of 1956, when the British and French fought an effective military campaign but Egyptian president Gamal Abdel Nasser gained control over the Suez Canal and gained broad Arab popular support. The United States refused to engage the political issues Saddam Hussein used to try to build Arab support.

Saddam Hussein appealed to a vast population whose memory is shaped by a deep sense of foreign domination and abuse. Theirs is a politics of resentment and anger. Many see their own governments as ruled by small families that amassed immense fortunes from oil production, invested that money in the Western—not in the Arab—world, and joined a U.S.-led military coalition that demolished and humiliated fellow Arabs and Muslims. They constitute a significant part of the bodies politic with whom future U.S.

relationships in the Middle East will rest.

The United States will not play an effective role in the world that is emerging if we do not recognize the realities that will shape that world. To begin setting the stage, two of those realities are described below.

Political Power

First: The nature of power and leadership are changing. If power is the ability to affect the course of events, then power will arise not only from military capability and economic capacity. Power will also arise from political ability to change political environments and to build, guide, and sustain coalitions and relationships necessary to accomplish tasks that no one nation can accomplish alone. Leadership will lie not in being number one but in being an effective first among equals.

In forging the international coalition to contain Iraqi aggression, U.S. leadership was essential. But sustaining that leadership in building the peace will require respect for the political objectives that coalition partners can support. Leaders must be able to fashion *common* purposes. What if others define objectives not only in terms of driving Iraq from Kuwait but in terms of building a more just Middle East and, for the first time, a relationship of equals between nations of that region and nations of the former imperialist world?

"Our interdependent world offers an array of political means for confronting aggression."

The new world that is emerging will place a greater value on *how* outcomes are produced than on the outcomes themselves, provided they are just. The reasons are realistic. In addition to needing a political alternative to nuclear, chemical, and biological weapons, we must also cope with the increasingly realistic prospect that the reactions of masses of people can destroy international relationships. The aim in this emerging world will be not just to block aggression but to block aggression in ways that do not inflict the costs of war on those opposing the aggression or on innocent pawns of a dictator's schemes. To do that will require developing a large array of neglected political tools.

When the first bomb dropped in the war to roll back Iraqi aggression, the hope of using the Gulf crisis of 1990-91 to establish a new world order was seriously undercut. The outcome reflects its achievement by the age-old tools of violence in what might be hoped to be the last of the twentieth-century wars against aggression. It will not have been achieved by political and therefore peaceful instruments; it will not have been achieved in ways even reflecting the experience of forty years of containment and Cold War. It will not have been achieved by policies that may be critical to global survival even before the twenty-first century.

Second: The real choice today is no longer between the poles of war and negotiation. Our interdependent world offers an array of political means for confronting aggression, resolving conflict, and generating change. In addition to learning that military force by itself does not produce only surgically defined results and is becoming prohibitively costly, we are also learning that negotiation and diplomacy alone do not initiate change. What President Bush called "diplomatic activity" in stating that the United States had exhausted all peaceful means is not the only or the primary instrument in the politics of international relationships. Until political leaders act in the political arena to change the political environment, diplomats and negotiators do not succeed.

Political options have largely been ignored—both more generally and in the choice of options following the Iraqi invasion of Kuwait. One could have imagined the Iraq-Kuwait crisis being wound down through a scenario of interacting political steps without a negotiated agreement. No one claims with certainty that it would have caused Iraq to withdraw; the point is that it was not earnestly tried.

When the war began, one could not imagine ending the conflict and building the peace without a political scenario. While war dashed the hope of resolving conflict peacefully, wars did not make moot talk of a political settlement. Without political vision and strategy, war had no point even in the old world order. Today's Europe was not built with weapons alone—but by men and women who said after a second world war: "Enough. There is a better way to conduct the affairs of humankind." Even in the Middle East, profound change has already come from a political process we called "the peace process"— a series of negotiations embedded in a larger political process. To argue for focusing on political settlement is to say that we must at least ask how we might build from those foundations.

The Concept of Political Settlement

Political settlement involves two main components. First is a picture of the settlement the parties could honorably live with. Second is a scenario of steps—a political process—for moving from a present situation toward that settlement.

Defining a settlement we could live with honorably begins with a discussion of *outer limits*. One way to begin the discussion is to offer the following principle: Iraq should not get anything in a political settlement that it could not have achieved peacefully. Aggression should in no way be rewarded. The one exception to this point is that no one can undo the damage and disruption that have been inflicted on Kuwait and the rest of the world; one can only rebuild.

There is both a practical and a moral dimension to the discussion. Is it possible to build barriers against future aggression peacefully? What is the moral justification of a war to destroy a nation's capability if it could be contained by peaceful means? Even if Iraq's nuclear or chemical programs have been set back will we not still need imaginative programs of international inspection? Is military attack the only option we will allow ourselves in preventing further spread of such weapons? Are we the ones to judge whose nuclear and chemical arsenals should be bombed?

One problem people have with this formula stems from the fact that it is in the nature of political settlement that everyone must be able to claim that he has achieved some important objective. Some react sharply: "Any appearance that Iraq has gained anything will undercut justice in the new world order—and will undercut the moral authority of the U.S." The response— again open to debate—is that unconditional surrender and punishment are possible options, but there are costs attached to them too. Some of those costs, if war is the instrument used to achieve the objective, are lives and treasure. Some are also costs in delayed progress toward the new world order, since one of its aims is to keep order and pursue justice by peaceful means. An aggressor can claim what he wants to claim; the world will make its own judgments about the price he paid.

"The causes as well as the symptoms of conflict must be addressed."

Developing the foundations for a political settlement starts with laying out an agenda of specific elements that must be dealt with in moving from conflict toward peace. Political exchanges during the crisis called the world's attention to a broad agenda in the Middle East. Before war began, it was possible to discuss a political scenario for dealing with that agenda as a possible alternative to war. After war began, it was necessary to discuss such a political scenario in the context of ending the war and launching another attempt to build a more just and lasting peace across the entire region. The substance of the agenda to be addressed might be sketched out under five points such as the following. *First: The territorial integrity, sovereignty, political independence, and national identity of every state in the Middle East must be respected.* The most immediate application of this point was total Iraqi withdrawal from Kuwait and restoration of the territorial integrity and sovereignty of Kuwait. The principle to be affirmed is that existing borders must be respected or be changed only through processes based upon genuine mutual consent. In the larger region, this suggests that Syria should not define a greater Syria and Israel should not define a greater Israel, to mention two other examples. (The Israeli-Palestinian case is dealt with below.)

Respect for national identity raises a less concrete issue. Within the context of restoring the territorial integrity and sovereignty of Kuwait, the nature of the government of Kuwait should be left for broadly based political processes involving the leaders and people of Kuwait to decide. The principle of self-determination should be applied. National identity reflects the total human experience of the people in the nation-state, and government must be responsive to who the people are and want to be.

This is a delicate issue in a region of traditional regimes. The purpose is not a mindless demand that monarchical governments suddenly be democratized; it is to suggest that orderly and productive change over time will depend on the ability of each people to reach into its own political experience to fashion a government responsive to its needs.

Second: Each state in the region has the right to live in peace with security against threats or acts of force. Security assurances must provide the most realistic guarantees possible against attack in all directions. A most obvious and immediate application of the point is the provision for a UN force on the Iraq-Kuwait border, as has existed on the Iran-Iraq border since the end in 1988 of the war between those two states.

Blocking Future Aggression

In addition to meeting pressing needs emerging from the Gulf war are concerns about blocking potential future aggression. The problem in the Middle East seems quite different from that in Europe during the Cold War. Whereas lines in Europe were sharply drawn between two blocs

threatening each other, the threat in the Middle East has tended to shift. Nowhere has that been clearer than in the Gulf: In the 1980s, Iraq was the threatening power and itself faced a possible threat of dismemberment by its neighbors. Who will be seen as the primary threat in the mid-1990s and later?

"The Gulf war focused attention on the larger political agenda of the entire region."

The problem of providing security guarantees in such a shifting situation has yet to be addressed seriously beyond the thought of trying to establish a new protective balance of power. In the early aftermath of the war, a continuation on a much smaller scale of some combination of the forces that fought Iraq might be an instrument for assuring that Iraq's other borders—with Iran, Saudi Arabia, Jordan, Syria, and Turkey—are not crossed in either direction. The Gulf Cooperation Council is another possible vehicle for marshalling a force. Any of this could be done under a UN umbrella. Beyond the early postwar situation, the challenge will be to establish a political authority for security forces that will be capable of shifting focus as the threat shifts.

Beyond the issues involved in securing borders is a complex of issues involving arms control in various forms. Basic are concerns among arms suppliers to find ways to limit the flow of so-called conventional arms to the Middle East, while respecting the needs of governments to defend their peoples. A corollary is the need to begin building understandings on limiting force levels into whatever peace agreements might emerge over time. Beyond this fundamental level are international efforts to limit the proliferation of chemical, biological, and nuclear weapons. Dealing with these problems involves, in part, the development and acceptance of far more intrusive inspection systems than previously known.

Third: As it is possible to move toward resolution of disputes, the underlying grievances, fears, and concerns as well as the concrete claims of each party must be considered thoughtfully and responsively. The causes as well as the symptoms of conflict must be addressed. The broadest possible approach must be taken to resolving disputes—not just by negotiating claims and counterclaims but by dealing with the issues that deeply divide people in the larger political arena. This is an argument for an organic, political approach rather than for the familiar, more mechanistic approach of bargaining over how to split the difference between conflicting claims. Such an approach is an essential foundation for developing political processes to change relationships in the region.

The Kuwait Invasion

Examples emerging from the agenda surrounding the Iraqi invasion of Kuwait included:

• Iraq stated that it needed two Kuwaiti islands to assure access to the sea. One could imagine the UN Security Council affirming Iraq's right to access to the sea and charging a UN peacekeeping force to assure that those islands not fall under the control of any party threatening that right.

• Iraq raised the question of the maldistribution of oil income in the Arab world. In doing so, Saddam Hussein attempted to exploit the genuine resentment of people in the Middle East who felt they had not shared in the benefits from oil production and who saw small ruling families investing oil profits in the Western industrialized countries rather than in the Middle East. Whether Saddam Hussein spoke out of conviction or from cynical motives, he tapped strong Arab feeling. In response, one could see bringing to fruition the initiative to create an Arab Bank for Reconstruction and Development funded by voluntary contributions from oil producers, including Iraq.

• Iraq expressed its resentment at Kuwait, in part, by charging that Kuwait had pumped oil from reserves that are rightfully Iraq's. Rather than dismissing that as a cynical claim, one could address that claim under the auspices of the World Court or an international commission to assure that any possible grievance is fairly heard.

"A political approach offers the possibility of actions not based mainly on firepower."

Fourth: All legitimate claims and debts must be settled by peaceful means in accordance with the United Nations Charter and in accordance with the principle that all serious grievances must be heard. Before Iraq invaded Kuwait, discussions dealt with repayment of Iraqi debts to Kuwait and Saudi Arabia incurred by Iraq to pay for its war with Iran. In addition to the legal merits of the case, mediators as well as the parties will need to take account in some way of the Iraqi feeling—however justified—that Iraq's prosecution of that war provided a shield defending the other Arab states of the Gulf against an aggressive Iran. In Iraqi eyes, that shield permitted other Arab oil producers to accumulate profits free from threat. The issues in a settlement even before the invasion of Kuwait might have been more political than financial.

Iraq's occupation of Kuwait added the complex issue of Kuwaiti claims for reparations to compensate for the destruction and looting of Kuwait. Closely related was the question of how long the embargo on Iraq's export of oil would be maintained after Iraq's military forces withdrew from Kuwait. It was conceivable to maintain that embargo for a period of time while other Arab oil producers continued to pump oil at high levels and, by some formula, donated a portion of their income to rebuilding Kuwait. They would, in effect, force Iraqi payment by channeling to Kuwait profits that Iraq might otherwise have received.

All of these issues need to be resolved—not just in financial negotiations but in a settlement broad enough to provide a foundation for gradually rebuilding some constructive relationship between Iraq and its neighbors. Another example from another part of the region is the difficult question of how to compensate Palestinian claims for property lost when they left their homes in 1948 while taking into account in some way Israeli claims for Jewish property lost as Jews felt forced to leave Arab countries at the same time. Again, debts need to be settled in ways that give each party a sense that its grievances have been heard and responded to. The calculation of what is fair might only be made in the context of shaping the relationship that aggrieved peoples were willing to try to build with each other, looking to the future.

"Printing the menu for a political settlement is not enough."

Fifth: New contexts for resolving regional conflicts must be created. During the 1990-91 crisis, Iraq called for resolution of the Israeli-Palestinian conflict in the context of ending the Iraqi occupation of Kuwait. Practicality argued in the eyes of many that the issues could not be formally linked because of their different characters and different time lines. At the same time, the fact was that the two situations became intertwined in many Arab minds—not always without reason. The issue became not so much whether the United States and its allies should agree to an international conference to deal with the Israeli-Palestinian conflict as a condition for Iraqi withdrawal from Kuwait. The issue was how to resume efforts to move toward an Israeli-Palestinian settlement begun long before Iraq invaded Kuwait in such a way as to contribute to a constructive political environment in the Middle East for dealing with that issue as well as a range of other important issues.

Discussion of this question gave rise to thinking about whether the traditional international conference for negotiation could provide the most fruitful context for the larger political task of changing relationships. That leads us to a larger discussion of the political process of moving toward more peaceful relationships.

A Larger Middle East Peace Process?

Printing the menu for a political settlement is not enough. Devising a scenario of political steps that could lead to changes in the situation is also essential to producing a political settlement.

In developing a scenario, one begins by analyzing the obstacles to moving toward a more desirable situation and then lays out a list of steps to remove or erode them. Next one looks at how those steps might interact. If one party could start with a small step, perhaps the other might respond with another, and so on. As those steps proceed, they change the political environment and the direction of events. The scenario never needs to be agreed on formally; it simply needs to produce action.

Whether or not to think about a scenario leading to a political settlement is a matter of choice. President Bush said in going to war that the United States had exhausted all diplomatic means—that Saddam Hussein had responded to no one. An alternative view would note that the United States helped create an atmosphere that blocked mediation—not one of containment, quarantine, and the possibility of dialogue. It was an atmosphere in which neither side could consider a political scenario.

Taking an alternative view, those who addressed the larger Middle East political agenda—either before or after the war—had a choice between two approaches. One was to take each of the issues and put it into its usual negotiating channel or diplomatic forum. The other approach was in addition to the first—not exclusive of it. This approach was to step back and bring the total complex of issues, negotiations, and diplomatic tracks into view and to try to understand their interactions in the larger political environment of the Middle East. The image was not so much of organist at the console with control over the playing of each note from the score, but of minds at work in the midst of a complex and murky situation—minds with a larger purpose and a full range of human and technical capacities for nudging the situation in a constructive direction step by step, dealing with the unforeseen and making mid-course corrections.

The Gulf war focused attention on the larger political agenda of the entire region. The challenge is to conceive a political process large enough to encompass that complex of disparate issues—a Middle East peace process. . . .

The suggestion here is to learn from these other experiences but to turn to one born in efforts to deal with conflict in the Middle East. The Arab-Israeli peace process became not just a series of negotiations but negotiations embedded in a larger political process. Troops disengaged following a war. Political relations were restored. Confidence-building measures between disengaging military forces were arranged to prevent another surprise attack. Mutually agreed measures for assuring compliance were put into place with little friction. Force limitations in certain areas were implemented. An oil embargo was ended. Joint economic commissions were formed. Disengagement agreements were superseded by a peace treaty. A sequence of negotiations was designed for bringing a Palestinian self-governing authority into being and then for shaping a long-term relationship among Israelis, Jordanians, and Palestinians. Attempts were made to relate global powers to the process. Peace was addressed both in its juridical and state-to-state forms and in the form of normalization of relations between peoples.

Increased Possibilities for Peace

The Arab-Israeli-Palestinian process remains uncompleted. Comparing thinking in 1971 about what is possible with thinking in 1991, one can hardly say that nothing has changed. Not as much changed as many had long ago hoped, but the possibilities for peaceful relationships have been enlarged. Even more important, the range of instruments available for changing relationships peacefully has been significantly expanded. Some of the new ways we have learned to think about peaceful resolution of conflict have been affirmed by what we have seen on the global stage.

In 1991 the challenge is to consider how in the wake of war the lessons of the Arab-Israeli peace process can be drawn on to build a larger peace process for the Middle East.

Those who oppose the course of political settlement argue that leaders who engage in lawless or even evil acts can only be confronted effectively with force. Indeed, anyone who has lived in the century of Stalin, Hitler, Pol Pot—and Saddam Hussein—knows tragically that there is evil in the world. The problem is that anyone who has lived in the nuclear age also knows that we are already in a world where some wars would destroy much of the world and so cannot be fought. We also foresee that more and more wars will very soon fall into that category.

"The Arab-Israeli-Palestinian process remains uncompleted."

The practical question is whether and how policymakers can devise ways of confronting lawless and evil acts effectively by using instruments that will not destroy what they are trying to preserve. We are not talking about what would be nice but about what will work to produce results we want at costs we are willing to pay. We are not talking about what is ideal but about what is realistic in a changing world. For many who are also concerned with the ethics of policy, a political approach offers the possibility of actions not based mainly on firepower but on the power that emerges from political relationships built on mutual consent and shared purposes.

The War Proves Military Force Cannot Solve International Problems

Katherine Boo

About the Author: *Katherine Boo is an editor of* The Washington Monthly, *a magazine of political analysis and public affairs that opposed the Persian Gulf War.*

The headless corpse of one of the [Iraqi] soldiers was on its back a short distance from the truck. Another body was wedged inside the engine compartment. Two more lay face up in the bed of the truck, their feet sticking grotesquely over the side.

—The Washington Post, March 3, 1991

As the ground war drew neatly to its close, it seemed the most perverse and peripheral of causes: a group of left-leaning reporters suing the government in federal court to open Dover Air Force Base to the public. They wanted us to see the body bags roll in. And in that desire, they were remarkably alone.

Just after the luckless plaintiffs lost the first court battle, the war in the Gulf was over, the issue all but moot. Yet, in a way, no episode better signifies the distance we've come since Vietnam. This time, we have no time for body bags. We're in love with the splendid little war.

A few years ago, prophets like John Mueller and Francis Fukuyama proclaimed that, in the future, first-world nations, obsessed with their

economies, would recoil from costly warfare. Today, Americans bear witness to the other extreme: a renewed faith in the power of the short, clean war—restorative, affordable, and preferably a few thousand zip codes away. It's a faith at least as old as Agamemnon, who believed Priam's city would be captured in a day. Yet as American troops suit up to become the world's policemen, historical parallels should make us a little nervous. "Fool," chided Homer, "who knew nothing of all the things Zeus planned to accomplish." From Troy to Tel Aviv, Berlin to Baghdad, leaders' faith in short, clean wars has wreaked havoc on humanity. In the midst of the revelry, one couldn't help remember the spate of brisk little conflicts—the Schleswig-Holstein, the Franco-Prussian, the Seven Weeks War—that convinced Kaiser Wilhelm that every modern war might be resolved in a matter of months. So in August 1914, he waved his troops off at Berlin Station, promising they'd be home before the autumn leaves fell.

I guess we could probably [estimate Iraqi casualties] if we really tried hard, but we don't really have that requirement.

—Brig. General Richard Neal, February 9, 1991

"In the wake of Vietnam, the courting of public support for American warfare has become a virtual religion."

Politicians, particularly, have had a hard time resisting the appeal of clean and easy wars; you could stock a dissertation with hapless folks like the Alabama congressman who in 1861 volunteered his handkerchief to mop up all the blood that would be spilled for Confederate independence. Still, most leaders have been unable to forego the optimistic forecast, for obvious reason. Effective warmaking depends not just on military and administrative prowess, but on widespread public support, as Clausewitz pointed out two centuries ago. And clean wars are the easiest sell—a truth Saddam Hussein himself understands. He started his war against Iran by promising his people a brief, decisive blitzkrieg. By war's end eight years later, there were 200,000 fewer Iraqis to remember that empty promise.

In the wake of Vietnam, the courting of public support for American warfare has become a virtual religion—one that includes such odd rites as open letters from the president to campus newspapers, pleading just cause. "Media campaigns increasingly decide whether or not there will be a war and, if there is one, how long it will last," reports James Dunnigan's manual, *How To Make War*. "The 'will to fight' can be sold like cornflakes, and increasingly it is." That lesson was not lost on Bush.

It is now clear that the president was committed to war as early as October 1990. The critical question was how to market the idea to the American people. So, like the makers of Fords or antiperspirants, he had to establish the obsolescence of the existing product—diplomacy. In December, the president who had touted sanctions a few months earlier suddenly declared that he had never believed they would work.

"Smart wars—even fast ones—can be just as messy as dumb ones."

By January 16, when George Bush announced the air strike, five months of sanctions had evolved into an "endless diplomacy." We've "exhausted all reasonable efforts," Bush intoned. "Exhausted every means." Consumers demanded a change. "The world could wait no longer."

The antidote to all this restlessness was, of course, war, which is not a simple sell, especially when it involves the liberation of an emirate 7,000 miles away. Fortunately, Bush's agents in the military, press, and the White House had been doing the advance work for months, peddling victory at discount prices. "It will be quick,

massive, and decisive," declared Vice President Quayle in December 1990. And quick, it was understood, would mean clean—a fact conveyed in the constant bandying about of "clean sweep," "precision bombing," and "surgical strikes." As the war got under way, Lt. General Charles Horner, commander of the U.S. Air Force in the Gulf and architect of Desert Storm, promised "a very efficient military campaign." And even General Colin Powell grew uncharacteristically giddy. "First we'll cut off the Iraqi army, and then we'll kill it." Victory in two fell swoops.

Killing Human Beings

Of course, the Iraqi army was a "them," not an "it." But after the first few days of the Storm, you'd be forgiven for forgetting. Objects in crosshairs exploded. Tanks were "killed." Only rarely—as when an Iraqi conscript, while surrendering, recognized a Marine from his old Chicago neighborhood—did humanity seem to impinge. Ties to Chicago somehow gave value to one Iraqi's life. It seemed strange, then, as British soldiers later sifted through the wreckage, that they found with the Iraqi corpses, not springs and gears and sprockets, but packets of processed cheese and coffee cups painted with flowers.

War is a blunt instrument. While by the end we could boast of "only" 323 American dead, the words short and clean seemed a little absurd. The war lasted a mere 43 days; cleaning the debris from Kuwait, as estimated by bomb-defusers, will take 40 years. The environmental damage may never be reversed. "I tell you, if I have anything to say about it, we're never going to get into the body count business," said Norman Schwarzkopf early on; now we understand why. News reports tallied up to 150,000 Iraqi dead, thousands of them civilians, thousands more blown up in retreat. Pentagon officials, meanwhile, offered a more palatable summary of the Iraqi casualties: 2,085 tanks, 103 aircraft, 962 armored vehicles, 1,005 pieces of artillery.

I am glad there were so few [American] casualties, but I would have liked a little more resistance.

—Sergeant Edward Swanson of Houston, Texas

The revolting carnage shouldn't surprise us; quick wars tend to be as ugly as long ones, perhaps because we've learned how to wage them so well. What should surprise us, perhaps, is our consummate detachment from the human cost—a coolness that begins in the way leaders plan and talk about their wars.

To ascertain the profitability of a proposed military action, the Greeks consulted oracles; the Romans read the entrails of chickens. Americans have cleverer tools: hundred-million-dollar computers on which whole conflagrations can be mathematically modeled. Our military analysts can enter one of a dozen air-conditioned simulation centers across the country, type a complex series of variables into a computer, and stage a dress rehearsal of any given war, deriving precise estimates of weapons effectiveness, troop mobility, casualty counts, and combat duration. So insulating is this sort of systems analysis that as bombs slammed into Baghdad, George Bush could consult his analysts and calmly claim, "We are on schedule," as if warfare were a luncheon with a queen.

"Most countries facing an alien army put up more resistance than the allegedly fearsome Iraqis were able to muster."

Only once during the war did Pentagon officials willingly deviate from their hardware-only accounting of costs to the other side. On February 24, they allowed a select group of reporters to screen-test a videotape of Iraqis being mowed down by Apache helicopters. The reporters blanched. The officials shelved the film, sticking with the tank kills. Today, in some Pentagon cubbyhole, there's an image the rest if us will never have to see: a group of young men dropping their dinners and fleeing in panic, before Apache cannon fire rips them in half.

As the carnage on the highway out of Kuwait further attests, smart wars—even fast ones—can be just as messy as dumb ones. That contemporary paragon of the short war—the Six Day War of 1967—left so many Israelis dead that rabbis were called in to consecrate the parks of Tel Aviv as temporary graveyards. Six years later, the Israelis entered the Yom Kippur War poised for an equally swift victory. Swift it was. "At the canal I saw a company of [Israeli] tanks disappear in less than a minute," wrote General Ariel Sharon later. "An entire battalion was engulfed and destroyed before they had time to report that they were being hit." Thanks to the efficiency of portable antitank missiles, two weeks of fighting produced casualties of more than 20,000.

Military Bullying

Perhaps because they happen so often, with little lasting international effect, these deadly, high-speed Middle Eastern wars aren't exactly emblazoned on the American memory. It's easier for us to recall the swift successes in Grenada—or Panama, about which one U.S. general would later boast, "There were no lessons learned." Of course, Bush did learn a lesson there, one that a year later helped propel us into the Gulf: Military bullying gets results faster than wearisome diplomacy. The question is, what results? Though Panama lasted only 14 days, the effort to capture one man left perhaps 4,000 Panamanian civilians dead. (That's the official Panamanian figure; the U.S. still refuses to release its numbers.) As the American press cheered the incursion, D.C.'s Spanish-language El Latino visited the Panamanian capital, where more than 10,000 homeless people were crammed into U.S. army hangars, five to a cubicle roughly the size of a condominium bathroom. A year after that glorious success, *The New York Times* reports that Panamanian cocaine exports are as heavy as ever.

You're superhuman. You're invincible. You're rolling into battle, and nothing can touch you.
—Lieutenant Eric Drake of Wilsie, West Virginia

Twenty-five hundred years ago, Thucydides

described another democracy's swelling infatuation with war. A swift, decisive onslaught by the Athenian superpower against the "mixed rabble" of Sicily, Alcibiades declared, would make his people master of all Hellas. The Athenians were quickly convinced.

> All alike fell in love with the enterprise. The older men thought that they would either subdue the places against which they were to sail, or at all events, with so large a force, meet with no disaster; those in the prime of life felt a longing for foreign sights and spectacles, and had no doubt they should come safe home again; while the idea of the common people and the soldiery was to earn wages at the moment, and make conquests that would supply a never-ending fund of pay for the future. With this enthusiasm of the majority, the few that liked it not feared to appear unpatriotic by holding up their hands against it, and so kept quiet.

The Athenians got creamed.

"When we finally 'won' it, the Gulf War had cost us perhaps $30 billion and 91 lives."

"By God," exclaimed President Bush a week after the war, "we've kicked the Vietnam syndrome once and for all." It wasn't hard to miss the subtext: This victory has restored our faith in weaponry as the wisest political tool. Yet as we retool and replenish for further world policing, it's worth remembering that most countries facing an alien army put up more resistance than the allegedly fearsome Iraqis were able to muster. Nowhere are predictions of clean war more misleading than in what historians call "asymmetrical wars": wars between Davids and Goliaths. To the weaker, conflict is not a cool calculus of risk, expense, and expectation, but a fight for national pride in which restraint and compromise are not options. A century after the fact, no military historian can adequately explain how, in the first battle of the Zulu-British war, 1,500 highly trained English riflemen were slain by native warriors bearing spears.

A few years later, American soldiers faced their Zulus in the Philippines, a place where, after the "splendid little war" in Cuba, few U.S. leaders expected to do any fighting at all. The object, explained Colonel Frederick Funston, was simply to "sit on and hold down the little brown brothers for a few months" until the Filipinos decided they didn't want independence after all.

Four months into the conflict, a stunned General Arthur MacArthur warned the White House that victory would be anything but easy. How in the world, he demanded, could one combat "the united and apparently spontaneous action of several millions of people"? (MacArthur's grim report caused the Springfield, Illinois, *Republican* to marvel, "Why did all this 'truthtelling' become available only *after* the election?")

Virtually the same sound track played in Vietnam, where boys in pajamas somehow managed to kill 60,000 exquisitely armed American troops. We won in the Philippines; in Vietnam, we lost. In both places, we earned an animosity that still haunts us. Yet as bridges and buildings smoldered in the Baghdad suburbs, as limbless corpses poked up through the sand, Bush could claim with finality a day after the Gulf war ceasefire, "This war is now behind us."

We don't find the [dog] tags around the neck very often—they've been blown away.
—A British lance corporal on burial detail in Kuwait, March 3

In late January, a senior Iraqi official was asked by the BBC how it felt to be losing so badly. "We have already won," the official responded coolly, "because it wasn't a two-day war after all."

Victory in the Long Run

That assessment, of course, doesn't touch us. For if the history of war is written by the victor, so is the definition of winning. At about the same time, Charles Krauthammer could define the impending U.S. conquest in terms, not of the Middle East, but of ourselves—a national psychotherapeutic cure: "If the war in the Gulf ends the way it began—with a dazzling display of American technological superiority, individual grit, and, most unexpectedly for Saddam, national resolve—we will no longer speak of post-Vietnam America. A new, post-Gulf America will emerge, its self-image, sense of history, even its political discourse transformed."

"Palestinians gathered on the rooftops of the West Bank, cheering the Scud missiles."

But as we revel in our psychic kill, it's worth considering the 12th-century Normans who, self-image enhanced by their easy conquest of England, planned a brisk overrun of the farmers and peasants of Ireland. Almost 900 years later, Irish bombs explode in Victoria Station.

If history has anything to teach us about war, it's that we should be wary of the term "clean victory," skeptical of mantras about "kicking ass."

Victory, as the Israelis learned in Lebanon, may be just another word for *bellum interruptum*. When we finally "won" it, the Gulf war had cost us perhaps $30 billion and 91 lives. For the Iraqis, the casualties may be more than a thousand times higher. Yet true victory—political stability, respect for human rights, democratic leadership, even stable oil prices—is no more assured in the Middle East, a region with more conventional weapons than all of NATO [North Atlantic Treaty Organization], than it was before we dropped 10 times the tonnage of Hiroshima on the Gulf.

In late February 1991, Palestinians gathered on the rooftops of the West Bank, cheering the Scud missiles as they arced toward Tel Aviv. A week later, Shiite fundamentalists stirred in Basra, armed by their Iranian brethren. Could it be that this new war, like the old ones, suggests another meaning for the Greeks' winged victory—something neither fleet nor transcendent? A promise, rather, that hovers just out of our grasp.

Chapter 4:

What Were the Consequences of the Persian Gulf War?

Preface

The 1991 Persian Gulf War had devastating consequences for Iraq, Kuwait, and other countries in the Middle East. Thousands of people were killed and millions of people were displaced during the Iraqi occupation of Kuwait, the war against Iraq, and the post-war civil conflict within Iraq. In addition, the war had profound environmental and political consequences for the region.

In Kuwait, the number of people Iraq took prisoner, tortured, and killed during its seven-month occupation is estimated to be in the thousands. Weeks after the liberation of Kuwait, more than 2,000 Kuwaitis were still missing. Another 1.6 million Kuwaitis fled to other countries. Many of these refugees lost their jobs, homes, and life savings.

The Persian Gulf War also had enormous human costs for Iraq. The U.S. Defense Intelligence Agency estimates that 100,000 Iraqi soldiers were killed during the war. An estimated 300,000 people, including 15,000 civilians, were injured.

Much of Iraq's human suffering resulted from the Allied bombing campaign. Bombs not only destroyed obvious military targets such as Iraqi army positions and missile sites, but also Iraq's infrastructure, including roads, hospitals,

power plants, water utilities, and irrigation systems. The destruction of these facilities made it nearly impossible for Iraq to provide for its population. Thousands of Iraqis were unable to receive necessary medical attention after the war. Military analyst William M. Arkin estimated that 74,000 to 101,000 Iraqi civilians perished from disease, malnutrition, and other causes attributable to the conflict. Thousands of others remained homeless and hungry.

Following the war, civil unrest broke out among Iraq's ethnic and religious groups, causing further human suffering. Shiite Muslims in the south and Kurds in the north of Iraq revolted against Saddam Hussein. Although the U.S. and other countries hoped a weakened Saddam would be overthrown, he managed to crush all of the rebellions. The number of people killed during these internal uprisings is unknown, but is believed to be in the thousands. Many groups were driven from the land, including more than one million Kurdish and Shiite refugees, who were forced to flee to neighboring Turkey and Iran.

In addition to human losses, both Iraq and Kuwait suffered much environmental damage. Egyptian geologist Farouk El-Baz estimates that a quarter of Kuwait's land mass was disrupted by bombings, movements of military vehicles, and the making of trenches and antitank barriers. The environmental devastation in the region was compounded by the destruction of Kuwait's main source of income—its oil wells. During its retreat, Iraq set more than five hundred Kuwaiti oil wells on fire. Months after the conflict was over, hundreds of wells were still burning, darkening the skies over Kuwait and consuming millions of barrels of oil a day. In addition, an estimated 63 million gallons of oil were spilled in the Persian Gulf by Iraqi actions and Allied bombings. Frank Barnaby, former director of the Stockholm International Peace Research Institute, called the conflict "the most environmentally destructive in history."

The Iraqi invasion of Kuwait and the resulting war also had dramatic political consequences, especially for the Arab world. For decades prior to the war, many Arabs in the Middle East had espoused Arab unity and denounced Western influences. But the Persian Gulf War divided Arab opinion and weakened these long-held beliefs. Most Arab governments supported Kuwait against Iraq. Some Arab governments also supported U.S. involvement in the conflict, while others were vehemently opposed. Finally, some nations, including Egypt and Saudi Arabia, fought alongside Western soldiers against Iraq. Middle East analyst Adel Malek writes that because of the war, "the traditional Arab order of old has been totally and irreparably shattered."

Whether the political stability of Arab nations and the decline of pan-Arab ideologies will continue after the war remains to be seen. *Washington Post* journalist Glenn Frankel writes that many divisions and sources of conflict within the Arab world remain. He concludes that the war has produced new wounds, fissures, and perceived betrayals that will haunt the Middle East for years to come. Deep divisions have been exposed within the Arab world between rich and poor, weak and strong, radicals and traditionalists—and between unelected governments and their own restless populations.

The Persian Gulf War is the latest in a long series of Middle Eastern conflicts. Evaluating its consequences may shed light on ways to achieve peace in the region. The viewpoints in this chapter cover these issues.

The War's Consequences Were Positive

Paul Starr

About the Author: *Paul Starr is a professor of sociology at Princeton University in Princeton, New Jersey. He is co-editor of* The American Prospect, *a journal of liberal opinion.*

Even before the jubilation in Kuwait City died down—indeed, even before the Gulf War ended in a decisive allied victory—many who warned that the war would go badly were warning that the war's aftermath would go badly. That is a safe prediction. No one has ever won a nickel betting on peace and harmony in the Middle East or gained a reputation for political clairvoyance by predicting that a war in the region would end its ancient conflicts.

But for all the postwar uncertainties, there ought to be no remaining doubt that the Gulf War was worth fighting and winning. In liberating Kuwait, we blocked the attempted murder of a country. In defeating Iraq, we averted the danger that an aggressive, militarist regime, hostile to liberty, might have continued to accumulate oil wealth, transform it into yet greater military force, intimidate and take over other nations in the region, and then—as it acquired nuclear weapons—reach a threshold of virtually impregnable power.

Preventing that concentration of self-reinforcing financial and military power in the hands of Saddam Hussein was the central, legitimate, national interest not just of the United States, but of the many other countries who joined us in the coalition. On that basis alone, the war was justi-fied, and our victory in it genuinely a victory for international security.

Yet the indirect effects of the war are also likely—with some notable exceptions—to be largely positive. The magnitude of Iraq's defeat may well cause another regional power to hesitate before undertaking aggression against a neighbor. I am not suggesting that the war will fulfill the Wilsonian hopes that President Bush has evoked in his talk of a "new world order." The Gulf War is no deterrent to aggression by one of the major powers, and it may lead another Iraq one day to believe it can avoid the fate of Saddam in Kuwait if only it has a better air force and nuclear weapons. Obscure conflicts in areas remote from the Middle East oilfields or other vital international interests are unlikely to mobilize world attention, much less an effective military response.

All the same, the war serves as a reaffirmation of the sovereignty of small nations and the elementary principles of international law for which Saddam showed contempt. Strict enforcement of those principles is unlikely. But the better they are observed, the safer are people everywhere. And the more strongly we affirm such principles, the more we create moral expectations that we will abide by them ourselves.

> **"The magnitude of Iraq's defeat may well cause another regional power to hesitate before undertaking aggression."**

Some who opposed the war, or at least the ground campaign, warned that our casualties would be so high that, instead of deterring aggression, the war would deter future counter-measures against aggression. This fear proved to be baseless. Had we gotten bogged down in a long and inconclusive stalemate, there would have been little deterrent value to our deployment of troops to the Gulf. But because we emerged victorious and with minimal losses, the

Paul Starr, "Collateral Gains," *The America Prospect,* Spring 1991. Reprinted with permission.

effort appears reproducible and, therefore, less likely in need of being reproduced.

Throughout the war, critics raised the specter of repercussions in the Arab street. This was, of course, one of the fears on which Saddam was counting; the excitement of Arab passions was partly his motivation for hurling Scuds into Israel and trying to cast the war in religious and ethnic terms. The effort did not succeed. Yet many of the war's critics in America were only too ready to accept Saddam's definition of the conflict as Arabs versus the West, even with Egypt, Saudi Arabia, and Syria as partners in the coalition.

"The defeat diminishes Iraq both as an ideological symbol and as a direct, political sponsor of violence."

The scenes of euphoria from the streets of Kuwait City after the liberation were perhaps the best answer to those concerned about the emotions that a war might release. And the mounting evidence of Iraqi atrocities against Kuwaitis—entirely in line with Saddam's record as a serial killer of his own citizens—are the best answer to the Baathist regime's claims to represent the forces of Arab brotherhood. The unequivocal defeat of Iraq and the discrediting of its moral claims provide a healthy antidote to whatever illusions some in the Arab world may have harbored, not just about Saddam, but about other "strong" leaders raised on revolutionary violence and bent on war.

So it is by no means clear whether America's role in defeating Iraq will stir stronger passions against us, strengthen radical pan-Arabism, and undermine moderate governments. Defeat has its disenchantments; none of the bluster from Baghdad in the days after the collapse of its armies could hide the disaster that Saddam brought upon his nation. The defeat diminishes Iraq both as an ideological symbol and as a direct, political sponsor of violence. Along with di-minished Soviet influence in the region, the war creates a new structure of power likely to have a positive impact in promoting moderate forces in Arab states.

War and Sanctions

Some may nonetheless still think that the war was unjustified because sanctions would have succeeded. In the congressional debate in January 1991 on the war resolution, Senate Majority Leader George Mitchell asked pointedly how, if we went to war, we would ever know whether the sanctions would have worked. But, in fact, from Saddam's refusal to give in after a month of dev-astating attacks from the air, we have a pretty good idea that he would not have yielded to a protracted economic embargo. The sanctions did not have the slightest promise, moreover, of reducing the scale of the Iraqi military. More than likely, had we continued with sanctions, American forces would have been sitting in the Gulf for a year and longer with no end in sight, suffering greater casualties from training acci-dents than they suffered in forty days of air strikes and one hundred hours of ground com-bat. . . .

For a generation Vietnam has been emblem-atic of the dangers of military intervention; many who opposed the war in the Gulf thought they were applying the lesson of Vietnam. But in fail-ing to recognize the crucial differences between the Vietnam and Gulf wars—the shared interna-tional interest in blocking Iraqi expansion; the clear moral foundations for the liberation of Kuwait; the weak hold of the Iraqi police state on the loyalty of its soldiers; and the practical advan-tages of fighting in a desert—the opponents of the Gulf War inadvertently ended up discrediting the lessons of Vietnam. If the next prospective in-tervention is more like Vietnam than Iraq, many Americans will simply not believe it. Or, if they do see a lesson, it may be the one conservatives draw—that we lost the Vietnam War because we reined in the military.

That was not, in fact, the cause for our defeat. We lost in Vietnam for one reason above all: we were fighting an indigenous movement that had its origins in anticolonialism and was able to mobilize nationalist passions against the United States. But during the Gulf War, some left-wing Democrats and many in the antiwar movement performed the parts conservatives might have assigned to them. By calling for premature cease-fires and limits on air and ground operations, they confirmed fears that if in power some day, they would so limit military operations as to prolong a war and increase our casualties.

> ## "Failing to recognize the crucial differences between the Vietnam and Gulf wars . . . discredit[ed] the lessons of Vietnam."

It is one thing to oppose entry into a war on moral grounds; that is an honorable view. But, once in a war, to oppose the military operations that will end it most quickly does not have the same moral or political weight. America does need a strong opposition to put every thought of foreign intervention to a hard test. Liberals will have the honor of remaining that opposition if in time of war we give the impression that our judgment is too colored by pacifist sentiment, too reflexively averse to the military, to be entrusted with ultimate responsibility for war and peace.

Faith in Government

If there is one positive domestic effect of the war, it is to restore some semblance of respect for the armed forces and, perhaps more generally, the capacities of government. Vietnam left behind an unhealthy distrust and disrespect for the soldiers and symbols of the United States. That distrust has been a deep infection in our public life. America's success in the Gulf War may encourage a dangerous overconfidence and overcompensation; it will probably undermine the effort to redefine national security in economic rather than military terms. But if in the aftermath of the war, we are more at peace with ourselves and have a renewed confidence in our capacities as a nation, we may be able to move on to put some fight into all those metaphorical wars—against drugs, against poverty, against economic decline—that we keep promising to win home.

The Persian Gulf War Devastated the Environment

John M. Miller

About the Author: *John M. Miller is coordinator of the International Clearinghouse on the Military and the Environment, an organization in Brooklyn, New York, that collects and distributes information on the environmental impact of military activities.*

"Unfortunately, war is not a clean business, everybody knows that," General H. Norman Schwarzkopf said at a briefing. The Gulf war is proving to be dirtier than most. While the full extent of Iraqi casualties is still unknown, they will continue to mount throughout the region as the environmental impacts unfold, long after the end of the fighting. Spilled and burning oil threatens Gulf ecosystems and human populations. Allied bombing of Iraq's chemical, nuclear and biological warfare facilities has released highly toxic materials.

In one of the worst oil spills ever, an estimated three to seven million barrels have poured into the Gulf from several sources. Initial estimates of the size of the spills were exaggerated and the exact amount spilled may never be known, but even at the lower estimate, the impact will be serious. While the US has accused Iraq of "environmental terrorism" for releasing oil from Kuwait's Sea Island Terminal, the Saudis estimate that at least a third of the spilled oil was the result of allied bombing. Iraqi oil storage and production facilities were systematically targeted by allied bombs, and much oil is probably still seeping into the ground, contaminating underground water sources.

John M. Miller, "Environmental Fallout from the Gulf War," *Fellowship*, April/May 1991. Reprinted with permission.

Efforts so far to clean up the spills have largely been ineffective and, as the oil spreads and disperses, will become even more so. Officials in Saudi Arabia and other Gulf countries are concentrating on protecting water desalination, oil-related, power and other industrial facilities from contamination. Ecologically sensitive areas are a low priority.

The Gulf, a shallow, enclosed sea with high salinity, is in many ways unique. Already burdened by natural and human-made factors, many species live at the limits of their tolerance. "The critical point is that this is already a highly stressed area. The wildlife that exists here is on the precipice as it is. They live in a harsh environment. They have adapted to the give and take of the Persian Gulf," says Thomas Miller of the Center for Marine Conservation in Washington, D.C. Richard Golob, publisher of a newsletter that monitors oil spills, says "that the most effective way to deal with an oil spill is try to contain and recover the spilled oil at the spill source. Here, the spill source is in a war zone, so it is impossible to mount a response there. As a result, you have to wait until the oil spreads out in a large slick. By that time, it is virtually impossible to contain or recover a significant amount of the spilled oil."

> ## "Spilled and burning oil threatens Gulf ecosystems and human populations."

Questions are being raised about what contingency plans, if any, existed to deal with a major spill. Iraq had used oil as a weapon during its war with Iran and allied strategy clearly included attacks on Iraq's oil infrastructure. A major spill should have been expected. Only when the size of the spill had become evident did equipment begin to pour into the region. A number of sensitive habitats are in the path of the oil, including vulnerable coral reefs, salt marshes, mud flats, seagrass beds and mangrove stands. These are important to a variety of species and a number of threatened species depend on them. Spawning areas critical to commercial fishing and shrimping could be damaged for years.

Around 600 oil wells in Kuwait were torched, most of them by the retreating Iraqi army. A deadly cloud of smoke, soot and chemicals from the burning oil caused massive local pollution in the form of highly toxic gases. An oily "black rain" was reported pouring on neighboring countries, and heavy smog was visible as far north as Turkey. Air pollution levels are reported to be seventeen times higher than normal in Teheran, threatening the health of the elderly, the very young and those with lung diseases.

Many scientists have predicted severe climatic changes as the wells continue to burn. Assessment of the damage to the wells is only beginning, but experienced oil firefighters say that it will take at least three years to extinguish all the wells. One possible impact is disruption of the critical summer monsoons over South Asia, a point confirmed by the British Meteorological Office. The result could be mass starvation. The largest number of casualties may be among poor Indians who had little or no stake in the war. Enough smoke could cause regional or global cooling, in essence a small-scale "nuclear winter." A study done for the Pentagon, while discounting any global impact, does say that the fires would be "a massive and unprecedented pollution event [that] could impact the ecology of the Persian Gulf and fall out on a wide swath across Southern Iran, Pakistan and Northern India." It argues that the smoke would not travel high enough to affect large areas of the Northern Hemisphere or cause a measurable temperature change, but, according to Dr. Carl Sagan and others, as the fires burn into the spring, solar radiation would loft the smoke high into the atmosphere, where it can not easily be rained out and may darken an area of unknown proportions.

Bombing Chemical Facilities

The destruction of nuclear, chemical and biological weapons facilities may also be causing major environmental damage. While the nerve gases are volatile and would have dissipated within hours or days, mustard gas can be quite persistent. Some nuclear materials can be poisonous for millennia. On January 23, 1991, General Colin L. Powell, chair of the Joint Chiefs of Staff, declared that Iraq's "two operating reactors . . . are both gone. They're down; they're finished." These were the first military attacks on operating reactors and risked extensive contamination if the radioactive fuel was still present at the time of the assault. General Schwarzkopf reported that thirty-one nuclear, biological and chemical facilities had been attacked and that over half of Iraq's facilities had been "severely damaged or totally destroyed."

"The destruction of nuclear, chemical and biological weapons facilities may also be causing major environmental damage."

Lt. Gen. Thomas Kelly, responding to a question at a briefing, was not so certain. Asked about any signs of contamination in Iraq around the nuclear or chemical facilities, he responded, "The initial assessment I saw was that, if there was any, it would be very localized. Precisely what it is, I don't know. I don't know the extent of it." Little information is available yet about what the consequences of these attacks have been. Dr. Matthew Meselson, an expert on chemical weapons and warfare at Harvard University, said that "if there was a temperature inversion and there was a big release [of nerve agent], and a slow wind driving that over a population center . . . you would kill everything from insects on up that doesn't have a gas mask." French, Czech, and German military sources have reported detecting traces of chemicals in the air near the Saudi/Iraq border. These releases were presumably the result of attacks on chemical weapons stockpiles. The incomplete burning of nerve agents and mustard gas would leave toxic byproducts, including dioxins, which persist in the environment.

General Stanislav V. Petrov, commander of the Soviet Union's chemical war troops, warned against targeting biological weapons storage sites: Destroying chemical weapons might not be that toxic beyond neighboring towns and villages; bombing biological weapon stockpiles could threaten neighboring countries. Unexploded chemical and other bombs will also cause problems years later. German mustard gas shells, lobbed during World War I, are still being discovered in Belgium. Unexploded conventional ordnance is still a major problem in Vietnam, sending numerous children and farmers to the hospital fifteen years after that war.

The massive movements of troops and armor have disrupted delicate desert ecosystems. Armies produce prodigious amounts of garbage, toxic waste and sewage. It is unlikely that much care has been taken on either side to insure that these are being disposed of properly. Traffic and digging have disturbed and destroyed plants and wildlife. John Cloudsley-Thompson, a London-based biologist and expert on the impact of war on deserts, says that "deserts are very fragile environments. Therefore, any movement—particularly of armored and heavy vehicles—cuts through the top surface and then erosion will set in and so the effects on the environment will last for centuries." With little water available, deserts can take years to recover. Tank tracks from World War II battles in North Africa are still visible.

"The massive movements of troops and armor have disrupted delicate desert ecosystems."

The United Nations Environmental Program (UNEP), after a long silence about the potential environmental impacts of a war, appealed in late January 1991 to the Gulf war combatants to provide information about the oil spills, and called for international action to prevent massive environmental damage to the Gulf. UNEP's executive director, Mostafa Tolba, expressed concern about the environmental impacts of releases from the destruction of nuclear, biological and chemical weapons facilities. "The environmental impacts of such releases could be as disastrous as the oil spill," he said.

"UNEP does not address the political components of the confrontation. Our business is the environment. And over that we are very worried." UNEP is now bringing together various governments and international agencies to coordinate a response to the environmental disaster in the Gulf.

While expressing concern for the Gulf environment, the Pentagon has moved to exempt itself from some US environmental laws at its military facilities at home. Early last August, the administration issued a wartime waiver of the National Environmental Policy Act (NEPA), that requires the Pentagon to study the environmental impact of its activities prior to implementation. NEPA has been used by groups to delay, modify or stop environmentally harmful activities. Activists are concerned that this precedent will be used to move ahead with controversial projects.

Energy Resources

The Gulf war was fought, in part, over control of energy resources. In response, many are calling for energy policies that stress the efficient use of energy and its conservation. Instead, the administration's recently proposed National Energy Strategy would *expand* oil drilling in environmentally sensitive areas, such as offshore and in wildlife refuges, and push for new nuclear power plants.

Ken Bossong, Director of Public Citizen's Critical Mass Energy Project in Washington, D.C, says that the administration's solutions will "expand our dependence on oil rather than trying to reduce it . . . ending up with a scenario where you are causing serious environmental damage, raising energy prices across the board and worsening problems of inflation. . . ." In the end, the energy strategy will, like George Bush's New World Order, lead us to future wars and greater environmental devastation.

The Persian Gulf War Had Enormous Human Costs

Eric Hooglund

About the Author: *Eric Hooglund is an editor of* Middle East Report, *a bimonthly magazine that analyzes events in the region.*

The human toll of the Persian Gulf war—as many as 100,000 deaths, five million displaced persons, and over $200 billion in property damage—ranks this conflict as the single most devastating event in the Middle East since World War I. At least three times as many people were killed during both the eight-year Iran-Iraq War and the 13-year civil war in Afghanistan, but the loss of life in those conflicts was spread over many years. In contrast, the majority of deaths in the most recent war occurred in a six-week period, commencing with the start of the American-led bombing campaign in mid-January 1991 and ending with the one-hundred-hour-long ground offensive in late February. A further period of massive bloodletting followed as the Iraqi army crushed popular rebellions in the south and north of the country.

It is also true that the continuing strife in Afghanistan has caused about five million people to flee their country, but their flight was spaced over years, allowing Iran and Pakistan, the principal host countries, to provide minimally adequate refugee assistance. In the Arabian Peninsula and Iraq, the confrontation uprooted millions of people in two large tidal waves, August-September 1990 and March-April 1991, catching both governments and international refugee relief agencies woefully unprepared to cope with even the most basic needs of the displaced populations.

Eric Hooglund, "The Other Face of War," *Middle East Report,* July/August 1991. Reprinted with permission of MERIP/*Middle East Report,* 1500 Massachusetts Ave. NW, #119, Washington, DC 20005.

Finally, the destruction of Iraq's and Kuwait's industrial and transport infrastructure was on a scale comparable to the devastation of central and eastern Europe during World War II. The consequences of this death, displacement and destruction, in a period of less than nine months, have seriously disrupted countries and societies throughout the Middle East and South Asia for years to come.

The one irreversible consequence of war is death. In this war there may never be an accurate account of the number of people who lost their lives. During the occupation of Kuwait reports circulated that the Iraqis had killed at least 4,000 civilians suspected of participating in the resistance movement. After Iraq was driven out of Kuwait, concerted efforts by human rights organizations to document the killings determined that the earlier estimates had been greatly exaggerated. Middle East Watch has ascertained that 300 of the 7,000-9,500 Kuwaitis taken out of Kuwait by Iraqi forces during the course of the occupation have been killed. This number may rise if some of the 2,000-2,500 persons still unaccounted for have in fact been killed. There are also reports of 28 civilian deaths in Kuwait during the allied bombing campaign; at least 30 foreign nationals murdered by Iraqi soldiers, apparently to cover up crimes such as robbery and rape; and up to 100 Iraqi soldiers assassinated by Kuwaiti resistance operatives.

> **"In this war there may never be an accurate account of the number of people who lost their lives."**

There are very precise statistics on the number of American casualties—144 killed and 479 wounded. Two deaths in Israel were directly attributable to Iraqi missile attacks; another dozen Israelis died of heart attacks or suffocated under their gas masks, while at least eight Palestinians died in the occupied territories because the Israeli-imposed curfew prevented them from getting medical treatment in time.

"The end of the war did not stop the killing."

There are no reliable data at all on Iraqi casualties. The United States, along with Saudi Arabia, assumed de facto responsibility for burying many of the Iraqi dead. The US unofficially estimates the number of Iraqi soldiers killed as a direct consequence of the air and ground war in January and February 1991 to be 75,000 to 105,000. Senior US military officials have said that 60,000 to 80,000 Iraqis died in bunkers during the air assaults and an additional 15,000 to 25,000 were killed during the ground offensive. (An Iraqi doctor working in the Basra area told relief workers in Iraq that he estimated between 60,000 and 70,000 Iraqi soldiers were killed in the withdrawal, and that half of these could have been saved had medical facilities and supplies been available.) Chairman of the Joint Chiefs of Staff General Colin Powell said that Washington does know how many Iraqi soldiers the allies buried, but so far he has declined to make that figure public. Iraq, whose commanders were cut off from their troops on the battlefield due to the effectiveness of the allies' bombing campaign, silently acquiesces in these US estimates.

The dead represent only part of the total casualties. Thousands more were maimed. There are no reliable estimates of the number wounded. The rule-of-thumb ratio of three wounded to each death, which dates back to World War I, suggests that as many as 300,000 Iraqis may have been wounded during the six-week campaign. Since the ceasefire, an unknown number of Iraqis and Kuwaitis have been killed and badly injured by mines and other unexploded ordnance.

The allied bombing campaign dropped over two million tons of explosive materials on Iraq and Kuwait. The US military's reference to civilian casualties as "collateral damage" camouflaged the impact of the air assaults on the noncombatant population. The Iraqi government has cited a figure of 7,000 civilians killed in the air raids, most of whom perished in Baghdad, Basra, Falluja and Nasiriyya. Subsequent eyewitness reports do suggest that civilian deaths as a direct result of bombing were probably in this range.

The end of the war did not stop the killing. During March 1991, thousands of Iraqi civilians and some troops and officials died in the unsuccessful popular uprisings against the government of Saddam Hussein. The estimates of those killed in southern Iraq start at 6,000. Reports of political killings in the south continued in late May 1991. The estimates of the number killed during the fighting in the northern Kurdish region are lower, beginning at 2,000. Since the fighting ended, however, an estimated 20,000, mostly children, have died from disease and exposure in the overcrowded, squalid refugee encampments along Iraq's borders with Iran and Turkey.

Altogether, at least 100,000 and possibly as many as 200,000 Iraqis, civilian and military, perished as a consequence of the US-led military campaign and subsequent civil strife.

Displacement Before the War

Once the dead have been buried, the survivors try to get on with their lives. This will be tremendously difficult for millions of people directly displaced as a result of the war.

In attempting to determine the number of refugees, one again encounters the problem of inadequate data. During the initial phase of the confrontation (August 2, 1990-January 17, 1991), more than 2.6 million persons were displaced. This figure includes at least 1.6 million refugees who fled Kuwait during the Iraqi occupation, as many as 700,000 Yemenis forced to leave Saudi Arabia, and as many as 400,000 foreign nationals, mostly Egyptians, who managed to leave Iraq before the allied bombing campaign began.

The first refugees came out of Kuwait. Iraq's occupation policies, combined with international financial measures such as freezing Kuwaiti assets, prompted 1.6 million people to flee the country. These refugees included Kuwaiti citizens and foreign nationals working there.

"Millions of people [were] directly displaced as a result of the war."

The experience of each group was very different. When Iraq invaded, the emirate's resident population of approximately 2 million included less than 700,000 citizens. The remaining 1.3 million—65 percent of the total—were expatriate workers and their dependents. An estimated 125,000 Kuwaitis had been outside the country on August 2, most on summer holidays, and chose not to return home. They were joined in exile by nearly 300,000 more fellow citizens. These 400,000 exiles obviously were generally spared the privations normally associated with refugee status, because the Kuwaiti government-in-exile provided monthly stipends of $1,000 to $4,000 per family. Following Kuwait's liberation, the extent of devastation compelled authorities to discourage these refugees from returning immediately, but by mid-May most basic services such as piped water, sewerage and electricity had been restored to some degree and restrictions on the refugees' return were lifted.

Kuwait's foreign nationals fared considerably worse, losing their jobs, their homes and their life savings. Some one million people, most of them breadwinners, saw their lives destroyed by Iraq's invasion. Their losses amounted to far more than simple personal misfortunes: hundreds of thousands of families throughout the Middle East and South Asia, financially dependent on the remittances sent home by these workers, were suddenly deprived of a primary source of income. There is no precise tally of the number of expatriates in Kuwait at the time of the invasion, since many foreign nationals were undocumented illegal aliens. Official government estimates for 1989 included 625,000 Arabs, 600,000 Asians, 60,000 Iranians, 3,000 Turks and 11,700 Westerners.

The largest group of expatriates was an estimated 350,000 Palestinians. After the Kuwaitis and Westerners, who held the most prestigious jobs, the Palestinians generally held the emirate's better paying, professional jobs. Most of the Palestinians sent regular remittances to families living in Jordan, Lebanon and the Israeli-occupied territories, many in refugee camps. About 200,000 Palestinian residents, including as many as 30,000 who were outside the country at the time of the invasion, fled Kuwait during August and September. The next largest group of Arab workers was an estimated 150,000 Egyptians, who sent home $500 million annually; approximately 90 percent of them fled Kuwait after the invasion. Together, Palestinians and Egyptians accounted for 80 percent of Arab expatriates in Kuwait. The remaining 125,000 Arabs included Jordanians, Lebanese, Yemenis, Moroccans, Sudanese, and Tunisians; at least 80,000 of these Arab nationals also fled.

Foreign Workers

Kuwait's 600,000 Asian workers principally came from the Indian subcontinent. The largest group were Sri Lankans, estimated at 200,000 and including several thousand Sri Lankan women who worked as maids in Kuwaiti homes. Other subcontinent expatriates included 172,000 Indians, 90,000 Pakistanis, and 78,000 Bangladeshis. From beyond the Indian subcontinent were an estimated 45,000 nationals from the Philippines, including several thousand women who worked as nurses in hospitals and maids in homes. The remaining 15,000 Asian workers were from Thailand, China, Indonesia, Taiwan, South Korea, Japan, Hong Kong, and Malaysia. More than 500,000 Asian workers fled Kuwait in the initial 10 weeks following the Iraqi invasion.

In addition, an estimated 100,000 to 150,000 Asians, 90 percent of them from the Indian subcontinent, were working in Iraq on August 2. The overwhelming majority of these workers were repatriated between August and November.

The remittances of Asian workers in Kuwait and Iraq not only sustained large families back home but also constituted an important source of hard currency for governments. The most severe impact was in Bangladesh. According to the United Nations Conference on Trade and Development (UNCTAD), 78,000 Bangladeshi workers in Kuwait lost an estimated $1.4 billion in wages, savings, and personal property when they fled. Thousands of destitute Bangladeshis were stranded at refugee camps in Jordan during August and September because Dacca said it did not have sufficient foreign currency to pay for their air fares home. Eventually Saudi Arabia footed the bill to fly them and thousands of other Asians home.

The flight of expatriate workers and their dependents included 65,000 who fled to Turkey (3,000 of them Turks), 60,000 to Syria (apparently including a large number of Iraqi deserters) and some 100,000 to Iran. The country most immediately affected was Jordan. Out of some 2.5 million foreign nationals in Kuwait and Iraq at the onset of the crisis, more than one million transited through Jordan. Most refugees were destitute and endured a grueling trek through the desert to the Iraq-Jordan border. Jordan was unprepared for such a flood of refugees, and received virtually no international assistance to deal with the problem. Thousands of Asians were stranded for weeks in the desert refugee camps where dehydration, diarrhea, scorpion bites and other ailments reached epidemic proportions. Eventually the Asians were repatriated. About 250,000 refugees, including at least 200,000 Palestinians, were citizens of Jordan and remained there. Their remittances, estimated at $400 million per year just from Kuwait, had been one of the country's major sources of income and foreign exchange.

Economic Blows

Dealing with the refugee crisis was only the beginning of Jordan's woes. As a result of developments related to the situation in the Gulf, Jordan suffered several devastating and simultaneous economic blows: (1) the loss of more than half its annual $800 million in remittances; (2) the task of absorbing thousands of working-age refugees when the country already was burdened with high unemployment; (3) the end of transit fees and the closure of export markets in Iraq, its primary trade partner, and Kuwait on account of UN-mandated sanctions, as well as in Saudi Arabia, which restricted Jordanian imports as a form of punishment for King Hussein's reluctance to join the anti-Iraq coalition; (4) the termination of low-priced oil imports from Iraq (because of the UN embargo) and Saudi Arabia (again, as a punishment); and (5) the retaliatory cut-off of $500 million in grants—supplying one-third of the state budget—from its main foreign benefactors, Kuwait and Saudi Arabia, who were displeased with Jordan's perceived sympathy for Saddam Hussein.

"The sheer number of refugees overwhelmed the ability of . . . relief agencies to care for them."

Jordan's economic difficulties spilled over into the Israeli-occupied territories. An unknown number of Palestinians possessing Jordanian passports actually resided in the West Bank. According to Palestinian economist Samir Hleileh, less than 1,000 Palestinian wage-earners from the Gulf were able to return to the occupied territories. The economies of the West Bank and the Gaza Strip heavily depended on remittances from the Gulf and wages earned by 120,000 workers who commuted daily to jobs in Israel. The intifada had already reduced remittances, estimated at $300-$500 million annually in 1987, to only $50 million per year by August 1990. Now even this amount was eliminated.

From the start of the crisis, Israel severely restricted the movement of Palestinian laborers who normally worked in Israel. During the six-week air war, when occupation authorities enforced curfews on the West Bank and Gaza an average of 21 hours per day, fewer than 20 percent of those Palestinians who had jobs in Israel were able to reach their workplaces on any given day, resulting in lost wages estimated at $2 million daily.

The displacement suffered by Palestinians is likely to continue. Those 150,000 who remained in Kuwait experienced along with Kuwaitis the brutality of the seven-month Iraqi occupation, and a few of them even participated in resistance activities. Nevertheless, the Kuwaiti mood has been directed not at showing appreciation to those who cooperated with the resistance but rather at harassing virtually all young Palestinians because a few did collaborate with the Iraqis. Amnesty International reported that as of early April 1991, of the some 600 Palestinians in prison, scores had been summarily executed, and at least 7 more had died as a result of torture during interrogation.

About 1.2 million foreign nationals, including one million Egyptians, were employed in Iraq when that country invaded and occupied Kuwait. The freezing of Iraq's assets and the international embargo on its trade led to widespread lay-offs that affected thousands of workers. After Cairo joined the coalition allied against Iraq, Egyptian workers were often harassed, prompting many of them to obtain the requisite visas to depart Iraq—a bureaucratic headache in the best of times. At least 350,000 Egyptians managed to get out of Iraq by mid-January. Including the estimated 135,000 Egyptian workers who returned from Kuwait, this meant approximately half a million extra workers looking for jobs in an Egyptian economy already plagued with high levels of unemployment, and the loss of hard currency remittances estimated at over $1 billion per year.

Economic Crises

Egypt was able to weather this economic crisis far better than Jordan or the countries of South Asia. Because it had joined what Jordanian commentator Rami Khoury calls the "cash register

coalition," Kuwait, Saudi Arabia, Qatar and the UAE [United Arab Emirates] rewarded Egypt financially by providing outright cash grants, forgiving more than $6 billion in accrued debts, and extending new low-interest loans. The US wrote off more than $7 billion in Egyptian military debt, and the Paris Club of Western creditor governments wrote off another $10 billion in late May. Nevertheless, the expatriate workers who returned home as refugees benefited little from this state to state largesse. The promise of hundreds of thousands of jobs for Egyptian workers in Saudi Arabia and Kuwait has yet to materialize.

"By one estimate, 80 percent of [Iraq's] electric power generating stations were destroyed."

At least 700,000 Yemeni nationals—out of more than a million living and working in Saudi Arabia—were forced out of the kingdom between September and December 1990 in retaliation for San'a's refusal to join the American-led coalition. Riyadh also cut off aid, loans, trade, and preferential oil shipments. Most of the Yemenis were able to take some savings and possessions with them, which helped cushion the blow of unexpected displacement. When personal savings are exhausted, these returned workers may become an economic burden and a source of political instability for the newly-unified country.

Thousands of other workers were also displaced. Virtually all of Kuwait's estimated 60,000 Iranian expatriates, most of them descendants of immigrants who had settled in Kuwait between 1935 and 1955, fled to Iran, leaving behind businesses and property worth up to $10 billion. According to private voluntary aid agencies, more than 35,000 Sudanese worked in Iraq and Kuwait before the crisis; they remitted an estimated $2.7 million per year back to one of Africa's most impoverished countries. According to Khartoum, Sudan also lost $3.4 billion in project loans because the Bashir regime failed to join the anti-Iraq coalition.

The difficult situation for the Gulf's expatriate work force pales in comparison to the refugee situation that developed after the war as a result of the unsuccessful uprisings in southern and northern Iraq. During March and April 1991, as many as 2.5 million Iraqis—14 percent of the country's total population—became refugees, fleeing from the soldiers of the Baghdad regime.

These uprisings seem to have begun spontaneously in the cities and towns of both southern and northern Iraq following the country's sudden and humiliating military defeat at the end of February. In the predominantly Shi'a south, hastily organized resistance groups attacked party headquarters, offices of the secret police and other symbols of repression in all the major cities, and destroyed many key government installations. Because Iraq's population is up to 55 percent Shi'a, senior US officials expressed concern that the Shi'a of southern Iraq were rebelling against the government in Baghdad because it was Sunni, and aimed to set up an Islamic republic allied to Iran. More likely, the people of southern Iraq disdained the Ba'th government, whose officials are of both Shi'a and Sunni origins, for the same reasons as their fellow Iraqis in the central and northern part of the country: they were tired of living in a police state, and weary from the two devastating wars this regime had started.

Southern Iraq

The people of southern Iraq felt emboldened after February 27 because they witnessed firsthand the disorganized retreat of the Iraqi military as the allied forces moved into the region. It is significant that the rebellion started in al-Zubair, a mainly Sunni town on the outskirts of Basra and the first town that soldiers retreating from Kuwait passed through. Many frustrated army conscripts were prepared to use their weapons against the government they believed was responsible for the debacle, and it was they who sparked the uprising. The rebels captured

virtually all cities and towns in the Tigris-Euphrates river valley, from al-Zubair north to Karbala, and took grisly reprisal against local Ba'th party functionaries, government officials, and suspected secret police informers. Their victories, however, were short-lived. Although Iraqi troops completely lacked the morale that would have enabled them to put up a fight against the well-organized and technologically superior American-led coalition, the regime's Republican Guard units did have considerable experience in suppressing poorly armed civilians and disgruntled draftees. Using brute force, they crushed the disturbances in the south within two weeks.

"Living conditions . . . throughout the Middle East . . . are deteriorating badly as a direct consequence of this war."

Estimates of the number killed during the civil strife in the south range around 6,000. Shi'as who participated in the rebellion claim the toll is as high as 100,000. Most nonpartisan observers accept the lower figure. Joost Hiltermann, an editor of *Middle East Report*, toured the cities of southern Iraq in April 1991, and concluded that "a few thousand deaths," rather than tens of thousands, likely occurred during the civil war in the south. Another 10,000 to 20,000 persons may have been wounded. Damage in residential neighborhoods was very extensive, especially in the cities of Najaf, Hilla, Karbala and Kufa, where entire blocks of houses were demolished.

As the army crushed the uprising, over 100,000 civilians fled. An estimated 40,000 sought refuge behind the American ceasefire lines in Iraq, and some 70,000 crossed into Iran. The status of these refugees, most of whom seem afraid to return to their homes, has been difficult to resolve. Both Iran and Saudi Arabia—but not Kuwait— have agreed to maintain refugee camps indefinitely.

The fighting in the Kurdish areas of the north

was far less intense than in the south. Kurdish casualties were considerably less than those in the south. The refugee situation that developed out of the collapse of the Kurdish rebellion, though, was horrendous. Iraq's Kurds number more than 3.5 million, more than 20 percent of Iraq's total population, and live predominantly in the mountainous north. They took over the main towns of Iraqi Kurdistan almost without a fight, and held them for two to three weeks. When the Iraqi army turned its attention from the south to the north at the end of March, the badly organized Kurdish fighters abandoned the towns for the mountains. Once the Kurdish population realized they were defenseless, they panicked and fled, literally overnight. In all, at least 2.3 million people, mostly Kurds but including some Iraqi Turkoman and Christian Chaldeans and Assyrians, headed towards the Iranian, Turkish, and Syrian borders. More than one million refugees had entered Iran by mid-April, and an estimated 450,000 more were camped on the roads leading to Iranian border checkpoints. At least 500,000 fled into Turkey, and an estimated 350,000 more were in the mountains overlooking the Iraqi-Turkish border.

"The war will result in deprivation for some 5 million children."

Why did so many Kurds flee? The one-word explanation of a Kurdish teacher—"Halabja"—may be the most plausible explanation. Halabja is the town in Iraqi Kurdistan that Saddam Hussein ordered bombed with chemical weapons in March 1988 during the final stages of the Iran-Iraq War. An estimated 5,000 Kurds, mostly women and children, died in that attack. This was followed five months later by the chemical bombardment of Kurdish guerrilla bases and the panicked flight of over 100,000 Kurds into Turkey and Iran. During the 1980s, Kurds had already watched Iraqi military forces destroy an estimated 3,000 Kurdish villages and disperse their

inhabitants. Since Halabja, virtually all Kurds are convinced that the Baghdad regime would exterminate them if given an opportunity. (According to reliable Iraqi opposition sources, Tariq Aziz acknowledged that the army had used a non-toxic gas to frighten the population in this latest campaign.) This is the kind of fear that drives millions of people to flee for their lives and to refuse to return despite regime assurances of their safety.

Refugees

The sheer number of refugees overwhelmed the ability of local and international relief agencies to care for them, leading to appalling camp conditions. Diseases swept the camps, claiming the lives of thousands of infants and children. The United States, which maintained throughout March 1991 that it would not get involved in Iraq's internal affairs, finally felt compelled to join its European allies in the establishment of a "safe-haven" zone in the north. By the end of May, the presence of US and European troops in a few small towns of northern Iraq had encouraged 350,000 Kurds to return to their homes or to resettle in special refugee camps, but the majority remained wary of returning to Iraq.

The uprisings and their consequences in southern and northern Iraq overshadowed the dislocations that had directly resulted from the allied war of January and February. According to the United Nations, which dispatched a special mission to Iraq to assess the humanitarian needs of the country in the aftermath of the war, as many as 72,000 people were left homeless by the war. Saudi Arabia evacuated several thousand civilians out of the Khafji area before it became a battle zone. Finally, there are three additional categories of displaced persons being handled by the International Committee for the Red Cross (ICRC). These include an estimated 16,000 Iraqi prisoners-of-war who refuse to be repatriated and remain in limbo at a POW camp in Saudi Arabia, up to 4,000 Kuwaitis still missing and believed to be in Iraq, and several thousand stateless persons—*bidun*—mostly tribespeople of Iraqi and

Iranian origin who had lived in Kuwait for decades without citizenship and whom the Kuwaiti government now will not permit to return.

Devastation

It remains to be seen if the Kurdish refugee problem can be resolved through repatriation and/or resettlement. At that point Iraq can get on with rebuilding its shattered economy. Authorities estimate that the destruction of bridges, roads, rail lines, port facilities, homes, shops, hospitals, factories and oil installations amounts to $170 billion. It is unclear whether this figure includes the considerable damage in both southern and northern Iraq inflicted during the postwar uprisings. Southern cities such as Karbala and Najaf, which were spared during the allied bombing campaign, were particularly hard hit during the anti-Saddam rising, and whole neighborhoods were demolished by tanks. More immediately serious has been the destruction of infrastructure directly related to the health of the population: water purification plants, sewerage lines, and electric generating stations. By one estimate, 80 percent of the country's electric power generating stations were destroyed. A 10-member Harvard University medical team visited Iraq in early May 1991 and reported that 18 out of Iraq's 20 generating plants were incapacitated or destroyed. In the three months after the ceasefire, Iraq has raised its generating capacity from 4 percent to 22 percent of prewar capacity. The inability to provide sanitary water, especially in the urban areas of southern Iraq, makes it difficult to contain potentially deadly communicable diseases such as gastrointestinal infections, typhoid fever and cholera, all of which had appeared in the Basra area by April 1991. The Harvard team's report stressed a direct correlation between this destruction and the subsequent breakdown in public health, and forecast that in the next year a minimum of 170,000 additional children under the age of five would die from infectious diseases as a result.

The damage in Kuwait was at least as extensive. Authorities have estimated that it will cost at least $60 billion to repair the damage to infrastructure, including streets, roads, electrical grids, medical facilities, the airport, harbors, and oil installations. It is expected to take as long as five years to restore the country to the status it was before the invasion. Even then, Kuwait may not be as well-off as before this catastrophe. The 600 oil wells that Iraqi forces set afire as they left the country were burning away around two million barrels of oil per day—more than Kuwait used to produce. As of late May 1991, less than a quarter of those fires had been extinguished.

Kuwait's burning oil wells are causing unprecedented environmental damage and affecting the health of millions of people in the area. The smoke darkens the skies over Kuwait, southern Iraq and southwestern Iran for the greater part of the daylight hours. It also pollutes the air with gases such as sulphur, nitrogen oxide and hydrocarbon that interfere with breathing, especially in persons with respiratory ailments and young children. These noxious pollutants are equivalent to ten times the average daily emissions from all US industrial and utility plants. The soot and gases from the oil fires mix with atmospheric moisture to form acid rain. This blackish and oily rain has damaged crops in both Iraq and Iran, raising concern for this year's grain harvests. The acid rain has spread as far as southern Turkey and western Pakistan.

"We can speak with alarming, grave assurance of a lost generation."

The acid rain also seeps into ground water supplies where chemicals such as lead and cadmium contaminate drinking water. World Health Organization director-general Hiroshi Nakajima reported in April that samples of drinking water from southwestern Iran contained levels of lead that were up to six times higher than what was considered medically safe. Regular ingestion of even small amounts of lead can cause mental retardation in children. Since the area of highest water lead levels, the flat plain extending from the Shatt al-Arab, borders southern Iraq, it is likely that Iraq's ground water supplies also are contaminated. As Kuwait's burning oil well fires are extinguished, the health risks from the toxic smoke and acid rain will diminish, but oil industry experts predict that it will take at least a year to put out all of the fires—a long enough period to build up unhealthy accumulations of dangerous chemicals in soils and water sources.

The several million gallons of Kuwaiti oil that the Iraqis spilled into the Persian Gulf in January will have long-term environmental consequences for the region. The largest oil slick, estimated to contain at least 3.3 million gallons of oil, continues to endanger the unique marine life of the Gulf: coral reefs, sea turtles, sea cows, shrimp beds, special fish species, and various local and migratory birds. The slick has remained in the northern Gulf, and so far has not threatened the major water desalinization plant at the Saudi port of Jubayl. It may actually be moving gradually westward, toward the Iranian coast. There are also dozens of smaller oil slicks in the northern Gulf. The slicks are beginning to take their toll on the fishing industry. In southern Iran, where fish constitutes an important source of dietary protein, complaints that fish smells oily and sometimes is inedible has sharply reduced the market for fresh fish, idling many fishermen.

This war has been an unmitigated disaster for millions of people in the Middle East and beyond. The many tens of thousands killed, the billions of dollars of property destruction, the millions of displaced persons and disrupted lives, the uncounted thousands with permanent physical and psychological scars, and the badly damaged economies are far more devastating than anything that has happened in the region in this century. Living conditions in Iraq, Kuwait and throughout the Middle East and South Asia are deteriorating badly as a direct consequence of this war, which has shattered the morale of millions of people. In Iraq and Kuwait, and even in nearby Iran, disease from contaminated water and polluted air will be killing and maiming innocent people for years to come. According to UNICEF, the war will result in deprivation for some 5 million children in Kuwait, Iraq, Jordan, Yemen and the occupied Palestinian territories. "We can speak with alarming, grave assurance of a lost generation," says UNICEF's Middle East regional director Richard Reid. The political, social and economic consequences of the US assault on Iraq, and the Iraqi regime's consequent assault on its own people, will afflict the region and the world well into the next century.

The War May Help End the Arab-Israeli Conflict

Martin Indyk

About the Author: *Martin Indyk is executive director of the Washington Institute for Near East Policy, a Washington, D.C.-based research institution that examines U.S. national interests in the Middle East.*

Saddam Hussein's devastating defeat in the Gulf war has left in its wake a sense of America's obligation to help resolve some of the Middle East's long-standing problems. One problem high on President George Bush's list of priorities is the Arab-Israeli conflict. As he told a joint session of Congress on March 6, 1991, "the time has come to put an end to [the] Arab-Israeli conflict."

Nonetheless, the Gulf war was fought to liberate Kuwait, not to solve the Palestinian problem. Although Iraq repeatedly attacked Israel with Scud missiles, Israel was not a belligerent in this war—at American insistence. Moreover, Hussein's threats to destroy Israel and his attacks on the Jewish state were fully supported by the Palestine Liberation Organization (PLO) and Palestinians in the occupied territories. This undermined what little trust had remained between Israelis and Palestinians. Nor has the war produced a new leadership on either side of the conflict capable of transforming the constituency-led politics of the past decade into the heroic politics of Anwar el-Sadat and Menachem Begin.

It is therefore not clear that this war has made the Arab-Israeli conflict any more amenable to solution. The opportunities for peace must be defined before new ideas for advancing the process can be developed.

Martin Indyk, "Peace Without the PLO." Reprinted, with permission, from *Foreign Policy* 83 (Summer 1991). Copyright © 1991 by the Carnegie Endowment for International Peace.

First, the defeat of Saddam Hussein represents the defeat of his world view. He had promoted the vision of a Hussein-led, pan-Arab superpower to counter American dominance of the post-Cold War world. He tried to give new credibility to the pre-Sadat method of settling the Arab-Israeli conflict—by threatening to destroy Israel. The war had the important side benefit of discrediting this approach.

The war also shifted the balance of power in the Arab world decisively in favor of the Egyptian-Saudi coalition that fought alongside the United States. Egypt and Saudi Arabia not only emerged from the crisis as winners, but also solidified their bilateral relations with a new bargain whereby Egyptian troops will help provide security for the Gulf Arabs in return for money to stabilize the Egyptian economy.

The devastating blow dealt radical Arab forces has left Syria, for the time being, with little alternative to staying with the winning coalition. The end of the Cold War cost Damascus its superpower patron: The Soviet Union has only been prepared to supply weapons for "defensive sufficiency," and President Mikhail Gorbachev has lectured Syrian leader Hafez al-Asad on the need to make peace with Israel, warning that Moscow would not support any Syrian military efforts to resolve the conflict. At the same time, the Gulf crisis has solidified U.S.-Israeli strategic ties, enhancing Israel's deterrent posture toward Syria.

> ## "The defeat of Saddam Hussein represents the defeat of his world view."

The defeat of Hussein also destroyed, for now, any Damascene dream of an eastern-front coalition (Iraq, Jordan, and Syria) capable of challenging Israel on the battlefield. As long as Egypt remains at peace with Israel and Iraq's offense is not rebuilt, Syria cannot contemplate waging a war on its own. The battlefield victory of Western technology over Soviet weaponry should also give al-Asad pause as he calculates the Syrian-Israeli military balance. Stepped-up American-Israeli efforts to upgrade the Patriot antimissile system and the Arrow anti-tactical ballistic missile should deflate Syrian hopes of holding Israel's civilian population hostage to stave off a battlefield defeat.

On the other hand, joining the coalition has already paid Syria dividends in the form of a free hand in Lebanon and Saudi financial aid. By enabling the coalition to engage in the peace process, Damascus can ensure that it becomes the focus of American diplomacy. Indeed al-Asad's assessment of the United States as the dominant power in the Middle East requires him to approach the Bush administration with new flexibility. But the United States also needs Syrian cooperation on postwar security arrangements and for a meaningful peace process.

> **"Iraq . . . demonstrated to the Gulf Arab states that they had more to fear from regional radicalism than from Israel."**

Syrian opposition to American efforts in either arena could complicate policy, providing al-Asad with some leverage in building the relationship he now seeks with Washington.

These trends suggest that inter-Arab politics is likely to be dominated for the foreseeable future by the new axis of Egypt, Saudi Arabia, and Syria—the largest, the richest, and the most nationalistic Arab states, respectively. This is an unassailable coalition should it decide to settle with Israel. However, whether this is in fact a dominant axis, rather than a triangle of tension, remains unclear. Saudi Arabia has a very modest conception of the Egyptian and Syrian roles in Gulf arrangements with the United States. For their part, Egypt and Syria are competitors for American attention and in their roles in the peace process. Cairo may feel it necessary to rehabilitate PLO Chairman Yasir Arafat; Damascus

wants to remove him from PLO leadership. And whether the capacity of these three Arab powers to make peace is matched by a willingness to come to terms with the Jewish state remains to be tested.

Postwar Opportunities

Still, there are some new reasons for cautious optimism. First, Iraq's invasion of Kuwait demonstrated to the Gulf Arab states that they had more to fear from regional radicalism than from Israel. Second, Israel's unexpected exercise of restraint in the face of Iraqi provocation demonstrated to the Gulf states that the Likud government is capable of acting rationally and, some aver, even wisely. Third, Egypt and Saudi Arabia should have a strong incentive to show the Arab world that they are better able to secure Palestinian rights through peace with Israel than Saddam Hussein could with his threats of destruction. And finally, Israel and Kuwait now share an antipathy for the Palestinians in general and the PLO in particular and, having recently regained their country, Kuwaitis are less inhibited about breaking taboos.

It is doubtful that the Palestinians share this same sense of realism and shared interests with Israel. Most Palestinians are bitter and frustrated with their mistaken dependence on yet another failed pan-Arab "hero." Arafat is responsible for committing the PLO to the Iraqi camp before Iraq's invasion of Kuwait, but his move was strongly endorsed by the Palestinian people. They were led astray, but they willingly followed. The Gulf Arabs do not sympathize with the Palestinians' choice. Gulf aid will not be restored soon and large numbers of Palestinian workers may be forced to leave the Gulf and return to Jordan and the West Bank. The Palestinian national movement will probably be in disarray for the foreseeable future amid score-settling and challenges to leadership.

The most significant repercussion for Arab-Israeli diplomacy is that the leading Arab states no longer insist on PLO representation in the peace process. Since the beginning of 1991, Egypt,

Syria, and the Gulf states have pointedly omitted any reference to the PLO in their joint communiqués. Arab state insistence on PLO involvement in the peace process and Israel's refusal to deal with the PLO have created a major roadblock to progress over the last decade. This sea change in Arab state attitudes offers potential for a breakthrough on the issue of Palestinian representation.

This PLO setback may combine with the impact of the *intifada* to shift decisively the balance of power in the Palestinian national movement from the headquarters in Tunis to a local leadership in the territories that would be more responsive to the local population. The decision of the local leadership to meet Secretary of State James Baker in April 1991 and break their own boycott on contacts with U.S. officials is the first manifestation of this potential. But if it is to be successfully developed, it will require the full cooperation of the Arab states. Those in the Gulf seem prepared to lend their support to the process, and Egypt and Syria are also willing to give the local leadership their backing for the moment.

King Hussein views the resuscitation of the PLO as a vehicle for Jordan's reentry into the peace process. That reentry has become a priority for Amman in its quest for rehabilitation in Arab and American eyes. But King Hussein is too weak and dependent on Palestinian sentiment to replace the PLO as spokesman for the Palestinians. Instead, he is likely to take advantage of the PLO's weakness to bolster his own efforts at reengagement.

Israeli Flexibility

There is reason to expect new Israeli flexibility in the peace process as well. Prime Minister Yitzhak Shamir has emerged from the crisis with his leadership strengthened and his relationship with George Bush reestablished. He apparently sees a golden opportunity to engage the Arab states in a peace process while the PLO is weak and Israel enjoys new popularity in the United States and Europe. Moreover, the desire of the

U.S.-led coalition to move on the peace process puts Shamir in the catbird seat since there can be no progress without Israel's cooperation. This became apparent soon after the Gulf war, when proposals for a U.N.-sponsored international conference were dropped because of Shamir's opposition.

"There is reason to expect new Israeli flexibility in the peace process as well."

With the pressing priority of raising some $35 billion to absorb about a million Soviet Jewish immigrants, Shamir has good reason to cultivate the United States and its Western allies. The near complete destruction of Iraq's offensive capabilities has also provided Israel with some breathing space in the military arena and an opportunity to prevent a new round of the arms race that it can no longer afford.

All these factors ought to renew Israeli interest in starting negotiations. But the war did nothing to shift Israeli attitudes on substantive issues. A public opinion poll taken after the war revealed an Israeli polity still deeply and evenly divided on territorial compromise. And a Likud-led coalition government of right-wing and religious parties is certainly no more willing to relinquish the West Bank. Israeli flexibility, therefore, will depend on an offer of genuine peace and acceptance of the Jewish state by the Arab states; such an offer would bolster Israel's sense of security within the region, thereby encouraging Israel to make a serious offer to the Palestinians. A key bearing the PLO's name could not open any Israeli door—all have been sealed shut by PLO endorsement of Saddam Hussein's threats against Israel. Rather, Arab states will need to support Palestinian interlocutors in the territories for an Israeli-Palestinian negotiation.

How the United States exploits this opportunity will be crucial to achieving a breakthrough. America has emerged from the Gulf war as the dominant power in the Middle East. All the powers in the region and all the interested parties outside the region are looking to Washington for leadership. The Arab Gulf states, in particular, will likely be responsive to U.S. peace process requirements. Egypt wants to play the role of strategic partner in the region. Syria is also keen to build relations with what it regards as the only superpower. And Israel seeks coordination with Washington to craft a process that meets its requirements.

In these circumstances, the United States now has a stronger hand in influencing the peace process than at any time since the disengagement agreements of the 1970s. And this influence is enhanced by Bush's tremendous authority, following what is seen in the region as his personal victory over Saddam Hussein.

"The war has generated some new flexibility on both sides."

But expectations of the United States are as high as its new reputation. In particular, the Arab states have come to believe that if the United States can liberate Kuwait in such short order, it is equally capable of liberating Arab lands occupied by Israel. And Israel's restraint during the Gulf war is generally viewed by Arabs as the result of American pressure rather than as Israeli forbearance. The president's March 6, 1991 speech to Congress, with its emphasis on "territory for peace" and its assertion that "in the modern age, geography cannot guarantee security," was welcomed in the Arab world as an indication that the United States was now preparing to deliver Israel. The president's 91 percent popularity rating in March 1991 is cited as evidence that he is no longer beholden to domestic political constraints.

In short, the Arab states are tempted to sit back and wait while Washington orders Israel out of the territories. And there is a similar urge to return to business as usual in inter-Arab politics as each power seeks to carve out new areas of influence in the Gulf and the PLO. Meanwhile, in the West Bank and Gaza, the cycle of Palestinian-Israeli violence could quickly sour the atmosphere between Israel and its Arab neighbors. In the absence of clear leadership from Washington, the window of opportunity will probably close rapidly. Conversely, if the United States takes the lead, it cannot hope to impose a solution unilaterally, but it may well be able to get the process of negotiations started. But they will need strong encouragement from Washington to take these steps.

Exploiting the Opportunity

The key to progress lies in quick exploitation of the opportunity that exists. The Gulf crisis has not moved the parties to narrow their differences on the substantive issues. The Arab states still demand complete Israeli withdrawal from the territories and the Palestinians demand an independent state. Israel demands secure borders, rejects an independent Palestinian state, and will not make a commitment to withdrawal before negotiations begin.

Nevertheless, the war has generated some new flexibility on both sides on procedural issues. First, the Arab states appear willing to accept the proposition that they, too, have to make peace with Israel through direct negotiations; an Israeli-Palestinian negotiation alone will not suffice. The willingness of Saudi Arabia and Kuwait to demonstrate their acceptance of Israel through confidence-building steps such as ending the secondary boycott, renouncing the U.N. "Zionism is Racism" resolution, and joining Israel at the negotiating table could help get the process started.

Second, Israel has indicated a willingness to attend a regional conference under the joint auspices of the United States and the Soviet Union as an opening for direct negotiations. This proposal comes very close to the Arab insistence on reconvening the 1973 Geneva conference. It might provide enough of the flavor of a multilateral conference to be acceptable to the Arab states and yet remain enough of a direct negotiation to appeal to Israel.

Third, the perennial problem of Palestinian representation might be more solvable in the post-Gulf war environment. Previously, Israel would not sit with the PLO, and the Palestinians would not come to the table without PLO authorization. The Arab states also insisted on a PLO presence in the negotiations. Now, with the Gulf Cooperation Council, Egypt, and Syria no longer designating the PLO as the "sole legitimate representative of the Palestinian people" and with the severing of financial support for the PLO, a consensus might emerge for Arab state-backed Palestinian interlocutors from the West Bank and Gaza.

This is a potentially decisive development. The Arab states created the PLO in 1964. A decade later at the Rabat summit they denied Jordanian claims to represent the Palestinians. From that time on, Arab state support has gone to the PLO and has been crucial for securing international legitimacy for that organization. If they are now prepared to back an alternative leadership in the territories and act as its custodian in negotiations with Israel, it may be possible to cut the Gordian knot on the Palestinian representation issue. . . .

"Every now and again in . . . the Arab-Israeli conflict a moment of opportunity arises. . . . The Gulf war has created such a moment."

The essential ingredient in this new recipe for Palestinian representation, however, is American leadership. Without a clear indication that Washington favors local representatives and is not interested in inserting the PLO into the local process, the Arab states are likely to pursue their own PLO agendas. But if the United States continues to reject unambiguously a PLO role, Arab anger with the PLO combined with desire to

please the United States will likely lead to support for this alternative process. Egypt, Saudi Arabia, and even Syria are tending in this direction already. King Hussein of Jordan, having no love for the PLO, has more interest in participating in the process than in insisting on PLO engagement.

The Right Time

This combination of American influence, Arab state engagement, Israeli procedural flexibility, and the potential empowerment of Palestinian leadership in the territories suggests that the time is auspicious for negotiations. Naturally, the negotiating road will be arduous. It is, nevertheless, possible to envisage an interim arrangement between Israel and a Palestinian delegation for Palestinian self-government in the territories. But, inevitably, there will be efforts, especially by Palestinian rejectionists, to subvert the process with terrorism.

Finding common ground between Israel and Syria on the Golan Heights will also be difficult, but progress may be possible in southern Lebanon instead. King Hussein of Jordan has an interest in the peace process if only to prove his value to the United States, but the current anti-American and continued anti-Israeli sentiments of his own people will make it difficult for him to move. The demands of the right-wing coalition will limit the Israeli government's negotiating position. And inter-Arab politics is likely to bedevil any effort to concert an Arab-state approach.

In short, negotiations may very well come to naught. But every now and again in the history of the Arab-Israeli conflict a moment of opportunity arises when the concerns of the parties overlap, if only slightly. The Gulf war has created such a moment. With American leadership, skill, and determination, a negotiating process can begin. It may be one small step, but in the Middle East it would constitute a major breakthrough.

The Persian Gulf War Increased Arab Resentment of the U.S.

Rami G. Khouri

About the Author: *Rami G. Khouri, a Palestinian, hosts a weekly political affairs television program in Jordan. He previously was editor of the* Jordan Times.

The relatively swift military defeat of the Iraqi army in the ground battle that never happened has shocked many people throughout the Arab world into momentary disbelief, concern and introspection. However, the scale and speed of the Iraqi defeat should not blind us to the deeper political and human reality that still characterizes the Middle East.

Understanding the contemporary frame of the Arab mind is essential in order to grasp the terms of reference with which we have viewed the conflict with the US, and thus the terms of reference that will dictate events in the aftermath of war.

The Arab world reached an historic turning point in the 1980s: People lost their fear. After the low-water mark of 1982, when the Palestine Liberation Organization and the Lebanese capital of Beirut were being shelled from the hills by Israel, supported by the American navy, during the Israeli invasion—which the high-minded Americans now seem to have conveniently forgotten—the Arab people were fed up.

The Arabs were so beaten down over the decades by their own autocratic leaders, by their inability to manifest their sense of pan-Arab unity, by their inability to do anything about Israel, by their inability to forge productive and honorable relations with the great powers, that they hit rock bottom.

Defeat seemed so total that renewal was the only way out. And as elsewhere in the world, such as Catholic Poland, large numbers of people turned to God when they gave up on the temporal order. From Jordan to Egypt, from Algeria to Lebanon, it was Islam that initially gave Arabs the strength to fight back.

No longer were Arabs willing to suffer the regional disequilibrium with Israel and the tradition of such western imperial military powers as Britain, France and the US playing games and drawing Arab borders based upon their own colonial interests or on the wishes of the Israeli lobby in Washington.

And no longer were Arabs willing to put up with domestic autocracy and tyranny or the economic and social inequity that characterized the Arab world for so many decades. Starting with the Palestinian and Lebanese Shiite resistance to Israel in southern Lebanon, the *intifada* and the struggle for democracy in Jordan, Algeria, Tunisia, Sudan, Lebanon, Yemen and other places, Arabs began saying in the 1980s that they were willing to take more destruction than an enemy or oppressor could throw at them, including, as in Iraq, death by high-technology machines.

Even though most Arabs didn't support the invasion of Kuwait, Saddam Hussein's fearlessness in standing up to our enemies, Israel and America, appealed to the new spirit of the Arab world.

"Saddam Hussein's fearlessness in standing up to our enemies . . . appealed to the new spirit of the Arab world."

Saddam Hussein is, of course no Santa Claus. He is a rough man. He kills people ruthlessly. He has lived by the gun all of his life. Yet, during the

Rami G. Khouri, "The Appeal of Saddam Hussein," *New Perspectives Quarterly*, Spring 1991. Reprinted with permission.

war, this unlikely, autocratic man became the very medium of a new Arab fearlessness aimed at casting off oppression from abroad. As the saying goes, he may be a son-of-a-bitch, but he is our son-of-a-bitch.

Indeed, the great paradox of this conflict was that in precisely those Arab countries where the people have started to achieve democracy and the freedom to speak out and express themselves—in Jordan, Algeria, Tunisia, Sudan, Yemen and among Palestinians—the support for Saddam Hussein was both fervent and widespread. The US was supported by only the mercantile autocracies. Egypt, as always, is an exception because of its obsequious political servitude resulting from dependence on American aid and its powerful self-reliance on its own national identity—that allows it, in fits of cash-laden confusion, to wander away temporarily from its greater home within the family of Arab nationalism.

"It was a source of pride to Arabs that Saddam could hit Israel with missiles."

Inconveniently for the west, the more free and democratic Arab countries become, the less sympathetic they will be to foreign designs for the region. They will also become more Islamic and anti-western.

Already, for example, the speaker of the house in the Jordanian assembly belongs to the Moslem Brotherhood, which holds a plurality there. In Algeria, the Moslem Brotherhood has a majority of local assembly seats. In both places, however, their success has depended on their agreement to play within a pluralistic framework and by the democratic rules.

Saddam was not the chosen leader of these Arabs seeking a new order. Ironically, it was the Americans who made him an Arab leader. After Saddam invaded Kuwait, every Arab country, without exception, far from praising him, called on him to withdraw at once. And many Arab leaders undertook immediate and fervent diplomatic action to secure such a withdrawal. But the Saudis and the Egyptians panicked and called in the Americans.

Iraq vs. the West

The minute American forces landed in the region, the whole equation changed. The issue was no longer Iraq occupying Kuwait. It was Iraq standing up to the arrogant west, holding out for a solution to the many regional economic and political problems that plague us.

It was a source of pride to Arabs that Saddam could hit Israel with missiles, as he promised. Of course the missiles did little real damage. But symbolically they were the equivalent of an Arab atomic bomb.

The crucial thing that the west refuses to see, perhaps through a combination of racism and ignorance, is that what is happening in the hearts and minds of most Arabs is the same thing that has been happening with South Africans, Eastern Europeans, South Koreans, Filipinos and Haitians. Like all those people, we too aspire to rid ourselves of unjust and irresponsible political orders. For most Arabs, Israel is the same as the white minority regime in South Africa.

For most Arabs, the western powers who carved up the Arab nation in their own interests are scarcely different than the Soviets who redrew the map of Eastern Europe. If the west continues to ignore this cry from the heart of 200 million Arabs in the aftermath of the war, it does so at its own peril.

Human beings cannot be suppressed over long periods of time without fighting back, standing up and grabbing for their dignity. Why has this lesson of 1989-90, learned so well in Eastern Europe and South Africa, been forgotten when it comes to the Arab world?

The west has money and high technology on its side. We have human nature and history on ours. Though we may have lost the war, we will inevitably win out in the years and decades ahead.

If, after the war, the US wants to keep a bevy of corrupt, undemocratic autocrats in power, try to destroy the rising Arab spirit and maintain by force of arms an inequitable and unstable political order that has failed the Arabs for three quarters of a century, it will have no more success than did Jaruzelski in Poland or Ceausescu in Romania.

"The west has money and high technology on its side. We have human nature and history on ours."

The initial signs in the postwar period are less discouraging than one would have thought. Western leaders are talking about the need to resolve the Palestinian issue.

Indeed, one rarely hears the words "Middle East" these days without the follow-up comment about the urgency of a more equitable economic balance in the region, the need for arms control agreements, the usefulness of democracy and human rights and the importance of justice as the foundation of stability.

Perhaps this morally and physically destructive war was the price that finally made people realize the need to attend to the festering wounds of the region, or else face another explosion.

This may be the unavoidable message of the mass madness that recently engulfed the Middle East and the world. What happens now will tell if we have finally learned the lessons not only of the last seven months, but of the last seven decades that led to this war.

The Persian Gulf War Resulted in Disaster for the Kurdish People

Peter W. Galbraith

About the Author: *Peter W. Galbraith is a senior adviser to the Senate Foreign Relations Committee. During March and April of 1991 he traveled to Iraq and surrounding regions to report on events following the Persian Gulf War.*

On February 27, 1991, at midnight e.s.t. [Eastern Standard Time], President Bush halted Operation Desert Storm after 100 spectacularly successful hours of a ground campaign. American forces had not only liberated Kuwait but were in occupation of 15 percent of southern Iraq and located adjacent to such southern Iraqi cities as Basra, Nasiryah, and Suq al-shuyukh.

The Iraqi army was decimated. Of a prewar size of 1 million, as many as 100,000 were dead. Most of its tanks, armor, and artillery had been either destroyed by coalition bombing or abandoned and captured during the ground war. Ordinary Iraqi soldiers, like the people in towns under U.S. military control, viewed the Americans as liberators. This attitude, graphically displayed in television images of defeated soldiers kissing the American victors, was combined with an intense hatred for the man who had inflicted so much misery in Iraq, Saddam Hussein.

On March 2, 2 days after President Bush halted the ground war, a surviving Iraqi tank driver in the southern city of Basra halted his tank before one of the 2-story high portraits of Saddam Hussein that hang everywhere in Iraqi cities. Through the portrait he fired a shell. This shell ignited a spontaneous rebellion that raged, like a nearby Kuwaiti oil fire, through the Shi'a-dominated cities of southern Iraq.

Within days anti-Saddam rebels controlled most of the populated areas of southern Iraq. The rebels were a motley group comprising military defectors, outraged citizenry, and, later, some Shi'a clerics. From Iran to join the rebellion came Iraqi Shi'a who had long been refugees in the predominantly Arab southwestern corner of the Islamic Republic. These Iraqis brought with them pictures of Baqir Hakim, the son of the Shi'a spiritual leader Muhsin Hakim, and a man whose six brothers had been executed by Saddam. As a result, Baqir Hakim, from his exile in Iran, became the most visible person associated with the Shi'a uprising. Yet he was neither its instigator nor its leader, and it is unclear how many of the Shi'a rebels would have associated themselves with him.

Also from Iran in the early days of the Shi'a rebellion came elements of the Badr Brigade, an Iranian-trained force of exiled Iraqi Shi'a. Inside Iraq the Badr Brigade was a disaster. It organized (perhaps with some local rebels) the execution of surrendering and captured Iraqi army units. These executions promptly ended the surrenders and the defections.

"For the last 2 weeks of March 1991 euphoria reigned in Iraqi Kurdistan."

As the Shi'a rebellion spread, the Iraqi regime pulled its forces out of northern Iraq to protect Baghdad and put down the rebellion in the south. This gave the Iraqi Kurds their chance.

Long suppressed by Sunni Arab regimes in Baghdad, Iraq's Kurds have almost invariably seized on weakness in the center as an opportunity for rebellion in the mountainous Kurdish areas of northern and eastern Iraq. Thus the Kurds took advantage of revolutionary confusion in

Peter W. Galbraith, *Civil War in Iraq: A Staff Report to the Committee on Foreign Relation, U.S. Senate*, May 1991.

Iraq in the 1960s and 1970s to rebel (a rebellion crushed after a U.S.-approved Iraq-Iran deal led to the cutoff of CIA [Central Intelligence Agency] assistance in 1975) and of the Iran-Iraq war to rebel in the 1980s. This time, however, the Kurdish leadership was more cautious.

"Hundreds of thousands of Kurdish refugees fled to the high mountains along the Turkish and Iranian borders."

The 1980s rebellion had been crushed with incredible ferocity. Beginning in 1985, the Iraqi regime had engaged in an accelerated program of destroying all the villages of Kurdistan. In March 1988 the regime used poison gas on the city of Halabja, and then in August launched a broad chemical weapons attack on more than 70 villages along the Iraq-Turkey and Iraq-Iran borders. With that rebellion taking the lives of more than 100,000 Kurds and costing another 2 million of their homes, the Kurdish leadership was reluctant to proceed without an assurance of success. To many in the Kurdish leadership the calls made by President Bush for the Iraqi people to overthrow Saddam Hussein and, in particular, the promise to shoot down Iraqi aircraft ("You fly, you die") provided such an assurance.

The spearhead of the Kurdish rebellion was not, however, the longtime leadership of the anti-Saddam Kurdish political parties. As in the south, there was a spontaneous popular uprising followed by the near simultaneous defection of some 300 officers of an all-Kurdish territorial military force. The defection of these officers and their units, locally known as the "jash" (or "mules") and long on the payroll of the Baghdad regime, effectively brought all the cities of Kurdistan under Kurdish control. It was only at this point that the two principal Kurdish leaders—Massoud Barzani of the Kurdish Democratic Party and Jalal Talabani of the Patriotic Union of Kurdistan—emerged to take control of the rebel

forces.

For the last 2 weeks of March 1991 euphoria reigned in Iraqi Kurdistan. The Kurds set up local administrations, restored basic services including electricity (Zakho in far north Iraq had electricity on Easter weekend; Baghdad did not), and prepared defenses. The Kurds inherited vast quantities of Iraqi military equipment including trucks, tanks, artillery, mortars, and light arms. They even captured an airfield with several Iraqi war planes.

For the first time the Kurdish population at large was exposed to the Kurdish insurgent movement and to the recent history of the movement. In the cities there were town meetings providing give-and-take between Kurdish leaders and community leaders and professionals. Movie houses showed video footage of the Halabja poison gas attacks, including documentaries made by Western television networks. Kurds were able to visit the torture centers of the regime as well as the 15 or more extravagant palaces owned by Saddam Hussein in the Kurdish mountains. Ba'ath party headquarters were torched, as were the local mukhabarat (secret police) offices. Abandoned army barracks were stripped of their tin roofs and valuables within.

The Kurds distributed weapons to every able-bodied man and claimed to have more than 400,000 men under arms. An observer could see that virtually every man in the Kurdish-controlled cities was armed but, as the Kurds discovered, an armed population is not an army.

Iraqi Prisoners

The Kurds also took large numbers of Iraqi prisoners. Jalal Talabani, head of the Patriotic Union of Kurdistan, estimated the total to be more than 100,000 but noted that the Kurds, having no food or other means to take care of them, could not hold these prisoners. Interestingly, the Kurds reported that their prisoners included more than 100 members of the Peoples Mojahideen, an anti-Khomeini Iranian group led by Massoud Rajavi, that apparently was fighting with Saddam Hussein in Iraq's civil war.

Kurdish euphoria proved short-lived. In the south, forces loyal to Saddam Hussein recaptured the main cities and engaged in a brutal campaign of repression. According to refugees, captured rebels typically were lined up, nooses strung from the lowered barrel of a tank gun were placed around their necks, and then the rebels were hanged as the gun barrel was raised. Shi'a holy shrines in Najaf and Karbala became abattoirs for the slaughter of rebels, clerics, and alleged sympathizers.

In addition to these activities, the Ba'ath regime apparently indulged its favorite pacification technique in the south. Whole neighborhoods were destroyed in March and early April, depriving urban rebels of sanctuary and punishing a hostile population.

The south's flat terrain, combined with the absence of experienced Shi'a guerrilla fighters, facilitated Saddam Hussein's repression of the southern revolt. The refugee flow out of the south—approximately 40,000 to the U.S. zone and 70,000 to Iran—did not compare to that which subsequently occurred in the north, in part because the Iraqi army was able to surround cities and close off exit points prior to initiating the slaughter. The plight of Iraq's Shi'as, while far less visible than that of the Kurds, is certainly more severe than currently depicted.

The Collapse of the Kurdish Rebellion

By March 28, 1991, the military tide was beginning to turn against the Kurds. Iraqi forces, backed up by helicopter gunships, launched a ferocious assault on the city of Kirkuk. As parts of the city were retaken, Kurdish insurgents reported that remaining residents of Kurdish neighborhoods were machine-gunned and slaughtered. Within days Iraqi army forces moved into other Kurdish cities and towns: Dihok and Irbil fell on March 31, Zakho and Sulaymaniyah on April 1.

The fierce Iraqi attack accounts in part for the Kurdish defeat. Cities were subject to intense bombardment. Dihok, for example, was shelled incessantly the night before it fell. Phosphorous shells, which can instantly cremate their victims, were used extensively and with maximum terror impact. Unlike the Iraqis, the Kurdish leaders were unwilling to subject their own people to this sort of devastation. Kurdish forces pulled out of cities not only because they believed they could not hold them over the long term, but also because they wanted to spare civilians and facilitate their flight to safety.

"The television images of these refugees . . . have shocked governments into action."

While the Kurds captured large quantities of Iraqi weapons, they were unable to make effective use of them. Artillery pieces were often idle for lack of firing pins. The Kurds had quite a collection of captured Soviet-made tanks (some disabled in the capture were restored by the Kurds) but did not necessarily have the ordnance to go with the tanks. All Kurdish military operations were hampered by a lack of gasoline and in some cases food for the guerrillas.

The Kurds also suffered from command and control deficiencies. Communication between commanders was often by written note and, when they had electronic communications, these were limited and not effectively utilized. Logistically, the Kurds had difficulty matching ordnance with weapons. Tank drivers, for example, would not necessarily know of a supply of ordnance stockpiled in a different part of Kurdistan.

From the cities of Kurdistan hundreds of thousands of Kurdish refugees fled to the high mountains along the Turkish and Iranian borders. The flight was not easy. After 8 months of sanctions and 2 months of war, little gasoline remained in Kurdistan. Thus, most refugees traveled by foot. The vehicles seen heading out of Dihok, presumably typical of the flight from other cities, were heavily overloaded. Dump trucks carried loads of 50 or more; private cars were filled and even carried adults and children in the trunks.

Not all the refugees were Kurds. Living among the Kurds in the north were more than 500,000 Christian Assyrians and Chaldeans. In Dihok, on Easter Sunday, Yacoub Yousif, an Assyrian leader, was eager to take his American visitor to the midnight service in an ancient Assyrian church, the first such service there since the Ba'ath regime had closed it years before. Heavy shelling of the city forced the priest to postpone the midnight mass to 2 a.m. and then, as the shelling continued unabated, to postpone it to Easter morning.

Easter morning the last of the Dihok residents were moving out and the Easter service was not held. And a day which Kurds, Assyrians, and Chaldeans hoped might be part of their national resurrection instead marked the beginning of a new chapter of suffering and death.

The Humanitarian Crisis

As the Easter weekend concluded, it was clear an immense catastrophe was about to overtake the Kurdish people. People walking to the mountains carried little food and not much with which to shelter themselves; adults shepherding children or assisting the elderly were able to bring even less. Those with cars and trucks were better off as they could carry more and arrived in the mountains less exhausted. However, even before the Kurds left their cities, little food was available. Typically a family group of 10 finding refuge in the high mountains on the Iraqi side of the border arrived on Easter Sunday with 100 pounds of rice and perhaps some other more perishable foodstuffs. It would be another 3 weeks before any significant international relief reached these people, and the Easter Sunday arrivals were the lucky refugees: they had come by truck or car.

Ultimately, some 800,000 Kurds actually reached the Turkish border while up to 1.5 million are in Iran or along the Iranian border. The television images of these refugees—desperate people living in filth, fighting for food, and burying their babies—have shocked governments into action. Yet they only represent part of the catastrophe.

Some unknown number of Kurds are still in the high mountains on the Iraq side of the Iraq-Turkey border, and perhaps on the Iraq side of the Iran-Iraq border. These are people camped out along the high Amadiyah-Zahko road, and on spur roads to the north. Almost certainly other refugees are camped along the road from Amadiyah to Rawanduz and in the mountains rising up to the Turkish border. These people are in areas where the Peshmerga, the Kurdish insurgents, operate, and of their plight little is now known, except that they are receiving no aid.

Another group invisible to the outside world but almost certainly in desperate condition are the residents of the so-called victory cities, concentration camps created by the Saddam Hussein regime to house the villagers made homeless by the regime's depopulation program.

Beginning in 1985 the Iraqi regime hit upon the ultimate solution to the persistent problem of Kurdish insurgencies: every village in Kurdistan was to be razed so as to deny the Peshmerga any base of support. During a 1987 trip through government-controlled Kurdistan, this author saw (and chronicled for the Foreign Relations Committee) the destruction process as it was under way. Along the principal highways in Kurdistan, villages and towns stood half destroyed. Sometimes the houses on one side of the road stood vacant while on the other side there was nothing but rubble. The villagers were being relocated to what the Iraqi officials described as "victory cities," really concentration camps under the watchful eye of the Iraqi army, the police, and the Ba'ath party. In 1987, as seen from the highways, these concentration camps were just under construction, piles of cinderblock laid out in vast grid patterns.

"The United States was unprepared for the peace that followed the gulf war."

Today there are no villages left in Kurdistan. Every village, including some that dated back almost to the beginning of civilization, has been dynamited and bulldozed into oblivion. Lost with the villages were schools, ancient churches and mosques, and a way of life for a proud, pastoral people.

Together with the villages, the Iraqi regime killed sheep and farm animals, and burned orchards. A particular target were the donkeys and few of these once ubiquitous beasts of burden can now be found in Iraqi Kurdistan. The donkey, like the village, was a key support system for the Peshmerga.

By destroying rural Kurdistan, the Iraqi regime also deprived the inhabitants of this pastoral land of any indigenous food supply. As a result, the Kurds have become entirely dependent on imported food, and in particular, U.S. rice and wheat. With the U.N. [United Nations] sanctions, the American war, and the civil war, these imported supplies disappeared. Kurds fleeing the cities at the end of March could find no food in the countryside and no village shelter in a still-freezing mountain environment. The absence of indigenous food and shelter has greatly exacerbated the humanitarian crisis overtaking the Kurds.

The Concentration Camps

Perhaps as many as 2 million Kurds, Assyrians, and Chaldeans were moved from their villages after 1985. The luckier ones went the cities to stay with relatives. There they were able to find employment or at least could live off the income of employed relatives. When the Kurdish military collapse came, these newly urbanized villagers, along with other city dwellers, had the food resources (often acquired at exorbitant black-market rates) and sometimes even the transport to flee.

Not so the inhabitants of the concentration camps, who number, according to Massoud Barzani, 1.1 million in 104 separate settlements. (This writer's independent estimate of the population was 1 million.) Mostly unemployed since the destruction of their villages, the concentration camp dwellers do not have the money to acquire food reserves.

In 1987 the Iraqi authorities would not permit a visit to the victory cities; in 1991 these concentration camps were liberated and thus accessible. They were also every bit as grim as they seemed from the highway 4 years ago. In a sprawling settlement of more than 10,000 near Zakho, a man was carrying grain treated with a vermin poison. To feed his family, the man intended to wash the poison off the grain. He said that several washings would be required.

In this particular concentration camp, there was just one well and it was highly polluted. Camp leaders said several children were dying each day of dysentery.

The plight of the 10,000 Kurds in this Zakho area victory city is emblematic of the 1 million or more concentration camp inhabitants. As of Easter Sunday, when catastrophe was just beginning to overtake other Iraqi Kurds, these people already had no food and their children were already dying.

The concentration camp inhabitants had no food resources to make possible an escape to Turkey or Iran and, unlike the city dwellers, there was no transport of any kind available to these people. Thus as the urban Kurds fled, the concentration camp people stayed behind.

The 1 million inhabitants of the concentration camps are the invisible victims of the Kurdish disaster. They are not seen on television but their plight may be worse than that of the more visible refugees. These invisible Kurds have no food, no sanitation, and are at the mercy of a vindictive Iraqi army.

"Iraq is a nation divided."

On August 25, 1988—5 days after the end of the Iran-Iraq war—the Iraqi air force launched massive chemical weapons attacks on Kurdish villages along the Iraq-Turkey border. The villages had been in areas where the Peshmerga operated, and because the Peshmerga had sided with

Iran during the war, the area was marked for retribution.

But in seeking retribution the Iraqi regime did not attack the Peshmerga camps on the mountains above the villages, camps presumably quite visible from the air on the barren Kurdish hillsides. Rather, the regime targeted villages inhabited almost exclusively by women, children, and noncombatant men. The terror impact of poison gas was thus maximized.

This history, and others like it, is well known to the people of Kurdistan. With the entire region under Kurdish control during the recent rebellion, entire urban populations feared a retribution aimed at maximizing civilian deaths. The actual experience of the March 1991 revolt—the shelling of cities, the use of phosphorous and napalm, the killing of Kurds in recaptured neighborhoods—seemed to justify these fears. . . .

United States Policy and the Kurds

The United States was unprepared for the peace that followed the gulf war. It did not comprehend the depth of popular anger inside Iraq at Saddam Hussein and therefore did not anticipate the uprisings either in the south or the north. The administration in its policy assessments seemed to mischaracterize the positions of the Kurdish and Shi'a rebels. As a result, an opportunity to overthrow Saddam Hussein in mid-March may have been lost. Further, neither anticipating the rebellion it had called for nor the brutal nature of the Iraqi response, the administration was unprepared to cope with the subsequent humanitarian crisis. Being caught by surprise may be directly traceable to a policy of no contact with the Iraqi opposition.

In April 1988, during a call at the State Department, the Kurdish leader Jalal Talabani met with the director for Northern Gulf Affairs, the Iraq desk officer, and the assistant secretary for Human Rights. (Talabani also met Foreign Relations Committee Chairman Claiborne Pell during the same visit.) This meeting, of which Secretary of State George Shultz was unaware, produced an explosive reaction from Iraq and

Turkey. Secretary Shultz felt blindsided, and an edict went forth mandating no contact with the Iraqi opposition. Subsequent developments—Iraq's use of chemical weapons on the Kurds, an evolution of Turkey's policy toward a more generous view of its own Kurdish population, Iraqi violations of international law, and even the invasion of Kuwait—did not change this policy. When Talabani came to the United States in August 1990, he met with Senators Pell and Kerry but was again cold-shouldered by the State Department.

"Other countries in the region were eager to assist the forces battling Saddam Hussein."

After the war began on January 16, 1991, the Iraqi opposition approached the administration with offers of military cooperation and of military intelligence. They were again spurned. Ultimately, a channel to provide military intelligence was established, by having information pass through the office of a Senate staffer. However, by the time this channel was established, the war was nearly over.

On the day the war ended, a group of Iraqi Kurdish leaders were meeting in Washington at a conference held under the sponsorship of Chairman Pell, in the Foreign Relations Committee hearing room. Both in the conference, in the side conversations, and at a private lunch hosted by the committee, these leaders gave a detailed account of developments in Kurdistan, of the depth of the anti-Saddam (and pro-U.S.) sentiment, and of the likelihood of a mass uprising. Subsequent developments thus would not have surprised a participant at these events. The administration, which again snubbed the opposition on March 1, 1991, was apparently unprepared for the uprising that began March 2.

Iraq is a nation divided on confessional and ethnic grounds. Fifty-five percent of the population are Shi'a, 40 percent are Sunni, and 5 percent are Christian. Ethnically the division is 70 percent Arab, 25 percent Kurd, 5 percent Assyrian, Chaldean, and others. The Iraqi opposition is as diverse as the country itself. However, it has achieved a degree of coherence that its critics (especially those who do not talk to the opposition) never imagined.

The Iraqi opposition consists of Shi'a parties, Kurdish parties, and ideologically based parties. The Shi'a parties include religious parties (the Dawa, or "Call" party, the Islamic Action party of the Ayatollah Mudarassi, and the Supreme Assembly of the Islamic Revolution in Iraq of Baqir Hakim) and secular independents, of which the London-based leader Ahmad Chalabi is the most articulate spokesman. The Kurdish parties include the Kurdish Democratic Party (KDP) of Massoud Barzani and Jalal Talabani's Patriotic Union of Kurdistan (PUK). The ideological parties, dominated by Sunni Arabs, include the Iraqi Communist party and a dissident Ba'ath party. The most prominent Sunni Arab opposition figure is Damascus-based former Iraqi general Hassan Nequib.

"Official Washington continued to see the [Iraqi] opposition in caricature."

In March these parties met in Beirut to forge an alliance and a common program. Brought together by a shared objective—the removal of Saddam Hussein—they achieved agreement on a broad program for a democratic and federal Iraq with very substantive provisions for Kurdish autonomy.

Strikingly, each of the parties in the Joint Action Committee—the cumbersome name the opposition coalition arrogated to itself—made tangible concessions in the interests of opposition unity. The Kurdish parties abandoned their dream of an independent Kurdistan, accepting that their rights can only be accommodated within Iraq. The Shi'a religious parties aban-

doned the idea of an Islamic state, recognizing the rights of religious minorities as well as those of the more secular Sunni Arabs and Kurds. The ideological parties accepted the idea of democracy in lieu of Fascist or Communist dictatorship.

The Beirut compromises reflect the reality of Iraqi politics. Based in the south and without a strong force in the army, the religious Shi'a could not hope to impose their will on all of Iraq. At a minimum they would need the assistance of the Kurds in the north, who would hardly subscribe to a fundamentalist agenda. The Kurds could never rule Iraq by themselves and likely could not obtain independence without either outside intervention or the acquiescence of the other Iraqis. The Arab Sunni opposition had a choice between Saddam Hussein (or a comparably repressive structure aimed at preserving the Sunni Arab monopoly of power) or a power-sharing arrangement with the more populous Iraqi groups.

Meanwhile, official Washington continued to see the opposition in caricature. The Iraqi Shi'a were viewed as pawns of Iran seeking to impose a Khomeini-style regime, in spite of a very different history. Theologically the Iraqi Shi'a follow the Najaf school of religious thought, Najaf being a more modern and influential center of Shi'a learning than the Persian holy city of Qom. Politically, the Iraqi Shi'a never responded to Iranian calls for rebellion during the Iran-Iraq war. And, unlike the strong tradition of anti-U.S. sentiment among the Iranian clerics, the Iraqi Shi'a parties, including the Dawa and the Islamic Action, have been desperately seeking U.S. support and military involvement in the effort to liberate Iraq from Saddam Hussein. (There are also many fewer clerics in Iraq than Iran, Saddam Hussein having killed most of them.) All this was apparently never comprehended in Washington.

Not Seeking Full Independence

Similarly, the Iraqi Kurds have long made clear their recognition that an independent Kurdistan is not realistic. To his followers in Dihok, Jalal Talabani made much the same statement as he had to the Foreign Relations Committee:

> It is very difficult to change the borders of five countries. We are not for an independent Kurdistan; we are asking for our national rights within the framework of Iraq. I know of dreams and reality. All Kurds dream of an independent, unified Kurdistan, but we have to face the reality.

Nonetheless, official Washington characterized Talabani as seeking the breakup of Iraq and of being antagonistic to Turkey. Interestingly, after being snubbed by the State Department on February 28, 1991, ostensibly because a meeting would upset Turkey, Talabani departed Washington for Ankara and a series of meetings requested by Turkish president Turgut Ozal.

An Opportunity Lost

As the anti-Saddam rebellion gained force in March, several strategically located Iraqi military figures contacted principals in the Joint Action Committee, according to both Arab and Kurdish opposition leaders. As the Iraqi military figures contemplated bringing possibly decisive force to the side of the rebels, they looked for a sign that the sponsors of the rebellion had the support of the United States, the one country preeminent militarily and politically in Iraq.

"The United States was unprepared for the humanitarian crisis."

No such signal was given. On the contrary, the public snub of Kurdish and other Iraqi opposition leaders was read as a clear indication that the United States did not want the popular rebellion to succeed. This was confirmed by background statements from administration officials that they were looking for a military, not a popular, alternative to Saddam Hussein. As one NSC [National Security Council] aide put it on March 1, "Our policy is to get rid of Saddam Hussein, not his regime."

Any potential defector to the rebel cause put everything at risk: his position, his life, his family's lives, the lives of his relatives. Given the negative signals from Washington, the potential military defectors sat on the fence. And while they did so, the anti-Saddam rebellion was crushed.

Other countries in the region were eager to assist the forces battling Saddam Hussein. Syria was the country in the region most strongly supportive of the anti-Saddam rebels and provided significant support to Shi'a, Sunni, and Kurdish opposition groups. Parties from all 3 ethnic/confessional groups make their headquarters in Damascus.

During the time the Kurds controlled northern Iraq, Syria generously permitted access to liberated Kurdistan through its territory. Syrian officials responded enthusiastically to suggestions of assistance from coalition countries to the Iraqi opposition to oust Saddam Hussein. However, Syrian officials were reluctant to go too far alone, and looked to the United States for leadership. None was forthcoming.

One reason suggested for U.S. reluctance to aid the anti-Saddam rebels was Saudi fears over the subversive impact of Shi'a or democratic success in Iraq. However, while the anti-Saddam rebellion was still under way, Saudi officials proposed that the United States and Saudi Arabia together militarily assist both Shi'a and Kurdish rebels. The Saudis indicated they had only recently developed contacts with the mainstream Iraqi opposition groups, but said they were prepared to support the Shi'a foes of Saddam as well as the Kurds. The Dawa party has sent Saudi Arabia a message assuring the Kingdom it has no intention of causing problems among the Shi'a in the strategically sensitive Eastern Province, and the Saudis expressly denied that concerns about the Shi'a would affect their plans to assist the rebellion.

According to the Saudis, the United States had not even responded to their proposal by the end of March. If a response came later, it was too late to tip the balance in favor of the rebels.

Having failed to anticipate either the rebellion

or the subsequent repression, the United States was unprepared for the humanitarian crisis that followed. Although clear warnings came from the U.S. ambassador in Turkey just 3 days after the March 31 Kurdish collapse (along with warnings from journalists and others escaping Iraq), U.S. government disaster specialists were still performing assessments 2 weeks after the crisis began. So little is known about conditions inside Kurdistan that relief officials continue to refer to "Kurdish villages," even though villages have not existed in Iraqi Kurdistan since 1988. At a congressional briefing on April 12, a senior U.S. government official responsible for the relief effort praised the Iranian Red Lion and Sun Society for its work, even though this society had dropped the Shah's Red Lion and Sun name and emblem in 1979 in favor of the Islamic Red Crescent.

The United States armed forces are doing an extraordinary job delivering food and other assistance to the Kurdish refugees. Because of the terrain, and because of limited road access to the mountains, the delivery of assistance is a logistical nightmare; only the ingenuity and dedication of U.S. servicemen and women is overcoming it.

However, it did take 3 weeks before these military operations were bringing adequate food to the Kurdish refugees on the Turkish border. Even now the mountain camps have inadequate sanitation and only limited water. Further, the much larger refugee population on the Iranian border has so far been excluded from U.S. assistance.

"The United States and its coalition partners are stuck in the Iraqi quagmire."

According to State Department estimates, Kurds are dying at a rate of 600 a day on the Turkish border. Another 1,000 or more may be dying on the Iranian border and, as always seems true with these megacatastrophes, the victims are the weakest of the community, the children and the aged. It is impossible not to conclude that this toll could have been much lower had the United States and other nations anticipated the uprising and its consequences. Instead, the Kurds were for too long a problem policymakers wished would go away. . . .

Saddam Hussein's Future

The developments in the 2 months after the end of Operation Desert Storm very much strengthened Saddam Hussein's position inside Iraq. He has defeated serious challenges in both the north and the south. The Kurdish autonomy deal threatens to split the unity of the Iraqi opposition, as it was a sine qua non of the Beirut declaration setting up the Joint Action Committee that there be no separate deals between opposition groups and the regime. Worse, the price paid in blood by Kurdish and Shi'a civilians is almost certain to deter potential opponents and coupmakers, absent a very strong likelihood for success.

In the immediate aftermath of Desert Storm, Iraq's army was dissolving and the regime's security apparatus fading away. Secret police went underground, as did many Ba'ath officials. Few wanted to risk the retribution associated with a doomed regime. Now that Saddam has survived the crucible of civil war, his instruments of control—the mukhabarat, the Ba'ath party, and the army—are rallying around him.

Having lost the best opportunities for removing Saddam Hussein both during Operation Desert Storm and the March rebellion, it now appears that the United States, the coalition, and the region will have to endure this dictator for some time to come. . . .

Unless the world community is prepared to consign the Iraqi people to a fate which many have fought to avoid, the United States and its coalition partners are stuck in the Iraqi quagmire. Only the removal of Saddam Hussein and his regime can get us out, and the best hope for this result has passed. Saddam Hussein just turned 54 and could be around for years to come.

The Persian Gulf War Left Kuwait with Many Internal Problems

Caryle Murphy

About the Author: *Caryle Murphy is a reporter for* The Washington Post.

The emir of Kuwait has announced that parliamentary elections will be held in October 1992, fulfilling a key promise he made when his country was liberated in February, but opposition leaders see the move as too little, too late.

Moving to quell rising discontent with his government since liberation, Emir Jabir Ahmed Sabah also ordered the National Council to reconvene to prepare for the election. By setting a firm election date, the emir is seeking to defuse opposition criticism that he was trying to delay the vote indefinitely. But opposition leaders complain that October of 1992 is too long a delay.

The election dispute is only one among scores of postwar problems that appear to be moving this tiny Persian Gulf emirate rapidly toward crisis. Although Kuwait is plodding toward physical rehabilitation after Iraq's seven-month occupation, its society remains torn apart, its people frustrated, and its ruling family facing serious challenges to its authority.

The malaise is not limited to opposition leaders. Kuwaitis from across the economic and political spectrum—businessmen, laborers and even members of the military—are complaining about the direction the country appears to be taking.

"The phoenix," one prominent Kuwaiti says with a sigh, "did not rise from its ashes."

Caryle Murphy, "Can Kuwait Survive the Victory?" *The Washington Post National Weekly Edition,* June 10-16, 1991, © 1991 The Washington Post. Reprinted with permission.

The country that the United States sent a half-million troops to liberate, many Kuwaitis say, is losing a historic opportunity to heal its wounds and solve its most pressing problems.

So deep is the crisis of confidence that Kuwait's national identity, which Iraqi president Saddam Hussein sought to rub out by annexation, seems equally endangered now by the disunity, listlessness and alienation of so many of its people. "[Hussein] has succeeded," says businessman Faisal Qasami, expressing the pervasive pessimism about this country's future. "By the year 2000, we will no longer see Kuwait as a country. And that's not far away."

Qasami says he hopes his jeremiad will prove exaggerated, but at the moment there are few trends bucking it.

The mood contrasts sharply with the frenzied jubilation after Iraq's defeat. Hundreds of Kuwaiti flags hoisted in celebration three months ago are today so blackened with oily soot their colors are barely visible. Nobody, it seems, cares enough to wash the national emblem, much less make the necessary changes to bring the nation's economy up to speed.

"The oil fires aren't emergency enough for them to alter their procedures," says a Western diplomat, alluding to the government's reputation for penny-pinching. "They squabble over $10,000 in dealing with $200,000 contracts."

> **"Although Kuwait is plodding toward physical rehabilitation . . . , its society remains torn apart."**

The slow restoration of government services is among the Kuwaitis' chief concerns. Government ministry offices, bereft of foreign workers who fled and of Kuwaitis not yet returned home, are working with skeleton crews. Most police stations remain shuttered, since there is no police force to speak of and, thus, no one to hear complaints about an upsurge of crime.

Wealthy merchants with intact financial assets are rebuilding inventories and signing contracts. But jobseekers find few openings, and small shopkeepers who lost everything to looters are stilled, awaiting government decisions on compensation.

To the dismay of some Kuwaitis who remained during Iraq's seven-month occupation, their fellow citizens are continuing to kidnap foreigners, especially Palestinians and Iraqis, subjecting them to beatings and torture. Western diplomatic sources say these abuses, which had been declining, have been rising recently as Kuwaitis return home, bent on personal revenge. Top on their list are members of Kuwait's Palestinian community, who often are accused of having collaborated with Iraqi occupation forces.

Prime Minister Saad Abdullah Sabah, the crown prince, has condemned these abuses and ordered a crackdown. But with no police force, many are skeptical that the vigilantes can be curbed. As a result, many of the 170,000 Palestinians still here—who are widely shunned in the job market—are planning to leave for Jordan.

No Army

Kuwait's armed forces, meanwhile, are nowhere to be found. Almost 90 percent of its pre-invasion army was composed of *bidoon,* longtime residents of this country who hold no citizenship. Since liberation, the government has made clear that these people, although some stood and fought the Iraqi invaders the first day, will not be taken back.

As for the Kuwaitis in the officer corps, "hundreds" of them, says one military source, are refusing to serve under the current military leadership because it failed to alert the armed forces to Iraq's invasion preparations, and then ran away. This was the message, several sources say, of a recent petition sent to the government by about 300 Kuwaiti army personnel.

The ruling Sabah family has returned to power with little change in its working style. It has not articulated a vision of a new Kuwait that inspires its citizens, beyond the slogan, "Kuwait for Kuwaitis." Nor has it recognized their demands, after the trauma of occupation, for a greater role in decisions, and for political appointments based on expertise rather than family connections.

Emir Jabir remains aloof, leaving administration to Crown Prince Saad, who has a reputation for rarely delegating authority. Despite repeated requests since August from Kuwait's opposition, he has refused to form a cabinet of technocrats, including some from the opposition. "He is like a basketball player who dribbles beautifully," says one official who has worked with Saad. "But dribbling is not playing. You have to score. He thinks that because he's busy, he's doing something."

Days often go by before action is taken on urgent problems by a leadership that many say is incompetent and inattentive to the nation's needs. "All Arab governments, without exception, have legitimacy problems," says a European diplomat. "And with this one, the problem has become acute."

If the government is taking note of these complaints, it is not saying so.

"First of all, there is no problem," says Deputy Prime Minister Salem Sabah. "Secondly, there are a lot of rumors around. . . . Things are normal now. Liberation being done, the government is functioning in its normal routine. People are trying to find little delays here and there . . . [and] magnify these normal delays in order to make out of them a fuss."

"The ruling Sabah family has returned to power with little change in its working style."

The most recent fuss was the international criticism, including from the Bush administration, over a 15-year prison sentence an Iraqi man received for wearing a Saddam Hussein T-shirt. Several days later, the judge disclosed in a statement that the defendant was also guilty of informing on Kuwaitis during the occupation.

When asked why these charges and the evidence were not presented at the trial, Salem indicates this is not a matter for his attention. "As a government," he says, "we don't follow the little details. . . . We talk to intellectuals. We talk to governments in the world. We talk to people who know what words mean."

"Tension has increased between the . . . Kuwaitis who remained during the occupation and those who fled."

Salem has not ruled out placing censors at newspapers, as was the case before the invasion. "Censorship is not as people perceive it," he says, likening a censor to "an elderly brother saying, 'For God's sake, this will embarrass the government or this might create a problem.' He's an adviser to them, more than a censor." The government, he says, does not object to newspaper criticism, "if it is constructive criticism."

One post-liberation paper has already been shut down by the government, and only one, whose Arabic name translates as "The New Dawn," is currently publishing inside Kuwait. Its pro-government stance has many people calling it "The New Dark." The more independent *Al-Qabas,* whose presses were stolen by the Iraqis, is to resume publication soon.

"I hope the government won't appoint a censor because we have nothing to hide in Kuwait now," says *Al-Qabas* editor Mohammed Saghr. "We are an open country. After what happened to Kuwait, there should not be censors." Besides, he adds, "the government says it believes in democracy and free press."

For most Kuwaitis, the Sabah family still is a symbol of unity for the country, and only a tiny minority wants it removed. But they also are demanding that the family revert to its legal role as head of state and sharer of executive powers with an elected parliament, as set out in the 1962 constitution. Emir Jabir suspended the constitution in 1986.

The return of this constitution and a demand for an earlier election date are the common denominator in an otherwise divided opposition.

The opposition now includes many young Kuwaitis who, in the absence of their government during the occupation, organized basic services and an armed resistance. From the first day of its return, the government angered many of these activists by refusing to work with them, either in distributing food or policing the streets.

Since then, tension has increased between the estimated 200,000 Kuwaitis who remained during the occupation and those who fled, as the "insiders" express resentment that those they derisively call "the runners" have not rushed back to help.

"They are there in their castles and palaces in Geneva and London," says Iqbal Qabandi, whose sister was killed by the Iraqis. "Let them come back here and build Kuwait. 'No,' they say, 'Too much smoke. It's bad for the children. No electricity, no water.' Why shouldn't they live like us? Sometimes I think our Kuwaiti blood means nothing to them."

The government says that about 10,000 Kuwaitis a day are returning. But these seem canceled by others leaving for summer vacations.

Future Conflict

Most Kuwaitis, however, are expected to return. . . . Unless the prevailing discontent and political divisions are resolved, many here fear that tensions could rise. And with the large number of weapons still in the hands of both Sabah supporters and their critics, there is also apprehension that any violence could lead the government, under the pretext of taming chaos, to impose emergency laws and postpone the elections beyond 1992.

"I just got my country back," says one Kuwaiti financial analyst who says he fears this scenario. "I don't want to lose it again."

Chapter 5

How Well Did the News Media Cover the Persian Gulf War?

Media Coverage of the Persian Gulf War: An Overview

Everette E. Dennis

About the Author: *Everette E. Dennis is the executive director of the Freedom Forum in New York City. The forum is the nation's first institute for the advanced study of mass communication and technological change.*

Editor's note: The American news media play an enormously important role in wartime. News organizations provide Americans with information they need to assess the progress of the war and the foreign policies of the American government. However, the news media face a difficult problem: They must attempt to communicate events fairly and accurately without revealing sensitive military information which could jeopardize America's war effort.

While all journalists acknowledge that some reporting restrictions are necessary to protect military operations, many journalists expressed dissatisfaction with the restrictions enforced by the American military during the Persian Gulf War. For example, at one point restrictions forced more than eight hundred reporters covering the conflict to compete for 125 spaces in press pools. Only members of press pools were allowed into combat areas, accompanied by military escorts, which often stifled the spontaneity of interviews conducted with soldiers on the field of battle. Unfortunately, the small size of the press pools made the rest of the press corps almost completely dependent upon pool reporters and military briefings for news. Reporters condemned the pool system for severely limiting the supply of reliable information about the war's progress.

Everette E. Dennis, "Introduction" to *The Media at War: The Press and the Persian Gulf Conflict*, a report published by the Freedom Forum Media Studies Center, New York, NY. Copyright © 1991. Reprinted with permission.

Ironically, the media's complaints about Pentagon censorship were apparently not shared by the American public, the presumed beneficiary of increased media access to information. For instance, a Time *magazine poll of February 4, 1991, indicated that 88 percent of respondents believed military censorship was necessary. Furthermore, 79 percent of respondents thought that despite the censorship they were getting enough information about the war.*

While the public's opinion on the adequacy of war coverage was generally favorable, media critics' detailed analyses of the quality of news reporting were overwhelmingly negative. Some critics charged that the media were far too nationalistic, blindly accepting the Bush administration's version of events. Others criticized the media, especially Cable News Network's Peter Arnett, for advancing the enemy cause by broadcasting Iraqi propaganda and exaggerating domestic opposition to the war. Some of the most discouraging assessments of the media's performance came from their own ranks. For example, on May 27, 1991, the editors of the Nation *magazine argued that "the main problem [with the war coverage] was with the mass media, not the government. Self-censorship, self-deception, unexamined bias and just plain cowardice subverted the facts, obscured history and occluded criticism better than any imposed regime could have done."*

> ## "In the 40-day Persian Gulf war the news media were much more than neutral observers."

The authors of the following chapter analyze the media's performance during the Persian Gulf War. The chapter begins with Everette E. Dennis's overview on the role of the media in wartime. Dennis examines the military's rules for protecting sensitive information, conflicts between the media and the military in wartime, and some of the praise and criticisms of media coverage of the Persian Gulf War.

In the 40-day Persian Gulf war the news media were much more than neutral observers. From the beginning of the war on the evening of January 16, 1991, media organizations were talked about almost as much as governments, generals and troops on both sides and across the 28-nation alliance that opposed the forces of Iraq. When President George Bush and his commanders were asked about early developments in the conflict, they often said they relied on "the media," and especially on CNN [Cable News Network]. And it was said that Iraqi leader Saddam Hussein was also watching the war on television, also relying on CNN and its remarkable international presence.

Media Were Misunderstood

If the media were much discussed in this war, it could also be said that they were much misunderstood. While there is evidence that the media competently performed a useful service in covering the war, this was done without much planning or reflection and certainly with little historical perspective on the role of the press in wartime.

At the same time, the military had made studious preparations for dealing with the press in this war, far beyond what it had ever done before. Since Vietnam, when the military thought its conduct of the war had been impaired by negative media coverage, people in the Pentagon had been simmering, planning and talking. In sessions there and in the war and naval colleges, the issue of "handling" the media was widely discussed and carefully understood. While the military assessment of the media's role in Vietnam and other wars may have been wrong—some of the most critical reporters in Vietnam, for example, were hawks, not doves—there was nonetheless a determination to be ready for the next war not only in strictly military terms but also in terms of public opinion.

The press, on the other hand, had grumbled about its treatment in the short-lived Grenada conflict in 1983, when reporters were initially barred from the battlefield and polls said the public mightily approved. But there was little collective effort to plan for covering future wars. Anything but. Most lacking was a clear sense of what the press typically does in time of war. With its lack of institutional memory, the press does not know the lessons of earlier war reportage as depicted, for example, in the leading book on the subject, Phillip Knightley's *The First Casualty*. While the military was planning for the next war in the years after Vietnam, giving young military officers training in public relations and communications strategy, the press gave relatively little thought to the subject.

The press has no such systematic approach to planning for war coverage or anything else. While there are common interests in covering war—such as access to the war zone and the freedom to transmit any information gathered—the media rarely speak with one voice because of their competitive nature. So while there might be objections made to information policies as promulgated by the Pentagon, there is little unified press effort to wage a successful war against them. In the Persian Gulf war, for example, when the editor of *The Nation* led several other journalists in filing a suit objecting to the Pentagon rules no major national media organizations either joined in the litigation or filed friend-of-the-court briefs. The military, conversely, generally spoke with one voice.

"War is always the ultimate news story."

While there was censorship in this and all wars, the press was not particularly effective in convincing the public that censorship was a bad thing. Quite the contrary, opinion studies show that most of the public strongly supported censorship and that people felt they were getting excellent or at least adequate coverage of the war. The media, meanwhile, complained on the one hand that they were doing an exemplary job under the circumstances while on the other that they couldn't get all the information they needed to inform the American public fully. Both views are probably correct, but precious little information was published to give the public any sense of what it might be missing. If there were categories of information, specific military operations, casualty figures, or other matters crucial to public understanding of the action, the press failed to say so, either during or after the war. Those would be essential ingredients in fostering more public support for the press in wartime.

War Is the Ultimate News Story

When it came to solving problems posed by censorship and natural media-government-military conflicts, once again the military was ahead of the media. After the Grenada affair, a commission headed by Major General Winant Sidle and made up of military and media people issued a report suggesting procedures, including a press pool that could be used for covering future wars. While thought to be a workable solution at the time, it was later claimed that the recommendations of this commission did not work, for example, in the short war in Panama in 1989. The press did not heed the warning of that conflict and failed to develop any mechanism for assuring access to information and limiting censorship in future military actions.

The failure was a regrettable one, for few journalists need any instruction in understanding that war is always the ultimate news story. In *The First Casualty*, Phillip Knightley quotes a young Peter Arnett saying in 1965 that the Vietnam War was "the best story going on anywhere in the world at the moment." Knightley adds that there is "no better place for a young reporter to put a gloss on a new career or for an old reporter to revitalize a fading one." A quarter-century later in Baghdad, an older and more experienced Arnett would again encounter "the best story in the world.". . .

While most reporters (and editors) assigned to this conflict had little or no prior experience with war coverage on the scale of the Persian Gulf conflict, they knew instinctively that this was likely to be "the story" of the decade and they wanted to be there. The organizations they worked for were also committed to covering the war and, in fact, some media outlets that rarely send people abroad committed resources to cover this story.

But while editors and electronic media executives talked about objective and impartial coverage of the war, they failed to realize that war, unlike many other news stories, is a one-sided affair. Reporters, whether they are Americans or from other countries, cover the action from the perspective of their country, mostly using sources on "their side" and aiming their reports at an audience within their own country. Covering war is unlike covering anything else, and it leads inevitably toward nationalistic accounts. Historically, the consequence of such coverage is cheerleading rather than critical analysis.

This is not to suggest that the media covering the Persian Gulf war or any other conflict have been mindless enthusiasts for battle, slavishly doing the bidding of their governments. Quite the contrary: Within the conventions and "rules" of reporting, war correspondents have tried to scope-out and monitor wars, often comparing official pronouncements with their own firsthand evidence. Then, too, the American journalistic article of faith says that media and government are often adversaries in the search for truth, leading correspondents to look for inconsistencies and conflicts between press briefings and the tale told on the battlefield. . . .

"The American journalistic article of faith says that media and government are often adversaries in the search for truth."

Peter Arnett who was with the AP [Associated Press] in Vietnam and CNN in the Persian Gulf war, became the central figure in the debate over what reporters could appropriately do in covering military conflict. Before the Persian Gulf war was over, Arnett's lone coverage from Baghdad would ignite the ire of Wyoming Senator Alan Simpson and others who would accuse him of helping the Iraqi cause. Perhaps more than any single case in the war coverage, Arnett's reporting for CNN underscored the role of censorship. In the autumn of 1990, when war talk heightened (although war itself still seemed unlikely to many observers), the Pentagon promulgated censorship rules aimed at protecting the lives of troops and preventing coverage that could even inadvertently interfere with military operations.

A Variety of Sources

American military censorship limited press access to U.S. officers and enlisted personnel, while official censorship by other nations as well as cultural taboos narrowed the scope of coverage that could come from Islamic countries like Saudi Arabia, Egypt or Jordan. Still, the massive amount of coverage that followed, both in electronic and print media, drew on a wide variety of sources. Leaders of the war effort, including President Bush, General Colin Powell, Defense Secretary Richard Cheney and General Norman Schwarzkopf, as well as other allied commanders from the 28-nation coalition, were regularly available. Other government leaders such as President Hussein of Iraq, Egypt's President Mubarak and Jordan's King Hussein, were also frequently accessible. Diplomats, military experts and others provided a flow of current information, and a mainstay of coverage was the regular briefing each day from Riyadh, Saudi Arabia, arranged and orchestrated by military authorities. There was also some access to commanders and troops in the field, which led to many local-color ("Hi, Mom!") stories that brought news of particular units to their hometown papers and broadcast stations.

But perhaps more than in any other war, in a fashion more like a political campaign, the media resourcefully developed their own non-official sources, mainly retired generals and admirals and other former members of the officer corps, who offered expert advice sometimes on a paid, consulting basis. Academic experts were also widely interviewed, especially those known as Middle Eastern or Islamic experts.

Although one conservative media study center said that early coverage was highly critical, sometimes skewering the president, state and defense departments, others doubted this, saying that most coverage was descriptive and generally positive in its portrayals, except for some interviews with members of Congress opposed to the war, or with representatives of the antiwar movement itself. Other commentators thought the war coverage was jingoistic, colored and, thus, too supportive of the war effort. Once the war began, members of Congress, once quite volatile during legislative debate, were notably quiet and apparently often unwilling to comment.

"The media resourcefully developed their own non-official sources."

In several addresses President Bush said the war provided a "defining hour" for the United States and U.S. foreign policy, but it was also a defining hour for the media. The war began like no other in history—live and on prime-time television just before 7 p.m. EST [Eastern Standard Time] on Wednesday, January 16—and with CNN carrying the first and subsequent live reports from Baghdad, much public attention was riveted on what had heretofore been the "fourth or fifth" network. The broadcast networks, after early continuous "real-time" coverage free of commercials, eventually confined their coverage to some special reports but mostly folded the war into regular news programs. They also responded with documentaries, longer news reports and the use of high-caliber news sources, some of them paid consultants. Clearly the emphasis of the networks was on quality of coverage and on editing otherwise disparate coverage into coherent, well-produced reports. CNN, meanwhile, not only held its own on cable systems but became "the network feed" for many independent stations throughout the country that could not get service from the Big Three. A few network-affiliated stations abandoned what they thought was sluggish coverage by their feed networks and also used CNN, at least for a time.

As networks redefined their coverage, so did newspapers and newsmagazines. Despite the early "death of print" predictions, both newspapers and magazines made circulation gains during the war. Still, newspaper editors had to contemplate seriously what people already knew from television as they rewrote interpretative and background reports; the persistent danger was in producing a newspaper so badly pre-empted by electronic news reports that it would arrive at readers' doorsteps stale, a recap of yesterday's news. Weekly newsmagazines had an even greater challenge to produce eye-catching reports and news summaries that would not be outdated before they got to the printer, let alone the newsstand. They succeeded. All print media engaged in public affairs news coverage reported increased newsstand and home delivery sales during the war. At the same time, however, the war seriously challenged the long-term viability of print media as a source of compelling, immediate news on which people depend, a view strongly reinforced by news sources themselves—presidents, generals and others—who admitted that much of what they knew they had learned from CNN.

A Preoccupation with Immediacy

Serious assessment of the quality of news coverage during the war still awaits a comprehensive study, but it was badly flawed by critics' preoccupation with immediacy. To a large extent immediacy, as represented by mere minutes, became a defining standard for the war and for media quality; CBS News took the opportunity to assess blame, firing executive producer Tom Bettag, a symbolic and real scapegoat for its slow start in the affair. It seems ironic that at the same time immediacy was touted as the only recognizable difference between television offerings, the print media, which lagged days behind in their production and treatment of news, inspired enough public confidence to boost sales.

Newspapers with national reach, notably the *New York Times, Los Angeles Times, Washington Post, USA TODAY* and *Wall Street Journal,* were cited for their energetic and exemplary coverage. Many critics said the *Los Angeles Times* had been particularly distinguished, but that few opinion leaders in the Northeast had read it. *USA TODAY* and the newsmagazines were the great packagers; maps, charts and other schematic data in *Newsweek, Time* and *U.S. News & World Report* were exceptionally useful in following the war.

"Presidents, generals and others . . . admitted that much of what they knew they had learned from CNN."

While the war coverage and its immediate aftermath greatly accelerated generalized coverage of the Middle East, critics rightly complained that other international news—in the Soviet Union, China and Eastern Europe, not to mention the nearly invisible developing world—had gone out of sight and out of mind. It raised questions as to whether the "new world order," as defined by the end of the Cold War and the forging of new understandings and alliances, was to be more than a political slogan or a rallying cry for the war. The answer to this question obviously is already an issue in postwar coverage of global affairs.

In a sense, when war occurs, even a relatively short one, almost all else stops in the world of the media, if not also the public. One report had President Bush devoting 70 percent of his time to the war between early January and late March 1991. The media, which typically let the president set the national news agenda, followed suit. Clearly the Persian Gulf war was covered extensively with every communication technology known to humankind. Whether the public is well- or ill-served by such practices is worthy of serious examination and discussion.

Media Coverage of the Persian Gulf War Was Accurate

Pete Williams

About the Author: *Pete Williams is the U.S. assistant secretary of defense for public affairs.*

Generals, it's been said, are always preparing for the previous war. In Operation Desert Storm, the same might be true of journalists.

The press arrangements for the gulf war were not, as some journalists claim, the most restrictive ever in combat. Some limitations were necessary to accommodate a huge press corps and one of history's fastest moving military operations. Even so, reporters did get out with the troops, and the press gave the American people the best war coverage they ever had.

What public, in what other conflict, can possibly have had as much information as the American people in this war? People responded to that coverage. A *Newsweek* poll found that 59 percent of Americans think better of the news media now than they did before the war.

Thanks to reporters, the American people could see what our troops, our commanders and our weapons were doing. Partly because of the thorough job the press did, respect for the military was enhanced. According to a *Washington Post*-ABC News poll, 88 percent of those surveyed thought the military gained respect during the gulf war. Ten years ago, the military had only half that public confidence.

Another part of the reason for the military's high credibility, of course, is that Secretary of Defense Richard B. Cheney and Gen. Colin L. Powell, chairman of the Joint Chiefs of Staff,

Pete Williams, "The Pentagon Is Not in the Censorship Business," *The Washington Post National Weekly Edition*, March 25-31, 1991. Reprinted with permission.

made the decision that we would say only what we knew to be true. We were careful not to get ahead of our successes. We waited for initial field reports to be confirmed.

Washington loves to talk about spin control. This was the first government operation I know of that had euphoria control.

The least loved aspect of coverage arrangements in the gulf was undoubtedly the press pools—groups of reporters who represent the rest of their colleagues and file stories for all, rather than just for their own news organizations. But it was just such a pool that got the first reporters to the scene.

Following Iraq's Aug. 2, 1990 invasion of Kuwait, U.S. forces began to arrive a few days after Cheney's meeting with King Fahd in Saudi Arabia. While the Saudi government considered whether to grant visas to journalists, they agreed to accept a small number of reporters if the U.S. military could get them in. So we activated the Department of Defense National Media Pool, to ensure initial coverage of the U.S. buildup. At the time, there was no other way to get Western reporters into Saudi Arabia. The number of journalists grew to nearly 800 by December 1990. Those reporters filed their stories independently, directly to their own news organizations.

"The press gave the American people the best war coverage they ever had."

After the president in mid-November 1990 announced a further buildup in U.S. forces, to give the coalition a true offensive option, the Department of Defense began working on a plan that would allow reporters to cover combat while maintaining the operational security necessary to ensure tactical surprise and save American lives.

News organizations worried in fall 1990 that they would not have enough staff in the Persian

Gulf to cover hostilities. They did not know how the Saudi government would respond to their request for more visas. They couldn't predict what restrictions might be imposed on commercial air traffic in the event of a war, and they asked us for a military plane to bring in journalistic reinforcements. We complied. A U.S. Air Force C-141 cargo plane left Andrews Air Force base on Jan. 17, 1991, the morning after the bombing began, with 126 news people aboard.

Ground Rules

In formulating the ground rules and guidelines for covering Operation Desert Storm, we looked at the rules developed in 1942 for World War II, at those handed down by Gen. Dwight D. Eisenhower's chief of staff for the reporters who covered the D-Day landings, and at the ground rules established by Gen. Douglas MacArthur for covering the Korean War. And we carefully studied the rules drawn up for covering the war in Vietnam. The ground rules were not intended to prevent journalists from reporting on incidents that might embarrass the military or to make military operations look sanitized. Instead, they were intended simply and solely to prevent publication of details that could jeopardize a military operation or endanger the lives of U.S. troops.

Some of the things that were not to be reported were:

• Details of future operations;

• Specific information about troop strengths or locations;

• Specific information on missing or downed airplanes or ships while search and rescue operations were underway; and

• Information on operational weaknesses that could be used against U.S. forces.

Reporters understand the reasoning behind these ground rules. Of all the aspects of the coverage plan for the war in the Persian Gulf, they were the least controversial.

The least understood was probably the system for copy review.

Reporters covering World War II wrote their stories and submitted them to a military censor. The censors cut out anything they felt broke the rules and sent the stories on. The decision of the censor was final. There was no such system of censorship in Operation Desert Storm. There was, instead, a procedure that allowed us to appeal to news organizations when we thought material in their stories would violate the ground rules. But unlike a system of censorship, the gulf rules left the final decision to publish or broadcast in the hands of journalists, not the military.

While the pools were in existence, 1,351 print pool reports were written. Of those, only five were submitted for our review in Washington. Four of them were cleared within a few hours. The fifth story dealt in considerable detail with the methods of intelligence operations in the field. We called the reporter's editor-in-chief, and he agreed that the story should be changed to protect sensitive intelligence procedures. This aspect of the coverage plan also worked well.

As the number of troops in the desert grew, so did the number of reporters, rising to more than 1,600 on the eve of the ground war. With hundreds of fiercely independent reporters seeking to join up with combat units, we concluded we'd have no choice but to rely on pools once the combat war started.

> ## "Our first obligation is to get reporters out with the action, so that journalists are eyewitnesses to history."

Before the air phase of the operation began in January 1991, news organizations were afraid that we wouldn't get the pools out to see anything. But we did. Reporters were on an aircraft carrier in the Red Sea to witness the launching of the first air strikes, aboard a battleship in the Persian Gulf that fired the first cruise missiles ever used in combat, at the air bases where fighter planes and bombers were taking off around the clock, and with several ground units in the desert. Those early days were not without problems. For example, the first stories written about the stealth fighters were sent all the way back to the F-117's home base in Nevada to be cleared.

Gulf War Was a Set Piece Operation

Now that the war is over and coalition commander Gen. H. Norman Schwarzkopf has described the plan, it's clear why the press arrangements for the ground phase of the campaign weren't like those in World War II. This was not an operation in which reporters could ride around in jeeps going from one part of the front to another, or like Vietnam where reporters could hop a helicopter to specific points of action.

"We must drop the pretense that the safety of journalists isn't the government's concern."

American ground units moved quickly—some of them by air. To cover the conflict, reporters had to be part of a unit, able to move with it. Each commander had an assigned number of vehicles with only so many seats. Although he could take care of the reporters he knew were coming, he could not have been expected to keep absorbing those who arrived on their own, unexpectedly, in their own rented four-wheel drives—assuming they could even find the units out west once the war started.

Nonetheless, by the time the ground war began, 132 reporters and photographers were out with the Army and Marines on the ground. Reporters were out with every division, and 27 more were on ships at sea or on air bases. The ground war wasn't like Vietnam, either, with minor skirmishes here and there and a major offensive every now and then. It was, as the world now knows, a set piece operation, with divisions from the Army and Navy moving quickly, supported by Air Force and Navy planes, and all of it carefully orchestrated.

In this sense, it was like something from a previous war—D-Day. Back then, 461 reporters were signed up at the Supreme Headquarters, Allied Expeditionary Force, to cover the Normandy invasion. But of that number, only 27 U.S. reporters actually went ashore with the first wave of forces.

Now that it's just about over, it's time to look back. There are clearly some things we could have done better. Here are some preliminary observations:

• We could have done a better job of helping journalists in the field. Judging from what I've heard from the reporters who went out in the pools, we had some outstanding escorts. But we must improve that process.

• Escort officers shouldn't throw themselves in front of the camera when one of the troops utters a forbidden word. We need to teach public affairs personnel how to do their jobs so that reporters won't feel their interview subjects are intimidated.

• Our first obligation is to get reporters out with the action, so that journalists are eyewitnesses to history. I've seen some excellent examples of that—some of Molly Moore's stories on the Marines for the *Washington Post*, for example.

We Must Do Better

But we must do better at getting stories back to the press center. Some units did well, using computer modems and tactical telephone fax machines. Others didn't do so well. I've heard from reporters who said their stories were delayed for several days. Although delivery problems would have existed whether the press worked in pools or not, we need to do better.

But part of the problem was the sheer number of journalists to accommodate. The government cannot decide who goes to cover the war and who doesn't. Maybe it's too much to expect as competitive an institution as the press to limit its numbers in a war, especially when local papers want to provide coverage to the hometowns where the troops come from. But it's worth raising.

Several bureau chiefs told me in fall 1990 that in planning for war coverage, the security of reporters was their concern, not mine. But that's not realistic, because we couldn't ignore that even if we wanted to. It's not morally possible.

> ## "Whatever else the press arrangements in the Persian Gulf may have been, they were a good-faith effort on the part of the military."

When a group of U.S. journalists was captured in Iraq after the cease-fire, four news industry executives wrote to the president, saying that no U.S. forces should withdraw from Iraq until the issue of the journalists was resolved. The issue was raised by the U.S. government with the Iraqis, and we succeeded in securing their release. Everyone is relieved they were freed. But we must drop the pretense that the safety of journalists isn't the government's concern.

Whatever else the press arrangements in the Persian Gulf may have been, they were a good-faith effort on the part of the military to be as fair as possible to the large number of reporters on the scene, to get as many reporters as possible out with troops during a highly mobile, modern ground war, and to allow as much freedom in reporting as possible, while still preventing the enemy from knowing what we were up to.

This was, after all, an enemy that had virtually as much access to American news reporting as people had here at home. From what we've been able to learn so far, Iraqi military commanders didn't have a clue as to which coalition forces were out there, where they were, or what they were up to. They appear to have been caught totally off guard by the quick move of the 18th Airborne Corps west of Kuwait, deep into Iraq. For the sake of the operation and the lives of these troops, we could not afford to let the enemy learn that.

Censorship Prevented the Media from Accurately Covering the Persian Gulf War

Michael Getler

About the Author: *Michael Getler is the assistant managing editor for foreign news at the* Washington Post. *He formerly covered military affairs for the newspaper.*

Along with the Iraqis, the civilian and uniformed leaders of the U.S. military did a pretty good job of mopping up the press in Operation Desert Storm. No one seems to care very much about this except several hundred reporters and editors who know they've been had. The war, after all, was successful beyond anyone's expectations: an overwhelming American-led victory with amazingly low allied casualties that ended after only 100 hours of ground fighting.

Many people by now probably feel they have a pretty good picture of what happened and may not have noticed or cared much if the news, details and pictures were a day or two or three late, or if a few things went uncovered, or if the war was over before they found out much. All's well that ends well. Indeed, the polls show a lot of people even think the press did a pretty good job.

But the military, and the civilians who are supposed to control the military, did a better job controlling the press than the press did carrying

Michael Getler, "The Gulf War 'Good News' Policy Is a Dangerous Precedent," *The Washington Post National Weekly Edition*, March 25-31, 1991, © 1991, The Washington Post. Reprinted with permission.

out its crucial, cranky function in a democracy.

The Pentagon and the U.S. Army Central Command conducted what is probably the most thorough and sophisticated wartime control of American reporters in modern times—what they could see, who they could talk to, where they could go, what they could tell the public and when they could tell it—a collection of restrictions that in its totality and mindset seems to go beyond World War II, Korea and Vietnam.

Because it all happened so fast and ended so happily, the implications of the Pentagon's victory over the press may not seem apparent or important. But had the war gone on longer or less well, the chances are that the restrictions would have been used to control and delay even more what the public knew about the fighting. The Pentagon has devised a system that tends to produce "good news"—and the Iraqis turned out to be a "good news" kind of enemy. But if allowed to stand as a model, the Desert Storm system runs the risk of seriously distorting reality for some uncertain time if the next war is a lot tougher.

There were many elements of the Pentagon's plan to control the press. They were there from the start of serious planning by the Defense Department in fall 1990. . . .

> **"The military . . . did a better job controlling the press than the press did carrying out its crucial, cranky function in a democracy."**

Censorship by delay: Perhaps the crucial restriction turned out to be what the Pentagon calls "security review" and what the press called censorship. The issue, as it turned out, was not really censorship. Correspondents told of many instances of foolish military attempts to delete material that had nothing to do with real security—earthy language or embarrassing scenes. Yet there seems to have been relatively little else removed from reporters' copy.

Indeed, this tends to back up the point that news executives repeatedly tried to make to the Pentagon: that reporters will agree to and abide by sensible ground rules about what not to report without the need for field censorship, a system that worked essentially flawlessly in Vietnam. Barry Zorthian, the former U.S. Mission spokesman in Saigon, has said there were only four or five violations of security—some unintentional—by some 2,000 journalists over a five-year period.

Lost Control

What security review did do, however, is force reporters to force their stories into their military minders in the field for review and transmission back to the military press headquarters in Dhahran, Saudi Arabia. Reporters totally lost control over their dispatches and the military gained the extraordinary power to delay transmission of news for unspecified amounts of time.

It is impossible to say for sure what happened to every dispatch or what every newspaper or network experienced. But the overwhelming evidence is that virtually all of these dispatches, or "pool" reports, were delayed because of tampering or various other reasons somewhere along the line by the military, at best one day but far more frequently by two or three days. Reporters who had risked their lives, along with soldiers, to ride through minefields and be exposed to Iraqi fire, and who thought they had sent their material on its way to readers or viewers, were almost always disappointed.

There were undoubtedly occasions where public affairs officers tried their best and where bad weather meant that helicopters that might have speeded the movement of stories could not fly. But the fact is the Army should not have been in the business of reviewing and transmitting stories and pictures.

"They don't know how to transmit copy just like I don't know how to drive a tank," says the *Post's* veteran foreign and war correspondent, Ed

Cody. Military officers have no incentive to rush back a story that they may not like, or to bug a senior officer to move it faster than a 20-hour "pony express" drive by truck, or to use the electronic means available to them.

The military refused to permit pool reporters accompanying troops to take their own vehicles, usually rented Land Rovers, or suitcase-sized satellite telephones out into the field. The phones could have given reporters direct access to their news desks.

New York Times reporter Philip Shenon, with U.S. armored forces, told the Associated Press his military hosts took 72 hours to transmit his stories, and that when reporters volunteered to go to a nearby Saudi telephone to file them, "we were given the ludicrous argument that we couldn't leave the base because there was a terrorist threat. They were supposed to help us file our story, but there seemed to be every desire to hinder us in getting the work out," Shenon says.

Contrast these delays with coverage of World War II. On June 7, 1944, within hours of the invasion of France, UPI [United Press International] reported "some of the first American assault troops storming the French beaches went down under a withering German crossfire. . . . They swarmed ashore over the bodies of their dead until they established a foothold. . . . At one point Nazi machine guns wiped out some of the first troops as soon as their landing craft swung open."

"The quality of the daily briefings in Riyadh, Saudi Arabia, led to what one reporter described as 'death by briefing.'"

There is, in my view, zero probability that that kind of accurate, timely and dramatic reporting would have been allowed to have been transmitted without serious delay by the presslords of Desert Storm.

Fortunately, there were no such scenes to describe this time. But there were also no accounts of the relatively few combat engagements of the war that reached here until the military either wanted them to, or the system got around to moving them, and that usually meant days late—in many cases, not until the war was over. There were few if any pictures transmitted during the fighting of wounded or dead GIs and very few of what must be thousands of dead Iraqis. There were only the fuzziest, delayed accounts of death by friendly fire of U.S. and British ground troops, perhaps understandably, perhaps also to let the bad stuff dissipate before it became public. Pool reporters were kept away from the first significant ground clash at Khafji, while briefers played down the role of U.S. Marines and played up the role of Saudi and Qatari forces.

Death by Briefing

The ground war, while it was underway, was described primarily by military briefers in the Pentagon and Saudi Arabia, which is what the Pentagon wanted all along—for them, not the pools or the press, to control the flow of news. The quality of the daily briefings in Riyadh, Saudi Arabia, led to what one reporter described as "death by briefing."

Those televised briefings helped the Pentagon's general press strategy in other ways. Reporters who regularly cover military matters generally know what to ask. A war, however, brings everyone into the briefing room and the briefers know it. So a lot of people get called on who may appear to a television audience to be ill-informed and pushy and that helps the view that those at the podium know best about what the public should know.

When the commanding presence of Joint Chiefs Chairman Colin L. Powell or Desert Storm Commander H. Norman Schwarzkopf were added for good measure, the questioners didn't have a chance on the public relations meter.

Until it was clear that the enemy was routed, the ground war was presented in much the same antiseptic way as the air war, in which videotapes of highly accurate smart-bomb strikes were shown to the public while repeated requests by reporters to go on raids or talk to crews of B-52s, which carry huge loads of less accurate bombs, were never acted upon.

As in Grenada and Panama, that first, potentially ugliest look at warfare, is what the Pentagon doesn't want anyone to see until it is on its way to doing what it wants to do.

When the ground campaign began, the first thing Secretary of Defense Richard B. Cheney did publicly was to announce a news blackout, which is known to have annoyed some U.S. generals in the field and which didn't seem to bother the British or French, whose reporters seemed to be getting more real-time information than were the Americans.

The Pentagon then partially relaxed its blackout within 12 hours so that Schwarzkopf could proclaim a "dramatic success" in the early going.

The other central element of the Pentagon's press control plan was the "pool" system itself, in which eventually about 150 reporters, cameramen and technicians out of more than 1,400 in Saudi Arabia at the time, were sent out in small groups with the armed forces to report back to their colleagues and the nation at large.

"We were like animals in a zoo, and the press officers were the zookeepers who threw us a piece of meat occasionally."

Contrary to some accounts, the pool system for Desert Storm was not signed onto by news executives of the major media organizations. It was a Defense Department plan, aspects of which drew consistent complaints from news executives in each of its variations.

The pool system originally grew out of a recommendation of the 1984 commission headed by retired General Winant Sidle that was meant to deal with press complaints of exclusion from covering the 1983 invasion of Grenada. Sidle recommended the pool approach to give reporters assured access at the start of conflict, proposing that the pool remain in place "for the minimum time possible" before switching to full press coverage, and that the Pentagon rely on "voluntary compliance" by the press with security guidelines established by the military.

Field Censorship

But in the invasion of Panama in 1989, the press pool was still kept away from the start of the conflict, and Desert Storm further violated Sidle's principles both by the crucial demand for field censorship and by keeping the pool system in place throughout the war.

The first published guidelines news executives saw in mid-December 1990 provided for something called Phase III, which meant that at some point open—or what the military called "unilateral"—coverage would begin. But Phase III, presumably on orders of Schwarzkopf's Central Command—which seemed to run everything including the civilian Defense officials in Washington—was dropped from the final guidelines.

Other aspects of the ground rules, in my view, also showed the command's determination to place unprecedented restrictions on how the war would be reported.

Early on, Pentagon spokesman Pete Williams allowed that reporters who went to the field on their own and happened to hook up with pools could join that pool. But the final guidelines said "news media personnel who are not members of the official CENTCOM [Central Command] media pools will not be permitted into forward areas. Reporters are strongly discouraged from attempting to link up on their own with combat units. U.S. commanders will maintain extremely tight security throughout the operational area and will exclude from the area of operation all unauthorized individuals."

Reporters had to have escorts with them at all times and at one point CENTCOM tried to make sure that all interviews were on the record,

both measures meant to deny reporters' freedom of movement and to ensure that whoever is interviewed doesn't say anything out of line. The military decided where they could go and who could talk to them—another form of censorship.

There is indeed an unavoidable tension between the military and the press simply because their roles in our society are so different. Yet many commanders, field grade officers and soldiers like having reporters around because they like to have their story told too, their courage and their part of the drama recorded.

The pool system is not without some merit. In a vast operation such as Desert Storm, with massive and swift movements of armor, hundreds of warplanes flying from Navy carriers and Saudi air bases, pools can provide a broader picture than we otherwise might get, certainly at the kickoff. But when, as in the case of Desert Storm, the system becomes a method of total control over what gets reported and when, that should be unacceptable for the news media—and untenable as well for the public when the news isn't good.

"There is indeed an unavoidable tension between the military and the press simply because their roles in our society are so different."

Some of the best coverage of the war came from those who bucked the pool system. One of those, and one of the newest reporters on the Desert Storm beat, was retired Army Col. David Hackworth, this country's most decorated living veteran.

Writing in *Newsweek*, Hackworth said as a reporter he had more freedom than a commander, "but I was very unhappy with the military's paranoia and their thought police who control the press. Although I managed to go out on my own, we didn't have the freedom of movement to make an independent assessment of what the military is all about. Everything was spoon-fed. We were like animals in a zoo, and the press officers were the zookeepers who threw us a piece of meat occasionally.

"I had more guns pointed at me," Hackworth added, "by Americans and Saudis who were into controlling the press than in all my years of actual combat."

Hackworth also had some critical things to say about the press, some of whom he called "irresponsible and unprepared" and who used the "power of the press for their own little trip."

"Desert Storm and its aftermath confront the press with many tough questions."

Indeed, Desert Storm and its aftermath confront the press with many tough questions. Should a newspaper or network decide not to take part in pools anymore to force the Pentagon to change the system? News organizations, by their nature, are competitive and don't work together. Nor should they. So how will they pressure the Department of Defense?

How would they have covered Desert Storm without the pool system? This newspaper sent six reporters and a photographer to the war theater, not to mention correspondents in surrounding countries. Will we and other big organizations each send 10 the next time, each with a leased Land Rover and $50,000 satellite phone, and tell them it's okay to drive across a vast, mined desert? And what will smaller papers do?

Sheer Numbers

Who should control the sheer numbers of reporters, cameramen and technicians that flock to a war zone? Bitter cat fights emerged in Saudi Arabia among organizations trying desperately to land the few places on pools, something military press officers undoubtedly enjoyed watching. Major news organizations with millions of readers and viewers—who invested lots of money in sending as many reporters as possible to the region right from the start and who are rich in military or Arab world specialists—naturally want the spots. But who is to say the reporter from a small paper in Missouri with a Guard unit in the war zone cannot go?

There are ways to do it better than Desert Storm.

Ed Cody summed it up succinctly. "Don't just take us along. Leave us alone."

The News Media Failed to Encourage Debate About the Persian Gulf Crisis

James Bennet

About the Author: *James Bennet is an editor of* The Washington Monthly. *The following article was written in December 1990, before hostilities broke out in the Persian Gulf. The article covers the period from August 1990 to November 1990.*

It's hard to recall now that in the first days after Iraq invaded Kuwait, sending any American troops—much less 430,000 of them—to the Middle East never seemed inevitable. In fact, it didn't even seem probable, since many lawmakers didn't like the idea. *The New York Times* reported on August 3, 1990, that "Senator Sam Nunn . . . expressed the prevailing view on Capitol Hill when he said that the proper response should be economic and political pressure and not military action." When reports did discuss the possibility of military action, the emphasis was always on air power, as in *The Washington Post* the following day: "'Carpet bombing is the phrase being used,' said one Pentagon official familiar with the planning. . . . Military leaders have recommended against sending U.S. ground forces to the Mideast." Why? Because "any plan for using American troops on the ground in Saudi Arabia, Kuwait or Iraq chills military experts," explained a *Los Angeles Times* story on August 5. "I think an economic boycott

James Bennet, "How They Missed That Story," *The Washington Monthly,* December 1990. Reprinted with permission from The Washington Monthly. Copyright by The Washington Monthly Company, 1611 Connecticut Ave. NW, Washington, DC 20009, (202) 462-0128.

can be effective," said Caspar Weinberger on "Nightline" the next day. "I think it would have to be backed up by a naval blockade to be sure that that was working."

Even in the early hours of the deployment, there was more than a whiff of potential disagreement over the type of force we should apply. *The New York Times* again called on Nunn: "'My hope is that we'll continue to confine our role to protecting air bases' and perhaps using American troops to mine highways from Kuwait on which Iraq might send tanks into Saudi Arabia, he said." But by the following day (same paper) "congressional opinion swung solidly behind the president's action," and none of the three national dailies mentioned above was able, evidently, to find someone to criticize either the president's goals or the means he'd chosen to achieve them—although 40 percent of Americans disapproved of the deployment. Just two days before, the *Los Angeles Times* had explained that "Bush and his advisers are wary of any military option involving a confrontation with the Iraqi armed forces because they realize that it would run the risk of an enormous loss of life, not only of U.S. military personnel but also of U.S. civilians in the region." But now, and for the next crucial weeks of the buildup, the notion of "an enormous loss of life" almost vanished from that paper's pages.

> ## "You don't have to oppose the American troop deployment in the Middle East to worry about the singular absence of public debate."

You don't have to oppose the American troop deployment in the Middle East to worry about the singular absence of public debate—in the House and Senate, in the major papers, on TV—during those first few weeks. You just have to believe that good debate makes good policy. The initial deployment and its subsequent spectacular growth came as surprises: We progressed almost magically from a projected ceiling of 50,000 troops to nine times that number. Likewise, we faded from "The mission of our troops is wholly defensive" (George Bush's words) into trying "to ensure that the coalition has an adequate offensive military option" (George Bush's words). Meanwhile, the national dailies and "Nightline" provided blow-by-blow accounts and occasionally ran some tougher stories analyzing U.S. interests in the Persian Gulf and the president's goals—whether we were preparing to fight only for oil, whether it was feasible to push for Saddam Hussein's ouster. On the op-ed pages, there was some grumbling back and forth as to whether those goals were worth chasing. But there was almost no discussion in any of these influential, supposedly adversarial sources of news about the *means* the president had chosen and what human cost they'd entail.

Muddled Alternatives

For example, the *Post* editorialized in early September that all those American troops have to be in Saudi Arabia because "the circumstances in Iraq's case would make complaisance there intolerably costly. Suppose that the United States and the others had not sent troops and ships or shut off Iraq's trade." OK, let's suppose if the *Post* had bothered to distinguish among those muddled alternatives, it might have found that they don't have to add up to "complaisance." Imagine that the U.S. had cut off Iraq's trade and, to contain Saddam (we were originally aiming for "wholly defensive" measures, remember), had sent ships and a) sent only a small "tripwire" force to Saudi Arabia, as other nations have done, or b) sent planes to Saudi Arabia, and only enough troops to protect them, since that nation has poor defenses. Or imagine that the U.S. had sent "no troops," but had relied on the naval embargo and on air power based on carriers and in Turkey, which has strong defenses of its own. It's easy if you try. For some reason, our national dailies and "Nightline" never did.

When Bush announced in early November that he was sending another 200,000 troops to the Gulf, the validity of the deployment—instead of the deployment itself—abruptly became news. Why were we risking so many lives? How could Bush be talking about taking the offensive? Congressmen were worried, columnists troubled, and reporters finally interested. But by then, we already had a quarter-million troops practicing offensive maneuvers in the desert who, according to the debate we were suddenly having, shouldn't have been there at all. Doing what many people now recognized was the right thing—reneging on Bush's new commitment and withdrawing some of the already deployed troops—would send dangerous signals to Saddam. As Al Haig, Henry Kissinger, and others pointed out, the horses had fled months before the press got excited about the idea of shutting the stable doors. Judging by a close reading of their coverage in the crucial first six weeks of the crisis, reporters for the *Los Angeles Times, The New York Times, The Washington Post,* and "Nightline" never asked the questions—Are any troops needed? If so, how many are enough? How many dead would be too many?—that would have jump-started the national discussion that we at last began in November. . . .

> ## "The horses had fled months before the press got excited about the idea of shutting the stable doors."

Of the three dailies, only one—the *Los Angeles Times*—published an editorial in the first six weeks that evaluated the size of the deployment. It's a doozy. "An anonymous Defense Department source is widely quoted as saying that contingency plans for the Persian Gulf 'could result in the insertion of up to 200,000 to 250,000 [U.S.] ground forces before it's all done,'" began the editorial on August 11. "These are sobering, not to say mind-boggling, thoughts.

Before they gain too much currency, it would be a good idea to freeze the frame and take a clear and realistic look at just what's being talked about." Ah, the omniscient voice of editorial reason, poised at last to tell it like it is. Read on:

Predictions about world events are best avoided, especially in an area as volatile as the Gulf, but here's one anyway: Hundreds of thousands of American fighting men are not going to be put into the ferociously hostile environment of Saudi Arabia. That won't happen because (1) Congress would refuse to approve such a commitment; (2) the American people wouldn't support it; (3) the Saudis would not invite or tolerate it; (4) probably no senior military official would propose it, and finally, (5) President Bush, if for no other reason than that he faces reelection in 1992, would not request it.

Well. This is, of course, wrong. But that's not why it's so interesting. After all, the editorial writers weren't the only ones being suckered by the Bush administration, which planned to send a massive force from the very beginning of the deployment, according to reports published in *The New York Times* and the *Post* in late August—none of which noted that the press had been duped. On August 10 in *The New York Times*, R.W. Apple wrote of the estimate of 250,000 troops, "One of the handful of senior policy planners in the administration described that figure as preposterous." On the same day in the same paper, Michael Gordon pooh-poohed the idea of even 200,000. (The failure to take a more critical look at these numbers is surprising given that many of the same reporters had bought the fallacious "carpet bombing" line at the beginning of the crisis. Gordon seemed to be expressing some frustration when he wrote the next day, after the official deployment figure had doubled almost overnight to 100,000: "The increased figure seemed less a reflection of a change in the Administration's plans, or its evaluation of the Iraqi threat, than a willingness among officials to discuss the size of the force with greater candor.")

The reason the editorial is interesting is that it hinted rather broadly that the *Los Angeles Times* thought a massive deployment of ground forces

would be a lousy idea. In fact, it went on to urge, "Bush and his advisers ought to be making clear that the Arabian oil fields can be defended without involving American troops in an open-ended land war in the Persian Gulf. *The key to defending Saudi Arabia and nearby smaller states is air and naval power.*" [Italics added.] If Bush doesn't come clean, American support could "fade very quickly under the impact of horror stories suggesting that 250,000 American troops could be sent to fight a long and brutal desert war."

"The editorial writers weren't the only ones being suckered by the Bush administration."

On August 22, the *Los Angeles Times* reported that the deployment "could grow to as many as 150,000 personnel." On September 3 it reported the force could grow to more than 200,000. Those new figures seem sufficient grounds for the editorial board to have revisited its earlier argument, either to announce that it had changed its collective mind or to attack the president's policy and push the air and naval power alternative. The *L.A. Times* did neither. No *L.A. Times* reporter wrote a story critiquing the buildup or exploring other options (on the *Times* oped page—which did a much better job than the other papers in presenting a range of views—Edward Luttwak of the Center for Strategic and International Studies twice slammed the Bush approach). The other newspapers didn't pursue that story either. As late as September 12, "Nightline" managed to do an entire program dedicated to "A Critical Look at U.S. Persian Gulf Policy" that focused on the boycott and never critiqued the troop deployment.

Bush's Response

In early September, the *Los Angeles Times* praised Bush for his "reasonableness" and "willingness to listen," and for "the George Bush style—on the slow side, on the cautious side, on the consensus side, on the pragmatic side." This about a man whose staff had misled the paper's reporters; who had made a monumental decision affecting the nation's future based on the advice of a handful of advisers; and who was pursuing a policy that the paper had called a "horror." Talk about appeasement.

On November 8, after the elections and while Congress was in recess, the consensus-building, slow and cautious Bush made the announcement that he was adding another 200,000 troops to beef up our offensive capability in the Middle East. That evening, Ted Koppel expressed some confusion: "I have a sense that we have taken sort of a major step forward from being . . . in a defensive posture to avoid an invasion of Saudi Arabia, to moving into a totally different kind of posture."

This shouldn't have come as such a shock, since for more than two months the nation's top dailies and "Nightline" had been running news that suggested American forces were preparing to attack, not only defend. Just as "Nightline" and the three papers never pointed out that the official size of the deployment was steadily ratcheting upward, none of them firmly came to grips with the fact that the initial line that the U.S. had deployed its forces for "wholly defensive" purposes had been crumbling from the get-go. *The New York Times*, at least, asserted in an editorial that "unilateral American military action may ultimately prove necessary." But in the first month and a half of the crisis, *The Washington Post* never went beyond endorsing defensive measures, and the *Los Angeles Times* declared, "Senator Sam Nunn . . . puts the issue clearly, leanly, and correctly: 'Our military mission is to defend Saudi Arabia.' Let's keep that in mind." Yet these papers never sounded the alarm as the true goals of the deployment became obvious.

There were clues everywhere that the mission was growing far beyond mere defense—clues like "In the early morning hours . . . troops practice offensive maneuvers" (*The Washington Post*, September 6); "Hostilities could also begin from the U.S. side" (*Los Angeles Times*, August 25);

"The question here has shifted from how well the United States and its allies would defend the Saudi kingdom to how well Washington and its allies might exercise an 'offensive option' to push the Iraqis out of Kuwait" (*The New York Times*, September 16); "The only thing keeping that [offensive readiness] from happening is the arrival of big U.S. equipment, particularly the M-1 tanks which are aboard these fast sealift ships and begin arriving next week" ("Nightline," August 24). I could find no article in any of the newspapers and no discussion on "Nightline" that pulled the pieces together—the excessive numbers of troops, the offensive maneuvers the troops were practicing—into a description of what the administration was really up to.

"In the first month and a half of the crisis, *The Washington Post* never went beyond endorsing defensive measures."

On August 29 on "Nightline," [Secretary of Defense] Dick Cheney told Sam Donaldson, "Well, again we'll come back to the proposition that our dispositions in the region are defensive. We're there to deter and to defend . . . but we're not there in an offensive capacity, we're not there threatening Iraq." Those M-1 tanks slipped Donaldson's mind, evidently, since he didn't pursue the issue. Koppel's astonishment on November 8 was no doubt feigned, but he was making an important point: No one (including Koppel) had been telling the average American that it was part of U.S. policy to prepare to launch an attack. That was a strategy, by the way, that a majority of Americans opposed.

The Best Attempt

The closest anyone came, in the words of the *Los Angeles Times* editorial, to freezing the frame and taking a clear and realistic look at just what was going on was Michael Wines of *The New York Times*, who kicked off an August 19 story with this promising lead: "In only 15 days, while Congress was scattered on summer recess and much of official Washington was on vacation, senior Bush administration officials have committed the United States to its broadest and most hazardous overseas military venture since the Vietnam war." Wines went on to point out that the administration had "deliberately kept vague" the length of the military commitment as well as the projected size of the force. He quoted Senator John McCain opposing the idea of a ground war, thereby—virtually for the first time among the three publications—introducing the concept of death into an analysis of the deployment: "'We cannot even contemplate, in my view, trading American blood for Iraqi blood.'" And Wines quoted a dazed-sounding Senator Joe Biden on the dimensions of the force, saying he was "struck by the size of this. This is a big, big deal. . . . I never contemplated talk of 250,000 troops." There should be, Biden said, "not only some consultation, but some extensive debate."

But Wines came to the conclusion that since massive deployment was inevitable, we might as well lie back and enjoy it: "In the atmosphere of crisis, there is no evidence that extensive debate or consultations would have changed the American commitment in any way." He pointed out that "the pivotal decisions have been made by Mr. Bush and a handful of his top advisers," but offered this astonishing reassurance to those like Biden, who worried about the absence of public discussion: "As the Vietnam experience proved, public debate and congressional action do not guarantee wise policymaking, several Bush administration officials and former government officials from the 1960s said in interviews."

When the United States first sent ground forces to Vietnam in March 1965, "You had overwhelming support in the public and the press," says Stanley Karnow, author of *Vietnam: A History.* "It's very hard to think of anyone—besides Izzy Stone—who objected." At the crucial moment in 1965, there was almost no dissent within the administration (Maxwell Taylor was the exception). Nearly 80 percent of Americans

favored the move—partly because they didn't understand what it would entail, since Lyndon Johnson's spokesmen were pursuing "a policy of minimum candor." Sound familiar? The questions—What are we fighting for?—and the debate started when Americans began dying. If you believe that the United States should have fought the Vietnam war indefinitely, then you might consider that debate to have been unwise. Otherwise, you might wish it had started a little sooner.

Exaggerating Public Support

As the Vietnam war progressed, Karnow argues, the press tended to trail public opinion, not the reverse. Johnson, watching Walter Cronkite report on the Tet Offensive, declared Cronkite would turn public support against the war. But by Tet, more Americans already were against the war than for it. Somehow, that news hadn't percolated up: "It was kind of like a wind tunnel, you know, with the press and the politicians talking to each other and not listening to anyone else," says Karnow. "Sort of like today, I guess."

"No one pieced together the president's actual policy toward Iraq."

Because no one pieced together the president's actual policy toward Iraq, throughout the first couple of weeks of the crisis the nation's leading newspapers couldn't help but overstate American support for the deployment. As the *Los Angeles Times* editorial quoted at length above makes clear, even Americans who closely followed the news (in fact, especially them, according to the polls) were tripping over each other to line up in support of a policy that was in fact not the one we were practicing. The pollsters were asking, as in a CBS News survey: "Do you approve of George Bush's decision to send U.S. troops to Saudi Arabia?" They weren't asking whether Americans approved of sending *250,000* of them to Saudi Arabia. Robert Shogan of the *Los Angeles Times* was one of very few journalists to make this elementary distinction. On August 19, he wrote, "Bush enjoys overwhelming public support for his decision to send U.S. troops . . . but he does not have a blank check." ("Nightline" for the most part didn't concern itself with public opinion, although Rep. Les Aspin did point out on the August 17 broadcast that "there is not, at this point, public support for using our military to invade Kuwait or to invade Iraq.")

Even taking the early poll results at face value, journalists—not just editorial writers or the flocks of hawkish columnists—repeatedly overstated the results. As late as August 24, by which time the size of the deployment and its offensive potential were becoming clear, E.J. Dionne led a story in the *Post* with: "After several weeks of nearly unanimous public support for President Bush's moves in the Middle East. . . ." The paper's own poll of August 10 had reported that, while most Americans support the president's "initial response," they "view the prospect of U.S. military engagement in the Middle East with a mix of skepticism, frustration, confusion, and outright fear." Sixty-eight percent said that the United States should not go on the offensive to liberate Kuwait. A *New York Times* poll published August 12 found that 40 percent of Americans thought Bush was "too quick to send troops." In another *Times* poll conducted over a week later, that 40 percent figure still held. By most standards, 60 percent doesn't qualify as "nearly unanimous support."

Small Minorities

What Dionne probably meant is that support seemed unanimous among "opinion leaders"—that is, the people top journalists interview. His story featured those opinion leaders—what he called "small minorities on the left and the right"—who were "beginning" to dissent from the president's policy: Patrick Buchanan, Thomas Bethell, Ramsey Clark (all of whom dis-

sented from the start). As another example, consider a story by Andrew Malcolm that ran in the *New York Times* on August 21. The teaser on the front page read, in part, "Little Dissent in U.S.: If war is in the offing, few Americans are voicing opposition." The headline declared: "FEW FROM LEFT OR RIGHT PROTEST BUSH'S BIG STICK." "So far," wrote Malcolm, "the critics of American military involvement in Saudi Arabia have been few and soft-spoken." It quickly becomes obvious that the piece is not about "Americans" in general but about a certain type of American: opinion leaders, like Buchanan, Walter Mondale, Coretta Scott King, William Sloane Coffin, Jr. And in fact in the course of the story these people voice quite a bit of dissent, arguing in general for deterrence and a negotiated settlement—a policy drastically different from the one Bush was implementing.

"Editorial writers and reporters . . . are too sophisticated to have children in danger of being gassed, shot, or blown up."

It's at the bottom of the story, however, that we discover what "little dissent" really means, when Malcolm refers to the *Times* poll and dials up a couple of Americans with unfamiliar names: "40 percent [of those polled] said the administration was too quick to send in the military and only 48 percent felt the government had tried hard enough to reach a diplomatic solution. . . . Deborah Huber, a 21-year-old housewife in Wichita, Kansas, was among those in the poll with doubts. 'This is really hitting home for us,' she said in a subsequent interview. 'My husband's brother, David, is being shipped over on the 24th this month.'"

When it comes to matters of war and peace, the troubled Mrs. Huber is what *The New York Times* would call "unsophisticated." In an August 12 editorial, the *Times* assessed the president's efforts to rally support to his cause. Though Bush had demonstrated he was "a superb crisis manager," as a communicator he was stumbling: "A *New York Times* poll shows that while most Americans endorse the president's action, half do not comprehend the dangers. . . . Why must the U.S. again bear a disproportionate share of the burden of defending oil . . . ?" The *Times* understands, but too many Americans don't: "Sophisticated citizens know how much the world depends on Saudi oil. It's up to the occupant of the bully pulpit to educate ordinary citizens, including parents of those G.I.'s, to these harsh realities." In other words, the views of the Mrs. Hubers are supposed to be changed, not taken into account.

Casualties

That editorial expresses an attitude that is certainly one source of the newspapers' repeated failure to give serious consideration to the opinions of the silenced 40 percent. The attitude is summed up by the opposition of "sophisticated citizens" and "ordinary citizens, including parents of those G.I.'s." Editorial writers and reporters and the talking heads they interview are too sophisticated to have children in danger of being gassed, shot, or blown up. Although by November others were waking up to that issue, in the first six weeks of the deployment, of all the columnists—hawks and doves—venting their opinions on the crisis day after day on the national op-ed pages, only one—Mark Shields—raised it.

One day in August, the celebrated op-ed by Alex Molnar, a Marine's father who didn't think the president's goals in the Gulf were worth dying for, appeared shoulder-to-shoulder with, of all columns, one by A.M. Rosenthal, a leading hawk. It's interesting to compare their tones. Molnar: "I kissed my son goodbye today. . . . You have ordered him to Saudi Arabia." Rosenthal: "The likelihood is that Americans will die in the Middle East. . . . In decency to them and the people of the Middle East and in pressing self-interest, the United States must now think

through and make clear two connected sets of war goals. . . . Saddam may still be able to kill thousands." If Molnar's tone struck many as melodramatic (and letters to the editor suggest that it did), Rosenthal's struck at least me as astonishingly breezy. The op-ed hawks purported to make their arguments out of common sense. The party line, as Rosenthal expressed it, was that "if Saddam is allowed to keep the missiles, poison chemicals, and nuclear potential . . . then one day he will murder far more people." The math is compelling, but it totally ignores—as almost all these columnists did—the possibility that other means than a ground war might accomplish the same ends. Without the pressure of knowing that your son or your brother-in-law could be among the "thousands," it becomes easier to overlook the "unsophisticated" question: "Couldn't there be a better way to do this?"

"No one explored the question of what the war would actually look like."

How else can you explain the total lack of interest the newspapers and "Nightline" expressed in the number of soldiers who might die? During the first weeks of the crisis, reporters occasionally referred to the prospective conflict as "bloody" or noted that "thousands" might be killed, but no one explored the question of what the war would actually look like. There were some clues, however. A doctor called up from the reserves told the *Los Angeles Times*, "There may never be another opportunity for me to see trauma cases like this." Without comment on page 22, in *The Washington Post* reported this chilling detail: "The department [of Veterans Affairs] has notified the Pentagon that it could make 9,200 [hospital] beds available within 24 hours, 18,321 within 72 hours and 25,000 within a month."

When 13 American servicemen died in a

plane crash in West Germany, the *Post* headline read: "CRASH OF GULF-BOUND JET REVIVES GERMAN FEARS." The story ran on p. 33. Later, the *Post* did a longer piece on the families of the dead, offering this observation: "Treatment of the crash has been somewhat muted, partly because of uncertainty about whether the 13 victims will become only an early and forgotten footnote in a much larger conflagration and perhaps partly because they did not die in the deserts of the Mideast." *The New York Times* ran about two inches of an inaccurate AP story: "10 Die in Transport Jet Crash."

Numbers Unimportant

On September 5, Joshua Epstein, a Brookings Institution military analyst, held a press conference at which he presented a model that projected the number of divisions the United States would lose if it attacked Iraq. The *Los Angeles Times* wrote it up in a short piece at the foot of page six. The reporter asked government analysts to translate the division numbers into human terms: "They said Epstein's model implies that American and Saudi forces would suffer casualties of 32,000 to 48,000 troops." Hmmm . . . 48,000 . . . hey—that's close to one-quarter as many as we suffered in the whole Vietnam war! And Epstein predicted that a Mideast war would be over in *one month*. Seem like important news? Well, you probably never heard about it, because nobody else touched the story.

"You never found yourself reading an authoritative analysis of the wisdom of the administration's means."

Also on September 5, CNN's "Crossfire" featured Richard Lugar and Les Aspin. Michael Kinsley pressed both guests to answer the question: "Is it worth 20,000 to 30,000 American casualties to get Saddam Hussein?" Both men—the chairman of the House Armed Services Committee and the ranking Republican on the Senate Foreign Relations Committee—said yes. Just for the record, here was Lugar's justification: "Finally we will come down to the point that if he exists and we're left out there in Saudi Arabia with our forces hunkered down, forever monitoring the situation, the casualties over the course of time will be greater or the loss of our national prestige and the whole world order will collapse in the process."

No newspaper or TV show picked up the story.

According to John Mueller, author of *War, Presidents and Public Opinion*, during the Korean and Vietnam wars, as casualties climbed from 100 to 1,000, support for the war dropped by 15 percentage points; as casualties rose from 1,000 to 10,000, support decreased by another 15 points. What would happen if U.S. forces suffered 20,000 casualties in the Middle East in a month-long war? "That would be catastrophic," he says. "That would be vastly more than were suffered in Korea in the first year. . . . I can even imagine impeachment." Unfortunately, like most journalists, pollsters haven't asked questions like, "Is it worth 20,000 to 30,000 casualties to get Saddam Hussein?"

Banalyses

The reporters who write "news analyses"—those who are supposed to bring a knowledge of history and a sense of proportion to bear on the news—are the ones who most let their readers down in the early weeks of the crisis. Generally based in Washington, these reporters tend to be those called on by the television talk shows to analyze events. Without exception in the first weeks, their analyses focused on the politics of the deployment and the view from D.C.: Could any cracks form in the president's domestic or international support? Does Brent Scowcroft or James Baker have the president's ear? What are the scenarios the military planners and armchair analysts think might be played out? Perhaps because these reporters don't have sand under their fingernails and some sense for which machines work, you never found yourself reading an authoritative analysis of the wisdom of the administration's *means*.

"When politicians close ranks . . . journalists must have the intellectual independence and imagination to supply the critical counterweight."

"Nightline" lagged far behind the print journals in this department. While the U.S. was in the first stages of building up its forces, ABC deployed Sam Donaldson to the Gulf, from where he was asked by the show's host, Jack Smith, if Iraqis really believed they could outfight Americans. "It's bluster, Jack," declared Donaldson. "The United States' conventional forces are such that once they are brought to bear in this area, all of them—the sea power that we are amassing, the land power—B-52s, as you know, can come from Diego Garcia and elsewhere—we could, with conventional forces, level Iraq. I think there's no question about that."

News Analysis

The newspapers were a bit more thorough. At times, they served up analytical pieces on the president's goals like the ones Thomas Friedman of *The New York Times* produced in the early days of the crisis that aggressively compared the administration's rhetoric with our real, historical interests in the region. But more typical were pieces that suggested that the photos of aircraft carriers and tanks and the president's angry rhetoric had caused their writers to lose a little perspective, like this chest-thumping, navel-gazing August 20 "news analysis" by R.W. Apple: "The obituaries were a bit premature. There is still one superpower in the world, and it is the United States. . . . There is a rush of excitement in the air here. In news bureaus and Pentagon offices, dining rooms and lobbyists' hangouts, the fever is back—the heavy speculation, the avid gossip, the gung-ho, here's-where-it's-happening spirit, that marks the city when it grapples with great events." Or when it grapples with itself.

Aside from journalists' lack of personal risk in a potential conflict, there are undoubtedly a number of reasons why stories appraising the size and strategy of the deployment didn't get written. For one thing, daily journalists rely on politicians to criticize other politicians' policies, and few in Congress had the guts to do that. For another, journalists can be patriots, too, and may have felt a duty to support the president's policy (whatever it was). On "Nightline," Koppel and Barbara Walters invoked the administrative "we" in interviewing the Iraqi ambassador, and the *Los Angeles Times* editorialized on August 27 that it would be "bad policy" for Congress and the White House to start "quarreling over U.S. policy in the Middle East." Furthermore, criticizing the deployment could put you at some risk, since charges of "dual loyalty" (by Richard Cohen), "second guessing . . . to encourage Saddam" (by Jim Hoagland), "anti-Semitism" (Rosenthal), being "for Saddam" (William Safire), and "appeasement" (just about everyone) were flying thick and fast. But whatever the reason, the "adversarial" press spawned by Vietnam let us down. The president's policy, right or wrong, left plenty of room for debate, and that room simply wasn't filled. When politicians close ranks behind a military action, journalists must have the intellectual independence and imagination to supply the critical counterweight on their own. If not, Americans will continue, over and over again, to find themselves crying over spilt blood.

The News Media Were Biased in Favor of the Persian Gulf War

Lewis H. Lapham

About the Author: *Lewis H. Lapham is the editor of the monthly periodical* Harper's Magazine.

Between the two campaigns waged by the American military command in the Arabian desert—one against the Iraqi army and the other against the American media—it's hard to know which resulted in the more brilliant victory. Both campaigns made use of similar tactics (superior logistics, deception, control of the systems of communication), and both were directed at enemies so pitiably weak that their defeat was a foregone conclusion.

The bombardment of Baghdad began on January 17, 1991, and within a matter of hours the newspaper and television correspondents abandoned any claim or pretension to the power of independent thought. It was as if they had instantly enlisted in the ranks of an elite regiment, sworn to protect and defend whatever they were told to protect and defend by the generals who presented them with their morning film clips and their three or four paragraphs of yesterday's news.

By the end of the first week I no longer could bear to watch the televised briefings from Washington and Riyadh. The journalists admitted to the presence of authority were so obviously afraid of giving offense that they reminded me of prisoners of war. The parallel image appeared on cue five weeks later when what was left of the Iraqi army stumbled across the desert waving the white rags of surrender.

The Iraqi troops at least had suffered the admonitions of gunfire. The American media surrendered to a barrage of propaganda before the first F-16 fired its first round at an Iraqi military target. The Pentagon's invitation to the war carried with it a number of conditions—no reporters allowed on the battlefield except under strict supervision, and then only in small task forces designated as "press pools"; all dispatches submitted to the military censors for prior review; no unauthorized conversations with the allied troops; any violation of the rules punishable by expulsion from the theater in the sand.

> ## "The American media, like the American military commanders, weren't interested in the accuracy of words."

The media accepted the conditions with scarcely a murmur of protest or complaint. Who could afford to decline even so ungracious an invitation? The promise of blood brings with it the gift of headlines, audiences, single-copy sales, Nielsen ratings, Pulitzer prizes, and a swelling of the media's self-esteem. A television network on assignment to a war imagines itself outfitted with the trappings of immortality. The pictures, for once, mean something, and everybody has something important to say.

On the fourth day of the bombing Dan Rather confirmed the Pentagon's contemptuous opinion of a media cheaply bought for a rating point and a flag. He appeared on a CBS News broadcast with Connie Chung, and after reading the day's bulletin, he said, "Connie, I'm told that this program is being seen [by the troops] in Saudi Arabia. . . . And I know you would join me in giving our young men and women out there a salute." Rather then turned to the camera and raised his right hand to his forehead in a slightly awkward but unmistakably earnest military salute.

The salute established the tone of the media's grateful attendance at what everybody was pleased to call a war. Had anybody been concerned with the accurate use of words, the destruction of Iraq and the slaughter of an unknown number of Iraqis—maybe 50,000, maybe 150,000—might have been more precisely described as a police raid, as the violent suppression of a mob, as an exemplary lesson in the uses of major-league terrorism. Although the Iraqi army had been much advertised as a synonym for evil (as cruel as it was "battle-hardened," possessed of demonic weapons and a fanatic's wish for death, etc.), it proved, within a matter of hours, to consist of half-starved recruits, as scared as they were poorly armed, only too glad to give up their weapons for a cup of rainwater.

But the American media, like the American military commanders, weren't interested in the accuracy of words. They were interested in the accuracy of bombs, and by whatever name one wanted to call the Pentagon's trade show in the Persian Gulf, it undoubtedly was made for television. The parade of images combined the thrill of explosions with the wonder of technology. Who had ever seen—live and in color—such splendid displays of artillery fire? Who could fail to marvel at the sight of doomed buildings framed in the glass eye of an incoming missile? Who had ever seen the light of the Last Judgment coursing through a biblical sky?

> ## "The Pentagon produced and directed the war as a television miniseries based loosely on Richard Wagner's *Götterdämmerung*."

Most of the American correspondents in Saudi Arabia experienced the war at more or less the same remove as the television audience in Omaha or Culver City. They saw little or nothing of the battlefield, which was classified top secret and declared off-limits to the American public on whose behalf the war presumably was being waged. The military command provided the media with government-issue images roughly equivalent to the publicity stills handed around to gossip columnists on location with a Hollywood film company. Every now and then the government press agents arranged brief interviews with members of the cast—a pilot who could be relied upon to say hello to all the wonderful folks who made the plane and the ordnance, a nurse who missed her six-month-old son in Georgia, an infantry sergeant (preferably black) who had discovered that nothing was more precious than freedom. But even this kind of good news was subject to official suspicion. A reporter who said of some pilots that the excitement upon returning from a mission had made them "giddy" found the word changed to "proud."

A Pentagon Production

The Pentagon produced and directed the war as a television miniseries based loosely on Richard Wagner's *Götterdämmerung*, with a script that borrowed elements of *Monday Night Football*, *The A Team*, and *Revenge of the Nerds*. The synchronization with prime-time entertainment was particularly striking on Super Bowl Sunday. ABC News intercut its coverage of the game in progress in Tampa with news of the bombing in progress in the Middle East, and the transitions seemed entirely in keeping with the spirit of both events. The newscasters were indistinguishable from the sportscasters, all of them drawing diagrams in chalk and talking in similar voices about the flight of a forward pass or the flare of a Patriot missile. The football players knelt to pray for a field goal, and the Disneyland half-time singers performed the rites of purification meant to sanctify the killing in the desert.

The televised images defined the war as a game, and the military command in Riyadh was careful to approve only those bits and pieces of film that sustained the illusion of a playing field (safe, bloodless, and abstract) on which American soldier-athletes performed feats of matchless daring and skill.

Like the sportscasters in the glass booth on the fifty-yard line, the newscasters standing in front of the palm tree or the minaret understood themselves to be guests of the management. Just as it never would occur to Frank Gifford to question the procedures of the National Football League, so also it never occurred to Tom Brokaw to question the ground rules of the war. When an NBC correspondent in Israel made the mistake of talking to New York about an Iraqi missile falling on Tel Aviv without first submitting his news to the local censors, the Israeli government punished his impudence by shutting down the network's uplink to the satellite. The embargo remained in force until Brokaw, at the opening of *NBC Nightly News*, apologized to Israel for the network's tactlessness.

Between representatives of competing news organizations the protocol was seldom so polite. The arguments were about access—who got to see whom, when, why, and for how long—and the correspondents were apt to be as jealous of their small privileges as the hangers-on attached to the entourage of Vanilla Ice. When Robert Fisk, a reporter for the British paper *The Independent,* arrived at the scene of the fighting for the town of Khafji, he was confronted by an NBC television reporter—a licensed member of the day's press pool—who resented the intrusion. "You asshole," the television correspondent said. "You'll prevent us from working. You're not allowed here. Get out. Go back to Dhahran." The outraged nuncio from NBC summoned an American Marine public affairs officer, who said to Fisk, "You're not allowed to talk to U.S. Marines, and they're not allowed to talk to you."

Even under the best of circumstances, however, print was no match for television. The pictures shaped the way the story was told in the papers, the newsmagazines, and the smaller journals of dissenting opinion. Although a fair number of writers (politicians as well as scholars and plain citizens) took issue with the Bush administration's conduct of the war, their objections

couldn't stand up to the heavy-caliber imagery delivered from Saudi Arabia in sorties as effective as the ones flown by the tactical fighter squadrons. *Time* and *Newsweek* followed the pictures with an assault of sententious rhetoric— "The greatest feat of arms since World War II. . . . Like Hannibal at Cannae or Napoleon on a very good day."

"Writing about the events in the Persian Gulf was distinguished by its historical carelessness and its grotesque hyperbole."

At the end as in the beginning, the bulk of the writing about the events in the Persian Gulf was distinguished by its historical carelessness and its grotesque hyperbole. The record strongly suggests that the Bush administration resolved to go to war as early as August 1990, almost as soon as Saddam Hussein made the mistake of invading Kuwait. If the war could be quickly and easily won, then the administration might gain a number of extremely desirable ends, among them the control of the international oil price, a revivification of the American military budget, a diversion of public attention from the sorrows of the domestic economy, a further degradation of what passes for the nation's political opposition, a cure for the mood of pessimism that supposedly had been undermining Washington's claims to world empire.

Hussein as Hitler

But none of these happy events could be brought to pass unless a credulous and jingoistic press could convince the American people that Hussein was a villain as monstrous as Adolf Hitler, that his army was all but invincible, that the fate of nations (not to mention the destiny of mankind) trembled in the balance of decision. It wouldn't do any good to send the grand armada to the Persian Gulf if the American people thought that the heavy guns were being wheeled into line to blow away a small-time thug.

The trick was to make the sitting duck look like the 6,000-pound gorilla. Much later in the proceedings Lieutenant General Thomas Kelly could afford to say, amidst applause and self-satisfied laughter at the daily press briefing at the Pentagon, that, yes, sending B-52s to carpet bomb a single Iraqi Scud site was, come to think of it, "a delightful way to kill a fly." But in the beginning the generals were a good deal more careful about the work of disinformation. By October 1990, Washington was besieged with ominous reports—about Hussein's chemical and biological weapons, about the price of oil rising to $50 or $100 a barrel, about the nuclear fire likely to consume the orchards of Israel, about the many thousands of body bags being sent to Saudi Arabia to collect the American dead. All the reports derived from government sources, and all of them proved to be grossly exaggerated.

The Advantage of Hindsight

The advantage of hindsight suggests that President Bush and his advisers chose Saddam Hussein as a target of opportunity precisely because they knew that his threats were mostly bluster and his army more bluntly described as a gang of thieves. The media never subjected the administration's statements to cross-examination, in large part because the administration so deftly promoted the fiction of a "liberal press" bent on the spiteful negation of America's most cherished truths. The major American media are about as liberal as Ronald Reagan or the late John Wayne, but in the popular mind they enjoy a reputation (undeserved but persistent) for radicalism, sedition, and dissent. The administration well understood that the media couldn't afford to offend the profoundly conservative sympathies of their prime-time audience, and so it knew that it could rely on the media's complicity in almost any deception dressed up in patriotic costume. But for the purposes of the autumn sales campaign it was necessary to cast the media as an antagonist as un-American as Saddam Hussein. If even the well-known "liberal press" could be brought into camp, then clearly the administration's cause was just.

The media loved the story lines (especially the ones about their own dread magnificence), and by Christmas every network and every magazine of respectable size had designed for itself some kind of red, white, and blue emblem proclaiming its ceaseless vigilance and its readiness for war. When the steel rain at last began to fall during the second week of January 1991, most of the national voices raised in opposition to the war had been, as the Pentagon spokesmen liked to say, "attrited." Through the five weeks of the aerial bombardment and the four days of the ground assault the version of the public discourse presented in the media turned increasingly callow. *Time* and *Newsweek* published posters of the weapons deployed in the Persian Gulf, and the newspapers gave over the majority of their editorial-page space to columnists gloating about the joy of kicking ass and kicking butt. Andy Rooney on *60 Minutes* struck what had become the media's preferred note of smug self-congratulation. "This war in the Gulf," he said, "has been, by all odds, the best war in modern history. Not only for America but for the whole world, including Iraq probably. It was short and the objectives of victory were honorable. In spite of all the placards, the blood was not for oil. It was for freedom. We did the right thing."

"The major American media are about as liberal as Ronald Reagan or the late John Wayne."

The return of the nation's mercenary army was staged as a homecoming weekend for a college football team, and the troops arriving in Georgia and California found themselves proclaimed, in the words of *Life* magazine, "Heroes All." Many of them had spent several uncomfortable months camping in the desert, but few of them had taken part in any fighting. The number of American casualties (125 dead in action, twenty-three of them killed by "friendly fire") once again posed the question of whether America had gone to a war or to a war game played with live ammunition. But it was a question that few people cared to ask or answer.

"I find it hard to believe that the American people feel quite as triumphant as they have been made to appear in the news-magazines."

Maybe the question is irrelevant. In the post-modern world maybe war will come to be understood as a performing art, made for television and promoted as spectacle. Maybe, as the producers of the charades on MTV would have it, Madonna is Marilyn Monroe, true love is a perfume bottle, and George Bush is Winston Churchill.

Certainly the administration succeeded in accomplishing what seemed to be its primary objectives. The cost of oil went down, and the prices on the New York Stock Exchange (among them the prices paid for Time Warner, the Washington Post Company, CNN, and the *New York Times*) went up. The country welcomed the easy victories in Kuwait and Iraq with band music, ticker-tape parades, and speeches to the ef-

fect that once again it was good to be American.

Still, I find it hard to believe that the American people feel quite as triumphant as they have been made to appear in the newsmagazines. The cheering rings a little hollow, as if too many people in the crowd were shouting down the intimations of their own mortality. The elation seemed more like a feeling of relief—relief that so few Americans were killed and that almost everybody, this time at least, got home safely.

Maybe the war in the desert was a brilliant success when measured by the cynical criteria of realpolitik, but realpolitik is by definition a deadly and autocratic means of gaining a not very noble end. The means might be necessary, but they are seldom admirable and almost never a cause for joyous thanksgiving. If we celebrate a policy rooted in violence, intrigue, coercion, and fear, then how do we hold to our higher hopes and aspirations? We debase our own best principles if we believe the gaudy lies and congratulate ourselves for killing an unknown number of people whom we care neither to know nor to count. How do we tell the difference between our victories and our defeats unless we insist that our media make the effort of asking questions other than the ones that flatter the vanity of the commanding general? Like the seal balancing the red, white, and blue ball on the end of its faithful nose, a servile press is a circus act, as loudly and laughingly cheered by a military dictatorship as by a democratic republic.

The News Media Were Biased Against the Persian Gulf War

Dwight D. Murphey

About the Author: *Dwight D. Murphey is a lawyer and faculty member at Wichita State University in Kansas. He is the executive director of University Professors for Academic Order, a group that opposes political activity and social activism on college and university campuses.*

It is one of the salient facts about American life—a fact that should never be lost sight of by anyone who hopes to understand our cultural slide and the neurotic nature of so much of our national discourse—that a deeply alienated intellectual subculture has long found expression not only within our universities but also within our dominant media culture and in the entertainment industry. Attempts were made by the media during the Gulf War to undermine the resolve of the U.S. public, but on this occasion they failed.

Those who base their thinking about our national problems on the very natural and easy assumption that we have a "normal" society are, in effect, operating on a false set of premises. If we ignore the cancer of the alienated intellectual culture, we live in a world of make-believe.

Mainstream Americans have been fully aware of liberal media bias for many years. But on the whole the great American majority—aptly characterized a few years ago as "the silent majority"—has allowed itself to be cowed into a submissive, albeit grudging, acceptance of the

Dwight D. Murphey, "The Gulf War's (Intolerable) 'New Journalism,'" *Conservative Review,* April 1991. Reprinted with permission from the Council for Social and Economic Studies, 1133 13th St. NW, Suite C-2, Washington, DC 20005-4297.

images and neuroses that are poured in upon it. How else is it that a movie like Oliver Stone's "Platoon," which pictured American soldiers as so utterly depraved, could have created hardly a murmur of protest?

But now there has been the stimulus given to patriotism by the recent war and by America's resounding military success in it. Perhaps in the new setting the time has come when the American mainstream will allow itself not only to feel anger, but to voice it. I hope so.

And angry it should be! The liberal media used the Gulf War to extend, formalize and institutionalize its wartime reporting in ways that deliberately eschew any loyalty to the United States. A "new journalism" was foisted onto the American people and the world. It is apparent that this was done concertedly and by conscious design by a predominance of the "major players" in the media, who no doubt have some confidence, however smug, that the new journalism will be allowed to crystallize into an established framework for wartime reporting.

The question that faces Americans today is whether we are going to sit still for this vast new extension of the bias. If Americans do choose to voice their anger, they will need first to arrive at a solid factual and conceptual foundation. For this, a dispassionate analysis is needed that will set aside the emotion, however temporarily. In what follows, I will seek to provide that sort of analysis through a series of steps:

> ## "Attempts were made by the media during the Gulf War to undermine the resolve of the U.S. public."

First, by delineating and illustrating the specific journalistic abuses that were committed during the war;

Second, by making clear the dangers that these abuses pose (and the terrible harm they might well have caused if the war had taken longer or had entailed more American casualties);

Third, by analyzing both the concepts behind, and the context of, the "new journalism;" and

Fourth, by reflecting upon the proper role of a free press during wartime.

"Throughout the war, American statements were offset, juxtaposed with, and contradicted by statements from the enemy."

CNN [Cable News Network] had commanded most of the attention. It is important to note, though, that the other television networks hoped to play the same role, but were simply far less successful at it. My review of press reports for the two months following the middle of January 1991 shows me that the main print media, too, molded their actions to the "new journalism."

1. *Reporting from Within Enemy Territory.* The single most obvious part of the new journalism, which immediately struck many of us as repugnantly odd, was that the media undertook to report from within enemy territory, even from the enemy's capital. CNN had obtained Iraqi permission for a special line. *ABC News* and *NBC News* were also there reporting from Baghdad—but lost their communications after the first few minutes of the air assault. CBS tried, but failed, to establish communication. Major elements of the print media also were operating within enemy territory, as is illustrated by an Associated Press reporter and *Newsweek* photographer's having taken a three-mile walk in Baghdad on January 18.

I intend to discuss later what precisely is wrong with this. But to keep it in perspective it is worth thinking about how astonishing it would have been if the American press had reported from inside Germany during the Allied bombing of that country or from Tokyo after Pearl Harbor.

2. *Providing a Platform for Enemy Propaganda.*

The war coverage was a mixture. Not all of it was negative, especially after the coalition's military successes became evident. But this shouldn't obscure the fact that a significant part of the coverage provided a platform—in this country and worldwide—both for blatant enemy propaganda (usually labelled "Cleared by Iraqi Censorship") and for empathetic presentations of the enemy's point of view (usually not so labelled).

One of the more egregious examples is Peter Arnett's January 28 interview of Saddam Hussein. Saddam sounded like a music teacher using CNN's podium to lead an international choir: "All of the people of Iraq are grateful," he said, "to all the noble souls amongst the U.S. people who are coming out into the streets and demonstrating against this war."

Arnett had already lent himself to Iraqi propaganda of the worst sort on January 23 with his tour of the so-called "infant formula factory," which the United States had bombed as a biological weapons facility. He said, as though it were fact, that "officials took me on a two-hour visit to a powdered milk factory *that actually makes infant formula.*" His conclusion: "It was innocent enough from what we could see."

When Washington peace activist Anthony Lawrence, a member of the Gulf Peace Team, visited Baghdad on January 30, Arnett provided him with what any activist dearly loves—an extended interview. Lawrence made optimum use of the platform: "I think that it is high time for the American people to join the peace movement and to demand that their government stop this war before we have many more than the eight Marines who were killed today lost."

Other Examples

It's a mistake, though, to focus entirely on Arnett. In Wichita where I live, the *Wichita Eagle* on January 17 reported an interview with a Palestinian-American. "I feel my family is a victim of this war," it quoted him as saying, "and the American administration is the murderer." Two days later, an item bearing a Nicosia, Cyprus, dateline said that "Iraq broadcast a call for terrorism today, telling Moslems that they should attack Western interests worldwide." A report from Amman, Jordan, quoted a Palestinian about the first Scud attack on Israel: "I can't begin to explain how happy I am. . . . It doesn't matter if I die now. . . . For the first time, I've seen casualties in Tel Aviv, caused by an Arab country.". . .

After the bombing of what the coalition said was a command-and-control bunker and the Iraqis called a shelter, the front page of the *Eagle* on February 14 featured large, bold-print quotes from Tariq Aziz, the Iraqi foreign minister (who said that "we demand that the U.N. . . . condemn this terrible crime"), and Abdalla Salch Al-Ashtal, Yemen's U.N. ambassador (who said "This war is illegitimate. This carnage is appalling. . . ."). The paper gave these quotes equal billing with those from defense secretary Dick Cheney and the Soviet U.N. ambassador.

"For those who would sap Americans' national resolve, there's nothing quite like bringing a dying American boy into everyone's living room."

There are many such examples. Throughout the war, American statements were offset, juxtaposed with, and contradicted by statements from the enemy and enemy sympathizers.

3. *A Constant Repetition of Charges about Alleged Attacks on the Civilian Population.* Perhaps the most continuous flow of enemy propaganda in the print media took the form of the almost daily reports from Jordan featuring interviews with refugees who told highly personalized stories of civilian casualties. . . .

A January 30 story from Jordan said that "repeatedly, refugees arriving here over the past 10 days have accused the United States and its allies of hitting civilian targets, but they have offered varying accounts as to the extent." The next day a report from Amman said that "an official from

the Jordanian Red Crescent . . . said he had seen a distraught Jordanian family that had lost two infants in a strafing attack." And the day after that the drumbeat continued, all reported dutifully by the Knight-Ridder News Service; a report from Amman said that "a Baghdad Radio announcer accused allied airmen of firing Gatling guns and missiles to kill 'very large numbers of women, children and old people in extreme cold blood.'"

Civilian Casualties

Then on February 4, a story from Ruweished, Jordan, took on an argumentative tone: "Despite U.S. statements that civilians are not targets of bombing raids, refugees crossing into Jordan on Sunday said allied warplanes are attacking and killing people fleeing Iraq."

The "civilian casualty" theme was picked up by the *Los Angeles Times/Washington Post* Service on February 8. In a story (from Washington this time) about former Attorney General Ramsey Clark's wartime visit to the Iraqi city of Basra, they reported: "Clark said he had seen residential areas, schools, a nightclub and a mosque that had been destroyed by the allied bombing. . . . 'You saw no military material being hit at all.'"

Two days later, on February 10, the *Wichita Eagle* had a headline "Allied attacks hinder Baghdad doctors" over a story from Amman, again by the *Los Angeles Times/Washington Post* Service. It was a long, personalized telling: "'It is very gloomy over there,' said Rizk Jaber Abu Kashef, a Palestinian surgeon. . . . Kashef said one doctor broke his leg when he tripped while climbing the stairs in the dark at the Red Crescent Hospital. Another was injured, he said, when their convoy was strafed by an allied warplane on the highway from Baghdad to the Jordanian border—despite the fact that the cars were marked with the symbols of the United Nations, the Red Cross and its Muslim counterpart, the Red Crescent."

All of this was followed by the pointing-with-alarm over the bombing of the Baghdad bunker (the alleged "shelter"), which was put forward with all the flamboyance of a scandal—with the United States cast in a defensive posture.

Sapping Americans' Resolve

4. *Visual Depictions of Suffering and of Dead American Soldiers.* From the Vietnam experience, we all know the soul-wrenching impact that a few seconds of televised heart-massage on a badly wounded soldier can have on people at home. For those who would sap Americans' national resolve, there's nothing quite like bringing a dying American boy into everyone's living room.

The media had relatively little opportunity to exploit this aspect of the war, but they certainly didn't eschew it. Once the ground campaign started, they began what they could along these lines. The front page of the *Wichita Eagle* on March 2 carried a 5-column-wide photo, taken by the *Knight-Ridder* Tribune News, of an American soldier crying while sitting next to another soldier whose eyes were bandaged; next to both of them was a dead soldier in a body bag. Back on page 10, another large picture showed soldiers lifting an American body, also in a bag, down from a Bradley Fighting Vehicle. (On the same page there was a picture of a boy in tears. The caption: "An Iraqi boy cries amid the rubble of Baghdad. . . .")

These depictions weren't inserted unthinkingly. *Accuracy in Media* reports that "when the Pentagon proposed press guidelines that would have barred showing wounded American soldiers in shock and agony, the media protested loudly. . . . The military, showing its own lack of psywar savvy, gave in and dropped the guideline."

5. *Showing of Many Filmclips Cleared by the Enemy.* A number of televised reports came out of Iraq marked "cleared by Iraqi censors." This became a hallmark of the new journalism: if reports were to be run that were "cleared by the U.S. military," then it was perfectly all right to run the enemy's propaganda so long as the viewers were warned with a label equivalent to that put on the U.S. reports.

The "cleared by Iraqi censors" filmclips could have no justification on the ground that the media were seeking objectivity, since everyone would agree that the filmclips clearly weren't "objective." It is apparent, therefore, that a desire for objectivity wasn't the prime rationale for the new journalism. Instead, the *ethos* was one of moral equivalence and of an attitude of loyalty to no nation in particular

But even this isn't what at first blush it appears to be. The presence of "open societies" and "enclosed societies" on the world scene (and in the war itself) means that the open societies were deluged with Iraqi propaganda while the closed societies, such as Iraq, that chose to bar the showing of U.S. military reports didn't let their people see them. The result is a stacked deck: the new journalism gives a worldwide platform to anti-American propaganda, but American perspectives are provided a vehicle only in nations that choose to show them. There is no real neutrality of treatment (even if "neutrality" by the media were an acceptable rationale while we are at war). Can we imagine that it is possible that American and the West's media don't realize this?

"The new journalism gives a worldwide platform to anti-American propaganda."

---

6. *Other Assorted Abuses Too Numerous to Mention.* I don't mean to suggest by the above enumeration that I have exhaustively catalogued all of the media's wartime abuses. We could, for example, easily include the CBS team's having gone off on its own into the "no man's land," where its members were taken prisoner, and then CBS's complaining bitterly that the Saudis were interfering in the search for them; or the publication of some bitterly anti-American letters-to-the-editor (reflecting the new *ethos* that it's perfectly all right, even desirable, for the

pros and cons of a war to continue to be debated even after the firing has started); or the lukewarm, often selectively negative, treatment that such a paper as the *Wichita Eagle* gave to the weekend "support-America" rallies that were put together by local citizens (including this author) who wanted to support our country.

The New Journalism

First, let us realize that what we are talking about, as in so many matters, involves a trade-off. An internationally minded, loyal-to-no-country wartime journalism, if truly committed to uncovering the truth, can no doubt have some valuable consequences. To some degree, facts will be dug out and falsehoods exposed; sensitivities will be raised; ideas will be batted about on a world stage, and no one (at least in theory) will be left undisturbed in his provincialism. Such a journalism might have done the world a lot of good during World War I.

It is easier, however, to recite these benefits than to have full confidence that they will accrue. I wish that I could look out on the world and know that the free-world's media had, over all these years of a free press's existence, uncovered and publicized Stalin and Mao's, and other assorted Communists', atrocities as fully as they did Hitler's. I wish that the world were as aware of the millions who were deliberately starved by Stalin in the Ukraine in 1933 as it is of the Holocaust. I don't know how many times I have read of "Hitler's attack on Poland" without being told that Stalin's Red Army participated, too, taking more than half of Poland's territory.

"The media's conduct . . . shows their desire for a journalism divorced from considerations of loyalty to the United States."

The point I am making, of course, is that a "free press," when governed by its own blindnesses and passions, as ours so continually is, is no guarantee that "the truth will out." Only in "Journalism 101," where "the First Amendment pieties" are taught so that media practitioners can mouth them unctuously for many years thereafter, is there any pure and naive confidence that wondrous benefits will accrue. (No one should conclude from this that I am against the First Amendment or a free press. It's just that journalists blatantly overstate their benefits while equally blatantly, much of the time, violating their spirit. Hypocrisy runs rampant in the journalistic profession more than in any other I know.)

"Harms" of the New Journalism

On the other side of the ledger—the side that deals with the "harms" that can flow from the new journalism—here is what we find:

1. *A Treasonable Undermining of American Will.* America's potential weakness is not, at least in the world today, in its military power. It is at home, in the minds and hearts of our own people. Saddam Hussein knew this when he went on CNN to praise the protestors; Ho Chi Minh knew it as North Vietnam followed the policy of attriting American resolve; and the adversarial American media know it.

This did not come home to roost during the Gulf War. The war was over far too soon, and with too few casualties, for that. But this does not mean that the media were not pulling out all the stops in their effort to turn the American public against the American government and the American prosecution of the war. They did their best to lay the foundation for feelings of revulsion, guilt and eventual loss of will. (And they did this even in a war where America's adversary evoked no particular sympathy from them.)

It is helpful that the sympathy factor was largely absent. By removing a variable, it makes it even clearer that the media's conduct during the Gulf War shows their desire for a journalism divorced from considerations of loyalty to the United States. It wasn't a special case based on sympathy for the other side.

2. *Adversely Molding Attitudes Among Diverse Peo-*

ples. CNN broadcasts to over a hundred countries. Peoples throughout the world see American television and are affected in their perceptions by the American media. And the press reports of the alleged American strafing of Red Crescent convoys no doubt reached millions. How many thousands, even millions, in the Arab nations and elsewhere drank it all in, accepting it in confirmation of their paranoia about and hatred toward the United States? The effects—especially long term—are incalculable.

3. *Disastrously Warping American Military and Political Policy.* In Vietnam, American presidents were forced, incredibly, to allow enemy sanctuaries; they were badgered into severely limiting target selection; they were led to fight the war on the very turf they were trying to protect, without taking the ground war to the enemy's own homeland; and eventually they felt it imperative to withdraw under conditions that left the North Vietnamese army entrenched within South Vietnam itself. In short, they fought the war under constraints that caused us to fight the war badly, slowly forfeit our national will, and eventually lose the war itself. Our media-induced national neuroses, and the anti-war movement they spawned, were central to this.

"[The new journalism] is a form of moral, perceptual bankruptcy."

Certainly the Gulf War was prosecuted vigorously enough to have avoided most of these warpings. At least, that's the conventional wisdom, and it's partly right. But we did refrain—did we not?—from bombing the Al-Rashid Hotel because of all the foreign journalists there, despite a conviction that it housed the final communication link between Saddam and his forces in Kuwait.

And we did limit quite unnaturally the political objectives for which we fought. Most amazingly, we called the cease-fire without having

seen to the ouster of Saddam from his dictatorship. This left Iraq in a state of chaos and continuing butchery that was out of our power to control. Since the future political condition of Iraq is of vast importance in the Middle East, this was an unthinkable gamble.

Subordinating War Objectives

Just as significantly, we subordinated our own formulation of war objectives. Far from putting the United States at the head of decisions about the war, we constantly referred back to the politically insufficient objectives stated in the United Nations resolutions. We have reason to be fearful, if this establishes the norm for how we as a superpower will act in the future. Cooperation with the United Nations is one thing; subordination of the United States to it is something of an entirely different order.

America in the past has fought two world wars with little regard for the shape the world would take after they were over. We have acted as though military success, not the attainment of political objectives, is the most important thing. Why did we, in the Gulf War, allow ourselves to take so crimped a view of our mission when that jeopardized extremely important geopolitical objectives?

The answer almost certainly lies in the fearful "look over your shoulder" reluctance to assert power that has become, largely through the impact of liberal intellectual and media culture, a part of the contemporary American character. In many ways, the Bush administration and the military deserve lavish credit for performing magnificently during the war. But this should not obscure for us the pusillanimity that undermined our strategic policy.

4. *Creating a "Moral Equivalency" Relativism.* A disastrous moral effect of a wartime journalism that carries everyone's propaganda, adds its own alienated slanting, reveals continuing skepticism toward statements of the American government and military, and seeks conspicuously to separate itself from any national loyalty is that it adds immeasurably to the attitude, held by America's

alienated intellectual culture and by many in Europe and the Third World, that there is a "moral equivalency" between the United States, as a free society, and whatever closed-society enemy we are fighting.

This, of course, is a form of moral, perceptual bankruptcy. In Ayn Rand's words, it is moral embezzlement because it robs the United States of its due; it is "moral counterfeiting" because it clothes Saddam, a despot guilty of the worst atrocities, with a moral standing he doesn't deserve.

Conceptual Mischief

There is no end to the conceptual mischief such a skewing can cause. We see it in small ways as well as large. In Wichita, the city's symphony orchestra played the "Star Spangled Banner" at the beginning of one of its concerts. The symphony's general manager was careful to announce, so there would be no misunderstanding, "that it's not meant to be a show of support for the war action, but just a recognition of our armed forces. . . ." At the same time as there were many fervent displays of patriotism, we also witnessed a widespread moral equivocation.

"In the future, if we have to tenderly protect journalists' lives, how many American soldiers will die because of it?"

---

5. *Undercutting the American Attempt to Establish a Precedent Against "Total War."* Earlier, we traced the propaganda that came out of Jordan and Baghdad, and from the likes of Ramsey Clark, charging the United States with indiscriminate bombing and strafing of civilians.

This propaganda was bad enough in itself, for the reasons we've stated. But we should go further and note that these charges were, in a special way, damaging to the world's future. The twentieth century has been a century of "total war" in which there has been little reluctance to

attack civilian populations. (I don't mean to suggest that this has been exclusively a characteristic of the twentieth century: Sherman's march through Georgia and Sheridan's through northern Virginia were nineteenth-century examples, and there are many others.)

But in the Gulf War, the Bush administration justly limited our targeting to military targets. If the international norm for the future can be to avoid the slaughter of civilians, that is a vastly significant move, I think, toward a heightened level of civilization.

The precedent was largely downgraded, however, by the "they're killing civilians" propaganda that flowed constantly into the world media. Will the world remember this war as one that set a valuable new precedent? Not if hundreds of millions of people give credence to the propaganda.

6. *Impeding U.S. Targeting.* We have already criticized, on other grounds, the physical presence of American and other Western journalists in the enemy country during wartime. It should not go unmentioned, however, that such a presence can (and did) constitute a direct interference with the United States' military efforts. Many Americans felt that our targeting should have paid no attention to the journalists' presence, and have killed them if need be. I agree. But we know—and so do the media, apparently—that that isn't going to be what an American administration will do. In the future, if we have to tenderly protect journalists' lives, how many American soldiers will die because of it?

Characteristics

We have noted that the "new journalism" has the following characteristics: an international flavor, involving media from other countries as well as the United States; a detachment from loyalty to the United States or, presumably, from any other country; a desire to be physically present even on enemy territory and in combat zones; a policy of dramatizing and personalizing the war's suffering, including that of American soldiers; a readiness to run all sides' propaganda, sometimes labelled as such; a belief that it is desirable, even during wartime, for policy options to be publicly debated and for opposition to be demonstrated toward the war effort; a willingness to question and to voice hostility toward the American government's and military's statements, motives, conduct and moral position; and a minimizing of concern over the effects on American morale, the passions of other peoples, or American policy.

Let us look at the conceptual foundations of this position:

1. *Detachment from National Loyalty.* We have already commented that the running of Iraqi propaganda, labelled as such, shows that the ostensible rationale for the new journalism cannot be that it seeks "objectivity." Rather, it seeks independence, which involves forsaking national loyalties. The theory is that this will lead to a vitally constructive international free press.

Wartime Measure

We have also already observed that in the context of open and closed societies this skews the wartime presentation of images and ideas in a way that is very favorable to the closed societies.

At its core, the new journalism is an extension of the absolutist conception of the First Amendment and of "free speech." This is a conception that holds that "free speech" far outweighs all other values (except perhaps for "politically correct sensitivity"), so that indeed a "weighing process" ought not to be engaged in at all.

This is an extremist position, although widely held within our intellectual culture. There is no reason for a supporter of a free society to embrace it.

Freedom of speech can be given a high value, as it must be in a free society, without losing sight of a great many other values that are also vital to such a society. (During wartime, one of these is, of course, the vital necessity of preserving the very society itself from military defeat.) Any time one value is made into an absolute in denigration of others, there is a serious loss of proportion. That is not something the theory of a free society demands. In fact, just the opposite is true: a free society requires the accommodation of many values.

"It would actually be a source of embarrassment for a journalist to accept at face value much of anything our government says."

I have noticed over the years that any viewpoint that absolutizes a single value has instant appeal. Many people insist on the black-and-white clarity of an unencumbered idea and are unable to deal with a more subtle consideration of many factors. In the debate over the new journalism, we are going to hear a lot about how conceptually unthinkable it "would be" to allow other considerations to impinge upon complete journalistic independence in wartime. This will involve an effort to cause us to forget that, at least until Vietnam, freedom of speech during a war was very much accommodated to other values without the sky falling in.

Anyone familiar with the ideological wars of the recent past will recognize, too, that the idea of a press that eschews national loyalty and that articulates a constant skepticism, almost a paranoia, has come to embody much of the worldview of the New Left counterculture. It is not coincidental that many journalists today were greatly influenced by the sixties. "The Establishment" evoked no loyalty, only contempt. In that context, it would actually be a source of embarrassment for a journalist to accept at face value much of anything our government says.

2. *Other Aspects of the Failure to Weigh Additional Values.* The downgrading of other values is an essential ingredient in the attitude of moral equivalence. It also underlies the argument that "even during wartime, the debate should go on."

Both of these reflect the atrophying of patriotic sensibility that has occurred among Americans since World War II. If the survival and welfare of the country were still guarded by a powerful mystique, it would not be an easy matter to subordinate national interests to an absolutized free speech, anti-establishment attitudes, perceptions of moral equivalency, or a willingness to indulge America-bashing protestors. It would be a certainty, say, that we would either be prosecuting Ramsey Clark or enacting legislation for the punishment of such conduct as his in the future.

3. *Never To Be Lost Sight Of: The Alienation of Our Dominant Intellectual and Media Culture.* Except at the very beginning of this article, I have discussed the new journalism without regard to the overriding fact of American intellectual life: that the "alienation of the intellectual" against a middle-class, market-oriented society has for many decades been a major given within America and throughout the world.

"The new journalism cannot produce a neutral result in a world of open and closed societies."

I doubt very much whether any of the ideological skewing that we have been talking about would be taking place if it weren't for this intellectual alienation. The antipathy toward "bourgeoisie culture" which includes most especially the United States and almost everything it stands for—has been the prime motive power behind the world Left for 175 years. It was a major factor in Nazism, despite Marxism's repeated assertion that German national socialism was "right wing."

I have cited the fact that the new journalism cannot produce a neutral result in a world of open and closed societies. Even more fundamentally, however, we must expect that journalism will not even strive for neutrality, other than as a facade. A constant factor will be hatred toward the United States (I don't mean by any individual reporter or outlet; I am speaking in the context of the predominant intellectual and media culture as a whole). Anybody who abstracts this aspect of modern reality out of the discussion is arguing with blinders on, or at least seeks to have his audience wear blinders.

Alienated Intellectuals

In the Gulf context, the alienation toward the West was there even though Saddam himself had little ideological attraction (other than to the extent that the Left has attached itself to the Palestinian cause over the past several years). If the war had become protracted or had involved many casualties so that it would have become possible for the Left to recruit a sizeable number of discontented people, the alienated intellectual culture would have been more than happy not only to erode American resolve, but to tear this country apart. The history of the Left has consisted of a constant search by the alienated intellectual culture for disaffected groups with which to affiliate itself.

The answer to this question is not to be found in a conceptually purist form. Freedom of speech ought at all times to be considered a principal player in an orchestra made up of the many values that are important to a free society. The significance of wartime is that it imbues some of those other values, such as national survival or the least costly prosecution of the war in terms of lives and treasure, with more than ordinary importance.

For the proper balance, I would simply have us look back in American history, such as to World War II, to follow the light of experience. Let that be the litmus test. If the American public would have been scandalized by a journalist's doing something—such as interviewing an antiwar activist from the enemy capital—during World War II, then it should be equally scandalous now. Only in that way can we free ourselves from the post-Vietnam echoes that the predominant media culture is seeking to extend into a new wartime journalism.

Media Coverage of the Persian Gulf War Jeopardized National Security

Ted Smith

About the Author: *Ted Smith is a professor of journalism at Virginia Commonwealth University in Richmond. This article was written before the cessation of hostilities in the Persian Gulf War.*

A favorite quotation of wartime journalists, endlessly repeated and paraphrased, is Sen. Hiram Johnson's 1917 lament that "the first casualty when a war comes is truth." Ironically, it now appears that the first casualty of the war against Iraq may well have been American journalism, maimed by a multitude of self-inflicted wounds.

Clearly, the conflict has elicited a maximum effort from the press, including two days of continuous coverage by CNN [Cable News Network] and network television, daily special sections (and even a few extra editions) in the larger newspapers, and the deployment of hundreds of journalists in the field. The result, thanks largely to the wonders of satellites, has been technologically awesome. But by most traditional standards of journalism, the quality of coverage has been appalling, especially on television.

Every beginning journalism student is taught that the first duty of a reporter is to provide accurate and reliable information. Yet coverage of the war with Iraq has been consistently, sometimes grossly, inaccurate. The most egregious errors occurred in the early stages of the conflict,

when all major television outlets offered extensive live coverage. Faced with the necessity of somehow filling days of air time, but possessed of little or no reliable information about breaking events, television adopted the simple expedient of reporting whatever came to hand. The result was a chaotic jumble of rumors, speculations, and outright falsehoods, sometimes lasting for hours at a stretch.

On the first night of the war, for example, euphoria over the unexpectedly low losses in the first wave of attacks was followed by wildly optimistic estimates of the damage inflicted. By 11:30 P.M., CNN's Wolf Blitzer had reported the destruction of the Iraqi air force, 100 airfields, and the Republican Guards; by 2 A.M., several networks were discussing the advisability of a bombing "pause" to allow Saddam Hussein to surrender.

Coverage of the first Iraqi missile attacks the next night was even worse. On CBS, Dan Rather insisted categorically and repeatedly that at least one of the Scuds that landed in Israel had carried a chemical warhead and that Israeli forces were "retaliating" against Iraq. Meanwhile, ABC and NBC were both reporting the arrival of nerve gas victims in Tel Aviv hospitals. Coverage of the first Scud attack on Dhahran was less hysterical but equally confused. Within a period of eight minutes, NBC claimed that a Patriot had intercepted a Scud, CBS flatly denied the intercept, and CNN denied that a Patriot had even been launched. Fifteen minutes later, on ABC, a report attacking the accuracy of the Patriot system was interrupted by the first video footage of the successful Patriot interception.

> ## "Throughout the first month of fighting, accounts of real events alternated with media hype and fantasies."

As the war settled into a routine and as live coverage of breaking events declined, reporting became more sober and restrained. But the inaccuracies continued. Throughout the first month of fighting, accounts of real events alternated with media hype and fantasies. For example, government attempts to set more realistic expectations, combined with the military's refusal to release detailed battle damage assessments, led many journalists to switch from unwarranted optimism to an increasingly ugly, sneering pessimism about the effectiveness of the allied campaign.

This trend climaxed on January 28, 1991, with publication of a syndicated feature article in which *Washington Post* writer Bob Woodward used detailed information from anonymous "well-placed officials" to challenge government claims of success. He said, for instance, that the allies had not hit Iraqi supply lines. Although fairly accurate in its overall assessment, many of such claims were false, as shown in Gen. Norman Schwarzkopf's January 30, 1991, briefing. . . .

Coverage also featured a continuous stream of shrill, almost apocalyptic, warnings of looming catastrophe due to deficient American equipment. Foremost among these were claims that wear-dated protective suits would soon lose their effectiveness and leave soldiers defenseless against chemical attack (they were simply replaced as planned) and that a transmission defect could cripple the Army's fleet of Bradley Fighting Vehicles in battle (a quick and simple inspection found only a few vehicles with possible defects). In these and other instances, the issue burst on the scene in a blaze of hyperbole, dominated coverage for a day or two, then disappeared as swiftly as the mythical force of 50 Iraqi tanks once reported defecting to Egyptian lines.

Finally, we must add to these larger inaccuracies the countless errors, misstatements, and non sequiturs that littered routine reporting. Typical examples include:

• Connie Chung's February 3, 1991, transformation of a Pentagon statement confirming a minimum of 68 Iraqi aircraft destroyed in hardened shelters since the beginning of the war to the claim that allied forces had destroyed 68 aircraft "today,"

• a February 6, 1991, graphic on CNN's Headline News showing the Republican Guards deployed along the Saudi border, and

• the gradual, mysterious growth in the size of the Iraqi tank corps, from 4,000 or less in mid-January 1991 to a high of 5,000 in a February 13 report on CNN.

Security vs. Censorship

The second serious deficiency in media coverage involves the intimately intertwined issues of military security and censorship. Long a matter of passionate disputation, discussion of this subject has become increasingly acrimonious in recent years due to the widespread belief among members of the military that the American press contributed to America's defeat in Vietnam and widespread anger among journalists at their exclusion from Grenada and the failure of the pool system in Panama.

"The second serious deficiency in media coverage involves the intimately intertwined issues of military security and censorship."

Cognizant of these problems, military information officials took unusual care in planning arrangements for the press to cover the Desert Storm campaign. Regardless, many journalists responded to the arrangements with outrage, and bitter denunciations of military "censorship" were a staple feature of coverage throughout the first month of hostilities.

It is tempting to dismiss the controversy as nothing more than the inevitable and irresolvable product of a fundamental clash between the journalistic imperative of providing accurate and timely information to the public and the military imperative of denying useful intelligence to the enemy. But this would be an error, in part because it misstates the nature of the problem. Posturing aside, all parties to the dispute agree that it is important to prevent the release of information that would damage operational effectiveness or increase casualties. Conflicts arise in deciding what types of information should be restricted and whether journalists or the military should make the decisions.

Given the performance of journalists in covering the war against Iraq, it is now possible to clearly resolve at least one of these questions. But this will require a careful analysis of the specific issues involved in the current round of controversy.

The best way to begin is to outline the military's plan to manage coverage of the conflict. At its core is a set of 12 "ground rules" designed to specify precisely which information "should not be reported because its publication or broadcast could jeopardize operations or endanger lives." All accredited journalists in the CENTCOM [Central Command] theater of operations are asked to sign a copy of these rules. In part because of the enormous number of journalists involved—more than 800 were based in Saudi Arabia by early February 1991—access to frontline units is restricted to members of officially designated pools. Reports from these pools are shared by all of the news media and, in the most controversial feature of the plan, must pass a security review in the field before being released. Finally, for the many reporters not assigned to a pool, the plan provides for daily, on-the-record briefings by senior military personnel in Riyadh and Washington.

Areas of Concern

Many journalists condemned these arrangements as an unwarranted intrusion on freedom of the press. Although few have bothered to enunciate specific criticisms, there appear to be four principal areas of concern. The first two involve restrictions on content implied by the 12 ground rules and the requirement that pool reports must be subjected to security review before publication. One concern could be that the

rules themselves are too broad; the other is that military censors might exceed their authority and prohibit publication of information that is critical or embarrassing but militarily innocuous. The remaining two involve issues of access. First, because subordinate commanders may refuse permission for a media pool to visit a particular unit, it is feared that the pool arrangement will be manipulated to ensure that only positive stories are reported while negative news is hidden in silence behind barriers of access. Second, because all other journalists on the scene are forbidden access to the troops, there is no way for anyone outside the official system to bring these hidden stories to light.

> **"In this latest conflict between the government and the press, the public clearly supports the government."**

The solution advocated by these critics appears to be a return to the situation that prevailed in Vietnam, in which there were few significant or systematic restrictions on either content or access. Several journalists, such as CBS reporter Bob Simon and his crew, backed their beliefs with action by embarking on "unilateral" reporting expeditions in direct contravention of the rules established by the military. Simon ended up under arrest in Baghdad.

Before examining these concerns, two preliminary observations are in order. First, even if the military authorities (and the Saudi government) were willing in principle to eliminate all restrictions on reporting, it is not at all clear how it would be possible for 800 or more journalists—including many women and many individuals of dubious physical resources—to roam at will in a crowded, remote, and environmentally hostile combat zone without disastrous consequences to themselves, the military, and the war. Second, in this latest conflict between the government and the press, the public clearly supports the government. A Times Mirror poll released on January 31, 1991, found almost 80 percent approval for existing restrictions, with 57 percent agreeing that they should be strengthened. Hence the supreme irony of journalists' demanding greater freedom in the name of the people while the people themselves clamor for greater control.

Potential for Damage

But what of the specific concerns about censorship that have been raised so often and so forcefully by journalists covering the war? There is no real disagreement that some restrictions on media content are required. This need is especially clear in the present conflict because there is every indication that the Iraqi leaders are relying heavily on CNN and other Western media to meet basic intelligence needs. Further, the widespread use of portable, satellite-based communications systems, which allow live reports from the field to be distributed instantaneously throughout the world, including the enemy capital, greatly increases the potential damage of any disclosure of significant military information.

In light of these considerations, it is difficult to see how the Desert Storm ground rules could be reasonably characterized as unduly restrictive. Limited in number and scope, they prohibit release only of detailed information of obvious military significance. It is also difficult to imagine how the security review process could be used successfully to suppress publication of unfavorable information. The same guidelines that mandate the review state that "material will not be withheld just because it is embarrassing or critical." More important, any journalist dissatisfied with a decision in the field has several avenues of recourse, including appeals within the military and, if necessary, to other democratic institutions such as Congress or the courts. In short, there is no reason to believe that the existing content restrictions pose any serious threat to the free flow of information.

Concerns about access are somewhat better grounded but hardly compelling. Given existing pool arrangements, it does seem possible that military commanders could hide certain problems, errors, or failures from public scrutiny. It also seems likely that at least some of these could be brought to light if journalists were given unrestricted access to search for them. The question is whether it is desirable to do so. One difficulty, suggested by the dismal record of accuracy established in coverage of the war to date, is that free-roaming journalists would undoubtedly discover far more "problems" than actually exist, thus diverting attention and resources from more pressing needs. But even when a real problem is found, it is not immediately obvious that the wisest course in time of war is to disclose its existence in the press. Aside from possible effects on military and civilian morale, it could well expose a vital weakness to the enemy. All of this suggests that reports of some problems should be suppressed.

This brings us back to the crux of the issue of censorship. Freedom of access for journalists requires freedom of movement. And freedom of movement, especially given modern communications technology, means freedom for journalists to determine the content of reporting without supervision by the military. The question is, Can they be trusted to make those determinations responsibly? Sadly, ample evidence exists that they cannot.

"Reports of some problems should be suppressed."

Shortly after 11:30 P.M. on January 16, 1991, the first night of the war, Dan Rather conducted a live audio interview with CBS photographer David Green. At the outbreak of hostilities, Green, apparently operating unilaterally, had traveled to the then-unknown town of Khafji to tour allied military positions in the vicinity of the border with Kuwait. What he found was electrifying. The town had been subjected to an Iraqi artillery barrage and, at least to Green's untrained eye, it appeared that the Saudi defenders had fled. In his words: "Unfortunately, every position between here and the border that was being manned by the Saudis is empty. There's not one Saudi between here and the border. They've all gone." Asked by Rather whether it was possible that the Saudis had merely redeployed, Green repeated and amplified his claim: "There's nobody between here and the border, the first eight miles. They could just walk in here, the Iraqis, if they wanted."

"American journalists are willing to risk their country's defeat . . . rather than curtail their search for the truth."

It is difficult to exaggerate the enormity of this incident. Although subsequent evidence strongly suggests that the Saudi troops had, in fact, executed a hasty redeployment to prepared positions to avoid needless casualties from the Iraqi barrage, it is clear from his statements that Green was convinced they had fled. Thus we encounter the amazing spectacle of an American newsman reporting live to the world during an active engagement what he perceived to be a major weakness in frontline defenses.

Nor was this an isolated occurrence. From the first moments of the conflict, when all the major news media announced the beginning of the allied air assault approximately 15 minutes before most pilots had reached their targets, reports from nonpool journalists have provided a constant stream of sensitive military information. Numerous stories have included specific details of allied deployments or operations. On the first night of coverage, for example, CBS anchor Rather listed all of the American ground units positioned around Dhahran. On the first day of allied air operations from Turkey, January 19, 1991, NBC's Diana Korlicke reported the exact number of combat aircraft stationed at Incirlik Air Base; some hours later, CNN relayed a BBC story announcing that more than 40 aircraft had departed from Incirlik at intervals of 90 seconds for a mission against Iraq. . . .

Potential for Damage

Whether through fortune or the weakness or ineptitude of the enemy, there is no evidence that these and other breaches of security led to allied failures or losses. But each carried the potential for damage, and thus their significance is clear. Whatever the benefits of uncensored reporting might be, journalists proved by their actions that they cannot be trusted to make responsible decisions about the release of sensitive military information. This does not mean that any American journalist would knowingly place allied operations or forces at risk. It does mean that many journalists, including some with years of experience, are simply ignorant of the military significance of what they report. Thus, censorship of their coverage is not only reasonable but necessary.

A third and final defect of coverage has already been so widely discussed that it requires little consideration here. For the first time in history, American journalists have provided daily reports from an enemy capital in time of war. Regardless of the philosophical justification for this practice or the quality of the material they have provided, there is no doubt that these journalists were permitted to remain in Iraq only because the Iraqi government was convinced they were serving its wartime goals. Worse, there is ample evidence that the coverage did increase the chances of an Iraqi victory by inciting unrest in the Arab world. This shows, at the very least, that American journalists are willing to risk their country's defeat in a just and popular war against a brutal totalitarian regime rather than curtail their search for the truth.

Chronology

1914-1918 Arab nationalists with British support revolt against the Turkish Ottoman Empire, which has ruled in the Middle East for four hundred years.

1920 Arabian lands formerly part of the Ottoman Empire are placed by the League of Nations under the mandates of Great Britain and France. The area under British mandate includes what is now Iraq and Kuwait.

1921 Faisal I, with the support of the British, is made King of Iraq, which is comprised of three Ottoman Empire provinces.

1922 At the Uqair conference, the modern borders of Iraq, Saudi Arabia, and Kuwait are drawn by representatives of the British government.

1932 British rule ends as Iraq is admitted to the League of Nations as an independent state.

1958 Faisal II, grandson of Faisal I, is assassinated. Gen. Abdul Karim Kassem installs himself as military dictator.

1961

June Britain ends its protectorate rule as Kuwait's independence is formally proclaimed. Iraq refuses to recognize Kuwait and masses troops on Kuwait's border. British troops come to Kuwait's aid and prevent an Iraqi invasion.

July Kuwait joins the Arab League.

September Arab League troops replace British troops in Kuwait.

1962 Iraq conducts major military operations against separatist Kurds led by Mustafa al-Barzani.

1963

January Kuwait elects a National Assembly of fifty members. Voting is restricted to literate adult Kuwaiti males.

February Iraqi leader Kassem is deposed in a military coup. The new leadership recognizes Kuwait as a sovereign nation.

1967 Iraq breaks diplomatic relations with the U.S. following the Six-Day War between Israel and bordering Arab states.

1979 Saddam Hussein takes power in Iraq in its thirteenth military coup since 1920.

1980 The Iran-Iraq War begins as Iraq launches a full-scale invasion of Iran. Kuwait provides financial support to Iraq.

1981 Israeli jets destroy an Iraqi atomic reactor near Baghdad that Israel claimed was a nuclear weapons facility.

1984 Iraq and the U.S. reestablish diplomatic relations, broken since 1967's Six-Day War.

1987

May 17 An Iraqi fighter plane fires on the patrolling U.S. warship *Stark* and kills thirty-seven members of its crew.

July The U.S. dispatches nearly fifty ships to and around the Persian Gulf to protect Kuwaiti oil tankers from attacks by Iran.

1988 A cease-fire takes effect in the Iran-Iraq War, ending eight years of fighting.

1990

April 3 Saddam Hussein threatens to destroy half of Israel with chemical weapons if Israel attacks Iraq.

July 17	Saddam Hussein accuses Kuwait and the United Arab Emirates of conspiring with the United States to keep oil prices low by exceeding their OPEC oil quotas.
August 1	Iraq-Kuwait talks concerning oil and border disputes break off.
August 2	Iraq invades Kuwait. The emir of Kuwait flees to Saudi Arabia. The United Nations Security Council passes Resolution 660 condemning the invasion and demanding Iraq's immediate and unconditional withdrawal from Kuwait.
August 6	The UN Security Council passes Resolution 661, which imposes a trade embargo and economic sanctions on Iraq.
August 7	U.S. pres. George Bush, after consulting with the leaders of Great Britain, the Soviet Union, Japan, Egypt, and Saudi Arabia, sends U.S. forces to Saudi Arabia to protect it from a potential Iraqi invasion. Bush calls on other countries to send forces to the Persian Gulf.
August 8	Iraq annexes Kuwait.
August 9	The UN Security Council passes Resolution 662 unanimously declaring the Iraqi annexation of Kuwait "null and void." Iraq seals off its borders to all foreigners except diplomats. An estimated 550 Americans are trapped in Iraq and 3,000 in Kuwait. Bush officially notifies the U.S. Congress of the deployment of troops to the Persian Gulf, but states he does not believe military conflict is imminent.
August 10	Iraq orders the closure of foreign embassies in Kuwait. Saddam Hussein calls for a holy war against foreign troops.
August 13	The United States and Great Britain begin a naval blockade of Iraq.
August 17	Iraq says it will move Western "guests" to military installations to discourage U.S. attacks on these installations.
August 18	The UN Security Council passes Resolution 664, which condemns Iraq for holding foreign nationals hostage and demands their immediate release.
August 22	Through executive order, Bush calls up U.S. reservists for the first time since 1968.
August 25	The UN Security Council passes Resolution 665, which outlaws all trade with Iraq and bars financial dealings between Iraq and UN members.
August 28	Saddam Hussein announces the release of all foreign women and children detained in Iraq and Kuwait.
September 13	The UN Security Council passes Resolution 666, which establishes guidelines for humanitarian food aid to Iraq and occupied Kuwait.
September 16	The UN Security Council passes Resolution 667, which condemns Iraq for violence against foreign embassies and diplomats in Kuwait. It demands protection for diplomatic and consular personnel.
September 23	Saddam Hussein vows to destroy Middle East oil fields if attacked.
September 24	The UN Security Council passes Resolution 669, which agrees to consider exceptions to Resolution 661 for shipment of humanitarian supplies to Iraq.
October 1	Both houses of the U.S. Congress pass resolutions supporting the U.S. military buildup in the Persian Gulf.
October 16	U.S. armed forces in the Persian Gulf reach 200,000.
October 17	U.S. secretary of state James A. Baker III testifies before a Senate committee that the Bush administration would not seek the approval of Congress before an attack on Iraqi forces.
October 29	The UN Security Council passes Resolution 674, which calls for the release of the hostages and holds Iraq responsible for the economic and financial damage caused by the invasion of Kuwait.
November 8	Bush orders a near doubling of U.S. forces in the Persian Gulf.
November 15	Saddam Hussein declares he is willing to negotiate with the United States, but will not withdraw his forces from Kuwait before the start of negotiations.
November 19	Iraq adds 250,000 troops to its existing contingent of 430,000 deployed in or near Kuwait.
November 29	In a twelve-to-two vote, the UN Security Council passes Resolution 678 authorizing the use of "all necessary means" to force Iraq from Kuwait if Iraq does not withdraw before January 15, 1991.
November 30	Bush, declaring he wants to "go the extra mile for peace," proposes meetings between the U.S. and Iraq.
December 1	Iraq accepts the idea of meetings but insists that a solution to the Palestinian problem be included in the discussions.
December 6	Saddam Hussein frees all foreign hostages.
December 9	Efforts to set up talks with Iraq are stalled. Saddam Hussein suggests that Baker visit Baghdad on January 12, 1991, while Bush insists talks take place no later than January 3, 1991.

1991

January 3	Bush proposes peace talks in Geneva, Switzerland, between Baker and Tariq Aziz, the Iraqi foreign minister. U.S. forces in the Persian Gulf reach 325,000.
January 4	Iraq accepts U.S. offer of peace talks. The talks are scheduled for January 9.
January 9	The Baker-Aziz talks in Geneva fail to resolve the crisis. The U.S. announces that its embassy in Baghdad will close on January 12, 1991. The State Department plans to evacuate all U.S. citizens from the Persian Gulf region.
January 12	By votes of 52-47 in the Senate and 250-183 in the House of Representatives, Congress authorizes Bush to use the armed forces to carry out UN Resolution 678.
January 13	In Baghdad, UN Secretary Gen. Javier Perez de Cuellar fails to persuade Saddam Hussein to withdraw Iraqi forces from Kuwait.
January 15	The UN deadline for Iraqi withdrawal from Kuwait expires.
January 16	Coalition forces launch massive air attacks on Iraq. Saddam Hussein declares that Iraq will never surrender.
January 18	Iraq attacks Israel with SCUD missiles, causing light casualties. The U.S. announces the loss of four American planes and seven crew members in the first forty-eight hours of the air war.
January 19	Three SCUD missiles hit Tel Aviv, Israel. The U.S. responds by sending troops to operate Patriot antimissile systems in Israel. Captured Allied pilots are displayed on Iraqi television. Antiwar demonstrations are held in Washington, D.C., and Los Angeles.
January 24	The number of Allied air sorties against Iraq and Iraqi forces in Kuwait reaches fifteen thousand.
January 25	A massive oil spill forms in the Persian Gulf. The U.S. charges the spill is caused by Iraqi sabotage of a Kuwaiti supertanker loading pier.
January 26	Large peace demonstrations are held in Washington, D.C., Los Angeles, and San Francisco.
January 28	The U.S. announces that more than eighty Iraqi aircraft have landed at Iranian airfields.
January 29	Iraq begins an incursion into Saudi Arabia in the first major ground offensive of the war.
January 30	Eleven U.S. marines are killed as Allied forces drive Iraqi forces out of Khafji, Saudi Arabia. Gen. H. Norman Schwarz-

	kopf, commander of the Allied forces, boasts that U.S. smart bombs and cruise missiles have "destroyed all of [Iraq's] nuclear facilities."
February 3	Allied air sorties reach forty thousand.
February 6	Iraq severs diplomatic ties with the U.S. and five other coalition members.
February 13	Several hundred Iraqi civilians are killed in Baghdad when U.S. bombs destroy a building where they were sheltered. The U.S. maintains the building was a military communications center.
February 15	Iraq says that it will consider withdrawing its forces from Kuwait, but imposes strict conditions. Bush calls the proposal a "cruel hoax."
February 18	Iraqi foreign minister Aziz visits Moscow, where Soviet president Mikhail Gorbachev presents a plan for ending the war.
February 19	Bush rejects Gorbachev's plan, calling it "inadequate."
February 22	Bush sets a noon, February 23 deadline for Iraq to begin a withdrawal from Kuwait or face a ground war.
February 23	The deadline passes and the multinational coalition launches a massive ground offensive against Iraqi troops.
February 24	U.S. general Schwarzkopf, commander of the Allied forces, announces that Allied casualties on the first day of the ground war were "remarkably light."
February 25	An Iraqi SCUD missile falls on a barracks in Dhahran, Saudi Arabia, killing twenty-eight American soldiers. Baghdad announces orders for Iraqi forces to withdraw from Kuwait. Iraqi troops begin to leave Kuwait City. The Allies say that more than six hundred fires are burning in Kuwait, including more than half the nation's one thousand oil wells.
February 26	Iraqi troops in Kuwait and southern Iraq are virtually surrounded. U.S. marines enter Kuwait City.
February 27	Bush declares victory over Iraq and announces the liberation of Kuwait. He orders Allied combat suspended at midnight. A permanent cease-fire is said to depend on Iraq's release of Allied prisoners of war and its compliance with all UN resolutions.
February 28	Iraq accepts Bush's terms.
March 2	The UN Security Council passes Resolution 686, which demands that Iraq cease all hostile and provocative actions by its forces against coalition members. It demands that Iraq rescind its actions regarding the annexation of Kuwait, ac-

cept liability for damage to Kuwait, release Kuwaiti and other detainees, release Allied prisoners of war, and return property seized from Kuwait.

March 3   A meeting is held between Allied and Iraqi military commanders to arrange terms for the official cease-fire.

March 4   Iraq releases the first ten prisoners of war. Civil unrest spreads throughout Iraq as a Kurdish rebellion begins in the north and Shi'ite Muslims rebel in the south. Throughout March and early April, the rebellions are brutally crushed by forces loyal to Saddam Hussein.

March 5   Iraq voids the annexation of Kuwait and frees thirty-five more prisoners of war. Thousands of Iraqis flee the civil unrest in the country. Kurdish refugees flee towards the Turkish border in northern Iraq and to Iran. Shi'ite refugees from the south flee to Iran and the marshlands of southeastern Iraq.

March 6   In Damascus, Syria, the foreign ministers from eight Arab countries in the Allied coalition agree to form a Gulf peacekeeping force. Bush addresses the U.S. Congress, praises the U.S. forces, and calls for peace in the Middle East.

March 8   Iraq frees 1,181 Kuwaiti citizens abducted as hostages. The first U.S. troops return home.

March 26   The Bush administration rules out shooting down Iraqi helicopter gunships that are attacking Kurdish rebels and civilians.

April 3   The UN Security Council passes Resolution 687, which establishes a formal cease-fire between Iraq and the UN coalition. The cease-fire resolution calls for Iraq's cooperation in identifying and destroying its chemical and biological weapons, ballistic missiles, and nuclear materials and components.

April 5   The UN Security Council passes Resolution 688, which condemns the repression of the Kurds and other Iraqi citizens, demands that Iraq end the repression, and insists that Iraq allow immediate access by international humanitarian organizations to all of those in need of assistance throughout the country.

April 7   U.S. Air Force transport planes begin dropping supplies of food, blankets, clothing, and tents for refugees and other distressed Iraqi civilians in northern Iraq.

April 10   In an attempt to protect the Kurds from Saddam Hussein's forces, the Bush administration announces that it has warned Iraq not to deploy aircraft or launch ground offensives north of Iraq's 36th parallel.

April 16   Bush announces that U.S. troops will enter northern Iraq to create a safe area for Kurdish refugees in the flatlands around the Iraqi border town of Zakhu.

April 18   An agreement is negotiated between the UN Secretary General's Executive Delegate for Humanitarian Assistance for Iraqi Refugees and the government of Iraq. It calls for the UN to provide humanitarian assistance throughout Iraq and requires the Iraqi government to facilitate relief efforts and allow the UN to work wherever it believes necessary.

May 7   U.S. deputy national security adviser Robert M. Gates states in a speech that economic sanctions will remain on Iraq until Saddam Hussein is removed from power.

May 16   The U.S. Department of Defense estimates that 170,300 refugees remain on the Iraqi-Turkish border, down from an original total of almost 500,000. An average of more than 10,000 refugees a day are returning to northern Iraq from Turkey. Approximately 1,000,000 Iraqi refugees remain in Iran.

June 28   Iraqi troops fire warning shots over the heads of UN inspectors who are trying to photograph heavily laden trucks leaving a base near Falluja, thirty miles west of Baghdad. It is believed that the trucks are carrying equipment used to make fissionable material for nuclear bombs.

June 29   Angered by Iraqi evasiveness about its nuclear capability, Bush tells the press that reports that he was considering renewed military action against Iraq were "not all warrantless." Bush accuses Saddam Hussein of "cheating and lying and hiding" on the issue of nuclear inspection.

July 14   Bush and Pres. Francois Mitterand of France threaten military action against Iraq should it persist in developing nuclear weapons.

July 15   The last of approximately 3000 Allied troops, who had been protecting and assisting the Kurdish refugees, withdraw from Iraq into Turkey. A rapid deployment force of 3000 troops, known as Operation Poised Hammer, is set up in the southern Turkish town of Silopi. The purpose of the force is to protect the Kurds against possible attack by Iraqi troops.

Bibliography

Books

Les Aspin	*The Aspin Papers: Sanctions, Diplomacy, and War in the Persian Gulf.* Washington, DC: Center for Strategic and International Studies, 1991.
Abdul-Reda Assiri	*Kuwait's Foreign Policy.* Boulder, CO: Westview Press, 1990.
Ted Galen Carpenter	*America Entangled: The Persian Gulf Crisis and Its Consequences.* Washington, DC: The Cato Institute, 1991.
Thomas C. Fox	*Iraq: Military Victory, Moral Defeat.* Kansas City, MO: Sheed & Ward, 1991.
Simon Henderson	*Instant Empire: Saddam Hussein's Ambition for Iraq.* San Francisco: Mercury House, 1991.
Efraim Karsh and Inari Rautsi	*Saddam Hussein: A Political Biography.* New York: Free Press, 1991.
Samir al-Khalil	*Republic of Fear: The Politics of Modern Iraq.* New York: Pantheon Books, 1990.
E. Lauterpacht et al., eds.	*The Kuwait Crisis: Basic Documents.* Cambridge, England: Grotius Publications, 1991.
Fu'ad Matar	*Saddam Hussein: The Man, the Cause, and the Future.* London: Third World Centre, 1981.
Middle East Watch	*Human Rights in Iraq.* New Haven, CT: Yale University Press, 1990.
Judith Miller and Laurie Mylroie	*Saddam Hussein and the Crisis in the Gulf.* New York: Times Books, 1990.
Stephen C. Pelletiere, Douglas V. Johnson II, and Leif R. Rosenberger	*Iraqi Power and US Security in the Middle East.* Carlisle Barracks, PA: Strategic Studies Institute, US Army War College, 1990.
Pierre Salinger and Eric Laurent	*Secret Dossier: The Hidden Agenda Behind the Gulf War.* New York: Penguin Books, 1991.
Micah L. Sifry and Christopher Cerf	*The Gulf War Reader: History, Documents, Opinions.* New York: Times Books, 1991.
Peter Sluglett and Marion Farouk-Sluglett	*Iraq Since 1958: From Revolution to Dictatorship.* London: I.B. Tauris, 1990.

Periodicals

David Albright and Mark Hibbs	"Hyping the Iraqi Bomb," *The Bulletin of the Atomic Scientists,* March 1991. Available from 6042 S. Kimbark Ave., Chicago, IL 60637.
Hossein Askari	"Restoring the Gulf's Health," *U.S. News & World Report,* March 18, 1991.
Fred Barnes	"Winners and Loser: A Postwar Balance Sheet," *The National Interest,* Summer 1991. Available from 1112 16th St. NW, Washington, DC 20036.
James Bennet	"Sand Trap," *The Washington Monthly,* April 1991.
Stephen Budiansky with Bruce B. Auster	"A Force Reborn," *U.S. News & World Report,* March 18, 1991.
George Bush	"Aggression in the Gulf," *Vital Speeches of the Day,* October 15, 1990.
George Bush	"Iraq Invasion of Kuwait: The Defense of Saudi Arabia," *Vital Speeches of the Day,* September 1, 1990.
George Bush	"The War Is Over: A Framework for Peace," *Vital Speeches of the Day,* April 1, 1991.
David Callahan	"A Dangerous Victory," *Nuclear Times,* Summer 1991.
Jimmy Carter	"The Need to Negotiate," *Time,* October 22, 1990.

Ahmad Chalabi	"Iraq: The Past as Prologue?" *Foreign Policy*, Summer 1991.
Tracey Cohen	"Covering the Peace Movement," *Nuclear Times*, Summer 1991.
Joe Conason	"The Iraq Lobby: Kissinger, the Business Forum & Co.," *The New Republic*, October 1, 1990.
Congressional Digest	"Persian Gulf Policy: Pros & Cons," March 1991.
Walter Cronkite	"What Is There to Hide?" *Newsweek*, February 25, 1991.
The Economist	"Kuwait: How the West Blundered," September 29, 1990.
Richard Falk	"Reflections on Democracy and the Gulf War," *Alternatives*, Spring 1991.
Maxim Ghilan	"Thoughts on the After-War Gulf," *New Politics*, Summer 1991.
Paul A. Gigot	"A Great American Screw-Up: The U.S. and Iraq, 1980-1990," *The National Interest*, Winter 1990/91.
Tony Gillotte	"Mountain of Sorrow," *In These Times*, May 1-7, 1991.
David H. Hackworth	"The Lessons of the Gulf War," *Newsweek*, June 24, 1991.
Fred Halliday	"The Gulf War and Its Aftermath: First Reflections," *International Affairs*, April 1991.
Hussein I, King of Jordan	"Let's End the War: The Legitimacy of Security," *Vital Speeches of the Day*, March 15, 1991.
Saddam Hussein	"Harvest in the Mother of Battles Has Succeeded," *Vital Speeches of the Day*, March 15, 1991.
Saddam Hussein	"The Justness of the Iraqi Position," *Vital Speeches of the Day*, March 15, 1991.
Julius Jacobson	"Pax Americana: The New World Order," *New Politics*, Summer 1991.
Elie Kedourie	"Iraq: The Mystery of American Policy," *Commentary*, June 1991.
J.B. Kelly	"Like a Wolf in the Fold," *National Review*, September 3, 1990.
Michael Kelly	"Rolls-Royce Revolutionaries," *The New Republic*, April 6, 1991.
Paul Lalor	"Report from Bagdhad," *Middle East Report*, March-April 1991.
John Langan	"An Imperfectly Just War," *Commonweal*, June 1, 1991.
Lewis H. Lapham	"Brave New World," *Harper's Magazine*, March 1991.
Michael Ledeen	"Operation Desert Shame," *The American Spectator,* June 1991.
Scott Macleod	"In the Wake of Desert Storm," *The New York Review of Books*, March 7, 1991.
Charles William Maynes	"Dateline Washington: A Necessary War," *Foreign Policy*, Spring 1991.
Muhammad Muslih and Augustus Richard Norton	"The Need for Arab Democracy," *Foreign Policy,* Summer 1991.
The New Republic	"Desert Shame," April 29, 1991.
Rod Nordland	"Saddam's Secret War," *Newsweek*, June 10, 1991.
Joseph S. Nye Jr.	"Why the Gulf War Served the National Interest," *The Atlantic Monthly*, July 1991.
Martin Peretz	"Unpromised Lands," *The New Republic*, June 3, 1991.
Daniel Pipes	"What Kind of Peace?" *The National Interest*, Spring 1991.
Jay Rosen	"The Whole World Is Watching CNN," *The Nation*, May 13, 1991.
Dick Russell	"War's Environmental Implications Go Beyond a Simple Desert Storm," *In These Times*, February 6-12, 1991.
Sheikh Jaber Al-Ahmad Al-Sabah	"The Invasion of Kuwait," *Vital Speeches of the Day*, November 1, 1990.
Eduard Shevardnadze	"The Rebirth of the U.N.," *Vital Speeches of the Day*, October 15, 1990.
Micah L. Sifry	"Iraq, 1958 to the Present: America, Oil and Intervention," *The Nation*, March 11, 1991.
Time	"The Gulf War: George Bush Leads the Allies to a Military and Moral Victory," March 11, 1991.
U.S. News & World Report	Cover Story, "The World's Most Dangerous Man," June 4, 1990.
Jim Wallis	"A Neither Just Nor Holy War," *Sojourners*, April 1991.
Michael Walzer	"Perplexed," *The New Republic*, January 28, 1991.
Frederick Warner	"The Environmental Consequences of the Gulf War," *Environment*, June 1991.
Albert Wohlstetter and Fred Hoffman	"The Bitter End," *The New Republic*, April 29, 1991.

Organizations
to Contact

The editors have compiled the following list of organizations that are concerned with the issues debated in this book. All of them have publications or information available for interested readers. The descriptions are derived from materials provided by the organizations. This list was compiled upon the date of publication. Names and phone numbers of organizations are subject to change.

Cato Institute
224 Second St. SE
Washington, DC 20003
(202) 546-0200

The Cato Institute, a public-policy research center, believes that America's vital interests were not threatened by the Iraqi invasion of Kuwait. It opposed U.S. involvement in the Persian Gulf War as a waste of American lives, effort, and money. Its publications on the war include books and policy papers such as *America Entangled*, "Should We Go to War for Oil?" and "Arabian Nightmares."

The Heritage Foundation
214 Massachusetts Ave. NE
Washington, DC 20002
(202) 546-4400

The foundation is a conservative public-policy research institute. It supported U.S. policy during the Persian Gulf War. The Heritage Foundation published position papers and reports on the war, including "What George Bush Now Must Do in Iraq," "The Future of Iraq," and "Winning a Real Victory Over Iraq."

Middle East Research and Information Project (MERIP)
1500 Massachusetts Ave. NW, Suite 119
Washington, DC 20005
(202) 223-3677

MERIP's mission is to educate the public about the contemporary Middle East. The project is especially concerned with peace, human rights, and social justice issues. It was critical of the decision to go to war against Iraq. MERIP's major publication is the bimonthly *Middle East Re-*

port magazine, which extensively covered the Persian Gulf conflict and its aftermath.

Mobilization for Survival
45 John St., Suite 811
New York, NY 10038
(212) 385-2222

Mobilization for Survival is a national network of groups that promote peace and justice. The organization works to stop U.S. military intervention in foreign countries and to end the arms race. It opposed sending U.S. troops to the Persian Gulf in the belief that their presence would only hurt the cause of peace and democracy in the region. Materials available from the organization include the brochure *The Middle East Peace Alternative*, and the quarterly magazine *Mobilizer*.

The National Association of Arab Americans
2033 M St. NW, Suite 300
Washington, DC 20036
(202) 467-4800
The National Association of Arab Americans lobbies Congress to create a U.S. Middle East policy that promotes justice and peace for all peoples in the region. It was opposed to the Iraqi invasion of Kuwait and supported the U.S. response to the invasion. Its publications include the monthly *MEPARC* update, *Voice* magazine, and *Focus*, a newsletter.

U.S. Department of State—Bureau of Public Affairs
Public Information Service
Room 5831
Washington, DC 20520-6810
(202) 647-6575

The Department of State—Bureau of Public Affairs, Public Information Service, works to develop public understanding and support of U.S. foreign-policy positions. It provides summaries of U.S. policy, speeches made by the secretary of state and the president, and background notes on foreign countries.

Index